Jane Addams and the
Dream of American
Democracy

Jane Addams and the Dream of American Democracy

A LIFE

JEAN BETHKE ELSHTAIN

BASIC
B
BOOKS

A Member of the Perseus Books Group

Published by Basic Books,
A Member of the Perseus Books Group

Designed by Cindy Young

Library of Congress Cataloging-in-Publication Data
Elshtain, Jean Bethke, 1941–
    Jane Addams and the dream of American democracy : a life /
Jean Bethke Elshtain.
        p. cm.
    Includes bibliographical references and index.
    ISBN 0-465-01912-9 (hc); ISBN 0-465-01913-7 (pbk.)
    1. Addams, Jane, 1860–1935.   2. Women social reformers—
United States—Biography.   3. Women social workers—United
States—Biography.   I. Title.

HV28.A35 E57   2001
361.92—dc21
[B]
                                                    2001043493

02 03 04 / 10 9 8 7 6 5 4 3 2 1

To JoAnn Paulette Welch

and

Christopher Matthew Welch,

beloved grandchildren;

and

to Robert Paul Bethke,

beloved grandson and son

CONTENTS

ACKNOWLEDGMENTS

A BOOK THAT HAS BEEN in progress as long as this one becomes encrusted with many layers of indebtedness. I ask forgiveness of any who assisted me over the years who through my oversight have gone unmentioned here.

I thank Robert Coles for supporting the initial idea; Christopher Lasch for urging me on and providing inspiration; and Merloyd Lawrence for giving helpful commentary and encouragement. My thanks also to my student assistants at Vanderbilt University and at the University of Chicago, who gave invaluable help in the research: Michael LeRoy, Suzanne Agnew, Joe Addams, John Carlson, Erik Owens, Melanie O'Hara, Jaimie Schillinger, and Christopher Beem.

I am grateful also to Louise W. Knight for sharing her thoughts about Jane Addams with me; to Beata Boodell for tracking down records of the Fortnightly Club; to Tom and Ida Lou Ennenga for showing me around the grounds of the Addams family homestead and inviting me in; and to Anne Firor Scott for generously sharing notes and papers of Jane Addams that she had collected as material for a book of her own.

The Guggenheim Foundation supported me in a first leave of absence from teaching, during which I made a start. The Pew Charitable Trust provided a cushion during a subsequent year's leave, as did a Fellows Grant to the National Humanities Center from the Lilly Foundation. I am particularly indebted to Bob Connor, Kent Mullikan, Robert Wright, and the extraordinary staff of the National Humanities Center, who provided space, materials, and other aid that allowed me to complete the writing.

Special mention must be made of Irene Rosenfeld, my wonderful landlady and friend, whose home became mine during my year at the National Humanities Center. She clucked over me; made certain that there was food in the refrigerator; reminded me to sleep; and taking up her famous blue pencil, edited the manuscript and offered candid, thoughtful suggestions for revision.

Without the support of the University of Chicago Divinity School, and particularly of Dean Clark Gilpin, I couldn't have taken that year off; and thanks to Dean Richard Rosengarten, I was able to implement the plan that Dean Gilpin had set in motion. My colleagues in ethics—William Schweiker, Frank Gamwell, and Don Browning—were unfailingly supportive.

My thanks also to Basic Books—especially to John Donatich, Jessica Callaway, and my astute editor Jo Ann Miller, for their patience and meticulous attention to detail; to my line editor, Rebecca Ritke, for her close reading; and to my agent, Glen Hartley, for jump-starting a project that had bogged down.

My deepest gratitude goes to my family—who tactfully stopped asking when the Jane Addams book would be finished, but who celebrated with me when it finally was. Particular thanks to my husband, Errol, and my son, Eric, for tracking down references and obtaining reprint permissions; and to Sheri, Heidi, and Jenny, for their generous understanding of their mother's obsession with Jane Addams. It is to our grandchildren JoAnn and Christopher Welch, and our grandson and son Robert Paul Bethke, that this book is dedicated. Jane Addams asserted that even if all we have to offer to the generations that come after us is a story of the way "life has marked us with its slow stain," that counts for a lot and might even be the beginning of a fragile wisdom.

CREDITS

Bob Dylan, "Shelter from the Storm," © Ram's Horn Music, lyrics reprinted by permission of the publisher.

John C. Farrell, *Beloved Lady: A History of Jane Addams' Ideas on Reform and Peace* (Baltimore, Md.: Johns Hopkins University Press, 1967), pp. 220–241 [bibliography of the works of Jane Addams], reprinted by permission of the publisher.

Plan of Hull-House and other photographic illustrations from the Jane Addams Memorial Collection at the University of Illinois—Chicago, reprinted by courtesy of the University Library, Special Collections.

CHRONOLOGY

1860	Laura Jane Addams born September 6, in Cedarville, Illinois
1863	death of mother, Sarah Weber Addams
1868	remarriage of father, John Huy Addams, to Alice Haldeman
1877	enrolls in Rockford Female Seminary
1881	graduates from Rockford Female Seminary (later renamed Rockford College)
1881	death of father
1881	registers at Woman's Medical College, Philadelphia
1882	awarded bachelor's degree from Rockford College
1882	health breaks down; winter of invalidism
1883–1885	tour of England and Continent
1885	baptized and joins Presbyterian Church
1887–1888	second trip to Europe
1888	attends springtime bullfight in Madrid
1889	goes to Chicago in January to look for a "big house"
1889	doors to Hull-House open September 18
1891	Edward Butler, Chicago merchant, gives $5,000 for an art gallery at Hull-House; Jane Club, a cooperative boarding-club for girls, founded at Hull-House
1893	coffeehouse and gymnasium built at Hull-House
1894	Pullman Strike

Note: This chronology closely follows that in Christopher Lasch, ed., The *Social Thought of Jane Addams* (Indianapolis, Ind.: Bobbs-Merrill, 1965), pp. xxix–xxxi.

1895	appointed garbage inspector for the 19th ward
1896	visits England and Russia; meets Tolstoy
1898	opposes United States' acquisition of the Philippine Islands
1901	defends anarchist Abraham Isaak, who was arrested following assassination of President McKinley
1905	first of many summers spent in Bar Harbor, Maine, with companion Mary Rozet Smith
1905–1909	member of Chicago School Board
1907	delegate to first National Peace Congress
1909	appendicitis
1912	delegate to Progressive national convention and member of platform committee; seconds nomination of Theodore Roosevelt
1914	First World War begins
1915	attends first congress of Women's International League for Peace and Freedom, in the Hague
1916	tuberculosis of kidneys; one kidney removed
1917	breaks with many Progressives over United States' declaration of war on Germany
1919	presides over second congress of Women's International League for Peace and Freedom, Zurich; tours postwar France, Holland, Germany; blacklisted by Lusk Committee, New York legislature
1920	votes for Eugene Debs for U.S. president
1921	attends third congress of Women's International League for Peace and Freedom, in Vienna
1923	travels around the world
1924	attends fourth congress of Women's International League for Peace and Freedom, in Washington, D.C.; votes for LaFollette for U.S. president
1926	attends fifth congress of Women's International League for Peace and Freedom, in Dublin; heart attack
1928	votes for Herbert Hoover in U.S. presidential election, due to his role in famine relief in postwar Europe
1929	attends sixth congress of Women's International League for Peace and Freedom, in Prague; resigns as president; elected honorary president for life

1930   awarded honorary LL.D., University of Chicago
1931   undergoes surgery (seemingly successful) to remove
        tumor; receives Nobel Peace Prize (with Nicholas
        Murray Butler)
1932   votes for Hoover again
1935   dies in Chicago on May 21, of cancer; buried in
        Cedarville, Illinois

BOOKS BY JANE ADDAMS

1902. *Democracy and Social Ethics*. New York: Macmillan.

1907. *Newer Ideals of Peace*. New York: Macmillan.

1909. *The Spirit of Youth and the City Streets*. New York: Macmillan.

1910. *Twenty Years at Hull-House*. With autobiographical notes. Illustrations by Norah Hamilton. New York: Macmillan.

1912. A *New Conscience and an Ancient Evil*. New York: Macmillan.

1915. *Women at the Hague: The International Congress of Women and Its Results,* by three delegates to the Congress from the United States, Jane Addams, Emily G. Balch, and Alice Hamilton. New York: Macmillan.

1916. *The Long Road of Woman's Memory*. New York: Macmillan.

1922. *Peace and Bread in Time of War*. New York: Macmillan.

1930. *The Second Twenty Years at Hull-House: September 1909 to September 1929 with a record of growing consciousness*. New York: Macmillan.

1932. *The Excellent Becomes the Permanent*. New York: Macmillan.

1935. *My Friend, Julia Lathrop*. New York: Macmillan.

1935. *Forty Years at Hull House, Being "Twenty Years at Hull House" and "The Second Twenty Years at Hull-House,"* afterword by Lillian D. Wald. New York: Macmillan.

Note: In addition to books, Addams's published work includes more than five hundred essays, speeches, editorials, and columns. Jane Addams's papers are housed at a number of sites, the most important being the Swarthmore College Peace Collection, and the Jane Addams Memorial Collection at the University of Illinois at Chicago. The massive, indispensable Jane Addams Papers on Microfilm, edited by Mary Lynn McCree Bryan (Ann Arbor, Mich.: University Microfilms International, 1985), contains most of the extant documentary and archival material.

HULL-HOUSE FIRSTS

First Social Settlement in Chicago
First Social Settlement in the United States with men and women residents
Established first public baths in Chicago
Established first public playground in Chicago
Established first gymnasium for the public in Chicago
Established first little theater in the United States
Established first citizenship preparation classes in the United States
Established first public kitchen in Chicago
Established first college extension courses in Chicago
Established first group work school in Chicago
Established first painting loan program in Chicago
Established first free art exhibits in Chicago
Established first fresh-air school in Chicago
Established first public swimming pool in Chicago
Established first Boy Scout troop in Chicago
Initiated investigations for the first time in Chicago of truancy, typhoid fever, cocaine, children's reading, newsboys, sanitation, tuberculosis, midwifery, infant mortality, social value of the saloon
Initiated investigations that led to creation and enactment of first factory laws in Illinois
Initiated investigations that led to creation of first model tenement code
First Illinois factory inspector: Hull-House resident Florence Kelley
First probation officer in Chicago: Hull-House resident Alzina Stevens
Labor unions organized at Hull-House: Women Shirt Makers, Dorcas Federal Labor Union, Women Cloak Makers, Chicago Woman's Trade Union League

Note: From the Centennial Annual Report of the Hull House Association, Chicago. (Note that although the association does not hyphenate Hull-House, Jane Addams always did; and I have followed her usage.)

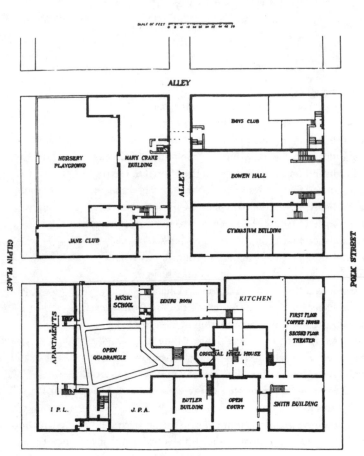

A plan of Hull-House buildings

Preface

❦

Interpreting a Life

THE NAME RINGS A BELL. Most Americans of middle age or older have heard of Jane Addams. Didn't she have something to do with immigrants and social work? "She was a socialist, right?" queried an academic friend when I told her I was at long last writing my "Jane Addams book." A vague sense of familiarity without any specific knowledge of who Addams was or what she did is understandable. Not only do Americans study far less history now than they once did, but Addams fell from public consciousness rather quickly following her death May 21, 1935, at the age of 74. Planned memorials faltered, and statues of her were never built. Yet at her death Addams was America's best-known and most widely hailed female public figure. Some went so far as to compare her to her hero, Abraham Lincoln. The mourning at her death was international. Tributes poured in from prime ministers and from ordinary men and women whose lives she had touched in some way by her life and work.

The reasons for Addams's posthumous eclipse are complex. Government-controlled and -administered welfare programs of the 1930s supplanted the settlement house movement Addams had pioneered, and altered settlement activities in such a way that they no longer conformed to her capacious vision. Addams thought of those who came and went at Hull-House as citizens, or citizens-in-the-making, not as clients or receivers of services. Although the names of settlements such as Hull-House were in some cases retained, the original model was transformed radically during the New Deal era and after. In addition, the costly battle against Nazism, followed by the long Cold War struggle with Soviet-style tyranny, made Addams's pacifism seem increasingly outmoded, or dangerously naïve. Thus, although Addams's vision and action provided a basis for later social programs, her reputation and her contribution to American life have gone largely unrecognized.

But we are in a new era. The Cold War is over. Traditional government welfare programs have been challenged from the left and the right. Concerns about America's civic health, voiced in recent public and scholarly debates, have brought to the fore the urgent need for a reevaluation of the status of democracy in the United States.[1] It is a propitious moment at which to reconsider Addams's life and legacy.

This book is an interpretation of the life's journey of an American woman as she made her way from a small town in rural Illinois to become the most famous female public figure of her time—an extraordinary pilgrimage, likened by some of Addams's admirers to that of Abraham Lincoln. Readers will retrace the evolution of Addams's powerful vision, a vision of generosity and hopefulness that made the American democracy more decent and more welcoming today than it otherwise would be. Our culture has become so cynical about public life that we may find it difficult to appreciate the significance of her vision and her contribution. My goal is to draw back the curtain of historic mist and dust that has obscured Addams and blurred her reputation. Using Addams's own method of "sympathetic understanding," I have interpreted her life primarily through her own writings, so that her distinctive voice can be heard above the din of our noisy, technology-invaded lives.

Any book about Addams will disappoint at least some of those with a proprietary interest in her legacy. She was a larger-than-life figure, of whom contemporaries, years after her death, still spoke with awe and reverence. One can never do justice to such a person. My comforting hope is that many readers of this book will go on to read Addams's own writings, in order to fully appreciate her intellect and her passion for civic life.[2]

Although Jane Addams has had her day, she has yet to receive her due.

INTRODUCTION

❧

Looking for
Jane Addams's America

To get to Cedarville (in northern Illinois, just south of the Wisconsin border), you follow Interstate 90 west to U.S. 20 west outside of Rockford. At the junction of 20 and Illinois 26, you turn north and proceed to Freeport, the site of one of the Lincoln-Douglas debates in 1858, which took place two years before Jane Addams was born. A few miles farther up the road you'll come to Cedarville, population 751. (The postmistress chuckled when I called to verify the population figures. "It depends on which road you drive into town on," she said, "but, yes, that's the population if you're driving up from Freeport.") A sign erected by the Illinois State Historical Society at the town limits in 1951 notes:

CEDARVILLE
BIRTHPLACE OF
JANE ADDAMS 1860–1935
HUMANITARIAN, FEMINIST,
SOCIAL WORKER, REFORMER,
EDUCATOR, AUTHOR,
PUBLICIST, FOUNDER OF
HULL HOUSE, PIONEER
SETTLEMENT CENTER,
CHICAGO, 1889, PRESIDENT
WOMEN'S INTERNATIONAL
LEAGUE FOR PEACE AND

FREEDOM. NOBEL PEACE
PRIZE, 1931.

Cedarville doesn't have a chamber of commerce or a mayor, but it does have a small historical society museum. The museum's first room is devoted to an exhibit of quilt-making past and present. The visitor next enters "The Addams Room," dedicated primarily to the life and times of Jane Addams but also featuring information about her family. Her father, John Huy Addams, is described as a "religious and civic leader in Cedarville and the most successful business man in the county." Noted is the fact that he was elected to the Illinois state senate as a Whig; that he helped found the Illinois branch of the Republican Party; that he served seven terms as the party's standard-bearer in the state senate, declining his party's nomination for governor and for the U.S. Congress.

A History of Stephenson County 1970, published by the Stephenson County government in Freeport, Illinois, affords glimpses of the Cedarville of Jane Addams's childhood, including details about her il-lustrious father—an abolitionist who was believed to have sheltered runaway slaves (Cedarville was on the Underground Railroad). The lo-cal fame and stature of John Addams were based in large part on his many successful business ventures, which included a farm; a linseed oil–extracting mill; the Second National Bank in Freeport, of which he was the first president; and a railway company. He led a campaign to link the county with the Galena and the Chicago Union rails, which later became part of the Illinois Central system, and invested his own funds heavily in the new railway. He also helped many of his neighbors estab-lish businesses of their own.[1]

John Addams's deep civic involvement clearly influenced his daugh-ter's development. He served as a member of the Cedarville School Board and as a trustee for the Rockford Young Ladies' Seminary, later Rockford College, where Jane Addams earned an undergraduate de-gree. He also played a central role in organizing the state Republican Party and in bringing a Lincoln-Douglas debate to Freeport. To his precocious, civic-minded daughter, he was a figure to admire and to emulate.

According to the county historians, Cedarville society provided a milieu that encouraged Jane Addams's further development in this direction.[2]

Stephenson County gave Jane Addams the rural advantage of a
very nearly classless society which was composed of people of a
wide range of economic and cultural advantages, from many places
of origin. . . . This was a time when, in contrast, the growth of the
cities had divided them [people of different origins and stations]
more and more clearly into economic and cultural classes, ignorant
of and distrustful of each other. Another advantage, one that she
considered essential to a child's healthy development, was the village child's closeness to nature which included intimate acquaintance with birth and death.

The Cedar Creek Mill, built by John Addams and central to the lore
his daughter wove around the figure she so revered, no longer stands.
But the museum includes fragments salvaged from its ruins. Sarah Weber
Addams, Jane Addams's mother, is described as a "saintly woman,
loved by everyone in the Cedarville area." When Sarah died in 1863,
after the stillbirth of her ninth child, her daughter Laura Jane (who
later dropped the first name) was only two and one-half years old. As
the youngest surviving child, Jane was doted on by the other members
of her very large family.

Jane Addams's personal possessions include a cradle made of a single
walnut board, and a full-length black dress in Addams's characteristi-
cally sober style. Adorning a tailor's form, the garment features loose-
fitting layers of impeccably tailored cloth set off by a three-tiered lace
bodice.[3] Even in the dog days of summer at the Bowen Country Club
(the Hull-House summer camp in Waukegan, Illinois), Addams wore
ankle-length black dresses, most often accessorized with a hat and
gloves.

I noticed a coin purse filled with artifacts that Addams probably had
collected in and around her family's Cedarville home site and mill.
These included shards of American Indian cooking pottery with char-
acteristic rows of indentations, identifying the items as destined for
home use rather than for trade. (Commercial pottery was brightly
painted and decorated.)[4] That Addams carried such talismans about
with her is a reminder of her sense of connection to her place of origin.
A clutch of memories likewise is embedded in her black drawstring
sewing kit with its basket-weave bottom. Addams embroidered and
crocheted for hours during trips and while listening to lectures. Exam-

ples of her craft on exhibit at the museum include an embroidered damask hand towel, probably intended as a gift for a friend; a delicate undergown with scalloped edges, painstakingly handcrafted for a friend's baby; and a pink knit baby sweater of tight weave—a gift for another friend who had just given birth. She had signed the gift cards, "With affectionate congratulations, Jane Addams."

My eyes next lit on a coarse-grained leather traveling medicine kit containing four silver-stoppered glass vials. What medicines Addams carried with her is not noted, but soporifics would surely have been among them, as Addams tells us that she was pitched into waves of debilitating nausea on sea voyages. Next to the medicine vials is a walking stick of unusual design that Addams used on trips abroad.

A selection of Addams's school memorabilia includes a gift to "Jennie Addams" (her nickname during her childhood and adolescence) from her teacher, dating from Christmas 1875. Addams was an earnest fifteen-year-old student at the time; and the gift presented to her was John Bunyan's *Pilgrim's Progress,* a book that played a role in shaping the narrative structure of her life as it did for so many of her contemporaries.

Addams's later fame as a cultural icon is represented by a can of "Jane Addams Mixed Vegetables," likely dating from the late 1910s or early 1920s. The Jane Addams brand reminds us of her impact on the popular consciousness as well as the fact that Hull-House attempted to interest the immigrants of the 19th ward, site of the settlement, in nutritious meals loaded with vegetables—with mixed success.

The archival lore in the exhibit also includes the minutes of meetings of the Hull-House Ladies' Club, dating from the early twentieth century, and the historic records of the Old Settlers' Association, of which Jane Addams's father was a founding member. In *Twenty Years at Hull-House,*[5] Addams recalled hearing her father address a meeting of the association:

> My father had made a little address of reminiscence at a meeting of the "old settlers of Stephenson County," which was held every summer in the grove beside the mill, relating his experiences in inducing the farmers of the county to subscribe for stock in the Northwestern Railroad, which was first to penetrate the county and to make a connection with the Great Lakes at Chicago. Many

of the Pennsylvanian German farmers doubted the value of "the whole new-fangled business," and had no use for any railroad, much less for one in which they were asked to risk their hard-earned savings. My father told of his despair in one farmer's community dominated by such prejudices which did not in the least give way under argument, but finally melted under the enthusiasm of a high-spirited German matron who took a share to be paid "out of butter and egg money." As he related his admiration of her, an old woman's piping voice in the audience called out: "I'm here to-day, Mr. Addams, and I'd do it again if you asked me to."

As I prepared to leave, I caught sight of an item of more recent vintage, a painting titled *Jane Addams with Children*, commissioned for the Hull-House centenary in 1989. It features Addams in a typical pose, seated and reading to children. The faces of her young listeners reflect our current concern with multiculturalism—they are Native Americans, Asians, and African Americans; but these communities, save for a small African American contingent, were not prominent among Addams's immigrant neighbors. If one were to select representative children from the 19th ward in 1889, when Hull-House opened its doors, the group huddled around Addams would feature Italians, Bohemians, Greeks, and Russian Jews, as well as more than fifteen other nationalities.[6]

Addams described the ethnic makeup of the neighborhood around Hull-House (near the junction of Blue Island Avenue with Halsted and Harrison streets) in her autobiography, noting the gradual outmigration of the more prosperous Irish and German immigrants, and the slow influx of Russian Jews, Italians, and Greeks in their place. Among the Italians, she differentiated between Neapolitans, Sicilians, Calabrians, Lombards, and Venetians. The Jewish population was largely Polish and Russian. These groups merged "into a huge Bohemian colony, so vast that Chicago ranks as the third Bohemian city in the world."[7]

That said, the mix of children seated around Addams nonetheless accurately reflects her attitude toward the great diversity of her neighbors. In the words of a Sunday school song surely familiar to Addams:[8]

JESUS LOVES THE LITTLE CHILDREN,
ALL THE CHILDREN OF THE WORLD.

BE THEY YELLOW, BLACK OR WHITE
THEY ARE PRECIOUS IN HIS SIGHT,
JESUS LOVES THE LITTLE CHILDREN OF THE WORLD.

The love of little children without regard to race, ethnicity, or cultural origin is central to the spirit of Christian universalism in which Jane Addams was raised. The painting embodies the belief that all children are to be valued without exception. On the way out, I examined an enlarged, framed photograph from the *Rockford Morning Star* (Saturday, May 25, 1935), headlined, "Throngs Pay Tribute to Noted Social Worker in Her Native Village Friday."

The townswoman "baby-sitting" (as she put it) the museum directed me to the Addams home site, a few miles away, on West Oak Road. Although the home is a National Landmark, it has been out of Addams family hands since 1956, when it was purchased by Mr. and Mrs. Thomas Ennenga. At the time, said Tom Ennenga (who had written up a history of the house and the story of its restoration for those interested in Jane Addams lore), the home was "a total wreck," having been rented out, "neglected and run down for more than thirty years." The Ennengas tell of squabbling between Jane Addams's heirs, one of whom received the land, and the other, the Georgian-style dwelling that had been built in two phases, the northern part in 1850, and the southern in 1854. As no member of the Addams family was living in Cedarville in 1935, when "Aunt Jane" died, the property gradually fell into disrepair. The task of restoring it devolved onto Tom Ennenga and his wife, Ida Lou.

The couple hired a Chicago architect who rebuilt the house completely (retaining only the outer walls, rafters, window casings, doors, and subfloors) while striving to maintain the style and character of the original homestead. The Ennengas were at first surprised by the number of people who appeared at their front door inquiring about Jane Addams, and as a rule, they did not permit visitors to enter the home. "It's amazing," Mrs. Ennenga told me. "We get someone here almost every weekend, wanting to come in, telling us Jane Addams gave them their start or personally helped them or their family in some way." The grounds, which visitors may tour at their leisure, are beautifully kept. One is also permitted to visit the original Pennsylvania bank barn 40 feet by 60 feet in dimension. "Notice the way it is finished off with wooden pegs in the classic style," Tom Ennenga pointed out. A mill-stone salvaged from the original structure adorns the side of the barn nearest the house, nestled amid a profusion of flowers and shrubs.

Ennenga enjoyed sharing a bit of Addams lore. "Her father was the most prosperous businessman in these parts, and he was a friend of Abraham Lincoln's," he told me. "Lincoln always called him 'my dear double-D'ed Addams' and told him that God only needed one D for his Adam." In *Twenty Years at Hull-House*, Jane Addams tells the thrilling story of the day when

> At my request my father took out of his desk a thin packet marked, "Mr. Lincoln's Letters," the shortest one of which bore unmistak-able traces of that remarkable personality. These letters began, "My dear Double-D'ed Addams," and to the inquiry on a certain measure then before the legislature, was added the assurance that he knew that this Addams "would vote according to his con-science," but he begged to know in which direction the same con-science "was pointing." As my father folded up the bits of paper I fairly held my breath in my desire that he should go on with the reminiscence of this wonderful man, whom he had known in his comparative obscurity, or better still, that he should be moved to tell some of the exciting incidents at the Lincoln-Douglas debates.

Addams's account of these events acknowledges that her abolitionist father had been present at the debate held in Freeport on August 27, 1858.

Tom Ennenga continued: "The $10,000 he put up for the mill and property was pretty steep in those days. Mr. Addams was a man of sub-stance. And you see that tangled bush area with the thickets and under-brush off to the side of the lawn?"—he gestured to a sloping expanse adorned with flowers of all sorts—"that was an area Miss Jane played in and it had a cave she liked to go into. She called it her fairyland. Not every child has her own fairyland."

Ennenga then gave me directions to the Cedarville Cemetery, a peace-ful, hilly site adjacent to the Addams property. The family plot is on the right of the cemetery as you drive in. An obelisk lists family members' names and the dates of their births and deaths. Individual graves are placed to the front of the obelisk and on either side. I noticed the names

Linn, Weber, and Haldeman, as well as Addams. Jane Addams's name appears on the back of the family obelisk. She is identified on her grave marker in simple words she selected before her death:

JANE ADDAMS
OF
HULL HOUSE
AND
THE WOMEN'S INTERNATIONAL LEAGUE
FOR
PEACE AND FREEDOM

The words etched into her gravestone have been worn nearly smooth by the elements and by the touch of those who over the years have made pilgrimages to her resting place. Although Cedarville is off the beaten path, a continuous stream of humanity has made this pilgrimage. Why do they come? Who is Jane Addams, that they should care? The answer may lie in the stories told to me by two women who grew up in the Italian immigrant neighborhood surrounding Hull-House.

On a brisk, sunny day in Chicago, I sat down in a room at the Chicago Hilton with Marie Thalos (née Bagnola) and Ruby Jane Delicandro (née Gorglione) to talk about Jane Addams.[9] Our conversation lasted four hours. The women were coy about their respective ages—both were in their seventies, I was told—but they spoke animatedly, completing one another's sentences as close family members tend to do. Ruby and Marie said they were at first reluctant to talk to me, as they mistrusted "experts or so-called experts" and what such experts had to say about Jane Addams. Ruby was especially wary. She confided to me, "I didn't want to talk to you because I thought, If this lady does what some others have been doing to Jane Addams, why, it's a great injustice."

What the two women found objectionable about much of what they had heard or read became clear as our conversation went along. When I asked them whether they had a specific worry, they told me they were stunned by others' comments about Hull-House, evoking images of the homeless and the derelict, of juvenile offenders, of unwed teenage mothers, and the like—the presumptuous superimposition of seemingly intractable, contemporary urban problems over the actual problems of turn-of-the-century immigrants in Chicago. Ruby and Marie recounted how after they told people about their Hull-House experience, those people looked at them as if they were "little criminals or something": "You say 'settlement house,' and they think 'paupers.'"

The women also voiced other complaints. They were upset about a recent television program on Jane Addams that devoted disproportionate attention to speculation about the libidinal lives of the female residents of Hull-House.[10] Exclaimed Ruby: "Why are they dwelling on that? *We're* the ones with sex on the brain, that's why." Marie: "Right ... and what she did for our community was just—" Ruby: "A miracle! It was a miracle." She added that she was glad Jane Addams wasn't alive to hear "some of the stupid things they are saying about her." She continued: "We've read stupid stories about how the neighbors were suspicious of Hull-House. But we *were* the neighbors. No one we knew was worried about taking her children to Hull-House."

Ruby had brought with her a well-thumbed scrapbook that she said she rarely takes out anymore to show to people because she couldn't abide their misunderstanding of what Hull-House was all about. When asked to describe Addams, she responded: "Miss Jane Addams was like a mother to us." Marie piped up: "Oh, to everybody." Marie enjoined me to be certain to note that the residents of Hull-House "never made us feel like paupers." She continued: "They treated us on an equal basis. Everything was top drawer. The best." Trying to capture the tone and texture of the place, Ruby spoke enthusiastically of how things were "so naturally done." "It was a way of life," she explained. "You walked through the door, and things happened. We wouldn't go to what they call Hull-House now. It's all changed. Our Hull-House was like a home, a well-kept home." Marie adds: "What we're saying is that Hull-House introduced us to so many things. It was such a rich environment. That's what everybody has forgotten."

Once the initial ripostes were out of the way, Ruby and Marie delved into their tales with gusto, perhaps having sensed the opportunity to set the record straight. "What happened when Jane Addams walked into a room?" I asked. Ruby proclaimed: "She was larger than life. White hair. Black dresses down to the floor. And big, big eyes. She always was a lady." Ruby recalled that she had first walked through the doors of Hull-House when she was five years old, around 1925.

Marie described her first encounter with Addams: "She came down the hall. My mother was with my brother and me. 'I'm going to a tea party,' she said. 'Would you allow me to take your children to it?' That was my introduction to Hull-House." She murmured, in a near-whisper: "Beautiful name. Miss Jane Addams. We always called her that. A beautiful name and a beautiful woman."

Ruby added: "In those days there was something called respect. She respected each and every one of us." Ruby then proudly described how she had become a star pupil of Edith de Nancrede, director of the Marionettes, one of the junior theater and dance groups at Hull-House. She recounted her role in the Hull-House production of *Merman's Bride*. Marie noted that her mother had helped sew costumes for this play. Ruby performed frequently. "I was Puck in *Midsummer Night's Dream*," she recalled. Marie said: "We had cellists, piano players, violinists. Many concerts. We even went to dance classes with Martha Graham. Everything was the best."

Ruby and Marie described the large, beautiful theater that was part of the Hull-House complex, and noted that they had paid their final respects to Jane Addams there, because that was where "she was laid out when she died."[11] The Hull-House that they had known had every imaginable facility for intellectual and physical development, including a huge gym as well as spaces reserved for music, dance, art, crafts (including weaving with giant looms), and literary groups. All of these activities "belonged to all of us," Marie said. "You had access to everything that was there." Marie told me several times over, just to be certain that I understood: "What Ruby and I are trying to say is that the children there were not little criminals, not delinquents, which is what some people seem to think nowadays."

Ruby and Marie had warm memories of their much-loved Italian neighborhood with its large family groups and robust social, cultural, and religious life. Hull-House enlarged but did not supplant the world of their immigrant community. Hull-House built on many activities and festivals native to Italy. The celebration they most loved was the annual enactment of Christmas tableaux, the singing of Christmas songs in many languages, and a tree with lighted candles. At the Christmas event, Jane Addams always offered a few words: "She was the one we listened to before the play, before we went on. She would always say, 'You're all a part of it.' And she emphasized the 'You're' part. She never said, 'This is mine,' no, she always said, 'You're a part of it.' And we were."

The welcoming intimacy of the Hull-House environment was personified by Addams. Marie recalled, "Her bedroom was immense, at least to us as children, and it was also used for people to dress before the plays." Ruby continued: "Every time you dressed in a costume, you would go to show her. The last couple of years she was bedridden a lot, so you would go into the room, and she'd say, 'Turn around and let me see you.' And then we'd go out to perform. But she more or less put her stamp of approval on us." Marie took up the story: "She had two rooms. One she called her office, but it wasn't really an office. It was a big room next to her bedroom, where she had these beautiful carpets and art work and two big desks. But she loved to be with us." Ruby and Marie recalled serenading Miss Addams and her coming out and smiling at them and blowing kisses.

The women told me that they grew up at Hull-House. It was their second home, from preschool through high school. They came and went, and life was full. Their mothers also were involved in Hull-House activities and felt supported in their own efforts with their children—or so Ruby and Marie surmised. They rambled pleasantly about "the Punch and Judy Club" and a painting club in which the teacher gave them the names of flowers. The most important thing, they said, was that they were treated as if they were the teacher's own children. Most of the teachers were unmarried, in their recollection. Ruby recalled receiving her first doll as a gift from one of her Hull-House teachers.

The word *respect* came up again and again: Jane Addams "respected us" and "she respected people's traditions." An important sign of this respect was that they were never yelled at or made to feel small. "None of the teachers lost their tempers," said Ruby. Marie added: "I never saw anybody lose a temper. I heard Miss Jane Addams raise her voice just once. She had a very gentle voice. But somebody came to the door and said somebody else had been accused of something, and it was all wrong. I was a child and I didn't know what it was all about. But she raised her voice that time. Then she calmed down. She could be firm, and she always got her point across, but never with shouting. Never. Without bullying anyone, you could say that she had a lot of power because everyone respected her."

Asked to elaborate on her experience of being respected, Marie recalled a painful childhood stutter. In her first play, *Puppet Princess*, she had two pages of lines to learn. "I cried and cried and said I wouldn't be able to do it. But Miss de Nancrede said, 'Marie, yes, you are going to do it,' and I did it. Every night I did it, I did it." Overcoming this stutter changed her life, she told me, as she lost her fear of people and of speaking. Ruby volunteered: "What we're telling you is that we hear a lot of stuff about Jane Addams that is just wrong. I don't know what all she did when she went to Washington or abroad, all I know is Miss Jane Addams of Hull-House, and she bettered the lives of thousands of people. When she died, the crowds streamed in for days. Our mothers were crying. She was such a simple lady. She never did anything with any ego of any kind. She would walk into a room and all us kids would run to her. And she would give us a hug. You'd better believe she'd give us a hug. She was wonderful. She was more of a mother for some kids than their own mothers. Her love rubbed off on all people."

Marie concurred: "She would never have had anybody around Hull-House who wasn't kind or who didn't want to teach a child in the right way, with respect. People learned music and went on to symphony orchestras. Maybe you know that Hull-House is where Benny Goodman got his start. You would pay 50 cents for a lesson—if you had it. Miss de Nancrede always told us that you have to go out in the world one day and not everything is free, so if you can pay something, you should, because that helps everybody else. At Hull-House, everything was beautiful. Clean, fresh, never slipshod or second-rate."

Learning was a part of every Hull-House activity, as illustrated by Ruby and Marie's account of their summertime activities at the Bowman Country Club, where they studied wildflowers and birds. Marie said: "They were teaching us all the time, even at camp. You didn't even know you were being taught. We'd go on stargazing expeditions at night and name the galaxies." Ruby nodded, adding: "It was all a part of experience. It wasn't social work. I don't know where that came from. It wasn't like that at all." Marie agreed: "Not at all. You know, Hull-House was a wonderful place. We try to get this across, but people just don't seem to understand."

Asked to sum up Hull-House and Miss Jane Addams, their words tumbled out: "She opened up a whole new world for us, is what she and the others did. . . . I see her as a great lady. All this controversy and stuff some people are saying, it just kills me. . . . She just had a way with children, a way with people. And she emphasized responsibility. 'You can do it,' she would say. 'You can do it,' and we did it partly because we didn't want to disappoint her. We did it out of respect. If you wanted books, the librarian would talk to you to find out what you were interested in, and then she'd say, 'This is for Ruby' or 'This is for Marie.' They paid attention to us as individuals. Everything was personalized. You weren't just some kid. They wanted you to be the best you could be. And a lot of the time you didn't even know you were learning, it was done in such a caring and loving way." Hull-House was, in Ruby's words, "the greatest experience of my life." Because of Hull-House, the two women completed high school and entered into a world of dance, art, theater, and reading that they have never abandoned. They say it helped to teach them respect for people different from themselves and made them more generous and broad-minded.

You weren't just another kid: that was surely the greatest gift Hull-House and Jane Addams gave to Ruby and Marie. "Miss Jane Addams never talked down to us," said Ruby. "She never used words you couldn't understand. But she and the others made sure you understood. They were teachers in everything they did. Hull-House was her life, her family." She recalled a campaign speech made in her behalf, when she ran for president of one of the clubs, and a little group singing campaign songs in Mexican, French, Bohemian, and German. Each culture was respected; they were all in it together. Marie volunteered, "Hull-House was the center," and Ruby echoed, "Yes, the center."

But our conversation ended on a rather somber note—without any suggestive questioning from me. Ruby and Marie brought up another grievance, having to do with Hull-House and race. They described being in classes with Mexican and African American children at Hull-House. "And we didn't give it another thought," notes Marie. "Hull-House brought us all together. We played and worked with everybody. Everybody was equal." Ruby continued: "We never heard racist stuff. But we read somewhere, or maybe it was on one of those programs on television, that 'Hull-House was racist,' and this made us furious. Our classes were all integrated. There were all kinds of people. We didn't even know this word 'racist.' You know, Miss Jane Addams never pointed a finger and said, 'You're Spanish,' or 'You're Italian.' We were Marie and Ruby. We were the Italian neighbors. We were children. She taught us to respect each other's traditions. *But the world now is a bunch of terrible words.*"

A bunch of terrible words: the phrase lingered in my mind as I said good-bye and set about listening to the four-hour tape and transcribing the conversation while it was still fresh. Unfortunately, scholars are not immune from contributing to, or even initiating, a bunch of terrible words from a stance of condescension or ahistorical present-mindedness, and adding thereby to the mountain of terrible words that bears down on our current civic culture. It is important to distinguish between keen, responsible criticism and gratuitously terrible words. Clearly, it is time to weigh the relative merit of the many wildly disparate evaluations of Jane Addams. But before we can do so accurately, we must first consider what all of these evaluations have in common: on what points do Addams's interpreters agree?

1

⌘

THE SNARE OF PREPARATION

JANE ADDAMS LIVED A quintessentially public life; there are no mysterious lost periods in her story. Records are sparse from the six months she spent bedridden following back surgery performed by her brother-in-law Harry Haldeman—probably due to her relative inactivity during this period and to her state of mind (she had reportedly suffered a nervous breakdown). But apart from this six-month period, her whereabouts and her actions are well documented. Born September 6, 1860, she was christened Laura Jane Addams; but throughout her childhood and youth, she was called Jennie by her close family members and friends. She was the eighth of nine children of John Huy and Sarah Weber Addams, and one of only four (three girls and one boy) to reach adulthood. Her mother died when she was two years old. She was cared for by her older sisters until 1868, when her father married Anna Haldeman, a widow with two children. Jane Addams entered the Rockford Female Seminary in 1877, and graduated in 1881. She was retroactively awarded a bachelor's degree in 1882, when Rockford Seminary became Rockford College and gained the right to confer that degree on students who had completed qualifying work in science.

The most important event of her young adult years was the death of her father in August 1881—an event that plunged her into a paroxysm of self-doubt ending in the breakdown of her own health and a long period of psychosomatic invalidism. During her early adulthood—the years that she called "the snare of preparation"—she made two trips to Europe: one in 1883–1885, and a second in 1887–1888. Her European trips were punctuated by a winter in Baltimore in 1884, where her stepbrother George Haldeman was pursuing graduate studies at Johns Hopkins University, and by two summers in her Cedarville home (1885 and 1886). During the first of those summers, she was baptized and joined the Presbyterian church in her village.

In January 1889, having hatched a scheme of moving into a "big house" in a "congested quarter" of Chicago in order to establish a settlement there based on the model of Toynbee Hall in London, Addams and her friend Ellen Gates Starr began their search for a suitable site. Hull-House opened its doors on September 18 that same year, and a period of rapid expansion followed, during which buildings sprang up and activities sprouted like mushrooms, seemingly overnight. Addams was hailed as one of America's most extraordinary and influential young women. Among Hull-House's residents were many who later played a foundational role in American social reform, including Julia Lathrop and Florence Kelley.[1]

By the turn of the century, Jane Addams's praises were being sung in every quarter. In one way or another, her name is attached to every major social reform between 1890 and 1925. But irritation also began to surface among some observers in response to her defense of anarchists following the 1901 assassination of President William McKinley. A few years later, her activities took a more partisan turn, when she served as a delegate to the national convention of Progressives and as a member of the party's platform committee in 1912. At the national convention, she seconded the nomination of Theodore Roosevelt for president. Her peace activities, at first lauded, later exposed her to public ridicule and scorn. She opposed U.S. entry into World War I in 1917 and broke with most of her fellow Progressives on this issue. She spearheaded the American Woman's Peace Party, which became a founding section of the Women's International League for Peace and Freedom.

At the first congress of the Women's International League, held in the Hague in 1915, Addams was elected president—a position to which she was reelected in every year following, until she stepped down from responsibility for direct, hands-on leadership (and even then she was named honorary president for life). Addams's wartime activities and her defense of immigrants and aliens earned her a blacklisting by the Lusk Committee of the New York state legislature in 1919. Interestingly, although she voted for Socialist Eugene Debs for president of the United States in 1920, Herbert Hoover earned her votes in 1928 and in

1932. She respected Hoover for his role in famine relief in postwar Europe—an effort in which she had participated. In 1931, the University of Chicago awarded her an honorary doctorate, and she received the Nobel Peace Prize (with Nicholas Murray Butler).

Her health was uncertain for many years, and she endured bouts of appendicitis, a heart attack, and a kidney operation. She died in Chicago on May 21, 1935, of cancer. All of Chicago was plunged into mourning. Expressions of sympathy and regret poured in from around the world. At her request, she was taken back to the village of Cedarville for burial. Her close friend and companion Mary Rozet Smith, who had signed on with Hull-House in its early years, taking on responsibility for the boys' clubs, had preceded her in death.

No one disputes these facts, although some have quibbled over a date or two (Addams's first biographer, her nephew James Weber Linn, was a bit haphazard with dates). However, a minor controversy arose around Addams's version of a bullfight she saw in Madrid, in April 1888, and later recounted in *Twenty Years at Hull-House*. Addams attended the bullfight with friends. She suggests in her autobiography that she was overcome with revulsion at her own attraction to the ritualized brutality. She describes her friends, who had left the fight early in disgust, as "stern and pale with disapproval of my brutal endurance," for she stayed to the very end, transfixed by the noise, the blood, the spectacle. But in a letter written at the time, she does not use the bullfight as an occasion for moral redress and improvement, and she makes no mention of friends leaving early even as she remained to the bitter, glorious end. According to historian Christopher Lasch, "[Her] autobiography almost invariably tends to read back more significance into earlier events than the contemporary records seem to warrant; more significance, at least, than she was aware of at the time."[2]

The matter in dispute—and it isn't much of a dispute—is Addams's reconstruction and interpretation of events in her life. Interpretive ambiguity is more or less inevitable whenever people put pen to paper to tell the story of a life, whether their own or someone else's. As attuned as Addams was to narrative structure, the requirements of drama, and the need to tether important ethical decisions to concrete and vivid events, it would not be at all surprising for the bullfight sequence to take on a more elaborate role when placed within a later narrative about her life at Hull-House. All of us tend to read particular significance into past events so as to make sense of what occurred after those events. Addams clearly believed that a sturdy self is a self that makes sense, not a self that is "all at sea" about life's meaning and purposes.

Being no doubt aware that no history, including that of one's own life, can reproduce things exactly as they happened, Addams must have appreciated that what she omitted or retold in a way that differed from a contemporaneous account was a sidebar, not the main story. Her primary concern was to close the gap between thought and deed, and her civic identity sprang from this concern. What use, she reasoned, are grand ideas if they can never be put into practice in some way?

Such pragmatism can, in some individuals, lead to brute reductionism and debasement of all complex, abstract thought. I do not see this tendency in Addams; however, others have, including Christopher Lasch, whose book *The New Radicalism in America* first piqued my interest in Addams. Although I do not entirely agree with Lasch's interpretation (in particular, with his chapter titled "Jane Addams: The College Woman and the Family Claim"), I was intrigued by his interweaving of Addams's personal emotional crises of lassitude, ennui, and despair with her public, active solution to those crises: Hull-House. His intuition of a deep conflict born in the interaction between the morally earnest eight-year-old Addams and her demanding, artistically inclined stepmother—a conflict mirrored in competing currents in American society at the time—is convincing. Such a conflict is implicit in Addams's omission of her stepmother from her official life story. Yet Addams also possessed the ability to depersonalize such conflicts and to perceive the wider cultural strands at work even in personal experiences. That being the case, it would be ironic indeed were the scholar writing about her to violate Addams's own sense of how a public self comes into being.

Although Lasch speculated about Addams's psychological motivation and identified a certain "anti-intellectualism" in her extolment of "applied knowledge," he did view her primarily as a theorist and an intellectual—"a thinker of originality and daring"—a conclusion that is borne out by my own analysis in this book. To his credit, Lasch got Addams's hard-won purposes right—"not so much . . . helping the poor as . . . understanding them," and "bridging the chasm that industrialism had opened between social classes." The fact that Addams did not write an omnibus theory of society "because she distrusted the dogmatism with which such theories are often associated," Lasch saw as a strength, not a weakness.[3] Lasch helps us get at the roots of Addams's identity formation and the motivation behind others' condescending treatment of her as a thinker, adopting her struggle—namely, sympathetic understanding—as his own. For Addams, this approach was the indispensable core of what might best be called the democratic character.

Lasch's attempt at sympathetic understanding is rarer than it should be. Sadly, many who have written about Addams have made no such effort. As a result, when we read most accounts that postdate her death and burial, we enter the strangely abstract and perpetually unsettled realm of criticism. No wonder Ruby and Marie are vexed.

The Politics of Criticism

Jacob Riis, a journalist with a reputation for devastating exposés of the awful conditions in America's early-twentieth-century cities, also penned these rare words of praise: "They have good sense in Chicago. Jane Addams is there."[4] This sentiment was not shared universally. In a 1934 tract titled *The Red Network: A Who's Who and Handbook of Radicalism for Patriots,* the mightily exercised Elizabeth Dilling described Jane Addams as a dangerous radical masquerading as a saintly champion of the poor. In Dilling's view, Addams was so "greatly beloved because of her kindly intentions toward the poor" that she was "able to do more probably than any other living woman (as she tells in her own books) to popularize pacifism and to introduce radicalism into colleges, settlements, and respectable circles." Dilling's warning to readers to avoid Addams's dangerous influence echoes the language used in World War I propaganda against aliens and seditionists: "One knowing of her consistent aid of the Red movement can only marvel at the smooth and charming way she at the same time disguises this aid and reigns as 'queen' on both sides of the fence."[5] Dilling claims to have been impressed by Addams's charming subterfuge during their only face-to-face encounter, which occurred in May 1933, at a legislative hearing in Chicago.

A different form of depreciation appears in a 1991 book by literary historian and theorist Tom Lutz, titled *American Nervousness: An Anecdotal History.* Lutz's interesting analysis of turn-of-the century diagnoses of nervous disorders including neurasthenia, with which Jane

Addams was diagnosed, is marred by his undisguised contempt for what he sees as Addams's insensitivity to other cultures. He describes Addams as one "of the haughty few" who interpreted their personal afflictions as the result of the debilitating effects of overcivilization on the well educated and who nonetheless felt a need to "civilize the masses." As evidence for this view, Lutz cites the fact that "Jane Addams, when she opened her settlement house in Chicago after years as a neurasthenic invalid, had as a prime ingredient in the routine for her *inmates* a course of reading in the classics of Anglo-American literature" (the italics are mine).[6] Reading this, I felt relieved that Ruby and Marie were unlikely to stumble on this tome and find themselves labeled "inmates." Jane Addams's neighbors, free to come and go as they pleased through Hull-House's open door, are turned into inmates of a coercive institution that cruelly subjected them to forced readings of Sophocles and George Eliot. Lutz apparently didn't know (or didn't care) that the literature classes were not only a vital part of the vast array of activities at Hull-House but were among the most popular. The classics of the cultures of the immigrant groups in the neighborhood were read, appreciated, and performed as drama. In Lutz's use of the word *inmates,* and in his disdain for the real suffering of those in Addams's time who were labeled "neurasthenic" (as if this were somehow a moral failure), one senses a disheartening tendency to condescend and demean. As nervous as Dilling and her contemporaries were about subversives, Lutz is contemptuous of purpose, meaning, and idealistic undertaking, seeing in such efforts only the harsh hand of hegemony. The diverse people who flocked to Hull-House out of curiosity, loneliness, fear, need, perplexity, pride, and a search for entertainment or intellectual possibility—all of them, young and old, become in his mind inmates confined to Jane Addams's asylum, a captive population for brainwashing. Such condescension is breathtaking.

Another book that taxes Jane Addams with a determination to generate homogeneity out of diversity is historian Rivka Shpak Lissak's *Pluralism and Progressives: Hull House and the New Immigrants, 1890–1919.* Lissak describes the immigrants living in the 19th ward as "helpless masses" rather than inmates and alleges that this is how Jane Addams related to her neighbors, although this characterization is unsubstantiated by Addams's own writings. There is no evidence that Addams considered people helpless—except, perhaps, infants. She clearly believed that many were bereaved, forlorn, exhausted, down on their luck, driven around the bend, laid up, and ground down by difficult circumstances, yes, but never helpless. Nor did she think of them as an uneducated group "to be passively led" (Lissak claims that this was Addams's "rationalization" for forcing them all into a single mold).[7] What Addams referred to as her incorrigible belief in democracy made her wary of paternalism, even as she believed that some individuals were called to help point the way for others.

Her view is similar to that advanced by African American scholar and activist W.E.B. DuBois, who was invited by Addams to lecture at Hull-House.[8] As sociologist Mary Jo Deegan notes: "The consistent misinterpretation of Addams's stance on immigrants is truly difficult to understand. Although condescending passages can be found . . . , her overwhelmingly more frequent and articulate stance against such attitudes far outweighs these other portions of her writings. . . . Addams found the American stress on homogeneous behavior and conformity to be stultifying."[9]

Although public criticisms similar to these were voiced during Addams's lifetime, the commentary was overwhelmingly positive before the outbreak of World War I and after the wartime fervor subsided. Addams notes that she was embarrassed by the often fulsome praise. Perhaps it was partly for this reason that she became involved in creating and controlling her official life story, which was written by her nephew James Weber Linn.[10] Addams read and authorized the first eight chapters of this biography; however, her death in 1935 prevented her from seeing the work through to completion. Linn's book, which was published in 1937, describes the extraordinary outpouring of public grief at Addams's passing (see chapter XXI, titled "She Goes in Peace"). Without his aunt's restraining hand, he occasionally gave in to the urge toward superlatives: "The death of no other citizen of Chicago, perhaps, ever provoked such grief; but it is quite certain that no other citizen of Chicago inspired such a sense of glory shared."[11] He was not alone in experiencing this urge: The Chicago City Council unanimously passed a resolution naming Addams "The greatest woman who ever lived." A former governor of Illinois and ex-mayor of Chicago, Mr. Dunne, commented in "broken-hearted" tones over the radio: "There was a great woman of the past, the Mother of God, whose name was Mary; and there is a great woman of the present, the Mother of Men, whose name is Jane Addams, and they stand alone in history."[12] In concluding, Linn wrote, if his aunt were "long remembered, it will be for the quality of her thinking, for her rightness as an interpreter of individuals to themselves and of social groups one to another."[13] Ironically, the very abilities that many contemporaries found in Addams have since been largely forgotten, neglected, or downplayed.[14]

Leaping from Linn's biography to *Life* magazine's fall 1990 tribute to "The One Hundred Most Important Americans of the Twentieth Century," we find Addams figuring as a suffragist and social worker. The two paragraphs on Addams include a description of Hull-House as a "center providing meals, job training, education and even a home for Chicago's immigrant poor"—making Hull-House sound more like a Great Society–era program rather than the complex intercultural space that it was.[15] Perhaps we are so accustomed to thinking of the poor as clients rather than citizens, as recipients of social provision rather than active architects of their own destinies, that we have lost a civic vocabulary rich enough to accurately and fully describe the reality of Hull-House. In any case, the real, three-dimensional Addams—the prolific writer and prominent intellectual and public figure—is worth nary a nod.

The *New York Times* also depicted Addams in this vein. In a 1989 article headlined "At Chicago's First Settlement House, Clients Are New but Problems Are Old," the language of clientage predominates. Portraying the old Hull-House of Jane Addams as a valiant but limited effort undermined by reliance on donations from wealthy benefactors, the article details the current annual budgetary needs of the contemporary enterprise that goes by the same name. Nowadays, the six sites in Chicago that have inherited the Hull-House name are staffed by "350 salaried professionals in the social services."[16] Whatever Addams might have thought of the current social programs, she would certainly have avoided the language of clientage. She would have opposed any suggestion of the dependence or subordination of the needy to those presumably in a position to satisfy their needs, for this was precisely the dynamic she warned against.

The Politics of Historic Assessment

Some distortions of Jane Addams's life and work are the result of change over time in popular images of American womanhood. What in the Catholic tradition is called a vocation—associated historically with vows of chastity, poverty, spiritual devotion, and a life lived in community with cobelievers—was embraced, altered, and mingled with potent maternal imagery in Jane Addams. Jane Addams's life of moral seriousness, lived in a community largely composed of women (although Hull-House was the first settlement to include both male and female residents), and her deeply felt maternalism (although she had no children of her own) are a combination we seem to find difficult to understand. Historian Allen F. Davis, whose *American Heroine,* a biography of Addams, appeared in 1973, interviewed one of the last remaining members of that extraordinary group of founding mothers of Hull-House, Alice Hamilton, who was in her nineties in 1963. He questioned her about the relationships among the women residents at Hull-House and reports: "She denied that there was any open sexual activity involving Hull House residents, but agreed that the close relationship of the women involved an unconscious sexuality. Because it was unconscious, it was unimportant, she argued. Then she added with a smile that the very fact that I would bring the subject up was an indication of the separation between my generation and hers."[17]

Hamilton was right. We are driven to expose what we take to be the most secret, hence truest (or so we believe), aspects of a person's life— as if tearing off veils, however gossamer-like, would reveal the whole truth.[18] But that impulse reveals more about us than about the object of our attention. That women in Jane Addams's era formed lifelong friendships; that those friends loved one another; that they expressed this love in effusive ways—all of this is well documented. Salutations in Addams's letters to her close friend and companion Mary Rozet Smith include *Dearie, Dearest, My Ever Dear,* and the like. The redoubtable Florence Kelley—a committed socialist, translator of Marx and Engels, and divorcée with three children when she came to Hull-House—addresses Smith in the same way. A letter from Kelley to Smith, dated February 14, 1899, begins *Dearly Beloved* and ends *Your loving F.K.*[19] The nature of Addams's relationship with the rather quiet Smith, who preferred to stay out of the limelight, is attested to by photographs, letters, memoirs, and the observations of contemporaries. There is no doubt that they had a special relationship. But *we* are the ones who insist on sexualizing it to conform to the political exigencies of our age.[20]

Every age reads its own obsessions into the record of ages past, but one should guard against this tendency rather than succumb to it. Writing about the controversy surrounding the writer Willa Cather, and about attempts over the years to either repudiate her or to embrace her depending upon whether she can or cannot be made to fit a particular political agenda, Joan Acocella could as well be describing Addams and her friends: "Crushes were common among college girls in Cather's day. And as feminist scholars have recently shown, women in the nineteenth century, the century in which Cather grew up, had far more effusive, more physical friendships than they have today. They wrote each other endearments; they snuggled, held hands, slept in the same beds."[21]

What exactly would be revealed, if definitive proof were discovered of carnal activity among Hull-House women? That Jane Addams's many close friendships sustained her in her public enterprises is significant. Her capacity for friendship and love and her ability to inspire loyalty and devotion in and from others helped make Hull-House and her civic role possible. That she and so many among this first generation of college-educated women did not marry is unsurprising. Being unmarried was unremarkable. For unmarried women to work together was similarly unremarkable. That we find it remarkable, and the public expression of a private secret, indicates not only a preoccupation with the sexual but also a tendency to reduce all social and political phenomena to either psychology or sex. Psychologized and sexualized caricatures of Addams omit her most salient features—those of a first-rate thinker and a gifted writer with extraordinary social and political influence.

A refreshing departure from this reductionist approach is that taken by historian John Farrell, whose *Beloved Lady: A History of Jane Addams' Ideas on Reform and Peace* demonstrates the author's recognition of Addams's power as a thinker.[22] Allen Davis's much better known book on Addams, in contrast, endorses the dominant opinion that she is "more important as a publicist and popularizer" than as a thinker with any claim to originality.[23] Social theorist Daniel Levine, author of *Jane Addams and the American Liberal Tradition,* concurs: Addams was "not an original thinker" but a "publicist" alive "to the currents of the day."[24]

In a number of influential social and cultural histories of the time, Addams is not even mentioned. In *The American Mind,* the great historian Henry Steele Commager completely ignores her.[25] Commager's foreword to a paperback edition of *Twenty Years at Hull-House* does take note of her "literary talent" and her "direct, lucid, and simple" style; but Commager erroneously interprets her writings as the effortless outpourings of a noble character, instead of the painstakingly worded, purposeful communications that they were. "She never thought of herself," he writes (again in error), asking, "Was there ever a more impersonal autobiography?" He concludes by burnishing the Saint Jane image. The real Addams—whose carefully crafted essays made her a leading public intellectual, and who thought frequently about herself and whether she was being good, fair, self-pitying, or self-centered—evaporates in favor of paeans to a noble and selfless life.[26]

Anne Firor Scott, a pioneer of woman's history, hails Addams's "clear convictions" but judges her mind not to be "the skilled instrument of the scholar or the logician, but one of intuitive wisdom." In Scott's words, "She was a mystic possessed of a devastating common sense who viewed everyday experience from a new angle of vision, distilling from it compelling insights into the human and social cost of industrial capitalism and international conflict."[27] I believe that Scott overstates the intuitive dimension of Addams's thought and underestimates her devotion to the craft of reasoned argumentation. (Addams sometimes worked ten hours a day when she was completing a writing project.) Addams was certainly no mystic—at least not in the traditional sense of the word—but she does share with Walt Whitman a lyrical evocation of American possibility, and that is no doubt what Scott has in mind.

Unlike Scott, historian Jill Ker Conway makes no attempt to understand Addams in the context of her writing and her life's work. As Conway describes Addams in an article published in 1965 in the influential journal *Dædalus*,[28] she was a driven woman who "desired a public life of restless activism, and saw fulfillment for these desires only in terms of extreme individualism"—a perplexing conclusion that runs counter to Addams's lifelong philosophy of sociality and her dedication to the collaborative community of Hull-House. In all of Addams's writings, too, her loathing of individualism and self-seeking is clear. Although crediting Addams with lucidity, Conway argues that she was a "popular writer" rather than a "systematic thinker." The feminist historian passes the harshest of judgments against Addams without defining her own criteria of systematicity.[29]

The world that Jane Addams hailed from is characterized by Conway as one of "comfortable barbarities." One wonders what Conway sees as barbaric: the abolitionist convictions held by Addams's father? Or the fact that the village lending library was located in the Addams's parlor? Or the small rural Illinois town itself? Conway does not tell us. Her fictive Jane Addams moves from the "comfortable barbarities" of her upbringing to "found a salon in a slum"—and a "sordid" slum, at that. The word *slum* is a denigration of the immigrant city. The implicit suggestion is that Jane Addams, college girl, was just going slumming with a few pals when she founded Hull-House. Addams is transfixed as a specimen exemplifying the very tendencies she spent her entire life opposing, especially "the philosophy of extreme individualism"; she is labeled "emotionally frozen," for that is the fate of all "ruthless individualists." The power and pathos of the complex journey that brought Addams to Hull-House is called "frenetic" and "pathetic." Conway uses a lot of terrible words in her strange assault on Addams.[30] But as Farrell notes, "Hull House stood first of all for social democracy"; and social democracy is not a philosophy of individualism.[31]

Addams's detractors are plentiful, however. Davis chides Addams for refusing to acknowledge "her administrative talent and her ability to compete in a man's world." These qualities "actually made her a success," he writes. What is the gist, then, of his complaint? We know that Addams could more than hold her own in fast political company and that she did so publicly on numerous occasions without tooting her own horn in the process. Numerous newspapers articles attest to her strategic abilities. The one excerpted below, published in the *Chicago Tribune* on April 15, 1905,[32] was written in a humorous vein and designed to show how Addams operated in political forums.

> Miss Jane Addams did craftily, underhandedly and feloniously deceive, perplex and otherwise bewilder the gentlemen who appeared at Springfield to assist in the passage of the child actor bill. She has for years been acquiring a reputation as a "reformer," and yet, behold, when the day of judgment arrives she shows a more intimate acquaintance with the theater than any of its authorized and accredited representatives. Some of the gentlemen who were furthering the interests of the children on the stage were Methodists and felt themselves under the necessity of admitting that they attended

the theater only occasionally and were more concerned in the general principle of the bill than in any particular application of it. This admission was made in Chicago before the descent on Springfield, and it led straight into Miss Addams' ambuscade. "Ben Great told me this, Sir Henry Irving told me that." "I became convinced of the following facts by watching the performance of such and such a play." "No there weren't seventeen children in that performance—there were twenty-three." What can be done with a "reformer" of this kind? She knows her own business and if she tries to reform somebody else's business she sets to work and studies it until she knows more about it that he does. People aren't accustomed to this kind of thing from "reformers." It takes them unaware and at a great disadvantage. By one display of real knowledge Miss Addams made the theater representatives at Springfield look ridiculous. She won her point. The child labor law will remain as it is and the field of labor for children on the stage will not be enlarged. But Miss Addams will never be trusted again. She may not be a sociologist but she is not harmless. She probably reads the Journal of Sociology, but when she goes after an abuse in real life she learns about it at first hand. This is why Miss Addams fails to please either the ultra conservatives or the ultra radicals.

Accounts such as this amply testify to Addams's skill and power. Why should she have focused on publicizing herself when she wanted the attention to be on her purpose instead? To demand this of her shows a complete lack of familiarity with Addams's sensibilities. Surely the evidence of her life is testimony enough.[33] Addams's sense that she was fated not to please either side in many disputes was borne out again and again, in her own epoch and in ours. In the chapter titled "Civic Cooperation," in her *Twenty Years at Hull-House,* her description of a conflict with the Chicago public school system supports this conclusion: "I was chairman of the School Management Committee during one year when a majority of the members seemed to be exasperatingly conservative, and during another year when they were frustratingly radical, and I was of course highly unsatisfactory to both."[34]

An inability to peg her, coupled with a determination to do so in the interests of one or another ideological agenda, has hampered most of Addams's detractors. Unlike them, Addams herself had a gift for speaking *to* the right, the left, and the center, without speaking *for* any camp in the narrowly consistent way so cherished by ideologues. Perhaps this ability was the hard-won product of her earlier struggle to define herself, during the period of her life that she later referred to as the "snare of preparation."

The "Snare of Preparation": Reading Jane Addams

Addams borrowed this phrase from an English edition of a work by the great Russian writer Leo Tolstoy, using it to describe the years of her young adulthood, when she was "all at sea" about her purposes. When she began to consider how she was being prepared for adult life, she became vexed with the inactivity, the seemingly endless waiting period, and the inability to "reduce"—a word she used in a sense we have largely abandoned, meaning to "distill"—her ideas into actions. It is unsurprising that she adopted the words of the great Tolstoy to describe her discomfort in this difficult period. What nearly all scholars and critics of Addams have missed or given short shrift to is just how much hers was a literary mind. Her sensibilities were forged in the generous company of literary personages who became companions in her struggles personal and political. Addams sought and found these companions in and through literary works, among living authors as well as protagonists who never lived except on the printed page.

A partial list of references appearing in the narrative of *Twenty Years at Hull-House* includes Ruskin, Carlyle, De Quincey, Browning, Plutarch, Irving (*Life of Washington*), Thomas Green, Gibbons (*Decline and Fall of the Roman Empire*), Emerson, Amos Bronson Alcott, Homer, Plato, Sombart, Maeterlinck, Darwin, Gray's *Anatomy*, *The Iliad*, Mazzini, H. G. Wells, Comte, Tolstoy, George Eliot, Hawthorne, Victor Hugo, John Locke, Pestalozzi, Beatrix Potter, Henry George, J. S. Mill, Schopenhauer, Engels, Masurek, Dewey, Goethe, Keir Hardie, G. B. Shaw, Sidney and Beatrice Webb, Karl Liebknecht, Luther, Graham Taylor, William Dean Howells, William James, *The Antigone*, Wordsworth, Walt Whitman, Galsworthy, Harnack, Ibsen, Yeats, Dante, Bakunin, Shakespeare, Gorki, Herbert Spencer, St. Francis, and so on. Addams had absorbed all of these works; they were part of the air she breathed, and they molded the dreams she dreamed. Although she was an avid reader of fiction, she was ambivalent about this interest, fearing that it might lead to an inability to engage the real world except through literary forms and allusions. She also found much of the fiction of her time—especially that aimed at women—frivolous, with an overly romantic or melodramatic depiction of life (an opinion shared by George Eliot, one of her favorite writers).

Herself a writer's writer, Addams has had few readers in recent years. Perhaps the tide now is turning. Although it would be premature to see the event as indicative of a renaissance of interest in her work, Addams's inclusion in the nineteenth edition of *The Norton Anthology of American Literature,* where she appears for the first time, is a good sign.[35] Addams was a practiced essayist, preferring that form over others because it best suited her purposes. Each of her books is a collection of essays on a particular theme. The narrative structure of some of her books—for example, *Twenty Years at Hull-House*—is chronological. In others, the essays are united only by their thematic subject (as in *Democracy and Social Ethics,* and *Peace and Bread in Time of War*).

For Addams, the essay was the perfect form within which to investigate a range of ethical and personal matters in a nondogmatic, exploratory way, a way that was both committed and open-ended. The essay was also the ideal genre in which to address her fellow citizens on the burning questions of the day as well as on more mundane concerns and events. In sum, the essay suited her complex and many-sided expository goals.

As a writer, Addams faced a number of daunting challenges: How could she write compellingly about quotidian concerns, the ordinary, the everyday, the eternal and pervasive—the life of woman in her role as "bread-giver" (as Addams envisioned woman's mission)? As I observe in my book *Women and War,* one frustration of pacifists is that war is more exciting than peace. War makes for a better story. It is an arena of heroic self-sacrifice.[36] Addams knew that great stories are often about stirring conflicts unto death; she herself loved the Greek classics and the Shakespearean tragedies. But what about being sentenced to life? To inexorable daily routines? Where was the dignity in that? Where was the adventure? Addams persistently sought and found dignity in the everyday tasks of tending to the well-being of the young and the old—sowing and sewing, planting and harvesting, covers for bodies, bread for stomachs, cool hands on fevered brows. But it was a struggle to convince others of the urgency, the importance of such affairs—and not only because they were viewed traditionally as women's work and hence devalued; the labor of the male peasant in the field or the factory worker in the assembly line was similarly unlikely to capture and hold many readers' interest.

Addams strove to show the adventure and conflict, the hope and despair, the little defeats and victories that are the stuff of life. Just as Greek tragedy was aimed at inculcating civic virtue and enhancing the capacity of citizens to act with foresight and to judge with insight, so Addams's narratives of daily life invite readers to similar forms of recognition and action. The mingling of stark terror and human indignity, the fusion of the small with the great in Addams's writing, opens up into a world as complex, terrifying, and conflicted in its redemptive power as anything devised by Sophocles. Here is but one example of her narrative skills and evocative power. I call it the Story of the Old German Woman Clinging to Her Chest of Drawers.[37]

> Some frightened women had bidden me come quickly to the house of an old German woman, whom two men from the county agent's office were attempting to remove to the County Infirmary. The poor old creature had thrown herself upon a small and battered chest of drawers and clung there, clutching it so firmly that it would have been impossible to remove her without also taking the piece of furniture. She did not weep nor moan nor indeed make any human sound, but between her broken gasps for breath she squealed shrilly like a frightened animal caught in a trap. The little group of women and children gathered at her door stood aghast at this realization of the black dread which always clouds the lives of the very poor. . . . The neighborhood women and I hastened to make all sorts of promises as to the support of the old woman, and the county officials, only too glad to be rid of their unhappy duty, left her to our ministrations. This dread of the poorhouse, the result of centuries of deterrent Poor Law administration, seemed to me not without some justification one summer when I found myself perpetually distressed by the unnecessary idleness and forlornness of the old women in the Cook County Infirmary, many of whom I had known in the years when activity was still a necessity, and when they yet felt bustlingly important. To take away from an old woman whose life has been spent in household cares all the

foolish little belongings to which her affections cling and to which her very fingers have become accustomed, is to take away her last incentive to activity, almost to life itself. To give an old woman only a chair and a bed, to leave her no cupboard in which her treasures may be stowed, not only that she may take them out when she desires occupation, but that her mind may dwell upon them in moments of revery, is to reduce living almost beyond the limit of human endurance.

In this vignette, Addams grips the reader's attention with a timeless story of old age and loss, reminding us that a life may be decocted to a cupboard or a chest of drawers—or in my grandmother's case, a sewing chest with neatly wound balls of thread and rickrack; small containers of buttons sorted by size, color, and shape; tiny pieces of cloth that might yet become a patch for a torn pants leg, or a piece in a colorful quilt. These she went over again and again in her twilight years, reminding us that she had built the drawers herself, for she was a carpenter as well as a seamstress. When my grandmother's wits deserted her, I imagined her dreaming of thread in tidy rows and bold pieces of cloth and all of the quilts she had lovingly made and given away over the years.

With stories such as these, in which we recognize our own lives' dramas, Addams calls us into empathy, humility, and large-heartedness of a sort that prepares us to travel into shabby rooms in decrepit buildings on a mission of discovering and ameliorating or mitigating (two of her favorite words). The tears shed on such occasions join the ever-flowing underground stream that gives life its inexorable sadness—the grief of "things as they are."

Jane Addams shared with George Eliot the staunch belief that—as Eliot writes at the conclusion of *Middlemarch*—the "growing good of the world is partly dependent on unhistoric acts"; and this belief perhaps best explains Addams's life and work. She found in the playing-out of her own ambition—in particular, the establishment at Hull-House of the settlement she had envisioned—a way of exerting her will toward the "growing good." At the age of twenty-nine, the year she and Ellen Gates Starr founded Hull-House, Addams wrote to her sister: "There's power in me, and will to dominate which I must exercise, they hurt me else."[38] She hoped to secure the necessary good of the unheroic by holding and containing it—giving it form—so that others could recognize it.

Addams rejected narratives she deemed frivolous, offering instead powerful nonfiction dramas of everyday life. In this sense, she fulfilled what the writer Flannery O'Connor considered the nature and aim of fiction—namely, a search for truth through a meaningful narrative.[39] Addams would extend O'Connor's claim about fiction to encompass all writing that aims to draw readers into closer contact with a complex social world—the sort of world she conveys in her essays. What does one see and hear and learn while living in Chicago's 19th ward? In her writing, Addams is an incarnational artist who bids us welcome into a world we would fain not enter (as she might put it). But if we have walked with her even part of the way, she assumes we will want to continue the journey, regardless of the difficulties.

For Jane Addams of Hull-House, as for Jennie Addams of Cedarville, life was a pilgrim's progress, and every step forward took all the courage, strength, and skill that she and her companions in pilgrimage could muster.

2

⚜

ONE PILGRIM'S PROGRESS

LIFE IS NEVER SIMPLE for the earnest child, alert to the ebb and flow around her; curious to the point of fearful insight into solemn events; driven to make sense, even of the senseless; wanting simultaneously to stand out and to blend in; seeking the self within available norms and conventions but also determined to bring forth new forms, new ideas, daring possibilities. Such a child often feels, in Jane Addams's words, an "excessive sense of responsibility." Because she is a child, she must search for appropriate targets for her ardent concern.[1] Her responsibility is not given to her in any simple way; indeed, her conviction that she *is* responsible is likely to outstrip the available outlets and avenues in and through which that responsibility can be made manifest. The earnest child is fated to have a "strict conscience, which she patrols like a sentinel so that no evasions of Christian duty slip by."[2] So it was for little Jennie Addams, who, as an adult, was insistent that "our genuine impulses may be connected with our childish experiences . . . where character is formless but nevertheless settling into definite lines of future development."[3]

Addams's story is that of a little girl sighing heavily from a precocious sense of responsibility. She was a painfully self-conscious child, describing herself as "ugly, pigeon-toed" with a "crooked back" that "obliged her to walk with her head held very much upon one side," an "Ugly Duckling." She would wake herself at three o'clock because that was when her father awoke. She would use the time to read every book in the "entire village library, book after book, beginning with the lives of the signers of the Declaration of Independence," as she believed her father had. She dreamed often of a dead world in which "I alone remained alive" and bore the responsibility to get things started again by successfully "making a wagon wheel." She heard stories from her father of big and little houses and how it came about that some have so little and others have so much more, leading her to declare that she would do something about that when she grew up.[4]

Her early letters reveal Jane Addams as a morally earnest and a *yearning* child. She longed for connection to all that was morally serious but she also possessed the saving gift of mild self-deprecation. Throughout her life she sustained a correspondence that generated thousands of handwritten notes of thanks to the ordinary people who had made contributions to Hull-House, however small; offering birthday greetings; acknowledging those who had sent flowers for some occasion or another, as "flowers are always welcome" to those who are "locked in struggle."

Addams is also revealed at a tender age as a *form-giver*—one who bestows shape, texture, and order to emotions, thoughts, intimations, and driving passions in every area of life, from the personal to the public. Her interest in politics, as one way in which a society expresses its most cherished norms and possibilities, had an early start. "I enjoy politics very much," she writes a friend, Vallie Beck, on March 21, 1877. In another letter to the same friend, dated May 3 of that year, she turns to the theme of friendship: "I am a great admirer of Platonic love or rather pure sacred friendship. I think it is so much higher than what is generally implied in the word love," for Platonic friendship affords a lofty form of intimacy, within which desire is sublimated. She was unstinting in her search for higher forms of friendship, thought, and action. But she also notes periods of lassitude, ruefully informing Beck, in a letter of August 3, 1878, that reading Edgar Allan Poe's "The Raven" prompted her to sit, perch, and "nothing more." She found this "occupation so delightful that I have continued to sit and do nothing ever since." One suspects that this mood didn't last long. Her correspondence with another childhood friend, Ellen Gates Starr, who became the cofounder with her of Hull-House, is suffused with self-reproach at not "having written promptly." To yet another friend, Eva Campbell, Addams indicates that the "state of my feelings" is "really of very little consequence" and she apologizes for having talked so much about them.[5] Addams embraced the hard work of disciplining her emotions by refusing to allow self-centered feelings to overtake her. She learned not to measure the world by the ups and downs of her inner barometer. The story of her childhood and young adulthood is, in large part, the story of a search for whoever and whatever would assist her in her self-appointed task.

Addams's youthful engagement with religious belief is instructive. She was not reared doctrinally. Her father called himself a Hicksite Quaker. In line with the generic liberal Protestantism of her day, Addams professed more interest in Jesus as a moral hero than in Jesus the Son of God. In 1879, she recommends to Ellen Starr a "little book by Horace Bushnell" on the "character of Jesus." The divinity of Christ, she flatly admits, perplexes her, although she confides to Starr, "I should be glad to believe it." She finds nothing illogical about Christ's divinity, but it is, for her, a hard pill to swallow.

Curiously, at about the same time as she was writing Starr, she drafted many letters to "My dear Ma"—her stepmother Anna—in which, having read Francis Bacon, she propounds a firm resolution "never to reason but . . . in the inductive method."[6] Just a few months later, however, she reports to her stepmother that she has never read anything as memorable as Homer: "I have never enjoyed the beginning and anticipation of anything as much as I have of that." To her sister, too, she enthuses about Homer, proclaiming that "although it sounds extravagant," she would be willing "to study Greek for ten years" if that would afford her the fun of reading Homer in the original. Milton also grips her imagination. The conflict between the apparent certainties of science and the grandeur, sweep, and penetration into the depths of the human heart found in Homer, Milton, and Charles Dickens—another of her schoolgirl favorites—gels in her adolescence to be one day resolved when she learns to turn the hard, cold facts about urban poverty and immigrant fears and alienation into literature, in a fusion of social science with art.

But neither Homer, nor Milton, nor Nathaniel Hawthorne, whose books she commends to friends, nor her beloved Dickens help her to resolve her torment over belief and unbelief. She reveals to Ellen Starr that she has embarked on a daring experiment—unmentioned in her autobiography—of not praying for three months. She is "shocked to find that I feel no worse for it." To Starr she confesses that she sees religion primarily through "understanding instead of by faith" and feels that she needs religion "only . . . in a practical sense."[7] God, she decides, didn't embody himself in Christ primarily in order to "reveal himself, but . . . he did it considering the weakness of man."[8] The human being "can occasionally comprehend an abstract deity but cannot live by one." An abstract center for faith may work for philosophers, but not for ordinary men and women. Starr found Addams's views on the inability of the ordinary person to live and think like a philosopher—to comprehend an abstract deity—trying; although Starr agreed in general "with the idea," she caviled at her friend's way of expressing it.

The path that Addams followed in her intellectual development was laid out early on. Her formidable, successful, politically active father, John Huy Addams, was the dominant influence in her life. It was to him that she dedicated *Twenty Years at Hull-House,* which was first published in 1910. At first glance, it seems paradoxical that Addams's father was the key figure in her life, given her own articulation of the sacred and social task of the woman as eternal bread-giver; her ample use of maternal metaphors to describe the work of Hull-House as well as her efforts after World War I to feed the hungry of devastated Europe; and her frequent references to the "great mother breasts of our humanity"—her poetic description of universal humanness. Yet Addams's autobiography attests that her father "held fast my supreme affection" and "drew me into the moral concerns of life."[9] "It is hard to account for the manifestations of a child's adoring affection, so emotional, so irrational, so tangled with the affairs of imagination," she writes, noting her "doglike affection" for her handsome, respected father.[10]

This desire to imitate the adored father extended to a quest for a "miller's thumb" like her father's, a thumb flattened and smoothed by the miller's repetitive rubbing of ground wheat between his thumb and fingers as it falls from the millstones. This "sincere tribute of imitation" becomes subtler in its manifestations as the child grows older. But the early, clumsy attempts at direct imitation, she claims, were "altogether genuine." Addams credits her father also for her aesthetic sensibility, although it was her stepmother who gave her early exposure to the world of art and music. She recalls the story of how her father had sown a stand of Norwegian pines in 1844, "the very year he came to Illinois, a testimony perhaps that the most vigorous pioneers gave at least an occasional thought to beauty."[11]

There are many reasons for her father's centrality to her life. Her mother, as noted in previous chapters, died when Jane Addams was two, and her father did not remarry until she was eight. But family history alone does not suffice to explain how her life became a "sincere tribute of imitation, which affection offers to its adored subject."[12] Addams turned to her father not only because she had been torn at a tender age from her mother's bosom but also because he embodied a world beyond the home and brought part of that world into the realm of domesticity. John Huy Addams offered young Jennie an expanded sense of the home.[13] For a time he ran a local lending library from the family's parlor.[14] He brought leading political figures through the portals to discuss their platforms and strategies. He shared portentous happenings with his daughter. For example, she recalls her father reporting gravely that Joseph [Giuseppe] Mazzini, an architect of the Italian *risorgimento,* or movement for Italian unification, had died. She had expressed skepticism about the significance of this event because she didn't understand what an Italian thinker and political leader could have to do with America. He helped her understand the connections.

The front door of the Addams home was never locked—something Jane Addams attributed to her father's Quaker background. The family's open door—a symbol of openness to and curiosity about the world—was a tradition that Jane Addams not only cherished but also maintained at Hull-House. The world's urgencies moved through its portals much as the churning currents of a river run between its banks. As guests entered the interior of the house, they were greeted by a beckoning, well-kept space, where they were treated with kindness, succored, sheltered, invited to learn and to teach.

The doors of Hull-House, once they opened September 18, 1889, were always open. Jane Addams often greeted visitors herself. "Hull House lived in a bracing, not a mawkish atmosphere. It met the world vigorously," wrote one observer who discovered Hull-House in 1906, when she was twenty-three years old.[15] Testimonials of this sort abound. Philip Davis, who immigrated from Russia to America around this time, describes in his autobiography *And Crown Thy Good*[16] a desultory existence until the day he entered Hull-House. He tells the story thus:

> The first time I approached Hull-House the door was open and I walked in. No one was in the reception hall so I sat down near a table, eyeing the books and magazines. Presently Jane Addams ap-

peared. From many pictures I had seen in the newspapers, I recognized her instantly. She greeted me cordially, then said: "Don't you want to read the *Atlantic Monthly* just out?" *The Atlantic Monthly* proved tough reading. After all, I came to see Jane Addams and Hull-House, not to read the *Atlantic Monthly*! Miss Addams passed through several times. Realizing I was lingering rather than reading, she tried conversation:

"Living around here?" she ventured.

"On DeKoven Street," I answered.

"Oh, then we are neighbors. You must come often," she said warmly. That was what I had hoped for.

Such was my introduction to Hull-House, the university of good will, good English, good citizenship. . . . Jane Addams had the happy faculty of liking people of diverse backgrounds. Unlike critics of the immigrants of that day, she encouraged us to build proudly on what was most valuable in our heritage. . . . Through such personal conversations with her neighbors on Halsted Street (with Greeks, Italians, Poles, Russians, and many others) she acquired an impressive knowledge of old-world cultures transplanted to this nation.

Drawn to Jane Addams's experiment, Florence Kelley, who later became a significant force in the history of American reform, was a resident at Hull-House before going on to become a leading crusader against child labor and the first Illinois Factory Inspector. She describes her initial experience of the open Hull-House door in similar fashion.[17]

On a snowy morning between Christmas 1891 and New Year's 1892, I arrived at Hull-House, Chicago, a little before breakfast time, and found there Henry Standing Bear, a Kickapoo Indian, waiting for the front door to be opened. [Note: The door was never locked, but it was closed during the night. And one was bidden to knock, as any good neighbor should.] It was Miss Addams who opened it, holding on her left arm a singularly unattractive, fat, pudgy baby belonging to the cook, who was behindhand with breakfast. Miss Addams was a little hindered in her movements by a super-energetic kindergarten child, left by its mother while she went to a sweatshop for a bundle of cloaks to be finished.

We were welcomed as though we had been invited. We stayed, Henry Standing Bear as helper to the engineer several months, when he returned to his tribe; and I as a resident seven happy, active years. . . . That first picture of her gently keeping the little Italian girl back from charging out into the snow, closing the door against the blast of wintry wind off Lake Michigan, and tranquilly welcoming these newcomers, is as clear today as it was at that moment.

Addams once tried to capture her philosophy of the open door in a poem.[18] Although her literary gifts did not lie in that direction, the poem does succeed in evoking the pensive mood made possible by Hull-House's provision of contemplative space, despite the constant bustle. Hull-House contained many moods, including the stirring of civic pride and sentiment. The poem, which became a Hull-House anthem, speaks

> *Of cities that shall be*
> *Within whose streets each citizen*
> *Shall live life worthily.*
> . . . .
> *Its doors are opened wide*
> *To all who come it bids "Good cheer,"*
> *To some it says: "Abide."*

It concludes that even through life's

> *hardest storm*
> *The shelter we together build*
> *Is all that keeps us warm;*
> *That fellowship is heaven-sent*
> *That it alone can free*
> *The human heart from bitterness*
> *And give it liberty.*

Addams alerts her readers here to a struggle against bitterness that would strangle the human heart, lock the doors, draw the blinds, and close the shutters. The house on the busy street, with its wide-open doors, is an opposing metaphor to a barricaded life that would make an idol of the gloomy, abject, needy self. Self-pity keeps us circling relentlessly in our own narrow orbit. Hull-House was no prison of refined domesticity but a parlor of affectionate and expansive worldliness. Its freedom was hard-won but was shared with others as a gift—a gift of the self.

Avoiding the Slough of Despond

Although Jennie Addams was at times "all at sea" about the course her life was taking, she never seemed to doubt life's central theme: a pilgrim's progress. Such an outlook is possible when a child's early and most basic affections are held fast and drawn into the moral life. Her father was the hub of that wheel, but there were many texts, literary and historical, that helped hold her affections and passions fast, molding in the process a character of sufficiently stern stuff that she *became* a self that would not wind up stuck in the Slough of Despond. She would be prepared to battle the monster Apollyon; to survive the torment meted out by the Giant Despair in the prison of his terrible Doubting Castle; to pass through the Valley of the Shadow of Death; to resist the seductions of Vanity Fair; and finally to enter the narrow Gates and join the heavenly city.

That the four personages who served as companions on this journey—Faithful, Hopeful, Timorous, and Pliable—must be further identified and explained to the contemporary reader is a measure of our distance from the world of Jane Addams's childhood. Although her father was a denominational latitudinarian who gave donations to every Protestant church in Cedarville, the flame of his moral convictions burned with a concentrated light. Apart from the Bible and the Declaration of Independence, no text did more to define the American character than John Bunyan's *Pilgrim's Progress*, first published in 1678.[19] It is difficult now to recapture the pervasive power and influence of Bunyan's tale "in the similitude of a Dream."[20] A work of moral edification, *Pilgrim's Progress* helped to create and to sustain the Puritan and post-Puritan temperament.[21] A religious allegory and a classic tale of moral heroism, *Pilgrim's Progress* is alive with vivid and frightening imagery. The reader suffers with the protagonist Christian, shares his desperation and his all-too-human backsliding, walks with him through sore testing, and tastes his final victory when in the company of his friend Hopeful he enters the Celestial City.

Given the course of Jane Addams's life, it is significant that Christian's entry into the Celestial City is made possible only with the help of, and in company of, a friend. Bunyan molded the dreams and fashioned the nightmares of generations of earnest Christian boys and girls. *Pilgrim's Progress* was part of the air Jane Addams breathed; she had received her own copy of the book at the age of fifteen years, as a gift from her teacher.

The book opens with Christian's "lamentable cry . . . 'What shall I do?'" as he peers over the edge of a yawning abyss. Those around him, including his wife and children (who are rescued for the Celestial City only in Part Two) are impervious to his deepening torment. Christian runs "from his own door . . . , his fingers in his ears, . . . crying, 'Life, life, eternal life.'" Fending off neighbors Obstinate and Pliable, Christian, with his load of burdens on his back, is directed by the Evangelist toward the Gate to the City. And thus begins the tale. Christian is hapless and falls into a terrible bog, wallowing in the Slough of Despond. Besmirched, he struggles out and continues on his way. Troubles mount up. But he will not be deterred by Mr. Worldly-Wiseman, who dwells in the town of Carnal-Policy, and who paints for Christian a fearsome picture of the obstacles he will meet as he makes his way to the Celestial City, including "wearisomeness, painfulness, hunger, perils, nakedness, sword, lions, dragons, darkness, and in a word, death."[22]

In this passage Bunyan is taking a swipe at the hollow rhetor who, like today's spin doctors, cunningly exploits and deepens the gap between saying and doing, between word and deed. Narrowing that gap was part of Jane Addams's lifelong project. Faithful denounces Talkative in the same words that Addams used later to attack the sort of abstract philosophizing in which concrete, embodied humanity vanishes. "Knowledge that resteth in the bare speculation of things, and knowledge that is accompanied with the grace of faith and love, which puts a man upon doing even the will of God from the heart: the first of these will serve the talker, but without the other the true Christian is not content."[23]

Having made it partway up the Hill of Difficulty, Christian speaks in verse:[24]

> *This Hill, though high, I covet to ascend,*
> *The difficulty will not me offend,*
> *For I perceive the way to life lies here;*

> *Come, pluck up, heart; let's neither faint nor fear:*
> *Better, though difficult, the right way to go,*
> *Than wrong, though easy, where the end is woe.*

A comparison with Jane Addams's favorite words of moral injunction to her Rockford Seminary classmates is instructive. She wrote on the flyleaf of a classmate's hymnal[25] the following exhortation:

> *Life's a burden, bear it.*
> *Life's a duty, dare it.*
> *Life's a thorn-crown? Wear it*
> *And spurn to be a coward.*

A young woman who expresses such sentiments has not been reared on a diet of literary pap. Like Bunyan's Christian, she takes the more arduous, interesting, and dangerous course. Like Bunyan, she keeps alive the immediacy of ongoing moral struggle through humor and vivid imagery. There are foul fiends, foremost among them the monstrous Apollyon, a horrible marvel and mix of species, with scales and wings, bear-like feet and a lion's mouth. When Christian was joined by Faithful (who meets his martyrdom before reaching the Gates), Bunyan tells us, they "went very lovingly on together, and had sweet discourse of all things that had happened to them in their pilgrimage."[26] It is this sweetness of discourse that sustains Christian, Faithful, and Hopeful on their way. When they are tired, Hopeful and Christian find that good discourse spares them from falling into a lethal slumber: "Saints' fellowship, if it be managed well, / Keeps them awake, and that in spite of Hell."[27]

Pilgrim's Progress is a storehouse of allegorical riches, biting commentary on human folly, and densely textured human fears and hopes. It is one of the texts that Jane Addams made her own. This text, with many others, helped create for her an intricate life of the mind and a sturdy yet supple identity given to action and to reflection on action. The fate of *Pilgrim's Progress* tells us a good deal about the American story. In Jane Addams's world, Bunyan was indispensable and inescapable, although the pitfalls and villains of that world were less obvious than those encountered by Bunyan's protagonist. It seems particularly significant that Christian abandoned domesticity in order to begin his pilgrimage: it

cannot have escaped the notice of this acutely intelligent, morally precocious young nineteenth-century woman that Christian had to leave
home on a journey in order to make his way to the Celestial City (as
well as to rescue his family from the City of Destruction, which he does
in the less-read second part of Bunyan's classic).

The Form-Giver

Jane Addams's life was a search for form, a way to give shape to her enthusiasms. She suggested the image of the bread-giver as a suitable symbol for the aspiring young women soon to graduate from the Rockford
Female Seminary. In a letter to her sister, January 23, 1880, Jane Addams explains the emblem on the class stationery—a design of wheat
and hops: "The hops I will admit are obscure but their significance is
deep. You know of course that Bread givers is the primitive meaning of
the word lady and there are sixteen girls in R.U.S. [the Rockford Semi-
nary] who mean to do all they can to restore the word to its original
sense—probably because they are so far off now from the accepted
meaning." Her 1880 oration as junior spokeswoman for the class of
1881 was entitled, simply, "Bread Givers." Noting the "change which
has taken place during the last fifty years in the ambition and aspirations of woman," she marks the passing from "the arts of pleasing, to
the development of her intellectual force, and her capabilities for direct
labor."[28] She hastens to add that woman "wishes not to be a man, nor
like a man, but she claims the same right to independent thought and
action."

As "young women of the 19th century" she and her Rockford classmates gladly claim privileges and opportunities; they "proudly assert"
their "independence." Yet they "still retain the old ideal of womanhood—the Saxon lady whose mission it was to give bread unto her
household." She continued, "So we have planned to be 'Bread-givers'
throughout our lives; believing that in labor alone is happiness, and
that the only true and honorable life is one filled with good works and
honest toil." Indeed, they would "idealize our labor, and thus happily
fulfill Woman's Noblest Mission."

One might read this ardent proclamation as a mere repeat of standard
images, a form of reassurance for concerned parents and teachers, that
these young women would proceed within acceptable, time-honored

lines of development. But this interpretation would be anemic. Jane Addams had an uncanny grasp of the human need for form and the companion requirement of balance. Unsurprisingly, her autobiography has been described by Leibowitz as a "masterpiece of balance—a trait that seldom inspires rapture." Leibowitz continues: "We secretly scorn balance as a dilution of feeling, a kind of static neutrality that lacks the thrill of adventure at the extreme—not the golden mean but the tinny average security of the bourgeoisie."[29] Doubting as we do that balance is worth very much, we tend to scorn just how difficult it can be to achieve it. For Jane Addams, balance—the balance of the Form-Giver as a type of Bread-Giver—means that the strong do not devour the weak; rather, they feed the weak without prejudice or condescension, offering sustenance for souls, minds, and bodies.

Addams's notion of form is generous in its wide humanity. Implicit in that notion is Addams's fervent belief that without cultural and social forms to contain and sustain human decency, the human heart would cast off all restraint and succumb to potent but chaotic and selfish enthusiasms. What Jane Addams hinted at early, and offered full-bloodedly later in her life and work, is a story of everyday life that permits one to display and to honor its complexity and dignity. For Addams, *in extremis veritas* is a seductive lie: in extremity there is only extremity, not truth unadorned.[30] Understanding full well the human "fascination with the brutal and the dangerous" and the "compelling place" it holds "in our culture's imagination," she resists this siren in much the way Christian battles Apollyon.[31]

Drawing attention to the life of the everyday, Addams urges us to focus on what nourishes a balanced imagination. Our actions are borne along on beliefs and concepts. Among these beliefs and concepts Addams would have included a belief that body and soul must be kept together, as the old saying goes. Her vision of what is good and excellent is a community of reconciliation in which differences are recognized but do not overwhelm a search for fellowship. She appreciated almost intuitively that too much fractiousness invites arbitrariness and a posing of harsh alternatives, such as, for example, that between the particularity of the one and the universality of the many. She would tether the one and the many together. Balance, again.

How did Addams arrive at such a tender age on a sense of balance and moderation that it takes many most of a lifetime to achieve? I have already noted her determination to rise at 3 A.M. as her father did and to use that time to read Plutarch's *Lives, The Odyssey, The Federalist Papers,* biographies of national heroes such as George Washington, and other fare unusual for one so young. She absorbed *Pilgrim's Progress,* Nathaniel Hawthorne, Ralph Waldo Emerson, and other great essayists. Her reading at Rockford Seminary is staggering by today's standards, ranging from Herbert Macauley to Milton, from Homer to Hesiod.[32] She drank up literature as a thirsty creature drains a pool of rainwater. She credits George Eliot and Charles Dickens with altering the course of her life by redirecting the flow and force of her sensibilities. While at the Rockford Seminary, Addams wrote regularly for and edited the *Rockford Seminary Magazine.* Reading her essay assignments for classes and her entries in the magazine, one is startled by the precocious gracefulness of the writing and its confident sophistication.

The subjects of her papers range from an exploration of rivers, to opium use in different cultural contexts, to defending the thesis "Blindness is preferable to deafness." The origin of chess is discussed, as is "The Present Policy of Congress." In the latter article, she uncharacteristically calls for the extreme remedy of "the knife not soothing herbs" as necessary to solve severe post–Civil War political problems. When she takes up nature, she falls into Wordsworthian lyricism, but she also notes nature's frequent appearance of hostility. The night sky may be "unfriendly and angry" and nature may "spurn her offspring." She embraces the thesis *Quid sum quia cogito* (which she translates as "What I am, I think"); for we know we exist, only because we think.[33] But she also criticizes thought as an end unto itself, expressing the worry that "rationalism is driving out all mysteries." She chides religion for growing too easy and requiring no self-sacrifice. Science comes in for criticism, too, as demanding only a type of thought rather than a full-hearted commitment.

The essay "High Winds Take the Trees" expresses her conviction that a society needs heroes, although great men are often "received with ill will" and face many struggles. Their contemporaries may see them as a threat. Often they are both hated and worshiped. Such men must possess "infinite courage" and "give up the comfort of being 'little.'" Here she has captured a fact of moral psychology: it *is* comfortable to be little and not to stand out too much. Littleness also means that one can wash one's hands of responsibility and insist that whatever goes wrong is the fault of others. These musings about society's ambivalence toward outstanding individuals are almost prescient; perhaps they helped prepare Addams for the adulation and the denunciation that were to be hers in abundance one day.

Speculating on "Unknown Quantities," she moves from the fortuities involved in the outcome of the Battle of Waterloo, with Napoleon's army bogged down because of heavy rain, to recounting how Egyptians valued their pharaohs according to their deeds, as the leaders' "aspirations, struggles and strivings are unknown quantities," and concluding with a proclamation that "the world and the mass of common people which is the voice of God, judge, not on what might have been . . . , not on the motive or the effort put forth, but on solely what *is,* and in this dread opinion 'we are what we must, not what we would be.'" This is stern stuff from the pen of a schoolgirl.[34]

A finely crafted essay on Savonarola helps explain Addams's enthusiasm for Eliot's *Romola,* in which the writer limns the character of the passionate cleric. Savonarola has often been presented in a sinister light, as a throwback to very dark ages, a puritanical denouncer of the Renaissance joie de vivre.[35] Closely following Eliot's characterization, Addams tells us that Savonarola brings us "face to face with a stern unflinching reality." His force is felt, his devotion to principles extolled; and we are "impressed with his terrible earnestness and feel that this strong and delicate character may, with truth, be called an *incarnate idea.*" Savonarola makes manifest what would otherwise remain latent. One might say that he crystallized public possibilities out of the materials of his epoch, and that the history of Florence, his city, therefore cannot be separated from his history, no more than Jane Addams's story can be severed from that of the city she embraced, Chicago. Addams's early recognition of the ways in which ideas become embodied, for good or for ill, was key to her later development.

A Philosophy of Murder

When we hear about a precocious child, we think of a would-be Mozart or a dazzling mathematics whiz. But there is a kind of moral precocity, too. A morally precocious child begins at an early age to ponder the whys, wherefores, and whatnots of ethical conduct. Such children typically express themselves with precision, clarity, wit, and descriptive power. This ability is linked to their need to express themselves for reasons of self-instruction and justification, although they often seek or presume a wider audience. Consider in this regard a remarkable essay on "The Macbeth of Shakespeare," written by Addams for the *Rockford Seminary Magazine* when she was nineteen years old and feasting on the yeasty works of Coleridge, Hawthorne, Thomas De Quincey, Walter Pater, Carlyle, Emerson, W. D. Howells, and others.

Apprising her readers of the plot and the basic story, Addams presents the famous three witches as seductresses offering Macbeth what his heart desires: "He starts, who wouldn't? The thoughts he has been thinking and thinking, have suddenly embodied themselves, and stand before him on the bold bare heath; they have all at once grown into definite purposes, have spoken out before a third person, Banquo, and he knows that ever afterwards he must acknowledge them, that they will pursue and harass him."

She universalizes Macbeth's experience by linking the tempting of Macbeth and the forging of thoughts into embodied deeds with these words: "We prepare ourselves for sudden deeds by the intuitive choice of good and evil, or, as our thoughts go forth never to be recalled, how they increase and gain enormous proportions until we lose all control of them." This is Macbeth's fate: "His thought grew so powerful as to assume form and shape, as to be endowed with life and a distinct physical existence to baffle and confront him." He is fearful, terrorized, tangled in "metaphysical confusion . . . lost in a maze of his own thoughts, he knows not what is real and what is fantastical, he is filled with horrible imaginings and doubts."

Arising before him quite distinctly is a phantom of his own creation but nonetheless real. The image "is murder, it takes a poetical man to call it an image, but Macbeth tries to deceive himself and keep his heart of hearts pure." Throughout the rest of the play, Macbeth struggles "with murder itself, invisible yet clinging and horrible." The phantom "pursues him until the last moment" and draws him to the deed as to "something inevitable." Thus "Macbeth is driven from murder to murder, ghosts and phantoms pursue him, he consults again the weird sisters, gains courage and is lost through his own daring—a poetical man doing the worst deeds in a poetical sense—the philosophy of murder."

The philosophy of murder is a rather stunning thing for a young woman's discourse, certainly in Addams's era. Placing her Macbeth essay side by side with her oration on women as bread-givers, one is struck by the power of form and embodiment as themes framing her foreboding recognitions (our phantoms can give rise to a philosophy of murder) and her solemn injunctions (we are enjoined to give bread, not to deal death).

Another of Addams's Rockford orations delivered at the Junior Exhibition, on the theme of Bellerophon in ancient Greek mythology, deserves special mention. The lesson she draws out is "that social evils could only be overcome by him who soared above them into idealism, as Bellerophon mounted upon the winged horse Pegasus, had slain the earthy dragon."[36] Bellerophon, a grandson of Sisyphus, was a great *tamer* of horses. He rode them, guided their power, urged them on in a disciplined way. Only with such taming could the glorious horse Pegasus, with Bellerophon on his back, fly faster than the wind and soar over land and sea. Together they fight and kill the Chimera, a fearful creature that doesn't know what it is, being a horrible combination of lion, serpent, and goat, and spitting fire from all three of its heads. In destroying the Chimera, Bellerophon and Pegasus bring peace and safety to the people of Lycia.[37] Eventually, because he tries to fly too high, Bellerophon falls to a sad earthly fate. The tale is one of idealistic rapture that, if it goes too far, and if one tries to fly too high, leads to an unseating and a life spent in brambles and in penury. It is instructive that Addams picked this tale for her oration. Later, directing the reader of her autobiography to the story, she no longer feels compelled to emphasize the play as a morality tale of excess; rather, she can surefootedly gesture to the idealistic enthusiasm alone, for by this time she herself has become a master form-giver, having brought into being a form—the Settlement House—a place of enthusiasms, yes, but enthusiasms tamed and contained.

A Wider Fellowship

Affection must be held fast. The sense of responsibility that enlivens it and helps hold it is laced through and through, from Jane Addams's childhood on, with a search for beauty and ritual, an aesthetic reconstruction of human experience. Raised without sacrament and ritual, she and her childhood playmate, her stepbrother George Haldeman, sought and found continuity—a story line—in their free-ranging games.

Their play was not constantly interrupted, as is that of children who must compete with traffic and pedestrians on city streets. Such disruptions in the continuity of urban children's play troubled the adult Jane Addams, who believed that they cut adrift the story line of young human lives. She was convinced that children need the opportunity to play complete stories, as she and George did. She depicts her childhood as a carefree romp through the landscape, occasionally tempting danger. She and George clapped their hands "in sudden joy over the soft radiance of the rainbow"; they "yielded to a soft melancholy when we heard the whippoorwill in the early twilight; . . . he aroused in us vague longings of which we spoke solemnly." They "erected an altar beside the stream, to which for several years we brought all the snakes we killed during our excursions, no matter how long the toilsome journey which we had to make with a limp snake dangling between two sticks."[38]

She and George Haldeman felt a strong compulsion that led them to initiate a ceremonial that expressed "their sense of identification with man's primitive life and their familiar kinship with the remotest past." She describes the ceremony they performed one autumn day upon their snake altar. They offered tribute, they knew not to what, by placing on the altar one out of every "hundred of the black walnuts which we had gathered, and then poured over the whole a pitcher full of cider, fresh from the cider mill on the barn floor. I think we had also burned a favorite book or two upon this pyre of stones."[39] The little book-burners were engaged in *sacrifice*, moved by a need to expiate, perhaps, but certainly also by a need to create a ritual of portentous meaning—all in companionship with nature.

Overcome as Jane Addams occasionally was by a fearsome sense of the demands of the moral life and "of solitude, of being unsheltered in a wide world of relentless and elemental forces," she sought out intimations of a deep if fragile humanity and universality that underlay life's often perplexing and doubt-filled torments. Anthropologist Mary Douglas reminds us that sacraments are "signs instituted to channels of grace," conduits in and through which the material world itself serves as a sign of grace.[40] As a child, Addams found fellowship with friends in play and with a comforting father, accessible to her despite his rectitude. He spoke to her as something of an equal, and he took her confidences seriously. She describes how he admonished her against wearing a beautiful new cloak, because it wasn't necessary to keep her warm and would only make other girls who had less feel bad. He praised her when she entered his room in the middle of the night to confess a lie. He comforted her when Polly, "an old nurse who had taken care of my mother and had followed her to frontier Illinois to help rear a second generation of children," died.[41]

The adolescent Jane Addams had been called to Polly's bedside after she fell ill while on her annual visit to her cousins' farm a few miles north of Cedarville. Young Jane kept watch and was present when "the great change came." On her way home, she was nearly overcome by the thoughts and emotions this experience had evoked, which later yielded what I call the Story of Polly's Death and the Laden Trees.[42]

> As I was driven home in the winter storm, the wind through the trees seemed laden with a passing soul and the riddle of life and death pressed hard; once to be young, to grow old and to die, everything came to that, and then a mysterious journey out into the Unknown. Did she mind faring forth alone? Would the journey perhaps end in something as familiar and natural to the aged and dying as life is to the young and living? Through all the drive home and indeed throughout the night these thoughts were pierced by sharp worry, a sense of faithlessness because I had forgotten the text Polly had confided to me long before as the one from which she wished her funeral sermon to be preached. My comfort as usual finally came from my father. . . . I felt a new fellowship with him because we had discussed it together.

Her father invited her into a wider fellowship because he paid attention to her stories and fears. He understood that children, too, would "eat their bread with tears." He is unashamed to display his sorrow to Jennie, even mourning over a stranger, as at the death of Mazzini in 1872. John Addams conveys to his daughter "a sense of the genuine relationship which may exist between men who share large hopes and like desires, even though they differ in nationality, language, and creed; that those things count for absolutely nothing between groups of men who are trying to abolish slavery in America or to throw off Hapsburg oppression in Italy." The daughter, in turn, is "filled with pride that I knew a man who held converse with great minds and who really sorrowed and rejoiced over happenings across the sea."[43] Happenings "across the sea"—how grand it sounds—a beckoning, great world, with circles radiating ever wider, from a hearth in Cedarville to Italy and beyond.

But to enter into this fellowship, one must repudiate what Jane Addams calls "the unpardonable sin of Hawthorne's lime burner," assuming (as she reasonably could at that time) that the well-informed reader would know which of Hawthorne's stories she had in mind, and therefore, what sin was unpardonable. Her reference to Hawthorne's limeburner comes up in the context of play. She and George had explored the dark, foreboding caves along the banks of the mill stream and also visited a "deserted limekiln" that she associated with the story of the "Lime-Burner," her way of identifying Hawthorne's short story "Ethan Brand." Hawthorne captivated Addams because he studied the human condition and spent time, as she later would, listening to "legends of the past from old women." Stories from old women would provide the basis of one of Addams's most famous essays decades later, on the devil-baby at Hull-House.

As Hawthorne's story begins, Bartram, a "rough, heavy-looking man, begrimed with charcoal," and his son watch over and stoke a lime-kiln that sits above a village. The smoke and jets of flame issuing from it "resembled nothing so much as the private entrance to the infernal regions, which the shepherds of the Delectable Mountains were accustomed to show to pilgrims" (another gesture toward *Pilgrim's Progress*).[44] There had been an earlier lime-burner, one Ethan Brand, who had led a solitary and meditative life, "before he began his search for the Unpardonable Sin," an "IDEA" [sic] that overtook him and drove him out of the village, into the night, and down an ever darkening road. Brand had become the butt of ridicule to the villagers. But on this particular night the phantom, Ethan Brand himself, reappears. He has discovered the unpardonable sin. It is one that "grew within my own breast.... A sin that grew nowhere else! The sin of an intellect that triumphed over the sense of brotherhood with man and reverence for God, and sacrificed everything to its own mighty claims! The only sin that deserves a recompense of immortal agony!"[45]

The triumph of intellect, of a system, an overarching philosophy— that was the unpardonable sin. Ethan Brand had cultivated an IDEA but lost his heart and soul. He had cherished his own powers exclusively. He would rise to the level of "star-lit eminence, whither the philosophers of the earth, laden with the lore of universities, might vainly strive to clamber after him. So much for the intellect! But where was the heart? That, indeed, had withered,—had contracted,—had hardened,—had perished! It had ceased to partake of the universal throb. He had lost his hold of the magnetic chain of humanity." And thus he "became a fiend," casting off Mother Earth, mankind, casting off his heart and soul. That night, as Bartram and his son sleep, he commits himself to the flames: "Come, deadly element of Fire, henceforth my familiar friend! Embrace me, as I do thee!"[46] All that is left in the morning are ashes that have taken the shape of a human heart.

"I Found My Father in Tears"

A parent's tears are powerful, intimating to a child the possible breakdown of an ordered world. If a parent can't hold things together, won't they most assuredly fall apart? When Jane Addams finds her father in tears, she is only four and a half years old, but she knows a world has ended. She had assumed, as children do, "that grown-up people never cried." But her father's tears, together with the white gate posts bedecked with American flags "companioned with black," told a story—the story of the death of the "greatest man in the world." Her response? It was "thrilling" and "solemn," for the world outside had once again entered her gate.[47] She is afforded a glimpse of the universality she craved; drawn out and into "that search for the heroic and perfect which so persistently haunts the young."[48]

From "the village world" to the "great world," borne along by the life and death of Lincoln, she is reminded of how her family had already brought that wider world within. There was a photograph of Lincoln in her father's room; another of Lincoln with "Little Tad" in "our old-fashioned upstairs parlor."[49] Her father had attended at least one of the Lincoln-Douglas debates, the one held at Freeport. Lincoln and her father blend in her mind; her "tenderest thoughts of my father" always fuse with those of Lincoln, and many lessons—including "charity for both sides"—radiate outward from that heartfelt core. Later she held Lincoln's Birthday celebrations at Hull-House and distributed copies of Carl Schurz's *Appreciation of Abraham Lincoln*—a classic text of Lincoln adoration, written by a German immigrant—to immi-

grant boys in the Hull-House boys' club.[50] Lincoln taught Jane Addams
that the past is not to be repudiated but retained and utilized; that immigrant children, driven to spurn their old-world mothers and fathers,
should not be "ashamed of the pit whence they were digged," she
wrote.[51] Lincoln invigorated and clarified. This was his power—this giant, this fresh breeze off the prairie.

But the glories of Lincoln's life and service are entangled in Addams's
memory with stories of the devastation the Civil War visited upon
Cedarville. Her most powerful reminiscence is what I call the Story of
the Forlorn Little Farm—an isolated farmstead in the environs of
Cedarville at the sight of which Addams and her chums "always fell
silent."[52] The house was empty, except for an elderly couple. In Addams's words:

> Five of their sons had enlisted in the Civil War, and only the
> youngest had returned alive in the spring of 1865. In the autumn of
> the same year, when he was hunting for wild ducks in a swamp on
> the rough little farm itself, he was accidentally shot and killed, and
> the old people were left alone to struggle with the half-cleared land
> as best they might. When we were driven past this forlorn little
> farm our childish voices always dropped into speculative whisper-
> ings as to how the accident could have happened to this remaining
> son out of all the men in the world, to him who had escaped so
> many chances of death! Our young hearts swelled in first rebellion
> against that which Walter Pater calls "the inexplicable shortcom-
> ings or misadventure on the part of life itself"; we were over-
> whelmingly oppressed by that grief of things as they are, so much
> more mysterious and intolerable than those griefs which we think
> dimly to trace to man's own wrongdoing.

This is not a brief against injustice. Injustice would be more tolerable
because something might be done about that. Rather, she offers here
unblinkered moral realism—the "grief of things as they are." This mor-
dant tale contains an entire moral philosophy. In its forlornness and
isolated gloom, it is worthy of Edith Wharton. Reading Wharton's
story of *Ethan Frome*, set in a bleak New England village called Stark-
field, one is overwhelmed by a sense of claustrophobic isolation, like
the isolation of Addams's two old people left to struggle alone, having

lost all five sons—a loss so overwhelming that it reduces those who pass by the forlorn farm to muttered whispers and sad, slow shakings of a downcast head. As with Jane Addams's elderly pair, "matters ain't gone any too well with" poor Ethan Frome, either.[53]

Jane Addams references Walter Pater in her Story of the Forlorn Little Farm as one of her guides to the brokenness of human life and to the sadness of things in themselves. Pater is a critic not much read any longer who took as his mission a determination to really *see* things clearly.[54] Pater was the master of a style of "self-restraint and -renunciation," hence a worthy object of Jane Addams's admiration.[55] He lodged protests "in favour of real men and women against mere grey, unreal abstractions," repudiating philosophies that made much too much of human rationality and too little of sense and sensibility.[56] Clearly, Pater strikes a theme that much preoccupied Jane Addams from 1881 to 1888, during the years of her neurasthenic crisis, including the theme of the ill effects of modern luxury causing people to grow "over-delicate" and to cease to engage the world on its own terms. Pater calls for self-restraint and a "a skilful economy of means . . . that too has a beauty of its own . . . that frugal closeness of style which makes the most of a word."[57] Good and worthy art enlarges "our sympathies with each other" and fortifies "us in our sojourn here." Prose, if it embraces and strives for a kind of poetry, helps redeem matter by incarnating and lifting up the dignity of a human life, however humble.

If her reading of the strenuous British writer Thomas Carlyle pushed Addams toward a heroic mode and the hero as a kind of divinity—all of those "Great Men" who are "modellers, patterns, and in a wide sense creators . . . the Great Men sent into the world: the soul of the whole world's history"—Pater was among those who helped keep her feet on the ground.[58] She tells us in *Twenty Years at Hull-House* that she had read Carlyle when she was bedridden for six months. She had been diagnosed with neurasthenia[59] and had received some form of treatment, or suggestions for treatment, from the famous physician S. Weir Mitchell in his Hospital for Orthopedic and Nervous Diseases in Philadelphia. This was followed by a spinal operation performed by her physician brother-in-law back in Illinois. Confined to bed following the operation, she ingested Carlyle's *Frederick the Great*.[60] But Carlyle gave cold comfort. The colossus who bestrides the world renders the ordinary and humble, the familiar and beloved, invisible. This is one of the lessons that Addams took with her from childhood—a lesson shaped by her encounter with Lincoln, as well as by her gregarious, interactive mode of reading, her attentive eye, and her anxiety about the unpardonable sin.

If she had any doubts that Lincoln's was the example to follow, these were laid to rest when she visited England in later years, after she had become famous as the creator of Hull-House and the brilliant spokeswoman for democracy. She spent several days in Oxford with a group of scholars and public figures closely associated with the nascent settlement movement,[61] and came away with a greater appreciation for American egalitarianism and that "refreshing breeze" that came off the prairies in the person of Lincoln. She felt humbled by the "fine analysis" of Abraham Lincoln given by Edward Caird, the Master of Balliol, who described Lincoln as a man who had dug "the channels through which the moral life of his countrymen might flow." Caird, a foreigner, gives Addams a finer, deeper appreciation of Lincoln, just as Caird's "Evolution of Religion"—she must mean his two-volume *The Evolution of Theology*—was of "unspeakable comfort to me in the labyrinth of differing ethical teachings and religious creeds," offering as it did a synthetic view, bringing together diverse perspectives in order to discover some "principle of unity in the universe."[62]

Addams concludes "The Influence of Lincoln," chapter II in *Twenty Years at Hull-House,* with a paean to him who "cleared the title to our democracy." Democratic government is "the most valuable contribution America has made to the moral life of the world." Like her great hero, Jane Addams was to become a channel through which the moral life of her country flowed. But it is important not to overlook her tumultuous yearnings, her struggles, her years ensnared in preparation. In *Twenty Years at Hull-House,* she tells a story of the dome of the Wisconsin capitol under whose protective orb lived for many years a great eagle, the symbol of the Eighth Wisconsin Regiment. As a child she had toured the capitol and had seen this much-admired bird, which had been dubbed Old Abe, and this journey came to symbolize for her "that search for the heroic and perfect which so persistently haunts the young."[63]

Returning years later to Madison, Wisconsin, to receive an honorary degree from its great state university, Jane Addams glanced down once again on that dome under which the little girl Jennie had once stood, and "dimly caught a hint of what men have tried to say in their world-old effort to imprison a space in so divine a line that it shall hold only yearning devotion and high-hearted hopes." There was only one other dome that "clutched my heart as did that modest curve"—namely, "the great dome of St. Peter's."[64] For an American child reared on a diet of Bunyan and generic Quakerism, this aesthetic and ethical flirtation with the expansive beauty of St. Peter's is touching and ever so slightly heretical. In Addams's mind, it was possible for Lincoln's fresh breeze off the prairie to mingle freely with the intoxicating mists rising from the Tiber and the sights and sounds of pilgrims, fused with memories of the blood of martyrs; and still possible to bow to the lure of flickering candles and lingering incense and the soft murmurings of the Hail Mary. All these Jane Addams had encountered as she traveled as a young woman and entered the protective bosom of a dome separated from that of the Wisconsin state capitol by thousands of miles yet mingling later in her memory and reflection as two distinctive homes for the human spirit.

"This Group of Ardent Girls"

Jane Addams had entered Rockford Female Seminary in June 1877, when she was not yet seventeen years old. At the time, Rockford Female Seminary was not officially a college. It did not become a college until 1882, as noted in an earlier chapter, when it began to grant bachelor's degrees. Although Addams graduated with the class of 1881, she and one of her classmates qualified for the degree of bachelor of arts, having taken courses above and beyond the seminary requirements. Addams returned to receive this degree in 1882, at which point she was in the throes of a crisis that would last for eight years and would resolve itself only with the founding of Hull-House in September 1889.

A family tumult had surrounded her enrollment at the Rockford Seminary. She wanted to head eastward, to attend the prestigious Smith College, to which she had been accepted. But her father insisted upon Rockford, where her older sisters had obtained their higher educations, and where he himself served as a trustee. Besides, he didn't want his beloved daughter too far from home. She yielded to this family claim, as she later described it, and jumped with gusto into the life of the seminary under the leadership of the redoubtable educator Anna Peck Sill.

Known as the Mount Holyoke of the West, the Rockford Seminary bubbled with an "atmosphere of intensity" and a "fever of preparation," for many students were bound for the mission fields, for lives as medical missionaries, as teachers of the blind, or as pioneer librarians. Later, it came as no surprise to her that the "most sympathetic and comprehending visitors we have ever had at Hull-House have been returned missionaries," for they knew what a life of service was and they understood what it meant to take up residence in a "foreign quarter."[65]

During Addams's years at the seminary, her teachers made various attempts to recruit her for the mission field, but she steadfastly resisted being drawn into a particular church affiliation or into missionary labor. Addams remained unmoved by such efforts, in part because "my father was not a communicant of any church" and "I tremendously admired his scrupulous morality and sense of honor in all matters of personal and public conduct, and also because the little group to which I have referred [a core of five hardheaded, intellectual girls] was much given to a sort of rationalism, doubtless founded upon an early reading of Emerson."[66] Looking back, Addams writes bemusedly about the girls' snobbish manner of distinguishing themselves from the unlearned and notes, with rue, "We were also too fond of quoting Carlyle to the effect, ''Tis not to taste sweet things, but to do noble and true things that the poorest son of Adam dimly longs.'"[67] These daughters of Adam also aimed for the noble. Addams's own ambitious yearnings left her chafing at the time she had to spend in preparation.

As part of that preparation, during one summer vacation, Addams and four of her friends committed themselves to reading a long list of books that included, in addition to Ruskin and Elizabeth Barrett Browning, Plutarch's *Lives* (which Addams had already gone through as a child); Irving's *Life of Washington;* Motley's *Dutch Republic;* and the entirety of Gibbon's *Decline and Fall of the Roman Empire.* This was heavy fare, for summertime reading, and only three of them, including Addams, completed the task. According to Addams, the curriculum at the seminary focused on the classics, languages, ethics (or moral science), and history. In *Twenty Years at Hull-House,* Addams proclaims that history was her "genuine interest" at this time, in part "because my father had always insisted upon a certain amount of historic reading." He had paid her five cents for each of Plutarch's *Lives* she devoured as a little girl.

To add piquancy to their routine, Jane Addams and the others—perhaps the same four who committed to the arduous summer reading course—"tried to understand De Quincey's marvelous 'Dreams' more sympathetically, by drugging ourselves with opium. We solemnly consumed small white powders at intervals during an entire long holiday, but no mental reorientation took place, and the suspense and excitement did not even permit us to grow sleepy." A teacher who was brought in on the scheme "grew alarmed . . . took away our De Quincey and all the remaining powders, administered an emetic to each of the five aspirants for sympathetic understanding of all human experience, and sent us to our separate rooms with a stern command to appear at family worship after supper 'whether we were able to or not.'"[68] This episode affords a glimpse into the transgressive, risk-taking side of Addams's nature. To be sure, opium was widely available at the time.[69] But it was certainly not routine fare for "ardent girls." Knowing of Addams's deep immersion in the novels of George Eliot, I find a fascinating similarity between Addams's description of this episode, and the rueful tale told by young Will Ladislaw, George Eliot's male protagonist in *Middlemarch*. Will, who is interested in all sorts of experiences, had "made himself ill with doses of opium. Nothing greatly original had resulted from these half-measures and the effect of the opium convinced him that there was an entire dissimilarity between his constitution and De Quincey's."[70]

Although Jane Addams references Thomas De Quincey's *Dreams,* his most detailed, even notorious dip into opium illumination (and opium-induced decline) is his *Confessions of an English Opium-Eater,* a text that traces De Quincey's early fascination with opium and his epiphany when, upon initially consuming it, his pains vanished and the "secret of happiness"—no less—seemed revealed.[71] Although De Quincey is no longer widely read, he was a prolific writer and one of a large company of nineteenth-century English essayists to whom Addams was devoted. It is easy enough to see why. His autobiography speaks of the affliction of childhood. Addams's reminiscences, filled as they are with the fears and forebodings of childhood, are sunny by comparison to De Quincey's tender years. De Quincey was an amateur psychologist of some insight, buttressing Addams's quest to discover how "our deepest thoughts and feelings pass to us through perplexed combinations of *concrete objects*," and how those experiences are compounded in such a way that they can never later be disentangled.[72]

The reported opium experiment at Rockford Seminary, whether hyperbolic or not, is not the only instance of Addams's having strayed from behavior considered acceptable for a Protestant young lady. She embarked on a "curious course of reading in medieval history," finding herself fascinated by "an ideal of mingled learning, piety and physical labor, more clearly exemplified by the Port Royalists than by any others."[73] At their apogee, the Port Royalists formed an extensive network of unorthodox Catholics called Jansenists. They created a flourishing community whose members bound themselves to imitate Christ in pursuing lives of "voluntary poverty, penance, and self-denial."[74] Combining meditation with labor, piety with practical service, the inhabitants of Port Royal had great appeal for Jane Addams, searching as she was for a way to "live in a really living world," an integrated, full-blooded life.[75]

She worked her way through Plato's *Crito* in Benjamin Jowett's English translation because the "Greek was too hard for me." She followed her father's political convictions, becoming an early supporter of the franchise for women. Her political interests come out in her writing and her oratory, although she treats her participation on an oratorical team at the seminary with gentle irony. This team, which had defined its mission as nothing less than "the progress of Woman's Cause," later placed "in the dreary middle" in an oratorical contest—a failure that was deemed by some of its more perfervid members as having "dealt the cause of woman's advancement a staggering blow," so "absurdly inflexible" were the harsh judgments of youth, Addams muses.[76] The story of the team's humiliation, significantly, becomes a segue into further musings by Addams on the inflexibility of the early socialists she encountered at Hull-House.

HULL-HOUSE, PLACE OF ENTHUSIASMS that it was, was open to propagandists of "divers social theories," some of which—she singles out the socialists—"used every method of attack" in their attempt to convert Addams to their cause. She notes, dryly, that one of their favorite methods was to proclaim her a real socialist at heart but just "too much of a coward to say so." Another decided she was somehow clearly "caught in the toils of capitalism."[77] Addams remained unmoved. The seventeen-year-old who had refused to yield to evangelizing undertaken by respected older teachers was not about to give way as an adult to zealous political missionaries for a secular political faith. She would not wander in the "wilderness of dogma"; rather, she would "select what seemed reasonable" from a variety of sources and inspirations—an approach she linked both to temperament and to sentiment, and one that permitted her to play the role of arbitrator in many heated, often terrible, disputes.

From an early age, she had decided that justice could come only through "broadened sympathies toward the individual man or woman who crosses our path; one item added to another is the only method by which to build up a conception lofty enough to be of use in the world"—much as a cathedral is built one brick at a time.[78] Only in this way could the inner consent of all concerned be secured. Otherwise the zealous would trample on those they considered insufficiently determined or riddled with false consciousness. Addams speculated that there may be something feminine about this cast of mind; but whether it was feminine or not, she had learned at an early age to "express herself without dogmatism," and she would continue in that mode for the rest of her life.

Addams illustrates the danger of dogmatism with what I call the Story of the Old, Crippled Employee, Broken in Spirit.[79] She used this story as a morality play about justice and the need for flexibility.

> I was called upon by a manufacturing company to act as one of three arbitrators in a perplexing struggle between themselves, a group of trade-unionists and a non-union employee of their establishment. The non-union man who was the cause of the difficulty had ten years before sided with his employers in a prolonged strike and had bitterly fought the union. He had been so badly injured at that time, that in spite of long months of hospital care he had never afterward been able to do a full day's work, although his employers had retained him for a decade at full pay in recognition of his loyalty. At the end of ten years the once defeated union was strong enough to enforce its demands for a union shop, and in spite of the distaste of the firm for the arrangement, no obstacle to harmonious relations with the union remained but the refusal of the trade-unionists to receive as one of their members the old crippled employee, whose spirit was broken at last and who was now willing

to join the union and to stand with his old enemies for the sake of retaining his place. But the union men would not receive "a traitor," the firm flatly refused to dismiss so faithful an employee.

The matter was thus turned over to arbitrators. Addams's life experience had prepared her well for such a role, and she and the other arbitrators worked hard to secure the "inner consent of all concerned." Frustratingly, she doesn't give us the specifics of the outcome—perhaps because she wished mainly to highlight the negative dynamics of unforgiving dogmatism, and the need for men and women of equable temperament to hold firm in their refusal to join one side or the other in such a way that their human sympathy freezes up and they cannot see things from another point of view.

A S ADDAMS'S FOUR YEARS at the Rockford Seminary drew to a close, she mused on the tragic possibility that she would be misunderstood by those around her. In her commencement oration on "Cassandra," she observed that one may be "always . . . in the right, and always . . . disbelieved and rejected."[80] She later attributed this statement to the "sublime self-conceit" of a schoolgirl who too readily believed that the world would strip her of her "precious ideals" unless she hewed to the narrow path of martyrdom and misunderstanding. This rare moment of self-pity passed quickly, for Addams had work to do. She was already hatching plans to study medicine, perhaps contemplating a Port Royalist vocation of service to the poor. The year after she left school, during "long vacations," she "pressed plants, stuffed birds and pounded rocks in some vague belief that I was approximating the new method, and yet when my stepbrother who was becoming a real scientist tried to carry me along with him into the merest outskirts of the methods of research, it at once became evident that I had no aptitude."[81] Nevertheless, having fulfilled the science studies required for the Bachelor of Arts degree, Addams returned to Rockford Seminary in 1882 (newly renamed Rockford College) to receive her degree. She was thus one of the first awarded a B.A. by Rockford College.

Overtaken by a sense of high purpose but perplexed as to how best to embody that purpose in deeds, Jane Addams spent the eight years following her graduation—from the summer of 1881 until she was energized by plans for Hull-House in 1889—in the wilderness. It was a rather privileged wilderness, to be sure, that included two extensive trips to Europe; but it was a wilderness of pain and confusion nonetheless. She who wished to "live in a really living world" by "refusing to be content with a shadowy intellectual or aesthetic reflection of it" could scarcely put one foot in front of the other—for the ground had been pulled out from under her. In August 1881, at the age of fifty-nine, her beloved father had died suddenly of an inflamed appendix.[82]

The young woman who was so eager to offer shelter from the storm to others now found herself tempest-tossed. Ralph Waldo Emerson's strenuous self-reliance and manly talk no longer served her well. "Inaction is cowardice," the great man had preached in his "American Scholar" address, adding that "there can be no scholar without the heroic mind."[83] In her lonely travail, Jane Addams found that she could not measure up to the Emersonian ideal of "Man Thinking," with its evocation of heroic self-assertion. She agreed with Emerson that "character is higher than intellect," but character did not dictate duty so simply.[84] Heroic sentiments could not fill the gaping hole that grew ever wider in her life and soul without her father's capacious "doublet" in which he had "wrapt me."[85]

Emerson claimed to offer a litany for the common man: "I embrace the common, I explore and sit at the feet of the familiar, the low."[86] But his words provided no comfort or reassurance to Jane Addams in her grief. She realized she could not share Emerson's certainty that man was "a sovereign state within a sovereign state." How could one practice self-reliance if the self was doubled over in pain and worn out by grief? In his bracing essay on "Self-Reliance," Emerson opined that travel was a "fool's paradise," a "symptom of deeper unsoundness affecting the whole intellectual action."[87] But travel Addams did, after several false starts. She first began medical school, then dropped out. She was bedridden with melancholia and back pain for six months. Then she spent twenty-seven months abroad, beginning in 1883 (in company with her stepmother, who receives nary a mention in Addams's autobiography). She returned to Baltimore, where George Haldeman was pursuing graduate studies in science at Johns Hopkins. Nothing suited. Nothing gelled. This was her absolute nadir. She took a second trip to Europe, during which she began at last to see a way through the "snare of preparation."

During her eight years in the wilderness, she no doubt read and reread one of her favorite poems, Matthew Arnold's "Rugby Chapel," written in November 1857.[88] It reads, in part:

> *Fifteen years have gone round*
> *Since thou arosest to tread,*
> *In the summer morning, the road*
> *Of death, at a call unforeseen,*
> *Sudden. For fifteen years,*
> *We who till then in thy shade*
> *Rested as under the boughs*
> *Of a mighty oak, have endured*
> *Sunshine and rain as we might,*
> *Bare, unshaded, alone,*
> *Lacking the shelter of thee.*
> *O strong soul, by what shore*
> *Tarriest thou now? For that force,*
> *Surely, has not been left vain!*
> *Somewhere, surely, afar*
> *In the sounding labour-house vast*
> *Of being, is practised that strength,*
> *Zealous, beneficent, firm!*
> . . . .
> *Then, in such hour of need*
> *Of your fainting, dispirited race,*
> *Ye, like angels, appear*
> *Radiant with ardour divine.*
> *Beacons of hope, ye appear!*
> *Languor is not in your heart,*
> *Weakness is not in your word,*
> *Weariness not on your brow.*
> *Ye alight in our van; at your voice,*
> *Panic, despair, flee away.*
> *Ye move through the ranks, recall*
> *The stragglers, refresh the outworn,*
> *Praise, re-inspire the brave.*
> *Order, courage, return.*
> *Eyes rekindling, and prayers,*

Follow your steps as ye go.
Ye fill up the gaps in our files,
Strengthen the wavering line,
Stablish, continue our march,
On, to the bound of the waste,
On, to the City of God.

Jane Addams's Celestial City was a bustling, raw, overflowing place, teeming with immigrants, energetic, democratic, corrupt, filthy, American to the marrow. Her discovery that you cannot be universal anywhere but in your own backyard came after much searching, some of it desultory, some of it exhilarating. She arrived at an ethic that "can better be enacted than formalized," an ethic that stresses "not the attractiveness of extreme risk or the darkest teachings of violence and domination" but instead a "celebration of the everyday, prosaic world, with its undramatic practices and values . . . a principled defense of the quotidian"—which she herself dramatizes so that it may be the more visible.[89] All of this, though, came to her only after much effort. First she had to find sufficient food for her own soul in order that she might feed and shelter others.

3

Imagining Hull-House

MIDNIGHT IN LONDON. A young American woman in a state of nervous depression finds herself on a train to Whitechapel, in the city's impoverished East End. It is November 1883, and a drama is about to unfold on the Mile End Road. Despite her "limited amount of energy," she records the event in the travel journey she turns to "in moments of deep depression when overwhelmed by a sense of failure." This is the Story of Pale Hands at Midnight.[1]

A small party of tourists were taken to the East End by a city missionary to witness the Saturday night sale of decaying vegetables and fruit, which, owing to the Sunday laws in London, could not be sold until Monday, and, as they were beyond safe keeping were disposed of at auction as late as possible on Saturday night. On Mile End Road, from the top of an omnibus which paused at the end of a dingy street lighted by only occasional flares of gas, we saw two huge masses of ill-clad people clamoring around two hucksters' carts. They were bidding their farthings and ha'pennies for a vegetable held up by the auctioneer, which he at last scornfully flung, with a gibe for its cheapness, to the successful bidder. In the momentary pause only one man detached himself from the groups. He had bidden on a cabbage, and when it struck his hand, he instantly sat down on the curb, tore it with his teeth, and hastily devoured it, unwashed and uncooked as it was. He and his fellows were types of the "submerged tenth," as our missionary guide told us, with some little satisfaction in the then new phrase, and he further added that so many of them could scarcely be seen in one spot save at this Saturday night auction . . . . They were huddled into ill-fitting, cast-off clothing, the ragged finery which one sees only in East London. Their pale faces were dominated by that most unlovely of human expressions, the cunning and shrewdness of the bargain-hunter who starves if he cannot make a successful trade, and yet the final impression was not of ragged, tawdry clothing nor of pinched and sallow faces, but of myriads of hands, empty, pathetic, nerveless and workworn, showing white in the uncertain light of the street, and clutching forward for food which was already unfit to eat.

Perhaps nothing is so fraught with significance as the human hand, this oldest tool with which man has dug his way from savagery, and with which he is constantly groping forward. I have never since been able to see a number of hands held upward, even when they are moving rhythmically in a calisthenic exercise, or when they belong to a class of chubby children who wave them in eager response to a teacher's query, without a certain revival of this memory, a clutching at the heart reminiscent of the despair and resentment which seized me then.

What, she wonders, is she to do? Can she act upon the dreadful lessons of that story, or should she instead avert her gaze and spurn those myriads of grasping hands? She walks through the London streets "almost furtively, afraid to look down narrow streets and alleys lest they disclose again this hideous human need and suffering." Strangely, the world turns as usual. Should it? Should the world not pause and take notice? The young American's comfort has been shattered. Life goes on despite the stark tableau enacted by the desperate players. There is nothing uplifting or ennobling about these poor. The scene witnessed and described by the twenty-three-year-old is unlovely; but she cannot erase from her mind the hands illumined by the moon as they reach for remnants that the world has cast off, the best of a bad lot of rotting vegetables—the bread of life, for the very poor.

"I Have Accepted the Advice
Given to Every Exhausted American"

It was 1883, and Jane Addams was in Europe on medical advice. Her father's death had plunged the entire family into crisis. She was "all at sea." Her stepmother was semi-invalided by grief. Her older brother, Weber, one of the four Addams children to reach adulthood, had suffered a nervous breakdown. Following her false start in medical school in Philadelphia in winter 1881–1882, Jane had undergone a back operation performed by her brother-in-law Harry Haldeman (husband of her older sister Alice). The half-year she spent bedridden after the operation is shrouded in mystery.[2] But plans slowly crystallized for a trip abroad on one of the great steamships that plied the North Atlantic route. Perhaps the grand tour would snap her out of melancholia. She was a college-educated woman who did not want to teach or go into missions. Marriage was an honorable and fitting estate, she believed, but it was not for her. There was something else she was meant to do, although what that was had not yet been revealed. Perhaps an unbidden event, as she called unexpected moments, would jolt her into clarity. So she joined thousands of other privileged Americans and embarked on a voyage.

The traveling party for what was to be her first European sojourn, which lasted two years (from 1883–1885), included Harriet and Mary Ellwood, Sarah Hostetter, and two chaperones, Mrs. E. Young and Anna Haldeman Addams. Jane Addams appears fragile, her face rather haunted and dominated by large, dark eyes, in photographs of the traveling party. A mere five feet three inches tall, she was also slight in build and weighed a mere ninety-eight pounds when the group embarked on the great ship *Servia,* out of New York Harbor, on August 22, 1883. The trip lasted twenty-one months and included the British Isles, Holland, Germany, Austria, Italy, Greece, and Switzerland, topped off by two months in Berlin and Paris. By that time, Jane Addams and her stepmother were traveling alone together, the other members of the party having departed for America.

The two women had planned meticulously for their two-year venture. Addams wrote of the time-consuming process of assembling the necessary wardrobes, which included a number of fashionable dresses with massive mutton-sleeves.[3] In Europe, Addams followed the routine that was customary for a young American pursuing cultural refinement: she collected art reproductions, studied languages, worked her way through museums, and wrote up her impressions. She brought to her European trips (this first trip was followed by a second, just a year before the founding of Hull-House) a vision of an America that kept faith with its best civic instincts. But could this vision be made a reality? And what part should she play—what role foreordained and blessed by the civic saints of American history, especially her beloved Abraham Lincoln?

These questions gnawed and nagged and sometimes wore her down as she read, wrote, and watched. Her stepmother needed close attention, cultivating one ailment after another. Addams missed home and her sisters; but still they stayed on. And in the pale hands she glimpsed one night, she witnessed a scene that, she sensed, placed her under an obligation. She had as yet no idea of how to meet that obligation. But because she was one of those persons in whom reasoning and imagining lead to action, she began slowly to forge a determination to emulate "the Man and His message," as she wrote (of Jesus of Nazareth) to Ellen Gates Starr on March 30, 1885, two years after witnessing the pale hands at midnight.[4] She would put the beatitudes into action. The stories she had recorded in her travel notebooks helped focus her determination. For it is only through stories like Christ's parables that one can best convey the real situation before one. Sympathetic understanding is made possible only if the descriptions of an event are sturdy and framed by a moral imperative. Then, perhaps, myriads of grasping hands may teach a lesson that cuts to the bone, and may even help a sheltered self become a strong, sheltering self.[5]

But to accomplish this, she must empty herself of self-pity, self-conceit, and self-pride—herein the sacrificial moment central to the Christian narrative—in order to be filled with the concrete reality of those standing before her.[6] Addams slowly came to the conclusion that her descents into desuetude were linked to a kind of selfishness: "I had been tied to the veriest ox-cart of self-seeking." It seems doubtful that an adamant self-seeker would write such words of self-indictment. But, one way or the other, Addams was on the road to Damascus, and she wanted her friends to walk along—through her stories and letters, if they could not be there in person. She knew that it would not be easy to get the stories right: The world is in relentless motion, only rarely permitting us to pause and to witness a scene in all its fullness; but unless we can do that, we are doomed to confusion as to whether what we are experiencing as real is "the inner pang or the outward seeming."[7] The problem is, how to grapple with difficult realities once the moment has passed; for these moments are likely to reappear as a sharp pain in the heart, making it hard to distinguish the "inner pang" from the "outward seeming."

Addams found herself in a shadowland. It would be years before she could even *imagine* Hull-House, much less make it happen.

After her vision of pale hands, the feverish search for culture begins to revolt her. She recovers some enchantment in Rome and the Catacombs, but her physician-sanctioned stay in Europe only throws into ever starker relief the yawning gap between the outer reality of a well-to-do young American abroad and her deep inner pain and emptiness; the abyss that separates outward seeming and interior sadness and yearning. "Weary of myself and sick of asking / What I am, and what I ought to be,"[8] she decides that she cannot be an aesthete living life through the prism of literature. For the episode of pale hands has trigged a literary reflection. She reminisces on De Quincey's "The Vision of Sudden Death" and comes to a recognition that the "lumbering" of her mind with literature only serves to "cloud" the situation. But there is irony in this recognition, as literature also offers her a form through which to understand what it means to see everything through the filter of literature: De Quincey tells the story of being confronted "one summer's night" with the appearance of two "absorbed lovers" who "suddenly appear between the narrow blossoming hedgerows in the direct path of the huge vehicle," a high mail coach on which he is a passenger, and who will surely be crushed "to their death." De Quincey would cry a "warning shout, but finds himself unable to make a sound" because his mind "is hopelessly entangled in an endeavor to recall the exact lines from the 'Iliad' which describe the great cry with which Achilles alarmed all Asia militant." "Strange it is," writes De Quincey, "that I should need a suggestion from the 'Iliad' to prompt the sole resource that remained. Yet so it was. Suddenly I remembered the shout of Achilles, and its effect."[9] Addams summarizes: "Only after his memory responds is his will released from its momentary paralysis, and he rides on through the fragrant night with the horror of the escaped calamity thick upon him, but he also bears within him the consciousness that he had given himself over so many years to classic learning—that when suddenly called upon for a quick decision in the world of life and death, he had been able to act only through a literary suggestion." She finds her own recollection of De Quincey struggling to recollect *The Iliad* "preposterous." She grows disgusted and feels stuck in a "hateful, vicious circle," unable to act.[10]

Recalling De Quincey recalling *The Iliad* is designed to tell us just how removed she and other well-educated women of her generation were from the "active emotional life led by . . . grandmothers and great-grandmothers." The "contemporary education of young women had developed too exclusively the power of acquiring knowledge and of merely receiving impressions; that somewhere in the process of 'being educated' [they] had lost that simple and almost automatic response to the human appeal."[11] Something was amiss; some thread of life-giving continuity that purposes a straightforward engagement with the world had been broken. But how was one to reweave the fabric of life? In the meantime, the travels continued; the impressions mounted; the frustrations built. The material she gathered in her notebook would one day offer her rich parables that would become central not only to her own transformation but also to that of hundreds of others. A second encounter with human hands is one such parable.

The Story of Reddened Hands with White Scars

Addams and her stepmother at last make their way to Germany. Here Addams discovers a deep and growing admiration for the prints of Albrecht Dürer, which she describes as stunning "human documents," "surcharged with pity for the downtrodden." The prints are impressive because they faithfully display the cost of "shedding of blood which is sure to occur when men forget how complicated life is and insist upon reducing it to logical dogmas."[12] Addams also reads German, and her admiration and affection for German culture are steadily growing.[13]

Yet all *Kultur* is as ashes in her mouth when she witnesses a scene of scarred, reddened hands. She takes note of the intimate details of the scene and responds to it emotionally and physically: she takes action. Captured in her vignette is a nascent philosophy, part pragmatism, part Christian witness-bearing. The scene speaks directly to Addams, and to us, because she describes it in a compelling, artful way framed by deep moral principles. Her vignettes are nodal points that bring together her strengths and gifts—moral ardor, acute intelligence, and a literature-shaped social conscience—adding up to what she describes as sympathetic knowledge and advocates as a way to approach human problems so that human beings do not disappear into a faceless, anonymous mass.[14]

> I recall one snowy morning in Saxe-Coburg, looking from the window of our little hotel upon the town square, that we saw crossing

and recrossing it a single file of women with semicircular heavy wooden tanks fastened upon their backs. They were carrying in this primitive fashion to a remote cooling room these tanks filled with a hot brew incident to one stage of beer making. The women were bent forward, not only under the weight which they were bearing, but because the tanks were so high that it would have been impossible for them to have lifted their heads. Their faces and hands, reddened in the cold morning air, showed clearly the white scars where they had previously been scalded by the hot stuff which splashed if they stumbled ever so little on their way. Stung into action by one of those sudden indignations against cruel conditions which at times fill the young with unexpected energy, I found myself across the square, in company with mine host, interviewing the phlegmatic owner of the brewery who received us with exasperating indifference, or rather received me, for the innkeeper mysteriously slunk away as soon as the great magnate of the town began to speak. I went back to a breakfast for which I had lost my appetite, as I had for Gray's "Life of Prince Albert" and his wonderful tutor, Baron Stockmar, which I had been reading late the night before. The book had lost its fascination; how could a good man, feeling so keenly his obligation "to make princely the mind of his prince," ignore such conditions of life for the multitude of humble, hard-working folk.

Addams's response to the scarred, reddened hands reassures her that she is still alive to the connections between image, thought, word, and deed. The situation before her invites a complex social analysis but also provokes her to immediate action on that wintry morning.[15] The challenge is to sustain such moments, to move beyond the merely episodic. Her attitude toward her grand tour grows ever sourer. She believes that her aesthetic tourism has become a gorging on "too much sweet dessert."[16] Italy distracts her from such dark thoughts and brings temporary relief. But her intense self-consciousness gives her little peace. She makes certain that she and several in her party walk "three miles in the hot sunshine beating down upon the Roman Campagna, that we might enter the Eternal City on foot through the Porta del Popolo, as pilgrims had done for centuries."[17] But even this act is fraudulent in her eyes: after all, she and her party had entered Rome the evening before, had stayed in a hotel, and had been driven beyond the walls in order that they might say, with ancient pilgrims, "Ecce Roma" as they caught their "first glimpse of St. Peter's dome." She calls this episode "melodramatic." Distrusting her advantages, she tells us that, nevertheless, "I wanted more of them."[18]

Through it all, she finds her mind returning to the scarred hands and the snowy morning in Saxe-Coburg. She sees the bowed backs of the women, their faces and hands laced by scalding brew as they plod back and forth. There are defining moments when one peers head-on at a bitter reality and is compelled to reflect and perhaps to act. For now, she can at least write down what she has seen, making visible to others the white hands grasping rotting vegetables at midnight, the women bent over hot tanks, their necks strained and their hands scarred. These scenes become her parables, preparatory to an ethics of realizable action made possible by sympathetic knowledge.

The Christ Spirit in Action

During an interlude in Cedarville, in the summer of 1885, she is baptized and joins the Presbyterian church.[19] She hastens to tell us that no conversion was involved in this decision: the baptism required no "assent to dogma or miracle," neither of which she credited (in this she was in tune with many others of her time). Although the ministers and church officers "were obliged to subscribe to doctrines of well-known severity," all that was demanded of her as a member of the laity was adherence to basic teachings and a good-faith effort to put them into practice. This form of faith without mystery made church membership acceptable to her, bringing her at last within a circle of fellowship, for which she had ardently yearned. Downgrading theology in favor of social action, she made "the ideals of democracy" the object of her "passionate devotion." Perceiving Jesus of Nazareth as a forerunner of the Founding Fathers, she recast him as a proto-democrat bearing a saving message with egalitarianism at its heart. Did he not lift up the fisherman and the slave? Surely *he* would not permit the privileged few to go unchallenged in tailoring society to their own measure! Thin though this theology may be, its message of democratic inspiration has been embraced by thousands of Americans over the years. The Social Gospel idea held that Christianity implicated believers in a new vocabulary of basic notions bearing requirements for action in the world, in the name of brotherhood and stewardship. The Social Gospelers of Addams's era aimed to retool Christianity, so to speak, so as to make it do lots of practical work.

That is why it was essential to embody the spirit of Christ. Addams's later correspondence shows how closely many identified her with that spirit, once she had decided on and begun to implement her plan of action.[20] In June 1897, for example, social reformer Graham Taylor writes Addams a long letter calling for Christianity to be put into action.[21]

> I cannot endure much longer the "moral dualism" between the clear ethical ideals of the Christian law of love—and the tacit acknowledgement of the necessity and the open participation in the "competitive order" which seems to be irresistibly forced upon everyone not willing to secede from the whole life of his day or desert the service to that life. It is coming to be nothing less than the moral self-stultification of the individual and collective Christian Conscience and is, I believe, the very paralysis of the church's power. What shall we think and do?

Similarly, George D. Herron, a professor of applied Christianity at Iowa College, writes Miss Addams that he is struggling with how to make his life a "true witness": "I do not see that Tolstoi has rightly answered it. At bottom, his is an *egoistic peace*. There is a better way. . . . It is peace for one's self, but not for the world. 'My peace give I unto you,' is something different."[22] Mary MacDowell, addressing herself to "Sister Adams" in 1898, proclaims that Jane Addams reflects "the Christ spirit as no one else does, and I am better after I have thought of you."[23]

But in 1885 such encomia lay in the future, and Jane's light was still bedimmed by self-doubt. Joining a local Cedarville congregation struck her as an exigent step. Why should she remain aloof from the modest "institutional statement" of Jesus's teachings in that "little village in which I was born"? Without humble and imperfect institutions it would be altogether too easy "for the world to slip back into the doctrines of selection and aristocracy."[24] Her induction into the church humbles her. She realizes that she must not stand apart awaiting the perfect embodiment of an ethic of universal fellowship. Although there is little doubt that she later believed that Hull-House came much closer to realizing that ethic than did any church, Hull-House was not yet even envisioned at this point. Addams would remain for three more years the "dupe of a deferred purpose."[25]

Europe Redux, 1887–1888

Jane Addams's lengthy snare of preparation included a second trip to Europe.[26] She was twenty-seven years old and had an independent, private income of $3,000 a year—substantial by the standards of the day. Ellen Gates Starr joined her, as did another friend, Sarah Anderson. There were more close encounters with human misery during this trip, this time in the organized form of meetings of striking London match girls as well as during a visit to Toynbee Hall, situated amid the urban detritus of London's Whitechapel area.[27] Toynbee Hall offered something new: In place of old-fashioned modes of relief to the poor, it provided mutual engagement across class lines and a broad education for working men and women. Run by the impressive Canon Barnett, Toynbee Hall emphasized the importance of art and culture to a "people's university." There were classes on hundreds of subjects. In 1887, a People's Palace opened in East London featuring a library, pool, gymnasium, and meeting halls. In its first year of operation, more than 1.5 million people—the majority between the ages of 16 and 25—used the facility. Toynbee Hall also contained a well-stocked library.

The settlement movement, of which Toynbee Hall was a product, had sprung up in England in the mid–nineteenth century. Inspired by the writings of social and cultural theorists and critics such as John Ruskin and Thomas Hill Green, the movement began with a desire on the part of the more privileged to share the lives of those less favored. In England the division between classes was particularly severe.

The beginnings of the settlement movement were humble. In 1875, Arnold Toynbee, an Oxford tutor, moved to Whitechapel, a rough, derelict part of London, in order to experience firsthand the notoriously poor living conditions endured by Londoners of humble means. Ten years later, Toynbee Hall, the first social settlement, opened. Two years after its founding, Jane Addams visited, and the visit changed her life, helping reinforce an idea that was already beginning to take shape—namely, that she and several friends should find a big house in a congested quarter in Chicago in which to make their own attempt at a settlement.

Addams was growing more resolute and focused in her anger at the way things were. She was seeking someone to blame for phossy jaw and other industrial illnesses, decrepitudes, and deformations, including the gradual, often invisible crushing of the human body and spirit. That longing for a clear villain behind the scenes was a fancy of the young, she later decided. The world was more puzzling that that, because even good people were part of structures whose outcome was misery. For a brief time, she attached herself to the Positivists, with their vague hopes for universal comity. A moment in the Ulm cathedral crystallized in her a notion of moral evolution and progress—a view she never abandoned, even in the cataclysmic regress that was World War I. But she had not yet discovered the context in which she could at last reduce her philosophy to deeds.

*   *   *

In early 1887, Addams and her traveling companions find themselves in picturesque lodgings outside Rome. Determined to cull useful experience, Addams resists the overly refined aesthetic engagement with Italy assayed by Nathaniel Hawthorne in *The Marble Faun,* a novel that had become a guidebook for Americans journeying to Italy to find culture, due to Hawthorne's detailed depiction of art, his "aesthetic or touristic model of reality."[28] Instead, Addams immerses herself in a study of the Catacombs—here are fellowship, purpose, deed-doing and suffering on a potent scale—but she is felled by "sciatic rheumatism." Tended by a trained nurse, she continues her recovery on the Riviera at her physician's advice. Many are those who would covet such luxurious invalidism! Here she bides her time, working on her Catacombs material in the hope of turning it into an "early interpretation of Christianity" that "*should* be presented to the poor, urging that the primitive church was composed of the poor and that it was they who took the wonderful news to the more prosperous Romans"[29] (the emphasis is mine). Her Catacombs lectures indeed are delivered to a deaconess training school during her first winter in Chicago, in 1889, following her return from Europe. By then she and Ellen Gates Starr have hatched their scheme to move into a big house in a "congested quarter."

Her interpretation of the early Christians helps one understand the absence of religious instruction at Hull-House. There was religion at Hull-House, she would later tell critics, but it was of the sort that *should* be offered to the poor—a story of their triumph through the *kerygma,* the good news of the Gospel. This was a radically transformed message. The good news of the Incarnation and Resurrection had been siphoned off, and Addams had refilled the wineskin with a social message, an account of Christianity's origins that offered the poor what she thought they needed: a serviceable story that promised comfort for the time being, strength for the journey, and hope of social transformation in the here-and-now.

That human beings do not live by bread alone Addams accepted; but the things of the spirit at Hull-House were art and drama, not worship. Great works of art and performances of great works of drama—the very culture with which she had been sated—were after all, she decided, a way to lift the spirit.[30] The rough-and-tumble social egalitarianism that, to her, was the heart and soul of the American democracy was fully compatible with beauty and a yearning for excellence in all things. Paring away the belief in the mystical and the miraculous was the route to a truly useful Christianity, she believed.

Here we bump up against a rare breakdown in Addams's commitment to sympathetic understanding. Her bare-bones ethical system in which Jesus joins company with other moral teachers and all else is let go leaves little space for sacred liturgy, saints, incense, the mystery of the mass— and these predominated among her Catholic Italian neighbors in the 19th ward. The Social Gospel is like a pair of sensible shoes for walking about and doing good works; but they are not a pilgrim's sandals with the soles worn paper thin by trudging miles to stand before a relic of the True Cross. A Christianity stripped of mystery had helped Addams find her way; unsurprisingly, she urged it on others, but not in energetic proselytizing. Rather, she tried to live out her creed and model a creative solution to the problems faced by educated young women, including those whose lives would be defined in part by what they did not do.

Lives Not Lived: Mission, Marriage, Society

Jane Addams's sojourn in the land of preparation did not entrap her in a life of inaction, as she feared it might during her lowest moments.

Each of us imagines the life we might have lived but did not, knowing as we do this imagining that we have one life only. The vocations open to middle-class women in the last three decades of the nineteenth century were marriage, mission work, and that vague but overpowering thing called society. Marriage was one entry point into society—depending, of course, on one's social class. Mission work was an honorable alternative to society. Young, unmarried Protestant women who became missionaries embraced something akin to a Catholic vocation. As mentioned earlier, Addams spurned the urgings of her teachers at the Rockford Seminary to take up mission work. She lacked the missionary's calling to risk life and limb in order to bring the gospel message to all nations. There were three missionary societies at the seminary, and they were the only "societies in which she never held an office."[31] She was already preaching religion in a practical sense, however. John Farrell points out that Miss Sill promoted a version of usefulness—"Christian Mothers and Missionaries for the evangelization of the world"—as revealed religion "was the basis of true moral culture and the bible the only test of practical morality."[32] Addams tenaciously resisted Miss Sill because she disagreed on a point of principle.

In many ways, Addams did create a mission field, but it was in the 19th ward of Chicago, and it didn't involve religious evangelizing; rather, democratic inculcation was the heart of her mission.[33] Just as Addams took the dominant themes and imperatives of her time concerning mission work and recast them in new forms, so she re-formed domesticity or housekeeping. Like other social feminists, she infused domesticity with a wider moral and social meaning, finding in it a way to serve others and to enact citizenship. Social feminism stressed the importance of women's ties to the wellsprings of tradition and extolled the centrality of family and children in women's lives; but the domestic arena was seen as a springboard into wider civic life rather than an inhibition to matters civic. Marriage seems not to have tempted Addams, although she was assiduously courted at several points. Her stepmother worked to engineer her marriage to stepbrother George Haldeman; but she chose to stay unmarried. A family story woven around her unmarried state held that the operation on her back left permanent damage that ruled out childbearing. Whether this is true or a sympathetic interpretation of the facts so as to avoid further probing is unclear.[34] Regardless of the reasons for her decision, Addams's creative redrawing of her household boundaries to encompass an entire city—her "civic housekeeping," as it came to be called—was a fascinating alternative to wedded domesticity.

It is difficult from our cultural perch to discern just how rigidly structured and stifling society would have seemed to an ardent, educated woman of Addams's day. The refinement of young women began early and was determinedly pursued through young adulthood. In the popular guide *The Girl's Own Book* (first published in 1834 and reprinted many times thereafter), Mrs. L. Maria Child expends nearly 300 pages detailing appropriate games, exercises, wordplay, and calisthenics for the properly bred and reared young woman. Mrs. Child presumes that the well-bred girl knows French. Several of the games involve queries and responses in French at a level of difficulty that presupposes years of tutoring.

The pre-scripted games, described as "great favourites in France," include "Cries of Paris," in which a child must take "the part of some of the numerous Parisian peddlers: one sells cherries, another cakes, another old clothes, another eggs," and so on. In another game, the girls form a circle, and a light feather or tuft of "unspun cotton, or silk" is kept aloft by the group's blowing. Mrs. Child finds this "droll" because the "whole circle" is "turning and twisting, and puffing, to keep up one poor little feather." There are instructive games and there are calisthenics, which some people think "dangerous, because they confound them with the ruder and more daring gymnastics of boys; but such exercises are selected as are free from danger; and it is believed that they tend to produce vigorous muscles, graceful motion, and symmetry of form."[35] Sketched is a young woman in long dress holding her arms aloft, bending over only so far as her waist, and then placing her arms at her waist.

To be sure, ladies were called to service of a circumscribed sort. Their world of service was meticulously severed from politics.[36] Ladies expressed sympathy, but action was denied them save of the Lady Bountiful sort—delivering parcels of food, taking part in sewing circles, bearing flowers to the sick in hospitals. A breakthrough occurred during the American Civil War, when women were hired by the tens of thousands to take up the slack as men went off to war. This was the era when women entered teaching, never to depart. But society and its strictures always loomed. If one were wellborn, especially among the East Coast elite, one's life was privileged but hemmed in by social conventions. Being a child of the prairie, Jane Addams experienced more freedom. Her small-town upbringing helped her avoid at least some of the hothouse restraints of society. Social distinctions in small towns were blurred and people mingled together, meeting and greeting one another in common places. The well-to-do, like John Huy Addams, were not segregated in remote estates sustained by a platoon of servants. Public education had an egalitarian effect. The world limned terrifyingly by Edith Wharton in *The Age of Innocence* would have been as strange to young Jane Addams as were the foreign cultures she visited and read about.

Newland Archer, Wharton's protagonist, is fraught with worry about offenses against Taste, "that far-off divinity of whom 'Form' was the mere visible representative and viceregent."[37] In this world of Taste, categories are rigidly adhered to, including the distinction between the woman a man loves and respects and women he enjoys or pities. Archer has fallen in love with the mysterious Countess Olenska, for whom he believes himself ready to abandon his approved marriage that solidifies several Society families, and he cries out to the Countess that he wants to escape it all, especially categories like "wife" or "mistress," and be simply "two human beings who love each other." Less romantic and more hardheaded than Newland Archer, Countess Olenska sighs, laughs bitterly, and asks Newland: "Where is that country? Have you ever been there?"[38]

Jane Addams would have appreciated the Countess's tough-mindedness. There are no cultures without categories, some of them rigid and cruel but always to a purpose. Throughout her life, Addams struggled to unearth the deeper logic that underlay categories. Working the way a cultural anthropologist works, Addams helped her contemporaries to see and thus to question much of what they had previously accepted on faith. With equal if not greater force, she insisted that ordinary people—who take on a kind of mystical quality for her from time to time (at least the women do)—are, deep down, wise. As a schoolgirl she had even called them the voice of God: *vox populi, vox Dei.*

"The Growing Good of the World Is Partly Dependent on Unhistoric Acts"

Jane Addams's experience of life convinced her that the past is always present in individual human beings and cultures. Perhaps if we explore the particularities of her history, we will better understand why she didn't turn out to be just another idealistic young woman out to do good in the world. Her early recognition that "there's power in me" identifies her as one of those earnest children who make very good use of their childhoods. This was especially important for earnest young women of Addams's day and social milieu because so many avenues for action were closed to them. Morally precocious youngsters could not afford to waste time. They were obliged to go through serious dress rehearsals for an adult life of purpose, meaning, and accomplishment. Some carried this burden lightly. Others were weighed down by it and become morbid. Jane Addams flirted with morbidity but finally wrestled that dire possibility to the ground.

She succeeded in rising from her bed of misery in part because she had moral tutors, as they were then called. Parents served in this role, first and foremost, followed by other family members, clergy, and teachers. But the wider surround in which children are raised is also, for better or worse, a moral guide. If norms are driven to the lowest common denominator, a society is likely in bad shape: cynical, narrowly self-interested. The flip side of the coin of moral relativism is, however, rigid moralism of a sort that makes little or no provision for human weakness and that squeezes out space for forgiveness and passion. Faithful to her lifelong search for balance, Addams attempted to negotiate the shoals between these two perils.

We glimpse Jane Addams's childhood intensity in her determination to rise at 3 A.M. as her father did and to use that time in the early morning dark to read Plutarch's *Lives, The Iliad, The Odyssey, The Federalist Papers,* biographies of national heroes such as George Washington, and other fare unusual for one so young. We know that she was a star pupil and a teacher's favorite. Her father was her first and foremost moral tutor, but her favorite writers were a close second. None was more central to her formation than George Eliot, both in the substance of Eliot's moral universe and in the many-layered, complex interplay between protagonists that Eliot used to convey moral struggle and moral truth.

Eliot finds a way to embody accounts of moral development and moral suffering without falling into the morass of victimization. A victim ideology was circulating in Jane Addams's day. To be sure, the cult of the victim had not overtaken the culture to the degree that today's obsession with victims has, but it was present in sentimentalized forms.

Henry James mocked the victim ideology he detected in one strand of nineteenth-century feminism. In his startlingly prescient *The Bostonians,* published in 1886,[39] his protagonist, Olive Chancellor, emphasizes in her rhetoric woman's universal, primordial, and ever-present suffering. Much of the suffering has been silent, she declaims, this "ocean of tears" that had been "shed from the beginning of time" as one age of oppression after another

> had rolled over them [all women everywhere]; uncounted millions had lived only to be tortured, to be crucified. They were her sisters, they were her own, and the day of their delivery had dawned. This was the only sacred cause; this was the great, just revolution. It must then triumph, it must sweep everything before it; it must exact from the other, the brutal, bloodstained, ravening race, the last particle of expiation!

To Olive, man was an "odious" ravager, a creature who "had trampled upon them [women] from the beginning of time, and their tenderness, their abnegation, had been his opportunity." By contrast, if women ran things, there "would be generosity, tenderness, sympathy, where there is now only brute force and sordid rivalry."[40] The ingredients of a distorting moral dualism are here contained: all evil is on one side; all good is on the other, inextricably bound up with perpetual victimization. One "race"—the male—is, in effect, tainted; the other—the female—is graced; and of all the horrors, none is harder to bear than the fact that the very marks of goodness make of woman a perfect patsy, easy to coerce, intimidate, manipulate, and cajole.

It is difficult to find coherent ground for a civic or political project in this moralistic reduction—then or now—for there is precious little to motivate the victim to give up a privileged status that confers both innocence and nobility without accountability. Recall here the young Jane Addams's insight that there was comfort in being little. But Addams would have none of it. To be sure, she shared a view of women as the carriers of a particular and universal morality; as the purveyors of an ethic of endurance, relationship, stability, and care. But they, along with men, were responsible, and they, along with men, could take action.

To Olive Chancellor's rhetorical celebration of victimhood, contrast Eliot's Maggie Tulliver, or her Romola, or the extraordinary Dorothea of *Middlemarch.* These are all women for whom difficulties arise and to whom terrible things happen. Maggie is impetuous and precocious. She picks up her dead father's copy of Thomas à Kempis's classic of Christian formation, *The Imitation of Christ,* and finds passages marked by him. One reads: "'Know that the love of thyself doth hurt thee more than anything in the world.'" If some seek ecstasy in gin or various enthusiasms, for the morally serious the struggle lay within their own souls, "one shadowy army fighting another, and the slain shadows for ever rising again. . . . So it has been since the days of Hecuba."[41]

Maggie understands that the foe is not *out there*; that she must fight her own demons. The moral life is a struggle, not a story of unblemished victory or victimization. Maggie Tulliver's struggle of conscience held much appeal for Jane Addams, who understood that moral struggle helps make us who we are and prepares us for public skepticism or even censure absent the comfort of littleness. Maggie Tulliver helps Jane Addams understand the challenges facing young people, for they, "like poor Maggie Tulliver, through many painful experiences have reached the conclusion that pity, memory, and faithfulness are natural ties with paramount claims."[42]

Reading George Eliot's novels, one is struck by the similarities between her philosophy of moral development as it is played out through her fictional protagonists and Jane Addams's philosophy of moral development and its unfolding in the creation and sustaining of Hull-House. Even as Eliot rejects overly abstract and systematized thought—as in her devastating portrait of poor Casaubon in *Middlemarch,* with his "Key to all Mythologies"—so Addams warns repeatedly against any attempt to fit everything into a tidy, orderly system.[43]

In *Daniel Deronda,* Eliot writes of childhood family memories and the need, in general, for a human life to be:

> well rooted in some spot of a native land, where it may get the love of tender kinship for the face of earth, for the labours men go forth into, for the sounds and accents that haunt it, for whatever will give that early home a familiar unmistakable difference amidst the future widening of knowledge: a spot where the definitiveness of early memories . . . may spread not by sentimental effort . . . but as sweet habit of the blood.

She adds that five-year-olds are not "prepared to be citizens of the world, to be stimulated by abstract nouns." It is only through seeding in familiar and family soil that universal aspiration can begin its tentative, frail sprouting.[44] The main lines of character are often laid down in these early experiences; and even before these experiences the newborn infant is morally awakened through her mirroring in a "loving mother's face."[45] Addams is more explicit on this score than Eliot, anticipating by decades what later child psychologists would call the failure-to-thrive syndrome, which results from neglect. As Addams writes in *Twenty Years:* "We are told that the 'will to live' is aroused in each baby by his mother's irresistible desire to play with him, the physiological value of joy that a child is born, and that the high death rate in institutions is increased by 'the discontented babies' whom no one *persuades into living*" (the italics are mine).[46] The malaise known as "hospitalization" had yet to be named by child development experts, but two nineteenth-century women had it nailed down. An entire theory of human nature is embedded in the profound fact that without human nurturance of a sort that goes beyond the provision of basics, the human infant languishes.[47]

Lessons Jane Addams learned as a child were powerfully reinforced by Eliot, including the conviction that sentiments that may "seem to be dying" may yet "revive into strong life" and that this may extend to entire nations.[48] This awareness is put in the mouth of her protagonist Daniel Deronda, who having learned of his Jewish heritage, expresses Zionist convictions about the need for the Jewish people to have a place to inhabit and to defend. This determination to nurture nations yet unborn may seem hopeless in the beginning. But the same yearning is implicit also in the dreams of others, including one of Addams's childhood heroes, Mazzini, with his goal of a new freedom for Italy and his efforts to "rouse the same feelings in other young men, and get them to work toward a united nationality."[49]

Eliot articulates universal themes through their concrete embodiment in characters, without reducing the greater themes to the merely subjective level. Addams imbibed, emulated, and added her own distinctive mode to this way of thinking and writing that was directly connected to action. The fictional and real-life protagonists who represent for Eliot and Addams, respectively, balked purpose and stunted growth, are those, like the villainous Tito Melema of Eliot's *Romola,* who acknowledge "neither moral order nor divine purpose in the universe" and who give themselves over to "unrestrained egotism." They are unable to get out of the box of selfish desires. They are criminals without consciousness of their crimes.[50]

Without a mooring in a moral purpose, life scatters, falters, and dries up. When we meet Eliot's Romola, she is living in and through devotion to her father, a blind scholar: here are echoes of Jane Addams's own stalwart devotion. By the standards of his day—the Florence of the Medici—Romola's father is a freethinker. When Tito, Romola's trickster husband, enters the novel, he is a poor but eager young man trying to make his way honestly. But he soon falls into treachery in order to achieve his ends. He tries to persuade Romola to jettison her father's library, despite the fact that "she was determined never to submit her mind on this question of duty to her father; she was inwardly prepared to encounter any sort of pain in resistance."[51]

The reason behind her determination is this: Eliot's Romola understands that sympathy and loyalty are the glue that hold the moral universe together. One who would "appropriate the widest sympathies" but has "no pulse for the nearest" is a fraud and "hopelessly shallow."[52] Romola finds this wider sympathy through Fra Girolamo Savonarola. She enters into communion with the Church after her father, her husband, and her brother have died, and in this way her moral hunger is at last satisfied. But it is the "sanctity attached to all close relations" that makes this wider morality possible, in contrast to the "light abandonment of ties, whether inherited or voluntary, because they had ceased to be pleasant, [which] was the uprooting of social and personal virtue."[53]

Addams's connection to Eliot is far-reaching. The two shared a deep belief in moral progress coupled with a fear that the abandonment of traditional religion—which Eliot and Addams both reject, remember— would lead over time to shallow utilitarianism and unrestrained egotism. Moral sentiments had to be rooted in some larger purpose. Both were convinced that human beings could not live on lofty, fleecy ideas, and that the moral life can only grow from the ground up. In both women's thought and writing, a dedication to social and economic reforms is tethered to an insistence that religion, science, and art are necessary components of *any* transformative vision. Human beings not only do not live by bread alone, they *cannot* live so. One thinks here of

Addams's determination to build an art gallery as soon as the money could be raised—an effort derided by many. Why do the immigrant poor *need* that? But, as if in direct response to the scoffers, the gallery drew enthusiastic crowds of 19th-ward immigrants once it was up and running.

Given her ethical and artistic sensibility, it is unsurprising that Jane Addams rejected the label of Hull-House as a laboratory experiment of a social sort. She loathed the phrase, applied by some urban sociologists, because she insisted that settlements "should be something much more human and spontaneous than such a phrase connotes." It was "inevitable that the residents [of Hull-House] should know their own neighborhoods more thoroughly than any other"; but that did not make of them scientists conducting an experiment *on* foreign-born immigrants as so many research subjects; rather, the residents and their neighbors shared a complex and sometimes difficult experience together, in and through which all would be changed.[54] Human life can only be understood through a sympathetic entry into its complexities: for George Eliot, through literature; for Jane Addams, through settling in a "congested neighborhood" and writing about it.

Both Eliot and Addams loathed the frivolous: Consider Eliot's famous criticism of "silly" novels by "Lady Novelists" who believed that "an amazing ignorance, both of science and of life, is the best possible qualification for forming an opinion on the knottiest moral and speculative questions"; and Addams's conviction that the flappers of the 1920s were making ill use of their freedom by heightening to an absurd degree one aspect of human experience—the sexual—and turning it into the very lodestone of existence.[55] Whether in silly novels or frivolous flappery, women were portrayed as embodying the triumph of *feeling* over the daunting complexities of educated and well-formed sensibilities.

Jane Addams's awareness of this celebration of quivering emotion over intellect is evident in her 1881 Graduation Day address at Rockford Seminary. In her speech, she warned "women of the nineteenth century" that the "weak woman" will veer off the arduous path into "spiritualism and clairvoyance" or become a "sentimentalist," and thus misuse the great gift of intuition. To be sure, Addams credits women with a "mighty intuitive perception"; but this is not enough. Women must study "at least one branch of physical science" in order that the "intuitive mind gain that life which the strong passion of science and study, feeds and forms." Latter-day Cassandras must learn self-denial and how to express themselves "not by dogmatism, but by quiet, progressive development." This is the path towards enlargement of the sympathies.

Jane Addams homes in directly on the dilemma Mary Ann Evans confronted by transforming herself into the great "George Eliot": The male persona had greater authority than the female, whatever his field of endeavor. The Cassandras of the world "have not gained what the ancients called *auctoritas,* right of speaker to make themselves heard," and without this their prophecies fall on deaf ears; their intuitions sputter and dim.[56] It is remarkable that Addams had hit upon this age-old dilemma as a twenty-year-old and had defined the issue as the absence not so much of power as of *authority.*

Addams understood that power does not confer authority automatically. If the powerful lose the legitimacy their authority confers, their power may crumble before their eyes. A ruthless strongman may have tanks, but an unarmed truth-teller may have more authority and may, improbably, disarm the depredators. Of course, the powerful who command tanks and hold dominion triumph often enough, but they cannot prevail indefinitely if authority is denied them. Authority grants the right not only to speak but to be heard.[57] How could the woman of the nineteenth century gain legitimate authority? Without the elusive but palpable power to be heard and thus to persuade, she could undertake no meaningful action to alter the course of events.

Jane Addams had her work cut out for her. George Eliot afforded her much of the material, the pattern, even the tailor's tools with which she worked. Addams borrowed directly from Eliot's metaphors and modes of expression. For example: Eliot's prose is riddled with watery metaphors—rivers, oceans, channels, rain. Maggie Tulliver dies, with her brother, in a flood. Others also perish or are lost in floods, including floods of emotion. They struggle to make their way to the surface and to channel their emotions; to change the course of the current of life. Eliot's imagery courses through Addams's writings. Jane Addams kept such close company with George Eliot that it is nearly impossible to prize the two apart. This goes much beyond borrowing or imitation, becoming something a psychoanalyst might call an "I-ideal"—a strong vision of what we aspire to become.

In the striving, we may become, at least in part, what we wish to be. For Jane Addams, sorting out the complexities of what she called the "family claim" was essential if she was to respond to the greater social claim. She decided that she would paint on a broad canvas and do so boldly, and her determination finally delivered her to the founding of Hull-House. But the haunting dilemma of the family claim and the social claim was never permanently resolved; instead it framed her entire adult life.

4

THE FAMILY CLAIM AND THE
SOCIAL CLAIM

THE DOORS OF HULL-HOUSE OPENED on September 18, 1889. Jane Addams had spent winter, spring, and summer 1889 in Chicago gathering money, paying social dues, garnering political support, and holding fast to her "scheme." Ellen Gates Starr, to whom she had first revealed the plan during their trip in Europe, 1887–1888, joined her, as did a housekeeper, Mary Keyser, when they took up residence at 335 (later, 800) Halsted Street, destined to become the most famous address in Chicago. In the quiet of the night before her open doors became a reality, Jane Addams no doubt mused on what had brought her to that moment. Convinced as she was that an old order was dying and a new one was struggling to be born, she aimed to contribute to the new by preserving the best of the old and creatively mixing the two.

The passing of an old way of life does not necessarily entail its obliteration, she insisted. Her sense of cultural renewal and moral evolution called for social amelioration, not violent upheaval. No responsible social reformer aims to wipe out all that has gone before. To the contrary, the basis of all progress, she writes, is to revere rather than to revile the best of the past. Addams hoped that "our American civilization might be built without disturbing these foundations [the examples of great civic heroes] which were laid of the old time."[1] The past haunts the present and works itself into its interstices. So it is that the modern woman carries forward in her own way the age-old story of woman as sower of grain, bearer of children, devoted steward of a domicile, by bringing new urgency to these ancient tasks. She must seek new cultural forms even as she recognizes the pathos of "the world of things as they are."[2]

Searchers in each generation are not content with skimming the surface of things. Instead, they plumb the depths *ardently*—a favorite word of Addams's that recurs hundreds of times in her writing. This begins with youth's ardent search to figure out "what I am and what I ought to be."

A House and a Home

When Jane Addams and Ellen Gates Starr set up housekeeping, they did it with all the flair of matrons creating a pleasing, welcoming home. Their enterprise was civic housekeeping, but it was also old-fashioned homemaking as well. Theirs was a "house constantly filling and refilling with groups of people."[3] Their home was ever metamorphosing as the neighborhood demographics altered. Hull-House was a permanent residence for Addams and Starr as well as for a number of others who lived and worked within its walls. Some residents stayed a few years and then moved on; others came and never left.

Addams brought to Hull-House most of her own possessions, including her books and heirloom silver. She dipped into her inheritance for the extensive revamping and restoration that the old mansion needed. She and Starr had acquired the residence in a token lease from Helen Culver, the cousin of its original owner, one Charles J. Hull. A year after the opening date, Culver, who supported the settlement idea, deeded the mansion, the land on which it stood, and other lots in the same block to Jane Addams. Culver's generosity enabled Hull-House to expand rapidly.[4]

Addams wrote long letters to her stepmother describing the early days.[5]

> Ellen and I live here alone with one servant. Miss Dow comes every morning at eight and opens the kindergarten at nine. We have twenty-four little people, about half of them Italians and other poor children whose mothers "work out" most of the day. We have a list of at least seventy more mothers who have applied and begged for

their children [to be admitted to the kindergarten]. Miss Dow takes lunch with us each day, and sometimes her two assistants come up. She is so young and pretty . . . every one is charmed with her. She gives her services of course as well as all the material used. Our piano was sent us with the rent paid for a year and an intimation that if the institution was thriving at the end of that time it would be given to us. Miss Trowbridge comes every night and stays until Sat. morning. She has a club of little girls. Miss Forstall has undertaken a "Home Library Ass" [sic] every Monday Aft, the books are kept at the house of one of the children with ten books and ten children in a circle. . . . We have two boys clubs every Tuesday. Miss Starr has hers down stairs and mine are in the dining room. I have twenty they are about to work at Fields and Walker's as errand boy and wrapping parcels most of them. I have one telegraph boy and two who are in machine shops. They are all so anxious to come and very respectful. The little ragamuffins down stairs are harder to manage. Miss Starr has help for tonight. Mr. Greeley came with his violin. There are so many applicants that we have started two overflow clubs for Thursday night. Mine on Thursday night are all Italians. Every Wednesday Mr. Sammons has a drawing class of twelve. . . . We have only taken those children who knew something about drawing, some who had left the Public Schools & one or two boys who were trying to keep on alone. One Italian, Frank Hardi, had had lessons in Italy and his great disappointment in America was that drawing lessons cost so much and he never could have any more. . . . On Friday evening we have older girls and on Sat. we are starting a Social Science club for men. . . . The House itself is a charming old thing and we are very fond of it. Our pictures look very nice and what furniture I bought was all handsome. Our dining room is very elegant and substantial. The Mason oak sideboard would be fine anywhere. Our table was a great bargain and I indulged in chairs at 5.50 a piece.

Visitors to Hull-House commented on its warm atmosphere and beguiling appearance. Marie and Rose (of Chapter 2) told me again and again that Hull-House was a "beautiful home" and that "everything was the best." The best, for Jane Addams, meant culture as well as décor and furnishings. In the early weeks a George Eliot reading group formed, and the first novel selected was *Romola,* read in Italian out of deference to the predominantly Italian neighbors. A woman who had been a resident at the Brook Farm experiment in communal living in Roxbury, Massachusetts, visited Hull-House and offered readings from Nathaniel Hawthorne.[6] If you were a resident, it would not be at all unusual in the course of a day to move from reading George Eliot to debating Karl Marx, to washing newborns, to readying the dead for burial, to nursing the sick, to minding the children. Participating in the "humblest services" helped residents share in what Addams declared those "simple human foundations" laid down long ago, without whose fulfillment no human life could exist.[7]

The statement of purpose in Hull-House's charter read: "To provide a center for a higher civic and social life; to institute and maintain educational and philanthropic enterprises, and to investigate and improve the conditions in the industrial districts of Chicago"; but this fails to capture the spirit and the manifold activities of Hull-House.[8] Addams refined this statement over the years. It was a "place for enthusiasms"; it helped "give form to social life"; it offered "the warm welcome of an inn"; it was a place for mutual interpretation of the social classes one to another; it responded to ethical demands and shared fellowship; it was a place for the life of the mind. Above all, it was the place Jane Addams and Ellen Starr aimed to "make . . . as beautiful as we could."[9] At the conclusion of her second autobiographical volume, *The Second Twenty Years at Hull-House,* Addams takes another stab at it: "It was the function of settlements to bring into the circle of knowledge and fuller life, men and women who might otherwise be left outside."[10]

In her final book—a posthumously published homage to longtime Hull-House resident Julia Lathrop, who was a close personal friend of Addams's and an indefatigable pioneer of reform efforts—Addams recalls a story from the early days, when the residents were still figuring out what they should be doing. A young woman had rushed through the door, shrieking that a baby was being born in their tenement to a girl who was "hollering something fierce." None of the neighbors would go to assist the forlorn girl because she was unmarried. No one called a doctor because the girl had no money to pay him. The girl's mother was at her job as a washerwoman. What I call the Story of Rushing into Midwifery[11] continues:

There seemed nothing for it but to go ourselves and Julia Lathrop and I set forth leaving a resident at the telephone calling up a friendly neighborhood doctor. We found the poor girl alone in her agony and by the time the doctor finally arrived, almost at the very moment that the girl's mother returned from her work, the patient was lying in a clean bed and the baby, having been induced to cry lustily, was having his first bath. As we left, the little mother feebly expressed her first word of gratitude by telling us that she would name the baby after us; but poor little Julius John died four months later on the Northwest side whither his mother and grandmother had moved because it would be easier in a new community to drape his existence with decorous fiction. I vividly recall through the distance of forty-five years that as we walked back from the tenement house stirred as we were by the mystery of birth, and seeing the neighborhood at its most attractive moment when the fathers were coming back from work, the children playing near the doorstep to be ready for supper which the mother was cooking inside, I exclaimed: "This doing things that we don't know how to do is going too far. Why did we let ourselves be rushed into midwifery?" To which she [Julia Lathrop] replied: "If we have to begin to hew down to the line of our ignorance, for goodness' sake don't let us begin at the humanitarian end. To refuse to respond to a poor girl in the throes of childbirth would be a disgrace to us forevermore. If Hull-House does not have its roots in human kindness, it is no good at all."

Those roots of human kindness gained expression in day nurseries, kindergarten classes, playgrounds, boys' and girls' clubs, a cooperative boardinghouse, theater workshops, music schools, language classes, reading groups, handicraft centers, and eventually a Labor Museum.[12] Jane Addams was on call the rest of her life, whenever she was at her Hull-House home. Newspaper clippings testify to the broad range of activities she was asked to take a hand in. Here is but one quirky example, drawn from the *Boston Transcript,* April 23, 1903:[13]

Chicago people look to Jane Addams of Hull-House in many emergencies. The other night the little woman was roused at midnight to meet a committee of firemen in the parlour. Stables had been burned in the neighborhood and horses were injured but not killed. There is a city law which requires a special order of court to shoot a horse within city limits. This order of court could not be obtained until morning. Horses were suffering with no hope of relief but death. "Miss Addams, can't you give us an order to shoot them?" asked the burly fireman. "I have no legal authority but I will take the responsibility," said the little woman. They drove with her to the place and she stood by to see the horses shot.

Clearly, Cassandra had become an acknowledged authority in nearly all matters, even in instances where she herself was rather doubtful that her knowledge—if not her authority—extended.

"Our Consciences Are Becoming Tender"

Hull-House had been up and running for three years when Jane Addams delivered what was destined to become a famous essay on "The Subjective Necessity for Social Settlements." This paper and its twin, "The Objective Value of a Social Settlement," provide a strong sense of Addams's passionate commitment, her ability to analyze social conditions critically, and her recognition that in hard, constructive work lay not only her salvation but that of many other educated young women. She—and they—were not traditional "charity workers": far from it. Instead, the gospel of Hull-House begins with "the theory that the dependence of classes on each other is reciprocal."[14] This "subjective necessity" derives from motives that are based on reasoned conviction and on passion. What young people seek and require is an "outlet for that sentiment of universal brotherhood which the best spirit of our times is forcing from an emotion into a motive."[15]

Three lines of "subjective pressure" pointed toward the social settlement idea: (l) the desire to make the social organism democratic; (2) the desire to share "the race life" (referring to the human race) and to bring as much social energy as possible to the task; (3) the desire to enact a "certain *renaissance* of Christianity, a movement toward its early humanitarian aspects." Building a democratic culture was the heart of the matter. Americans of Addams's time had democracy in a political sense, for the "gift of the ballot" had at last been given to "the negro." But African Americans and many others lived in "social ostracism," and women languished outside the franchise altogether—a fact that Addams does not stress in this essay, but one that fits. We offer the franchise to the immigrant man, she writes, but then we "dub him with epithets deriding his past life or present occupation, and feel no duty to invite him to our houses." Our democracy has not yet realized its full social possibilities.

Addams doesn't have socialism in mind when she speaks of socializing democracy here and elsewhere; rather, she is referring to a process that breaks down artificial barriers between people and makes it possible for human beings to realize their full sociality. "Our consciences are becoming tender in regard to the lack of democracy in social affairs," suggesting that America is entering a "second phase of democracy" in which Americans seek common places in which to meet and to offer hospitality to one another: clubhouses, libraries, galleries, and semi-public conveyances. These should be available to all. Otherwise, for immigrant men at any rate, the "only place of meeting is a saloon"; and in her ward, "a local demagogue" frequents the saloons, trying to drum up political support for his own narrow agenda.[16] Unless the good we seek is "secured for all of us," it will be a precarious and uncertain thing.

What Addams saw as undeniably good included the many blessings she associated with education and cultivation. Some would cavil at this now, finding blinkered elitism at work. Addams would plead not guilty to elitism in a political sense, but guilty as charged to an unabashed sense of what is good, worthy, and fine in a painting or a text. Most important, she believed the human soul yearns for knowledge; that we can be set afire mentally and ethically; that learning must not be confined to schools but must go on in villages and extension movements, among dock-laborers in New York harbor and in small towns in New England and the Midwest. Education can deliver us, she wrote—by which she meant, vouchsafe to us transformed bodies and minds. Her hero Giuseppe Mazzini is referenced again here, for he had proclaimed education a "Holy Communion with generations dead and living," by which the learner "fecundates all his faculties." Without this, we are but beasts.

She also further refines her definition of a settlement. She had previously referred to the settlement as "one manifestation of that wide humanitarian movement which, throughout Christendom, . . . is endeavoring to embody itself"; and now she calls it a "protest against a restricted view of education," and part of the effort to "socialize democracy." This means that a settlement must "never lose its flexibility, its power of quick adaptation, its readiness to change its methods as the environment may demand." The settlement speaks to broad and generous yearnings for a fuller life and use of the faculties. The "great mother breasts of our common humanity" must not be withheld from any of us. And starving the faculties can kill: Addams draws upon her own story as an illustration of how young women are taught to consider the good of the whole but then denied a way to participate in bringing it about. The resulting sense of uselessness is a shock to their systems and leads inexorably to an "atrophy of function." Addams's analysis suggests an image in which the senses wither, the faculties withdraw their tendrils and entwine inward upon themselves, and the growing tree is slowly strangled before it has a chance to branch out.

The Hull-House gospel isn't philanthropy or benevolence but a "thing fuller and wider than either of these." It is nothing less than a Christian impulse to "share the lives of the poor" in the way the Good Shepherd would have us do, in a manner both "blithe and gay . . . the hart no longer pants, but rushes to the water brooks."[17] Addams's Jesus is one who calls us to action, for it is only in putting ideas into action that we can truly receive the truth. In line with the general contours of the Social Gospel, Addams associates Christianity with social progress and with a deepening of human affection, even as early Christians "longed to share the common lot that they might receive the constant revelation." She does not associate Christ's message with "the religious consciousness" ("whatever that may be," she says rather curtly); but it is to be "proclaimed and instituted." Educated young women should be agents of this resurgence of Christian humanitarianism. Indeed, that was already happening, "in Chicago, if you please, without leaders who write or philosophize, without much speaking but with a bent to express in social service, in terms of action, the spirit of Christ."

It is always difficult to analyze a living thing, and that is what a settlement is: it is experimental; it aims to succor and to educate. A settlement is not political in a narrow sense; rather, it gives "the warm welcome of an inn"—and all her listeners knew which inn that would be—to those who preach propaganda, by which Addams refers to social and political ideologies. "The one thing to be dreaded in the Settlement is that it lose its flexibility, its power of quick adaptation, its readiness to change its methods as its environment may demand. It must be open to conviction and must have a deep and abiding sense of tolerance. . . . It must be grounded in a philosophy whose foundation is on the solidarity of the human race, a philosophy which will not waver when the race happens to be represented by a drunken woman or an idiot boy." Nowadays we wouldn't say "idiot boy," and "drunken woman" would be considered insensitive; but the wider point remains, there *is* room at this inn. Addams's "subjective necessity" essay displays the American Social Gospel movement at its most attractive: full-throated, open-hearted, filled with hope about human and democratic prospects.

Addams's approach avoided many of the shortcomings of the Social Gospel movement, including its often vague sense of generalized benevolence and blithe presuppositions of Protestant cultural dominance. She never forgot what it meant to be frightened and all at sea. If one remembers this fright, perhaps it is easier to open one's heart to others. In a letter to Ellen Gates Starr, written when Hull-House lay two years in the future, Addams wrote: "If you don't take charge of a child at night you can't feel a scared trembling little hand grow confiding and quiet as soon as it lies within your own. If you don't take little children out in the yard to spend the morning you simply can't see their unbounded delight and extravagant joy when they see a robin taking his bath." Joy in one's surroundings and the comfort in a small hand enfolded within a larger one is central to the family claim. The family claim is no private matter: it is a social claim of the most basic kind. Addams's challenge was to see the family as part of a web of social imperatives and forces without ever losing sight of that one little hand.[18]

The Objective Claim As an Urban Dream

What of the settlement's objective value—the subject of the second paper Addams read to her listeners at the School for Applied Ethics in Plymouth? You cannot take the measure of a social institution unless you describe it vividly and provide as much detail as possible. Objective value cannot be toted up like a bank balance; rather, one must burrow inside the situation if one would assess it objectively. It is worth quoting one particular long paragraph from Addams's essay,[19] because it affords a vivid description of Chicago's 19th ward in 1892—a model of a method of social analysis that relies on thick description:[20]

Hull House is an ample old residence, well built and somewhat ornately decorated after the manner of its time, 1856. It has been used for many purposes, and although battered by its vicissitudes, is essentially sound and has responded kindly to repairs and careful furnishing. Its wide hall and open fires always insure it a gracious aspect. It once stood in the suburbs, but the city has steadily grown up around it and its site now has corners on three or four more or less distinct foreign colonies. Between Halsted Street and the river live about ten thousand Italians: Neapolitans, Sicilians, and Calabrians, with an occasional Lombard or Venetian. To the south on Twelfth Street are many Germans, and side streets are given over almost entirely to Polish and Russian Jews. Still further south, these Jewish colonies merge into a huge Bohemian colony, so vast that Chicago ranks as the third Bohemian city in the world. To the northwest are many Canadian-French, clannish in spite of their long residence in America, and to the north are many Irish and first-generation Americans. On the streets directly west and farther north are well-to-do English-speaking families, many of whom own their houses and have lived in the neighborhood for years. I know one man who is still living in his old farm-house. This corner of Polk and Halsted Streets is in the fourteenth precinct of the nineteenth ward. This ward has a population of about fifty thousand, and at the last presidential election registered 7072 voters. It has had no unusual political scandal connected with it, but its aldermen are generally saloonkeepers and its political manipulations are those to be found in the crowded wards where the activities of the petty politician are unchecked. . . . The streets are inexpressibly dirty, the number of schools inadequate, factory legislation unenforced, the street-lighting bad, the paving miserable and altogether lacking in the alleys and smaller streets, and the stables defy all laws of sanitation. Hundreds of houses are unconnected with the street sewer. . . . An unscrupulous contractor regards no basement as too dark, no stable loft too foul, no rear shanty too provisional, no tenement room too small for his workroom, as these conditions imply low rental.

This word-portrait brings the Hull-House neighborhood to life: we smell the smells; sense the hustle and bustle, hear the babel of tongues overlapping with tongues; slip in the refuse; seek comfort in the saloon; try to rest, exhausted from lousy work and low pay, perhaps collapsing in a dank bedroom in an ill lit, poorly ventilated, and noisy tenement. How does Addams connect this scenario to the settlement's objective value? Standing outside and looking in, what Addams sees is the benefit derived for America if she treats newcomers with hospitality and welcomes what they have to offer: "One thing seemed clear in regard to entertaining [they are guests, remember] these foreigners: to preserve and keep for them whatever of value their past life contained and to bring them in contact with a better type of Americans." The reader no doubt winced at the phrase "better type of Americans." But this isn't class snobbery on Addams's part so much as a hardheaded acknowledgment of the fact that many immigrants' first encounters with the new world were with the worst it had to offer: unscrupulous operators out to fleece them; tenement owners out to gouge them; and factory operators out to overwork and underpay them.

My immigrant grandmother remembered a store clerk's attempts knowingly to give her incorrect change when she had made a purchase, the clerk assuming that this little foreign girl who couldn't speak English wouldn't know the difference. (They didn't know my grandmother!) She recalled jokes made at her expense when she sought assistance, once asking for a board at a lumberyard by using her hands to sketch the size of the board she needed. Because her pronunciation of the word *board* sounded a lot like *bread,* she was laughed at and told to go to a bakery. Small acts of humiliation. Small, but not forgotten sixty years later.

Newcomers are often confused and bewildered, and some among the better established will take advantage of this bewilderment. But those who cherish their citizenship and what America has to offer at its best recognize that immigrants are active, seeking people who yearn, like everybody else, for individual opportunity and communal solidarity. In order to lessen the newcomers' bewilderment, Hull-House offered an information and interpretation bureau. The immigrants' yearning for knowledge and beauty was met with "large and flourishing" math classes, a branch reading room of the Chicago Public Library, and the Butler Art Gallery, completed in 1891 and visited by 3,000 people, on average, each week. Human pride and dignity are serious issues for those who often face humiliating situations, including a lack of facilities in which to wash. Many immigrants were dirty because there were so few bathtubs in the crowded tenements. Seeing this, Addams built five bathrooms in the rear of Hull-House and made them available to the neighborhood. The bathtubs were as popular as the art gallery: They were constantly in use. Addams reports, "The number of baths taken in July was nine hundred and eighty." The day nursery and crèche hosted thirty to forty children daily, and this "nursery is not merely a convenience in the neighborhood; it is, to a certain extent, a neighborhood affair." Given Addams's strong views about the importance of hands-on parental (especially maternal) care of children, the closer the child care to the mother and to the family's home, the better.

Hull-House was a center for organizing union activities. Four women's unions met regularly there: the bookbinders, the shoemakers, the shirtmakers, and the cloakmakers. In spite of itself, Addams reported, Hull-House also did a good deal of legal work. The cases involved deserted women, "insurance for bewildered widows, damages for injured operators, playing something of the role the big brother does to protect his little brother from neighborhood bullies."

At Hull-House, the "zest for discussion" was always at full throttle. "Chicago is full of social theorists," Addams wrote without exaggerating; these social theorists hawked their wares regularly at Hull-House. Even though she might have found some of their wares unappealing, to suppress and to bottle them up would have been unwise, for then "there is danger of explosion." Addams continues, "Nothing so disconcerts a social agitator as to find among his auditors men who have been through all that, and who are quite as radical as he in another direction." Thus far, however, Hull-House had not succeeded in getting the "capitalist and the working-man" to "meet as individuals beneath a friendly roof"; but Addams was still hopeful.

All of Hull-House's many activities pointed toward one goal: the building up of a social culture of democracy. Addams insisted that the residents were neither philanthropists nor charity visitors nor social workers. Rather, they were citizens—although most of them, being women, did not have the right to vote. Hull-House's objective value lay in its capacity to help create strong citizens through a variety of means, methods, and media. If this sounds archaic or even corny to us, that is probably because we do not share Addams's sense of urgency about the creation of strong citizens. Seeing no subjective necessity for settlements, we find it difficult to assess the objective value of a Hull-House or any other experimental institution that responds to, and enriches, civil society. To begin to imagine what it would mean to commit ourselves to democratic social life, Addams insists, we must begin at the beginning—namely, at home.

"The Destruction of Either Would Bring Ruin"

In order to understand the struggle and the claims of necessity involved in family life on the one hand, and the potent claims of freedom implicated in social life on the other, one must first understand the nature of the family claim and the social claim. One never jettisons a legitimate claim: one works to refract and reshape it to the needs and exigencies of one's time. To repudiate either the family claim or the social claim invites tragedy that goes far beyond the routine sadness that often accompanies the "world of things as they are."

Jane Addams had learned this lesson at a tender age, having been compelled to negotiate the changing exigencies of a home in which her mother had died and a new mother had taken up residence a few years later; and from which a beloved father, the epicenter of the family claim, had been taken away by sudden illness and death, leaving his youngest daughter reeling and feeling like a spoke in a wheel that has lost its hub. Death marked the Addams family claim as it did many families of that era. Four of the initial brood of nine died as infants. Of the five who survived—Mary, Martha, Weber, Alice, and the baby Laura Jane (Jennie)—a number seemed star-crossed. Mary, at age seventeen, had assumed much of the care of the younger children (Martha was thirteen; Weber, ten; Alice, nine; and Jennie, only two) when Sarah Addams died. Martha died suddenly of typhoid fever at the age of sixteen; and Mary herself, the mother of the family in many ways, also died young, in 1894.[21] The wife of a Presbyterian minister, Mary had named her sister Jane as the guardian of her youngest child, a boy— James Weber Linn—who "practically grew up at Hull-House."[22] Another nephew of Jane's, Stanley, and a niece, Marcet, the daughter of her sister, Alice, also paid visits. Jane Addams was thirty-four years old at the time of Mary's death.[23]

Addams chose an unusual context in which to describe the circumstances of her beloved Mary's death—a chapter on "Labor Legislation in Illinois"—and she does this without once mentioning Mary's name. The story of Mary's death illustrates how familial lives and claims can become ensnared in large and sometimes dreadful events. Chicago was in the throes of the Pullman Strike in May of 1894.[24] The strike had brought rail travel to a virtual standstill, and this fact in and of itself had spurred the "growth of class bitterness."[25] Hull-House, true to form under Addams's firm tutelage, had kept open "avenues of intercourse with both sides," in the hope of providing arbitration—thereby displeasing both sides, because each believed in the absolute rightness of its cause and sought support undiluted by any consideration of compromise, without any awareness that there may be some truth to the matter on both sides. Jane Addams "had known Mr. Pullman and had seen his genuine pride and pleasure in the modern town he had built with so much care"—what we today would call a company town. The strike had embittered Pullman. Negotiations were stalled, and no compromise seemed possible. Addams was appointed to a Citizens' Arbitration Committee, but still matters dragged on. In the midst of this civic upheaval, something terrible happened, yielding the Story of a Death Free from Bitterness.[26] Addams recalls that a

> very intimate and personal experience revealed, at least to myself, my constant dread of the spreading ill will. At the height of the sympathetic strike [others going out on strike in sympathy with the Pullman strikers] my oldest sister who was convalescing from a long illness in a hospital near Chicago, became suddenly very much worse. While I was able to reach her at once, every possible obstacle of a delayed and blocked transportation system interrupted the journey of her husband and children who were hurrying to her bedside from a distant state. As the end drew nearer and I was obliged to reply to my sister's constant inquiries that her family had not yet come, I was filled with a profound apprehension lest her last hours should be touched with resentment towards those responsible for the delay; lest her unutterable longing should at the very end be tinged with bitterness. She must have divined what was in my mind, for at last she said each time after the repetition of my sad news; "I don't blame any one, I am not judging them." My

heart was comforted and heavy at the same time; but how many more such moments of sorrow and death were made difficult and lonely through out the land, and how much would these experiences add to the lasting bitterness, that touch of self-righteousness which makes the spirit of forgiveness well nigh impossible.

By drawing together family tragedy and social upheaval, Addams reveals (one of her favorite terms) the often hidden dimensions of visible events, and does so without pushing a strained analogy. Here a family claim of the most dire sort—the wish of a beloved mother and sister to say good-bye to her family before she dies—is denied as a result of the legitimate, not illegitimate, grievances of labor. Addams thereby shows how equally valid claims may conflict.

Jane Addams surely found death a too-frequent family visitor. Death was also accompanied by madness, as it was then called. When Anna Haldeman became John Huy Addams's second wife and Jane Addams's stepmother, she brought into the family two sons: Harry Haldeman, who later married his stepsister Alice and became a physician (it was he who operated on Jane Addams's back and in whose home she spent her pain- and bedridden convalescence). Harry died of acute alcoholism in 1905, at the age of fifty-seven.[27] The story of Anna's other son, George Haldeman, Jane Addams's boon companion in childhood, turns sad. Anna was eager for a marriage between Jane and her son. He too was keen; Jane was not. This further soured Jane's already tense relations with her stepmother, and it seems to have played a part in plunging George into a deep melancholia, from which he never rebounded.[28] He had been shy and withdrawn as a child. As an adult, he became ever more remote and reclusive and would spend days at a time holed up at the Addams's homestead, seeing no one. Photographs from this period show him with a long, unkempt beard. Apparently disoriented, he once disappeared for three weeks. He wandered off and walked all the way to Iowa, more than a hundred miles from Cedarville, stopping only to work on a farm for a week. He apparently had no change of clothing and no visible means of support. A local newspaper clipping reports that the Freeport sheriff and Harry Haldeman "finally found him near Waterloo, shuffling along the road looking 'ragged and dirty and . . . out at the head and feet.'"[29] George died when he was forty-eight years old.

Given to foreboding reflection on life and death as a child, Addams was surrounded by reminders of life's fragility and of her entanglement with that fragility. Because human beings need reminders of mortality and fragility lest they grow arrogant and overbearing, Addams had little use for those who abandoned the family claim. Addams's admiration for George Eliot's protagonist Romola surely derives from the fact that Romola refuses to acquiesce to a situation in which she must either break the marriage tie or abandon a solemn vow to her father. No decent person throws "aside all obligation for the sake of her own selfish and individual development. The man, for instance, who deserts his family that he may cultivate an artistic temperament, or acquire what he considers more fulness of life for himself, must always arouse our contempt."[30] Of course, one must take account of human weakness. All human beings violate legitimate claims at one time or another. But this is different from renouncing a claim and doing so in a way that assails its general legitimacy.

The Tragedy of Goosie, with Small Feathers in His Hair

If families are working well, they free human beings for a wider world and avoid too narrow a definition of the family claim. At the same time, the social claim—the claim asserted by the public world of responsible human action—must respect and respond to the family claim: the realm of eating, sleeping, finding shelter, being born, dying, and rearing children. One cannot resolve tension and conflict between the two through abstract logic. Instead, the relationship must be worked out in practice. If the social claim ignores or tramples on the family claim, the outcome can be tragic. Addams illustrates this point with a heart-tugging drama about what happened to one family when a harsh and unforgiving social claim—in this case, the demands of poorly paid work for long hours, necessary to put bread on the table—cruelly trumped the family claim. This and many other tragedies involving children of her immigrant neighbors were directly traceable to the fact that women were forced to leave their children untended and to work for long hours at low pay.

Goosie's sad tale is told in large part through the voice of his grieving mother.[31] *Goosie* was the nickname given by Hull-House residents to a little boy who was "brought to the nursery wrapped up in his mother's shawl," which had collected a number of "small feathers from the feather brush factory where she worked" and transferred them to the little boy's hair. Having set the stage, Addams continues:

> One March morning, Goosie's mother was hanging out the washing on a shed roof at six o'clock, doing it thus early before she left for the factory. Five-year-old Goosie was trotting at her heels handing her clothespins, when he was suddenly blown off the roof by the high wind into the alley below. His neck was broken by the fall and as he lay piteous and limp on a pile of frozen refuse, his mother cheerily called him to "climb up again," so confident do overworked mothers become that their children cannot get hurt. After the funeral, as the poor mother sat in the nursery postponing the moment when she must go back to her empty rooms, I asked her, in a futile effort to be of comfort, if there was anything more we could do for her. The overworked, sorrow-stricken woman looked up and replied, "If you could give me my wages for to-morrow, I would not go to work in the factory at all. I would like to stay at home all day and hold the baby. Goosie was always asking me to take him and I never had any time." This statement revealed the condition of many nursery mothers who are obliged to forego the joys and solaces which belong to even the most poverty-stricken. The long hours of factory labor necessary for earning the support of a child leave no time for the tender care and caressing which may enrich the life of the most piteous baby.

Addams is incensed by Goosie's fate. It is stupid, she insists, to compel mothers of preschool children to stand on their feet all day long in brush factories or to labor all night, leaving their children alone, in order to creep home, bedraggled and exhausted, as dawn breaks and their children begin to stir. It is inconsistent to force mothers into such situations, for "this generation has placed upon the mother and upon the prolongation of infancy" a great emphasis. Widely read in theories of child development, Addams is struck by the simultaneous existence of scientific evidence concerning the importance of early child nurture and the role of the mother and the denial to hundreds of thousands of such mothers the possibility that they might spend time with their children.

Addams reinforces this point with a second tale, told in a tone of palpable indignation—the Story of Breast Milk Mingled with Dirty Scrub Water.[32] What makes this story so powerful is that Addams taps into the unconscious cultural symbolism that touches on primordial notions of taboo—here, the mingling of elements that should be kept separate (breast milk, scrub water) in order to avoid contamination that may presage doom for a person or a group.

> I cannot recall without indignation a recent experience. I was detained late one evening in an office building by a prolonged committee meeting of the Board of Education. As I came out at eleven o'clock, I met in the corridor of the fourteenth floor a woman whom I knew, on her knees scrubbing the marble tiling. As she straightened up to greet me, she seemed so wet from her feet up to her chin, that I hastily inquired the cause. Her reply was that she left home at five o'clock every night and had no opportunity for six hours to nurse her baby. Her mother's milk mingled with the very water with which she scrubbed the floors until she should return at midnight, heated and exhausted, to feed her screaming child with what remained within her breasts.

This child was probably left unattended throughout the night, or placed in the care of older siblings who were just children themselves, or entrusted to the haphazard attention of a neighbor asked to listen for the baby's cries. How can society demand that this mother tend to her maternal responsibilities even as economic need drives her to work at any job and under any conditions?

Once again, Addams illustrates general socioeconomic themes through a powerful vignette. And there were so many desperate stories from which to choose: of children sent outside to play in the streets all day, whatever the weather, when their mothers left for work; of children locked in their rooms for twelve hours or more at a time. There is the terrible fact that the first three crippled children whom Addams and Starr encountered in the neighborhood had incurred their injuries while their mothers were at work: "One had fallen out of a third-story window, another had been burned, and the third had a curved spine due to the fact that for three years he had been tied all day long to the leg of the kitchen table, only released at noon by his older brother who hastily ran in from a neighboring factory to share his lunch with him."[33] The same harsh economic necessity lay behind all of these awful stories. The "poor little mites" paid the price directly, but the degradation of the family claim radiated outward like a slowly spreading fungus to coarsen all human social relations. Those who lived comfortably and at a great distance from such distress were, in an intangible but very real way, corrupted by the presence in their midst of unnecessary human misery of a sort that was *not* traceable to the losses and distresses that are the general human lot. It is not built into the order of things that mothers must be taken away from their children both day and night, without provision being made for the care of those children.

Even as some mothers are gone much of the time, others are trapped all day *with* their children, being ensnared in the web of the system of sweated labor, forced to work up to eighteen hours a day either in a sweatshop or in their own poorly ventilated and dimly lit rooms. These women compelled even their "incredibly small" children to work all day and often well into the night in order to scrape by. Addams offers details: "I remember a little girl of four who pulled out basting threads hour after hour, sitting on a stool at the feet of her Bohemian mother, a little bunch of human misery." No child should wind up a "little bunch of human misery." If society is to tend to the requirements of the family claim, Addams asserts, it must structure the social claim in such a way that no child must endure such misery.

The mothers in Addams's stories are neglectful but are not guilty of neglect. The world has closed in on them. In order to put food on the table, they must give succor short shrift. But there are other stories, too, of parents—often fathers (Addams's capacity for sympathetic understanding here is stretched to the limit)—who torment their children by demanding that they do the adult job of supporting their family. Addams tells of immigrant parents who found it only too easy to live on the earnings of their children. Perhaps these parents initially sent their children out to work due to their own bewilderment and inability to use English. Over time, what started out as a necessity turns into an expectation.

Addams muses that the South Italian peasant who finds himself in Chicago's 19th ward "cannot see at once the difference between the outdoor healthy work which he has performed in varying seasons"—

with his children toddling along after—and the very different "factory work which his child encounters when he goes to work in Chicago." She continues: "An Italian father came to us in great grief over the death of his eldest child, a little girl of twelve, who had brought the largest wages into the family fund. In the midst of his genuine sorrow he said: 'She was the oldest kid I had. Now I shall have to go back to work again until the next one is able to take care of me.' The man was only thirty-three and had hoped to retire from work at least during the winters." Or consider the tragedy of the "girl of thirteen, a Russian-Jewish child, employed in a laundry at a heavy task beyond her strength" who "committed suicide, because she had borrowed three dollars from a companion which she could not repay unless she confided the story to her parents and gave up an entire week's wages. . . . Her child mind, of course, had no sense of proportion, and carbolic acid appeared inevitable."[34] Addams makes it clear that there are cases where the failure of parental responsibility is the source of the trouble. She distinguishes such instances from those attendant upon harsh economic realities.

Pale, listless children, emerging from factories as if from tombs: these are the indelible images Addams makes visible to her readers. She reveals the world of the immigrant, working poor in the broken neck of Goosie and in the "little bundle of human misery" in the corner. What saves these stories from descending into bathos is the hard-headed analysis that frames them. This analysis is captured most famously in another of her Addams's early essays, "Filial Relations," chapter III in her *Democracy and Social Ethics*, published in 1902. Already well-known as the young founder of Hull-House, Addams became famous as a result of the enthusiastic praise garnered by this book. This essay is founded on her assumption, then widely shared, that the human race is moving toward a "higher social morality." This quest is marked by conserving what is worthy, including legitimate claims, but adapting them to new circumstances. Sometimes this means broadening and extending those claims in the service of a distinctive social morality.[35]

With a democratic faith nurtured in the bosom of the Social Gospel, Addams sees in this practice of higher virtue the direct application of Christianity. One must ease some of the demands of "the current standard of individual and family righteousness" in the interest of meeting other demands. This does not entail the abandonment of ethical standards, ethics being "but another word for 'righteousness,' that for which many men and women of every generation have hungered and thirsted, and without which life becomes meaningless."[36] Problems arise if the "instinct to conserve" is "combined with a distrust of the new standard" (a reference to the social claim), leading to a "constant difficulty in the way of those experiments and advances depending upon the initiative of women, both because women are the more sensitive to the individual and family claims, and because their training has tended to make them content with the response to these claims alone." Once a woman attempts to respond to a wider social claim, she may be pitched into moral conflict that depletes her energy. It is likely that her perplexed parents will see her determination to "undertake work lying quite outside of traditional and family interests" as a "foolish enthusiasm." In a sense, Addams puts a query to her society: Why press forward with higher education for women, if the social avenues through which that education might be used are blocked?

The social claim, like the family claim, is a dignified one. But in seeking to meet its challenge head-on, the woman is often seen as "setting up her own will against that of her family's for selfish ends." She is regarded as "wilful and self-indulgent." The family is prepared to relinquish a daughter to marriage, when her purpose is to found another family. But suppose that she seeks to go beyond this elemental and vital claim in order to fulfill the other imperatives she has absorbed as an educated American woman? Suppose that she wants to play a direct role in the American democratic experiment?

Addams seeks the adjustment of the familial and the social in such a way that no legitimate claim is abandoned. There is a difference between the temporary violation of a legitimate claim in the service of some other vital claim and its repudiation altogether; the latter is destructive. What do you do when there is a "collision of interests, each of which has a real moral basis and a right to its own place"? What do you do with "the struggle between two claims, the destruction of either of which would bring ruin to the ethical life"?

Society has at least begun to recognize the possibility of tragic conflict, but it seems not to have found a way to place these claims together and to give each its due. From the beginning of recorded history, the "claim of the state in time of war has long been recognized, so that in its name the family has given up sons and husbands and even the fathers of little children." To a life-risking purpose based on a claim widely regarded as legitimate, society sends some of its children forth to die and, even worse, to kill. Why not send children forth to sustain life? If men can, and have, acted conscientiously in behalf of the social claim, why not women?

Grown-up sons are also citizens: they are familial and civic beings. But what of grown-up daughters? We send a few to college, and then we confine them to a narrowly defined domesticity because the family cannot let them go. The family will permit its daughter a pale aesthetic existence—she may play the piano and serves as hostess—but the family seems incapable of thinking of her in relation to outside duties. Perhaps all of this was workable when girls were not educated. But the genie is out of the bottle: the educated young woman of the nineteenth century would do more than "grace the fireside" in her parents' home until she moves out to take charge of her own hearth. Much of the conflict into which she is pitched is totally unnecessary; indeed, most of it is, Addams assumes confidently.[37]

Perhaps the family claim triumphs because it is concrete and exigently represented and felt. But would the family claim be dissipated if it were extended beyond the domestic hearth? Is the social claim really that abstract? Is it not also a "demand upon the emotions as well as upon the intellect," the suppression of which lowers a young woman's "springs of vitality"? Her "health gives way under this strain"; and what does the physician advise? Rest. But this is not what she needs. "What she needs is simple, health-giving activity, which, involving the use of all her faculties," brings her satisfaction, because she has found a way to think communally rather than just individualistically.

To this end, she must be brought into contact with the harsh realities that are now hidden from her because they are considered too strenuous for woman's delicate constitution. As a result, she does not see "the feebleness of childhood, the pathos of suffering, or the needs of old age." But, like a young man, she dreams of "self-sacrifice, of succor to the helpless and of tenderness to the unfortunate." Why must these dreams be distrusted unless they fall within the well-worn grooves of a traditional family claim? Why not have some confidence that human beings are too closely bound up with one another to rest content for very long with individualistic anthems and purposes?[38]

King Lear of Chicago

Addams concludes her essay "Filial Relations" with a reprise of the conflict between familial and social claims, viewed through the lens of the tragedy of King Lear. She draws directly on her observations of the Pullman Strike of 1894.[39] Lear's tragedy derives from his absorption in "his own indignation" and his subsequent failure to "apprehend his child's thought." In his anger, he loses his affection; indeed, "he had lost the faculty by which he might perceive himself in the wrong." So it was with the famous Mr. Pullman, for whom "domination and indulgence" went together, as they did for poor King Lear.

The Pullman Strike, as I noted above in connection with Addams's account of her sister's death, roiled Chicago during summer 1894. Chicagoans were "confronted by a drama which epitomized and, at the same time, challenged the code of social ethics under which we live. . . . It sometimes seems as if the barbaric instinct to kill, roused on both sides, the sharp division into class lines, with the resultant distrust and bitterness, can only be endured if we learn from it all a great ethical lesson."[40] Addams assumes Mr. Pullman's philanthropic intent as one motive—certainly not the only one—in creating a town within which his workers and their families could live, shop, go to church, and educate their children. But George Pullman also exercised direct, near absolute control over his village. Everything in the town was "responsible to the Pullman corporation." According to one historian, Pullman "refused to brook any sort of political opposition" in his town. Labor organizers and those considered too radical were "barred from the town by the simple expedient of denying them the right to rent or use public halls."[41] To understand Pullman, Addams resorts, as she frequently has before, to literature. Shakespeare's great drama brings her closer to a sympathetic understand of Pullman and of his striking workers.

The events surrounding and flowing from the strike remind us that the social claim and its modes of expression are as unsettled as the family claim appears settled. But this family claim has changed, demonstrating that societies can adjust to new exigencies. When we reflect on Lear, we find his relations to his children archaic, Addams claims. We know that our morality around family ties has moved beyond parental domination based on a dreadful power to give and to take away the means of livelihood. In Lear's case, as he is a king, this power extends to bestowing land or sending a child into exile. Lear illustrates the playing-out of "mal-adjustment between individuals" in a "personal and passionate" way. The modern tragedy is more complex, for it involves "two large bodies of men, an employing company and a mass of employes." But there are significant parallels.

Lear and Pullman both feel the sting of what they interpret as ingratitude. Lear is cut to the quick by his favorite daughter Cordelia's inarticulateness and lack of effusiveness in stating, when Lear demands it, her affection for him. Addams faults Cordelia's "lack of tenderness" and the cold way she ignores her old father's plea for indulgence. But he is the one who brings the tragedy on. He goes overboard in his anger and sinks into a pit of self-pity and recrimination that leads to madness. Eventually he does come to his senses; but by then it is too late. Pullman, a man "dined and feted throughout Europe as the creator of a model town, as the friend and benefactor of workingmen," finds himself inexplicably "execrated by workingmen throughout the country." His refusal to give the representatives of his workers even ten minutes of his time testifies to the selfish motives hidden beneath his brand of industrial relations. The latent dictatorial possibilities in Pullman's position rise to the surface, just as they did with Lear, and everything falls apart. Pullman speaks the language of an individualist ethic. The workers had learned that "the injury of one is the concern of all," and "brotherhood, sacrifice, the subordination of individual and trade interests to the good of the working class" had become their bywords. (Addams no doubt downplays the fierce rhetoric of insult and injury that was part and parcel of the workers' arsenal as well.)

There is little doubt which side Addams is on, but she takes that side with a heavy heart, because the individual virtues that enabled Pullman to rise in life—especially, hard work—are real virtues, but they are also insufficient to this new day. Being good to people in a paternalistic way is not the same as trying to understand them. To be sure, the interests of labor and capital are not identical; but must they be openly hostile, the political equivalent of war, with the unconditional surrender of one side the only alternative? Here, as elsewhere, Addams warns against class hatred and the rhetoric of war and martial fervor as catalysts of social change.

A narrow definition of emancipation plagues the workingman, too, especially if what he seeks is what the employer has. In this case, the upshot of a successful social conflict would be a new boss just like the old one. An astute moral psychologist, Addams is attuned to the fact that resentment is a degraded motive for social change, for it leads to a mere turning of the tables rather than to a transformation of the situation in such a way that no one has authoritarian power over the lives of others. Many workers are captured by a false doctrine of emancipation. Nonetheless, on the question of Pullman's despotic control over his town, it is the workers who are right. Over the long run, however, the claims made by, and in behalf of, workers and all who toil must be governed by the democratic ideals of consent and dedicated to "slow but sane and strenuous progress." Otherwise, failure is certain.

Addams concludes "Filial Relations" by associating her views with those of Mazzini and Lincoln, her reliable, revered heroes. She draws heavily upon Mazzini's best-known text, *The Duties of Man*.[42] Mazzini placed duty before rights. Rights, he argues, "cannot exist except as a consequence of duties fulfilled, and . . . one must begin with the latter in order to arrive at the former."[43] In her essay, Addams defines "duties to humanity," vague though the phrase may be, as a primary duty. One rises to this duty on the back of other duties, including those of son, husband, and father—Mazzini's examples, to which Addams would add daughter, wife, and mother. Being a citizen of one's own country also helps one to aspire to an even wider citizenship. The issues posed by the Pullman Strike pit a narrow understanding of a paternalistic familial ethic (for Pullman thought of himself as a benevolent if controlling father) against a wider understanding of the nascent social morality embedded within the new industrial relations. This new ethic will take years to crystallize. Hull-House is one vital embodiment of the new claim—a creative, nondestructive way to mediate the legitimate claims that tug on us and either pull us apart or help us achieve a wider, more balanced, more capacious life. Later in life, however, Addams came to recognize that not all cultural transformations of subjective necessities are for the better.

Against the "Imperious Claims of Sex"

Confident as Addams was of slow but certain moral evolution in the direction of a more social ethic, it was also clear to her that cultures, like individuals, could backslide. Perhaps for this reason Addams does not call our attention to the challenge posed to her theory of moral evolution by the flapper generation, although she was greatly vexed by that generation's misdirected ethos of personal freedom, which she interpreted in *The Second Twenty Years at Hull-House* as enacting the urgency of the claims of desire over and above any notion of civic responsibility. First published in 1930, this follow-up volume to *Twenty Years at Hull-House* shows Addams deeply troubled that so many women of the younger generation had succumbed to a strange post-Freudianism that invited an "astounding emphasis upon sex."[44]

This was the more incomprehensible to her in view of the roles that educated, unmarried woman of her generation had played just a few decades earlier, in the latter half of the nineteenth century. Addams describes the choice faced by a young woman of her generation as either marriage or career:[45]

> She could not have both apparently for two reasons. Men did not at first want to marry women of the new type, and women could not fulfill the two functions of profession and home-making until modern inventions had made a new type of housekeeping practicable, and perhaps one should add, until public opinion tolerated the double role. Little had been offered to the unmarried women of the earlier generations but a dependence upon relatives which was either grudged or exploited, with the result that the old maid herself was generally regarded as narrow and unhappy and, above all, hopelessly embittered.

This situation had changed for the better. Women with "pioneer qualities," driven by "the divine urge of intellectual hunger" and "devoted to their fields of activity," moved into the wider social world—met the social claim—with forthrightness and verve. They did this without abandoning the family claim, instead reforming and extending it. Jane Addams never regarded the family claim as "dreaded," as one recent author claims.[46] Rather, she searched for creative ways to meet that claim, knowing that once a culture begins to educate women fully and well, those women are going to want to use their newfound powers to their fullest capacity.

So it is unsurprising that Addams is worried, as the 1920s end, by the cultural displacement of both the family claim and the social claim among a gaggle of "half-baked" pseudo-Freudian lecturers who are running all over the country preaching the gospel of the repressive evils of self-control.[47] "Reckless youth" took this message to heart, and the irresponsible advocacy did much damage. A gospel of frankness triumphed, holding that natural impulses should be expressed without inhibition. It was not the "revolt against Victorian prudery" that Addams found most troubling but the new "cult of frankness," in which duty was derided and replaced by a will to power. In practice, this did not lead to a new and better self but to a more conformist self that lacked the capacity for self-discipline and self-criticism. Too often, those who took the new gospel to heart paradoxically became less free, insofar as they saw themselves as the playthings of "blind forces beyond their control." Not the devil but the libido made one do it. "The fear of missing some emotional stimulus may well become a tyranny worse than the austere guidance of reason," she warns.[48] Perhaps, she muses, the pendulum must swing back and forth: one can get too dogged about duty, too enchained to service. The liberty of the self seems to offer a corrective. Advocates of "unlimited opportunities for self-development" promote a distorted view of freedom, however. This freedom of uninhibited individualism generates its own conformities and restrictions. But publicists of the "cult of frankness" are not driven, as Addams and her generation were, to interpret critically the dominant themes and demands of their culture, because these come wrapped in the gaily decorated package of freedom. Such freedom leads to an obsession with sex and distorts human life by exalting that dimension of experience above all else. Moreover, the overemphasis on frankness, exposure, and acting-out sexually ensures that everything else in human life will be explained in light of that one dimension.

Addams writes to one of her accomplished friends, Emily Greene Balch ("who for twenty years had been head of the Department of Economics in Wellesley College, and who through years of study in Europe and as the first secretary of the Women's International League knew the women in many countries"), and asks her help in explaining what is going on. Balch's response[49] is intriguing and uncannily apropos to our own moment:

> Men had normally given hostages to fortune in the shape of families. Professional women were far freer in general to risk their jobs for the sake of unpopular principles and tabooed forms of activity.

They had, too, a quite special spur in the desire to prove incorrect the general belief that they were congenitally incapable. They found a tingling zest in discovering that it is not true, as woman had been brought up to believe, that she was necessarily weaker and more cowardly, incapable of disinterested curiosity, unable to meet life on her own merits. Much good feminine energy went astray in proving that women could do this and that which had been marked taboo, when perhaps this or that was not the most desirable thing to do. There was also another incentive in the sense of opening the way to others and the sharing of an interesting experiment. Is it compatible with modern theories about sex that two generations of professionally trained women lived, without vows or outward safeguards, completely celibate lives with no sense of its being difficult or being misunderstood? Some of them later married; most of them did not. Now they are old or oldish women, how do they feel about it? They are a rather reserved lot, but quite willing to admit that it has been a serious loss, certainly, to have missed what is universally regarded as the highest forms of woman's experience but there is no evidence that they themselves or those who know them best find in them the abnormality that the Freudian psychoanalysts of life would have one look for. They are strong, resistant and active, they grow old in kind and mellow fashion; their attitude to life is based upon active interests; they are neither excessively repelled nor excessively attracted to that second-hand intimacy with sexuality which modern science and modern literature so abundantly display. It is, however, strange to them to read interpretations of life, in novels, plays, and psychological treatises that represent sex as practically the whole content of life; family feeling, religion and art, as mere camouflaged libido, and everything that is not concerned with the play of desire between men and women as without adventure, almost without interest. If the educated unmarried women of the period between the Civil War and the World War represent an unique phase, it is one that has important implications which have not yet been adequately recognized by those who insist upon the imperious claims of sex.

The "imperious claims of sex" hold us yet in thrall. What is peculiar about the present cultural moment is the insistence that sexual activity makes us happy and therefore sex must have its way with us—although nowadays this sexual activity can be disconnected altogether from love, devotion, and affection. Without sex, even if it is self-sex (and the glories of masturbation, especially for women, have been extolled over and over), you are bound to be a shriven sort of creature, thinking lurid thoughts and tempted by puritanical crusades because you are sex-obsessed but are "in denial" about this obsession. Sex is natural, and whatever is natural should or will have its way, we hear preached daily. But Jane Addams, and the many with whom she shared cherished friendships and collegialities, believed that natural impulses were to be shaped, made beautiful, and interpreted: this was the work of culture. The unthinking, formless discharge of an impulse was destructive. If one is "on the job" sexually at every moment, one's interest in the world beyond the realm of libidinal claims is greatly diminished.

Addams and Balch and the other college-educated women of their generation struggled with the claims made upon them by families and the wider social world, recognizing legitimacy in each of these claims and knowing that their working-out was bound to be difficult, often "more or less tragic," as Addams put it. That could not be helped—not in a world that marks you with its "slow stain." But the saving grace was fellowship: finding a place you could call home that also gave you a site from which to speak and to act. One doesn't permit impulses to take over; rather, one uses impulses as a sculptor uses a block of stone or wood—first, identifying the immanent possibilities within that object, and then hammering and scraping and pounding and chipping away at it until a recognizable figure emerges. Celibate lives need not be lonely lives or distorted lives but could be full of love, friendship, and joy—and so they were, for Jane Addams, for Emily Balch, for Ellen Gates Starr, for Addams's companion, Mary Rozet Smith, and for many other college-educated women of their day.

The winding road down which Jane Addams had traveled from little Cedarville kept bringing her back home again—back to a very different sort of home, but a home nonetheless. Home was a place where the needs of children were tended to, where children were free to satisfy their "insatiable desire for play."[50] But what if their playground was the city street? This was a challenge to which Addams, as a woman and a form-giver, felt called to respond.

5

COMPASSION WITHOUT CONDESCENSION

The Child and the City

In Egypt, in late winter of 1912 to the early spring of 1913, Jane Addams found herself thinking about death. As she reflected, she sensed a tensile strand of memory and experience stretching across a vast distance—from the pyramids of Giza to the village cemetery in Cedarville, Illinois—and threading together past and present time. Something odd was happening, something that she "was totally unprepared to encounter." She observed that she was accompanied "by a small person with whom I was no longer intimate, and who was certainly not in the least responsible for my present convictions and reflections."[1]

Rather than shooing the small person (the child-self standing alongside her adult-self) away, she opened herself to experience anew a part of her life that had long lain dormant. Can like moods link generations and connect diverse cultures? Her answer is Yes; but a precondition for this possibility is the patience to pay close attention to sensory experience, remaining in a receptive mode. Her encounter with the ancient tombs and her musings on the Theban hills revealed to her that some how she—and indeed all mortals—had been where the Egyptians had been, preoccupied as they were with the "presence of death."[2] It occurred to her then that a "sincere portrayal of a widespread and basic emotional experience, however remote in point of time it may be, has the power overwhelmingly to evoke memories of like moods in the individual." The vivid and unsettling images and emotions aroused in Addams by the sights and sounds of this place convinced her that emotional messages can transcend the barriers of time and space—can connect an Egyptian nobleman preparing for his own entombment in the time of the pyramids with a frightened small person in Cedarville, Illinois, ca. 1865. Each is preoccupied with death. What happens to the body? Where does the spirit go?

Addams writes of her earliest memories of death in what I call the Story of Death's ABC's.[3]

> I was a tiny child making pothooks in the village school, when one day—it must have been the first flush of Spring, for I remember the crab-apple blossoms—during the afternoon session, the A B C class was told that its members would march all together to the burial of the mother of one of the littlest girls. . . . The cemetery was hard by the schoolhouse, placed there, it had always been whispered among us, to make the bad boys afraid. Thither the A B C class, in awestruck procession, each child carefully holding the hand of another, was led by the teacher to the edge of the open grave and bidden to look on the still face of the little girl's mother.
>
> Our poor knees quaked and quavered as we stood shelterless and unattended by family protection or even by friendly grown-ups . . . we kept an uncertain footing on the freshly spaded earth, hearing the preacher's voice, the sobs of the motherless children, and, crowning horror of all, the hollow sound of three clods of earth dropped impressively upon the coffin lid.
>
> After endless ages, the service was over. . . . But a new terror awaited me even there, for our house stood at the extreme end of the street and the last of the way home was therefore solitary. I remember a breathless run. . . . I took a circuitous route to the house that I might secure as much companionship as possible on the way. I stopped at the stable to pat an old horse . . . , and again to throw a handful of corn into the poultry yard. The big turkey gobbler who came greedily forward gave me great comfort because he was so absurd and awkward that no one could possibly associate him with anything so solemn as death. I went into the kitchen where the presiding genius allowed me to come without protest although the family dog was at my heels. I felt constrained to keep my arms

about his shaggy neck while trying to talk of familiar things. . . . I
wanted to cry out, "Their mother is dead; whatever, whatever will
the children do?"

Surely the children must fight the "horrible thing which had befallen
their mother," but what can defenseless children do? Addams found no
solace in the hope of a reunion in eternity, whether as a child or an
adult. As a child, she had spurned the view that the unchurched, no
matter how good they were, could not share in eternal life. Her attitude
on this matter approached truculence. God's grace played no role in her
thinking; it was the call to stewardship that counted. Addams was preoccupied with the fears and hopes of children; their nighttime terrors
and daydreams; their escapades that may turn deadly; the arduous labor they are forced into that might kill their spirits, in contrast to forms
of play and work that would unlock their longing for what is good and
beautiful and true and steer them away from the tawdry, salacious, and
morally lax. These are some of the themes that reverberate in the sustained thoughts of Jane Addams on what she called the spirit of youth.
Her own childhood provided the template on which she strove to understand sympathetically the very different childhoods of the teeming
throng of young people in the 19th ward of Chicago, and by extension,
the entire city and the world beyond.

Addams begins, as always, with concrete experiences. Along the way,
she discovers that there are experiences that belong to others but that
she can take in as her own. So it was with the tombs and the strange
style of drawing that is "naturally employed by a child"—stick figures—but the Egyptians had "deliberately stiffened it [this style] into an
unchanging convention." The earliest tombs resemble a child's efforts
to place stones one on top of the other, and the vastness of the pyramids taps the child's attempts to defeat death by finding a safe haven.
Perhaps one can keep death at bay through creating massive defenses:
the pyramids of Giza are for her a case in point. Perhaps death can be
outwitted by the bewildering labyrinths, as she calls them. But deep
down we know that we, too, must go through the devastating experience. All the more important, therefore, that we cherish as a "precious
possession . . . the belief that no altar at which living men have once devoutly worshipped, no oracle to whom a nation long ago appealed in
its moments of dire confusion, no gentle myth in which former genera-

tions have found solace, can lose all significance for us, the survivors," if we are but open to "an almost mystical sense of life common to all the centuries, and of unceasing human endeavor to penetrate into the unseen world." She continues, "These records afford glimpses into a past so vast that the present generation seems to float upon its surface as thin as a sheet of light which momentarily covers the ocean and moves in response to the black waters beneath it." St. Bernard of Clairvaux insisted that we all stand on the shoulders of giants. Our indebtedness to those who have gone before—and this alone—gives us a vantage point from which we can see more and farther than if each of us stood alone, peering into the historic haze.

Through a method of interpretation involving reminiscence, Jane Addams illustrates a fundamental human solidarity. She was insistent that certain experiences are shared on a deep level by all human beings. If we open ourselves to understanding, then we who are separated by vastly different sorts of childhoods, political systems, and even historical eras can find common ground. The quest for understanding is never for naught; one doesn't cast one's net into the waters and come up empty.

The task of understanding was no ancillary activity for Addams, nor was it peripheral to the work of Hull-House. Nearly every major piece of social legislation or civic initiative having to do with the well-being of children from 1890 until the New Deal bears the Hull-House stamp in one way or another; and this legislation, at its best, began life as sympathetic understanding, a determination to enter into lives that were not one's own, without falling into the arrogant pretense that one understood the lives of others better than they did.

"The Girl Announces to the World That She Is Here"

Her 1913 experience in Egypt reinforced Jane Addams's conviction that it was possible to penetrate to the truth of things, whether on the Theban hills or in the congested quarters of the 19th ward. Her entry points were primarily the experiences of women and children.[4] She was especially confident that she knew what was going on with children, and that her growing-up years in a small town had afforded her a perch from which she could understand the experiences of immigrant children in the city.

From her deft pen flow tales that bear in their wake an embedded theory of moral development. That theory holds that we are all creatures born with blind, unformed appetites. These appetites yield to moral motives slowly, through a process of education that touches the heart. The heart is touched through the senses at first; but gradually, appetites yield to psychic impulsions. These impulsions, in turn, are mingled with reason as the child grows up and are transformed into moral motives. If children suffer from violence and neglect, if their spirits are crushed and their inventiveness is stymied, they might well be doomed to a shriven existence, even if they have no external, visible impediments.

Such a child may well be impervious to what Jane Addams called the "gentler aspects" of life. To the extent possible, parents, teachers, and the entire society should avoid magnifying and deepening, through neglect, abuse, and unreasonable expectation, the fears of childhood. For it was the particular yet prototypical fears of childhood that were triggered in Egypt. If adults could but remember the terrifying fears of each and every child—of abandonment, of death, of being lost—and if cultures could find ways to allay the sadnesses and tragedies over which human beings do have a measure of control, then we should have made gentler the aspects of our shared world and have blighted fewer vulnerable, growing minds and bodies.

Toward this end Addams asks: What *is* the concrete situation? Addams and her Hull-House associates always assessed the empirical reality in which parents and children found themselves. They saw that parents under terrible economic and cultural stress often compelled their children to labor at horrible tasks under unhealthy and even dangerous conditions without surcease. Children were pressed to the breaking point; and if the pressure persisted, they might well grow into resentful adult victims of the habit of resentful obedience. There is such a thing as normal growth for a child. For an adult to compel an immature child to take on tasks beyond that child's strength is disastrous. Addams describes such situations in dire and dismal terms. In contrast, appeals to the child's senses, particularly the sense of adventure and the longing for beauty that all children share, help mold the moral motives that enable the child, as an adult, to live out such motives, now cast as solid habits in his or her own raising of children, in participating in democratic citizenship, in determined labor and work, and in service to a church or a community. We can be saved for fellowship, but we are also saved *through* fellowship, from birth to death.

That Addams drew general significance from Cedarville norms—norms that she insisted were not particular to Cedarville—put her on a collision course with many nineteenth-century giants of political and social theory. For example, one of her contemporaries, Karl Marx, asserted in his polemics that rural life was idiocy. Marx probably had in mind the ancient Greek view of the noncitizen as one who lived only for himself, as an *idiot,* trapped in his own life or *idion.*[5] Marx was also convinced that rural life, or small-town life, could not serve as the staging ground for the full socialization of life through labor, which would eventually bring about the ultimate revolution and inaugurate all the glories he imputed to classless society. In this process, all useless persons, societies, and cultures (as Marx defined them) would be swept away into the dustbin of history. Addams was never much interested in grand, apocalyptic theories that did violence to lived life, belying the concreteness of particular places and ways of being. Grand theories wiped out stories and reduced human beings to faceless anonymity. Addams never trafficked in such categories as "proletariat" and "bourgeois." She never talked about "mass society," being concerned lest the individual become lost in the crowd. She had learned her small-town lessons well.

In an interview published in the *Chicago News* on April 10, 1899, Addams extolled the bicycle as a form of exercise. When asked if this was particularly beneficial to the poorer and middle classes, she said: "There is where I wish to make an exception. I object to that word *class.* It is unAmerican. There are no classes in this country. The people are all Americans with no dividing line drawn. But I think the bicycle is a good thing for the workingman. . . . It gives him recreation and exercise and while riding to and from his work he enjoys the open air." Whatever one thinks of Addams's hope that tired workingmen might find their health improved by bicycling, the most interesting moment is her truculent dismissal of the word *class.* Of course, there were dividing lines in America. It was one thing to acknowledge an empirical reality that separated people; it was another to use a collective category to classify hundreds of thousands of people, and in so doing, to obliterate their distinctiveness. Americans should think of one another as neighbors and fellow citizens who have had vastly different experiences. We are obliged to interpret ourselves one to the other and to do all we can to ease the situation for those who are hard-pressed. Jane Addams practiced what she preached when it came to being attuned to the uniqueness of each and every person, however insignificant he or she might seem.

A letter from Ellen Gates Starr to Jane Addams's stepmother, written during the second of Addams's tours of Europe, shows just how intensely Addams had absorbed the notion of the dignity of each person. This generalized notion derived in large measure from the seepage into the groundwater of the American culture of the basic Christian insistence that we are all precious in God's sight. Ellen Starr writes to Mrs. Addams:[6]

> Jane devoted most of her time at table to an absurd old Missourian who wore a flannel shirt and a paper collar, speared his bread with his fork ... and picked his teeth at table, and whom nobody else near him would take the trouble to talk to. I never admired her more. She talked to this man as she would have done to a man of the world. I don't know what I would not give to have what prompts her and makes it possible for her to act in this way. I suppose what I would not give is the moral effort and self discipline which is required to develop a character like hers. It seems more beautiful to me as I know it better, and would be worth more to me than all Europe if I could become only a little like her.

Jane Addams absorbed lessons in paying attention to the concrete and particular person from growing up in the cauldron of small-town life, where anonymity is not an option, for better or for worse.[7]

Just as Addams's way resisted Marxian grandiosity, so it resisted mid-twentieth-century absurdity. For Jane Addams, human beings were not poised in terrible oppositions to one another; they did not live in that bleak universe limned by twentieth-century existentialists, such as Jean-Paul Sartre, to whom every man is an enemy to every other ("Hell is other people"), in which every moment is a struggle for existence and for appropriation of what is not one's own.[8] The routine and seemingly spontaneous cooperation Addams saw around her while growing up— and later found in the poor who helped one another in their "teeming quarters"—convinced her of that.[9] Her childhood gave her a secure foundation of rough-and-ready social egalitarianism.

The trajectory of Jane Addams's life is described perspicuously in the official history of Stephenson County as "From the Ward to the City and Beyond"; but one might more aptly describe it as "From the Village to the Ward to the City and Beyond," because for Addams there was continuity, not rupture, in the transition from rural village to urban neighborhood. Her journey was made complete with her return to the soil of Cedarville after her death. More important, her experiences, with their sense of life-giving continuity, helped her penetrate the bathos of the ruptured lives of immigrants. Her life was devoted to helping heal those ruptures. This is much of what she meant by a "dedication to social amelioration."

The small town afforded the child an encompassable universe in which she could sort out the complexities of human society; could learn when to yield and when to stand apart, without any resentful, harsh, or violent dismissal of "the other." Who is this "other," after all? No abstract artifact of discourse, but rather, one's neighbor. Likely your mother borrowed a cup of sugar from her yesterday. Possibly your father needs to return to that same neighbor the tool he borrowed last week. You go to school with the neighbor's kids. Do you really want to cause a permanent rupture? Probably not. Her childhood also struck themes of adventure and spiritedness, raised questions of meaning and purpose, and stoked fears. Flannery O'Connor once observed that if you've survived childhood and lived to be fifteen or so, you have enough material to write a lifetime's worth of novels. Most social theorists do not take childhood to heart. Jane Addams did, and that helps account for the richness of her thought.

To Addams, reminiscences were the raw material of both personal and social formation. When one compared reminiscences, one was struck by their irreducible singularity *and* their universal recognizability. This recognition entered into all of her life and work, including what critics found the inexplicable or even lamentable emphasis at Hull-House on art, music, and theater.

New Temptations and Ancient Evils

The reader may recall Jane Addams's emphasis on revelation—not revelation in the theological sense but in what might be called the anthropological sense: the importance of revealing what is human in general, and adding thereby to the storehouse of human knowledge. One of the most severe effects of poverty was the way in which it stymied or hid the unique and irreducible features of a living human being, affording no possibility of their revelation. Given this conviction, it is not surprising that Addams and Starr from the start put so much emphasis on Hull-House as a place of interior beauty and grace, on teaching the arts and giving children the opportunity to participate in a variety of artistic activities. These goals were realized in part by the creation at Hull-House of the Butler Art Gallery and by the extensive instruction provided in theater, dance, orchestral music, folk music, sculpting, painting, pottery, and literature.

Starr is worth more than a passing mention in all of this, as she was a person of artistic temperament. She also agitated for unions and at one point decamped to England to learn classical bookbinding, returning to Hull-House in order to set up a bookbindery—adding yet another enterprise to the dozens of activities already going on.[10] Starr penned a discussion of "Art and Labor" for the book *Hull-House Maps and Papers,* published in 1895. This was the first volume that afforded a sense of Hull-House's complexity as a site for initiating painstaking social science *and* as a place that accommodated social enthusiasms of all sorts. The article's title makes it sound like a tendentious piece of socialist realism; but it is, instead, a potent rejoinder to any reductionistic treatment of art, expressing beautifully the aesthetic rationale underlying Starr's and Addams's stress on the arts *despite* their functional uselessness from a utilitarian viewpoint (a perspective that pertained among most socialists, for example).

Ugliness and beauty to Addams and Starr were ethical categories as well as aesthetic ones.[11] Starr speaks of the "hungering individual soul" that suffers if it passes "unsolaced and unfed." The young especially respond "to what is beautiful" and reject "what is ugly." This "renews courage to set the leaven of the beautiful in the midst of the ugly, instead of waiting for the ugly to be first cleared away."[12] Ugly, for example, would be mountains of uncleared garbage—an offense to the eyes and nostrils and an assault on the human soul, which says that the city cares so little about taking away this garbage because it regards the human beings compressed into the 19th ward as refuse, too. Add to this the horrific odor emanating from the Chicago stockyards; the often visibly dirty drinking water; the shabby, unkempt, poorly ventilated tenements. What is naturally beautiful—including children—grows be-grimed and besmirched in this environment. Children become apa-thetic, and their eyes lose luster.[13]

In the 19th ward, much that should be beautiful is converted through a perverse alchemy into an eyesore, is uglified—people's homes and streets, first and foremost. Hull-House would not wait for the ugly to be cleared: it would create beauty in the midst of things, roses among the thorns, in order to sustain a sense of form and wonder and in order to keep alive the yearning that Addams and Starr assumed lay at the core of every human being, every child. The denial of expressive space to peoples and cultures may have devastating effects. As Starr makes clear in *Hull-House Maps and Papers,* if human beings are denied space in which to reveal themselves, the self is strangled and cannot thrive.

Anticipating the work of mid-twentieth-century critical theorists such as Walter Benjamin, Starr notes the effect of turning human beings into adjuncts of machines. Modes of mechanical reproduction also di-minish the human being.[14] Because we human beings are creatures cre-ated for love and gifted with yearnings, we experience pleasure that ei-ther degrades us or lifts us up. There are many ways to feed the hungry, and one way is to feed them with good and beautiful things: "The soul of man in the commercial and industrial struggle is under siege. He is fighting for his life. . . . [A settlement] must work with all energy and courage toward the rescue of those bound under the slavery of com-merce and the wage-law; with all abstinence it must discountenance wasting human life in the making of useless things; with all faith it must urge forward the building up of a state in which cruel contrasts of surfeit and want, of idleness and overwork, shall not be found."[15]

Toward this end, Hull-House included exhibitions of pictures, a working people's chorus, Sunday Concerts, the Paderewski Club of in-struction in piano, summer excursions so that nature's beauty might be experienced, a mandolin club, and on and on. Working people had a right to enjoy what was excellent and met the highest possible stan-dards of technical adroitness and beauty of execution. Addams and Starr were repelled by what came to be called socialist realism, with its crude fusion of the heroic (fantastically construed) and the "photo-graphic."[16] The desire for beauty can be stifled—denied—but with dire effects. The young person's search for beauty, adventure, excitement—

all features of the authentic spirit of youth—clashes frequently with the parents' desire for safety, prudence, and keeping the child beholden and under thumb (in the case of immigrant parents, imperatives often born of bewilderment, perplexity, and fear).

Addams worked very hard to interpret youth to their frightened and angered elders. She understood the young person's search for excitement as a protest that often goes awry, a protest against a life that is dull, gray, and deadening—the life the working young faced each and every day. Sympathetic knowledge is on full display in Addams's 1909 text *The Spirit of Youth and the City Streets,* said to be her favorite among her books.[17] It captures youth's ebullience and the need for that vivacity to be held within capacious, life-sustaining forms if it is to enhance life over time rather than to sputter out in a flurry like a moth diving into the destroying flame. There may be great romance in the notion of youthful ardor snuffed out in a spasm of creativity, or orgiastic love, or equally orgiastic political activity that brooks no compromise, or the terrible beauties of that most terrible of activities—war.[18] This is romance that destroys rather than builds, and its undoubted allure is not for Jane Addams. More important, it is ardor of a sort ill suited to the building of a democratic political culture that is *not* a warrior culture. There may, from time to time, be a need for heroes. If a culture is forming citizens with a sense of responsibility and duty, heroes will rise up when they are needed—or so Addams believed.

What did turn-of-the-century Chicago offer the spirits of immigrant youth? For Jane Addams, it was a dispiriting picture. The city was formless, out of control, and thus incapable of carrying the burden of civic formation and the creation of selves. There were no clear channels through which civic life and aesthetic life and adventure might flow. There were no safe places for children to play. There was no regulation of low-paid jobs: workdays sometimes lasted sixteen hours. There were no limits to how old or young a worker might be, and even children as young as four years were taxed beyond limit and destroyed in the process. There were no sanitation standards, and sweatshops were often hotbeds of smallpox and tuberculosis—diseases that spread from worker to worker, and to the population at large via the articles produced. Even a necessity as basic as water was allowed to become filled with pollutants and bacteria that could be deadly, especially to the very young, the old, and the ill.

A kind of order pertained in city administration, but because it was corrupt, it was also capricious. Many honest judges, policemen, and alderman who tried to uphold the law were disgraced through set-up scams, designed to get them out of the way so that profitable avenues of graft could remain open. Worse, argued Addams, there was the terrible confusion and anomie of peasants, thrust from the fields of Calabria to the garbage-packed streets and refuse-strewn alleyways of Chicago. Their young men drifted, courting disaster or crime. Their young girls were duped into believing that in America girls got married by just moving in with someone. In this way, she claimed in *A New Conscience and an Ancient Evil*, they were drawn into the pit of vice and disease, often trailing home only to die in disgrace from syphilis or gonorrhea.[19]

Given her emphasis on form, Jane Addams defied the age-old myth of the woman as one who is always threatening to disrupt order (Nemesis, Fortuna); who is given to outbursts and nonsensical cravings; who cannot handle the ordered complexities of law and citizenship (a Fury rather than an Athena); and who finds serious responsibility too great a burden. Throughout the history of Western political thought, women are construed frequently as an internal threat to order—indeed, to the very form of public life. The frustration is that you cannot kick them out and have a republic at all. So women's tasks must be assigned carefully and circumscribed efficiently.

But along comes young Jane Addams, reversing the equations: it is the men who run Chicago and who are the antic princes presiding over a veritable riot of disorder in the name of order. They are the industrialists who desire to keep labor as cheap as possible and workers as disorganized as possible; to tax human beings, especially women and children, to their very limits, and force women into the kinds of jobs they say women are not really suited to, even as they separate women from the tasks they insist women *are* suited to—namely, nurturing children. To organize schools and playgrounds is to create social forms—institutions—against the denizens of formlessness.[20] Addams believed the city should be a thing of beauty for all its citizens—in the building of its buildings, including its schools; in the provision of free public libraries; and in the generous dotting of the city with theaters—for theater was a major Hull-House undertaking. Addams joined like-minded persons to protect the wandering shore of Lake Michigan from speculative private development—an activity one might call form recognition, protecting a natural wonder that was provided freely for all to enjoy, shoring it up (literally), and enhancing it for generations to come.

But how could a form be created that, in contrast to regimented law and order, offers greater freedom in the channeling of energies over the long term? Human potential is maximized if enthusiasms are shaped and directed rather than allowed to spill out in many directions at once (which has the same deadly effect upon the human psyche as uncontrolled bleeding has on the human body). Hull-House was known primarily for its attunement to the young (a kindergarten was its first organized undertaking), but Addams was insistent that education should continue throughout life. She illustrates this point with what I call the Story of the Old Woman Who Picked Plaster Off the Walls and Spoke Gaelic.

In this anecdote, Addams describes an elderly woman whose daughter left her alone all day while she was at work. The older woman had a persistent habit of picking plaster off the walls. Landlord after landlord refused to have her for a tenant, and the beleaguered mother and daughter were forced to move again and again. Then one of the Hull-House kindergartners taught the old woman how to "make large paper chains and gradually she was content to do it all day long, and in the end took quite as much pleasure in adorning walls as she had formerly taken in demolishing them." The old woman's enjoyment in making the paper chains was unsurprising; they represented continuity with the unquenchable spirit of youth, although bedimmed by age. Then something truly surprising happened. This elderly plaster-peeler, at first thought to be babbling nonsensically, was later discovered to be speaking Gaelic: "And when one or two grave professors came to see her, the neighborhood was filled with pride that such a wonder lived in their midst. To mitigate life for a woman of ninety was an unfailing refutation of the statement that the Settlement was designed for the young."[21]

Freedom Only Through Self-Control

Addams is unstinting in her presentation of the many ways human beings over the centuries have satisfied their need for charm and beauty and their "insatiable desire for play."[22] But the modern industrial city makes the satisfaction of this desire very difficult, as she explains in her book *The Spirit of Youth:*[23]

> Never before in civilization have such numbers of young girls been
> suddenly released from the protection of the home and permitted to
> walk unattended upon city streets and to work under alien roofs;
> for the first time they are being prized more for their labor power
> than for their innocence or their tender beauty, their ephemeral gai-
> ety. Society cares more for the products they manufacture than for
> their immemorial ability to reaffirm the charm of existence. Never
> before have such numbers of young boys earned money indepen-
> dently of the family life, and felt themselves free to spend it as they
> choose in the midst of vice deliberately disguised as pleasure.

In Addams's view, it was a bad deal all around; indeed, a "stupid experiment" was under way. Because play was unrecognized as a need, it
had fallen into the hands of those who pandered to the worst rather
than the best instincts. Society washed its hands of the matter, as if the
city had no obligation to provide for a basic human need. The upshot
was that the unscrupulous rushed in to fill this yawning gap in the order of things, recognizing that the love of pleasure, which could not be
stifled, could be bent to their own profit.

In *A New Conscience and an Ancient Evil,* Addams delivers up a series of lay sermons intended for the civic church of her city and her
country. Should people not look at the situation before them? If they
ceased to avert their gaze, they would see cheap gin palaces that over-
stimulated the youth, poisoned a few of them with bad stuff, and emp-
tied their pockets, forcing desperate boys and girls alike into debt. To
pay off that debt, the purveyors of cheap pleasures offered the boys
good money as procurers or decoys to lure the girls into vice. To the
girls they offered the chance to meet a few men, get paid for it, and get
out of debt quickly. The die was cast, and some young lives would be
doomed.

Some of Jane Addams's critics assaulted her sermonizing in *New
Conscience and Ancient Evil.* Walter Lippman, for example, described
it as hysterical and puritanical. But Addams makes clear that she's no
puritan in the sense he implied. After all, it was the "soldiers of
Cromwell" who "shut up the people's playhouses and destroyed their
pleasure fields." Ever since that time, "the Anglo-Saxon city has turned
over the provision for public recreation to the most unscrupulous members of the community."[24] As a result, joy had become confused with

lust, and gaiety, with debauchery. This confusion invited the debauched to sell debauchery, and sell it they would and did: even in Addams's day the traffic in vice was a multimillion-dollar affair. Addams understood that an absolute interdiction of vice was a utopian fantasy. Her worry was that too many young people, yearning for their house of dreams and with their young selves in the throes of often tumultuous development, would be dragged down into an orb of vice from which they would not have the power and strength to extricate themselves.

Addams associates her civic sermons with a Social Gospel message. After all, the "good news" of Scripture is a source of "inexpressible joy." Why do so many Americans forget this and permit the lambs to be "caught upon the brambles," entrapped in the sordid and joyless, where joy instead should be. Addams makes a pitch for joy that affirms life and permits it to perdure—in contrast to outbursts of pleasure that are intense momentarily but that coarsen the spirit over time.

The modern city degrades what should be exalted.[25] It is responsible, first, for the "wrecked foundations of domesticity," as families implode from the pressures that come from all directions. Generations are driven apart. Men feel helpless and useless and desert their families. Women and young children are driven into soul-killing and body-weakening labor. Their surroundings are rodent- and insect-infested, dark, dirty, and unsafe—an aesthetic and health catastrophe as well as a firetrap. Imaginations run wild in what Addams frankly calls degenerate directions, given the horrible overcrowding, the absolute lack of privacy for intimacy, and the overagitation of the youth, who cannot really comprehend what they see and hear but are vaguely excited by it all.

When girls go wrong, they often tremble at the prospect of turning to their families in their time of trouble, for fear of censure and punishment. So Hull-House served as what we might call today a battered women's shelter. It took in many a woman, often a young, inexperienced woman, lured by the promise of her own home away from the tenement only to find herself trapped. Here is the Story of a Slender Figure Trembling with Fright,[26] told with the vivid physical detail that makes Addams's tales so potent:

> I can see her now running for protection up the broad steps of the columned piazza then surrounding Hull-House. Her slender figure was trembling with fright, her tear-covered face swollen and blood-

stained from the blows he had dealt her. "He is apt to abuse me when he is drunk," was the only explanation, and that given by way of apology, which could be extracted from her. When we discovered there had been no marriage ceremony, that there were no living children, that she had twice narrowly escaped losing her life, it seemed a simple matter to insist that the relation should be broken off. She apathetically remained at Hull-House for a few weeks, but when her strength had somewhat returned, when her lover began to recover from his prolonged debauch of whiskey and opium, she insisted upon going home every day to prepare his meals and to see that the little tenement was clean and comfortable. . . . This of course meant she was drifting back to him, and when she was at last restrained by that moral compulsion, by that overwhelming of another's will which is always so ruthlessly exerted by those who are conscious that virtue is struggling with vice, her mind gave way and she became utterly distraught.

Apply Jane Addams's moral theory to this sad tale, and it goes like this: the young woman's brutalization and her obedience in a coercive situation had become habitual. An authentic human virtue—caring for another human being and tending to the needs of another—was misdirected toward one who not only betrayed her trust but brutalized her again and again, and who might one day come to the point of killing her—because he, compulsively, could do nothing else, certainly not without help. Torn by the counterexample of Hull-House and with her mind wracked by conflict, the slender young woman trembling with fright could not focus her will. She was doomed, it seems, to repeat rather than to reach for a life-sustaining alternative. She could not seize the true bond that should hold families together, a bond that "blends the experience of generations into a continuous story." Hull-House observed many tragedies. It could always provide succor. It could not always effect a change for the better.

The path to freedom open to all in America could not be denied to the young, Addams understood, but that path was "made safe only through their own self-control."[27] Addams saw no way to make freedom safe but for all Americans to rely on a strong code of inner-directed conscience and the formation of such a robust sense of ethics that one need not be guarded or chased around to be certain one was in compliance. The youth's quest for adventure should be neither crushed nor permitted to degenerate into vice. It should be recognized as societies have long done by sustaining complex rites of initiation into the adult community, often accompanied by communal affirmation and celebration. The spirit of adventure was once the purview of "the hunt, of warfare, and of discovery"—at least, for young men.[28] Camaraderie, danger, adventure, beauty—how could a young person not be attracted to their allure? But the city provided few channels for the realization of adventure. Youth were educated and then driven to distraction by what was expected from them as it was often so shriven, so boring, so repetitious: the world's dour restraint clashes with their high hopes and their ardent desire to make something of themselves. Addams empties a bushel-basketful of stories illustrating the spirit of adventure gone awry, which she collected from records of the juvenile court (which she and Hull-House played a central role in creating). These case files make for interesting and often amusing reading, although too many of the stories have unhappy endings.

Here's a sample from actual court records of misdeeds that landed their perpetrators before judges—much of which seems rather innocent by today's standards. Addams's aim in compiling what I call the Stories of Boys Being Boys was not to shock and outrage but to illustrate the unquenchable nature of the spirit of adventure—which, one way or another, will find expression.[29]

> (l) Building fires along the railroad tracks; [Addams observes that boys are drawn to the railroad tracks by the sense of power, movement, adventure, and escape] (2) flagging trains; (3) throwing stones at moving train windows; (4) shooting at the actors in the Olympic Theatre with slingshots; (5) breaking signal lights on the railroad; (6) stealing linseed oil barrels from the railroad to make a fire; (7) taking waste from an axle box and burning it upon the railroad tracks; (8) turning a switch and running a street car off the track; (9) staying away from home to sleep in barns; (10) setting fire to a barn in order to see the fire engines come up the street; (11) knocking down signs; (12) cutting Western Union cable.

Addams challenges her city to redirect the boys' legitimate yearning for adventure into pathways that are not destructive of themselves and others. She charges the city with failing to even try to enter with sympathetic understanding into the world of youth. The problem, at base, was one of refusing to interpret the experiences of youth in a way that reveals what is going on and that invites a complex variety of responses rather than the simplistic reaction of taking them to court.[30] Of course, something must be done if the spirit of adventure goes haywire. But must that reaction take a punitive form only? Without imaginative ways to channel all of that youthful energy and desire for risk and danger, there will be tragedies—especially if the city caters to the most destructive impulses of the human heart.

Addams tells of boys enacting a scene they saw in the theater, who wind up killing a poor delivery man, and of children driven around the bend by opium. With horrific stories like these piling up, her sense of moral evolution was greatly challenged; it seemed as though society was being dragged back toward a norm of brutality that she had previously thought was being replaced by culture. For her the evolutionary imperative was first and foremost a moral imperative: Had Western society not repudiated heinous practices such as child abandonment, and would future generations not look back on the present ill use of children in a similar light? How could the soul not shudder at the wreckage, the little balls of human misery folded up in musty corners, pulling out basting threads hour after hour?[31]

Girls are also seized by the spirit of adventure, and they wind up picking pockets, desirous as they are of the lovely and unattainable goods they see all around them. Thousands of girls labor standing on their feet all day, with perhaps a half-hour lunch break, clerking for horrible pay yet required to buy and maintain their own uniforms. The upshot: In Chicago, in 1908, fifteen thousand young people under the age of twenty were arrested and brought into court. They had broken the law "in their blundering efforts to find adventure and in response to the old impulse for self-expression."[32] If we try to understand, we see that this demand for excitement is a "protest against the dulness of life," which we should all understand because we, too, were once young and dreamed of adventure and romance and daring and saying to the world, "Here I am."

The modern city caters to this need with the magic of plays; and Hull-House, the mother-house of Chicago theater, recognizing this, put on plays in its 750-seat Bowen Auditorium before packed crowds. By

1900, Hull-House theater had achieved international acclaim.[33] Addams was a meticulous reviewer of Hull-House productions, evaluating them on the basis of their artistic merit. If a performance improved, she approved. In her view, artistic discipline enhanced self-improvement. Addams's moral theory dictated that to improve one's performance in a complex practice such as theater was to better one's life. But it was very hard to compete with the houses of dreams, as they were called, that sold cheap sentiment and romance at a nickel a ticket. Some young people became addicted to the theater—it was more real than the ugly streets and factories. If life was too unbearable, there was an alternative drama unfolding before them. Theater can serve powerfully to shape and form the emotions of love and jealousy, of revenge and daring, and can warn us of a road down which lies madness or destruction or defeat. But too often the purveyors of cheap melodrama sold only tawdry tales of vengeance and betrayal.

One example Addams highlights is the story of a thug "killing the father of the family and carrying away the family treasure. The golden-haired son of the house, aged seven, vows eternal vengeance on the spot, and follows one villain after another to his doom." Each execution, Addams tells us, is "shown in lurid detail," but the overall message is that the hero thanks God "he has been permitted to be an instrument of vengeance."[34] Vengeance is celebrated rather than challenged. Impressionable minds are filled "with absurdities which certainly will become the foundation for their working moral codes"— of this Jane Addams has little doubt. Children reenact much of what they see. The problem is that the constant vulgar titillation of an instinct inhibits its development into something deeper and richer. Theater becomes a factory churning out cheap everything: love, heroism, revenge. Starved imaginations will be fed, one way or another, if only on debased forms of the dramatic arts.

The Spirit of Youth and the City Streets is elegiac in its recognition of youthful yearnings. *A New Conscience and an Ancient Evil* is grim in its depiction of what happens when adventure and desire go astray: these books are the two sides of a single coin. Complex and well-crafted drama, in contrast to sleazy houses of dreams or even elegant department stores that have become wish-generating factories, "provides a transition between the romantic conceptions which they [the young] vainly struggle to keep intact and life's cruelties and trivialities

which they refuse to admit. A child whose imagination has been cultivated is able to do this for himself through reading and reverie, but for
the overworked city youth of meager education, nothing but the theater
is able to perform this important office."[35] On March 29, 1902, Addams spoke on "What the Theatre at Hull-House Has Done" before a
crowd gathered at the Assembly Hall of the United Charities Building.
She credited the "people of the neighborhood," because they "for the
most part have been the actors upon the stage." The theater was established, she tells us, because "of the influence this institution has upon
the working people, all of whom attend as frequently as they are able
to afford the small admission fee charged at the cheaper places of
amusement. The theater is a strong force in the life of the ordinary
working boy, and has its influence upon all members of the social class
of which he is a part. It forms to some extent their concept of morality,
and in a greater degree shapes their outward manners and conduct. It
rivals the schools in its influence, which, indeed, is protracted far beyond the school age."[36]

For this very reason, theaters should perform plays that speak to
great and tragic possibilities—not didactically and dogmatically but in
an aesthetically powerful and beautiful way: Schiller, Shakespeare,
Molière, the great Greek dramatists. It was Hull-House that staged the
first production of Sophocles' *Ajax* in America—not "the great University
of Chicago." Writes a reporter for the *Kansas City Star*:[37]

> Few things would ordinarily be less associated in the public mind
> than a social settlement and Sophocles, yet we have come to know
> that at Hull-House and under the guidance of Miss Jane Addams
> all things seem possible. And this phenomenon of a Greek play,
> acted not by academically trained students, with approved accents
> and gestures, but by more or less uneducated modern Greeks, with
> no training but a natural enthusiasm. This is another manifestation
> of the strong belief held by Miss Addams that the foreigners whom
> the social settlement seeks to assist can be best helped by being en-
> couraged to give in their turn of their best instincts and powers for
> the common center, in this case Hull House.

Small wonder that novelist William Dean Howells, in a letter to "My
dear Miss Addams," enthused that the Hull-House stage "seems to me

Jane Addams, age 6, 1866. Already apparent are her beautiful, penetrating eyes, commented on over the years by friends, family, and journalists.

John Huy Addams. His rectitude is evident in one of the few available photographs of Jane Addams's much beloved father.

Jane Addams's birthplace in Cedarville, Illinois. The home has been restored by its current owners and is not open to the public.

Jane Addams with her stepmother, Anna Haldeman Addams, and stepbrother, George Haldeman, c. 1876. George Haldeman ended his life as a recluse. Jane had refused a marriage between her and George that Anna Haldeman had pushed energetically.

Jane Addams, c. 1887, at the time of her second European tour. She wears one of the elaborate dresses with giant mutton sleeves that so riled Leo Tolstoy when Addams visited him at his home a decade later.

Jane Addams was determined that the interior of the Hull-House mansion be a beckoning, beautiful, well-furnished home where all could be greeted warmly and offered hospitality.

Ellen Gates Starr, Jane Addams's friend, who became a co-founder of Hull-House and resident for many years. A passionate advocate for labor, Starr eventually left Hull-House after establishing a book-bindery and leading literature and reading classes. She and Addams remained good friends.

Mary Rozet Smith, daughter of a prominent Chicago family, had traveled extensively as a teenager and was looking for something useful to give her life to when she helped found Hull-House in 1890 at the age of twenty. For the remainder of her life—the next forty-three years—she devoted herself to Hull-House and, most particularly, to befriending and helping to care for Jane Addams.

One of Jane Addams's many creations at Hull-House was the Labor Museum, which displayed the arts and crafts of immigrant men and women. She hoped in this way to bridge the gap between immigrant parents and grandparents and their Americanized children.

The Hull-House nursery school provided high-quality day care for children whose mothers worked. Hull-House pioneered in well-baby care, preventive medicine, and inoculations. Notice the reproductions of fine art in the room, an effort later commentators found affected. But Jane Addams insisted that being surrounded by beauty helped to develop the mind.

"Rear Tenements at Hull-House Neighborhood," one of the original sketches by Norah Hamilton featured in the original edition of Twenty Years at Hull-House.

Edith de Nancrede, director of the Hull-House Junior Dramatics Group, The Marionettes, insisted that drama was a powerful force in "awakening and stimulating interest in intellectual and beautiful things." Shown is a scene from Merman's Bride, *which premiered at Hull-House.*

This lively bunch represents the Hull-House Boys' Club shown near and on their club house. Most of the famous photographs of Hull-House, including this one, were done by Wallace Kirkland who served, from 1923, as director of the Hull-House boys' and men's clubs.

A boisterous greeting for Jane Addams in Japan during her around the world tour of 1923. Her reputation had not suffered internationally, even as it had plummeted nationally because of her pacifistic stance during World War I.

Addams, c. 1930–1935, reading to an ethnically mixed trio of children as other children busy themselves with what appears to be an art project.

Hull-House courtyard, May 23, 1935, jammed with mourners at Jane Addams's funeral. As many as 6,000 people an hour filed past her bier in the Bowen Theater, part of the Hull-House complex. Stores shut down, even saloons closed their doors, for the funeral.

a real Theatre Libre, and provides an opportunity for a conscientious drama which is quite unequalled in America, so far as I know." He hopes to create something "worthy of the Hull House stage."[38]

Addams advocated not only theater but public festivals, beautiful, safe parks, street processions, marching bands, orchestral music in public squares or parks—all of this has magic power—and at least some of it is being implemented in today's city, although we caught on rather late to the need for human beings to experience beauty in fellowship. Celebrate holidays; celebrate the changing of the seasons. There are all sorts of reasons for public festivals. The many foreign colonies "afford an enormous reserve of material for public recreation and street festival."[39] Addams's characterization of the higher function of art may from time to time soar into the ether. But there is something stirring in it, too, especially her recognition of the need and "possibilities for public recreation and for the corporate expression of stirring emotions. After all, what is the function of art but to preserve in permanent and beautiful form those emotions and solaces which cheer life and make it kindlier, more heroic and easier to comprehend; which lift the mind of the worker from the harshness and loneliness of his task, and, by connecting him with what has gone before, free him from a sense of isolation and hardship?"[40]

In Addams's mind, the search for righteousness and the quest for beauty were linked. She was convinced that all human beings have deep within them an unformed desire to share in a common life and to protect and cherish weaker things. We would never have survived as a species were this not the case. These impulses can be driven out of us or go into hiding. But it is the task of adults to nurture these tendencies in the young.[41] City youth must share in the "common inheritance of life's best goods." Toward that end, moral authority should speak "with no uncertain sound if only to be heard above the din of machinery and the roar of industrialism." Then and only then can it exert "itself as never before to convince the youth of the reality of the spiritual life"—a reality that should be charming, beautiful, and in its own way seductive.[42]

Families and Their Travail

Given Jane Addams's social feminism and her moral theory, it is unsurprising that so much of the focus of Hull-House was on children and on those responsible for caring for children in the homes, the factories, the churches, and the streets. The family was no isolated institution but one profoundly affected by the surround in which it was nestled. Addams's emphasis on the community helps us understand not only her concentration on art but her focus on health as a public matter, not simply a private one.[43] She worked with the Board of Health in the fight against a long list of childhood diseases, many of which, before the advent of antibiotics, were potentially fatal, including smallpox. During the smallpox epidemic of 1893 to 1894, Addams made Hull-House available to city inspectors as a base of operations in their war against smallpox.[44] She also derived a notion of the purpose of the state from the smallpox epidemic. She argued that the state should embody "the commonality of compassion." The smallpox inspectors were the human face of that compassion.[45]

Just as disease broke bodies, so too did sweatshops, which generated serious health hazards. It has been estimated that in the decade of the 1890s alone, Addams made a thousand speeches on child labor and the need to abolish sweatshops.[46] In her approach to the child as in all else, Jane Addams was resolutely empirical: What is the situation we face? What is the evidence? It is from the basis of solid factual evidence that social interpretation and sympathetic understanding proceed. The story of "huge and foul tenements" isn't just an account of overcrowding and stench. It is a story of the denigration of the human person and of a protracted assault upon human souls and spirits. Reform efforts must, first and foremost, prevent harm. But they should also lift up and encourage human beings. Children should laugh and move about, not cough and wilt and walk the streets like slow-moving mannikins with pallid faces.

What sorts of public policy remedies did Addams seek? These varied widely. In some cases, she wanted to strengthen extant institutions; in other cases, to create institutions—such as the juvenile courts, which she overoptimistically hoped would primarily help protect wayward youth rather than punishing them. It is easy to identify problems with the juvenile courts from today's vantage point. But the concrete situation Addams faced was that of hundreds of children being hauled before criminal courts for minor infractions and jailed with adult criminals. The community longed for a change, she argued. She knew this because she insinuated herself within the montage of frantic human voices—most often, those of mothers—pleading that their children be spared prosecution.[47] Hull-House residents played the part of what we would now call an advocate or parental surrogate for children when they appeared before a judge. Often the children were remanded to the responsible Hull-House resident, who then functioned as something of a probation officer. All of this was revolutionary at the time.[48] But it comported with what one might call the founding Hull-House directive: a response to the child's fearful query, What is to become of me?[49]

Hull-House's attempt to respond to that question involved the institution in politically controversial activities such as union organizing, although Addams lamented strikes as a lingering example of a martial spirit in civic life.[50] Hull-House became involved in unionization efforts on the assumption that if parents were depleted and exhausted, children suffered. Addams was a staunch supporter of the idea that mothers of young children should be able to stay home with their children and that public reforms should be directed along those lines.[51] Hull-House ran what we today would call a well-baby clinic, and taught basic hygiene and diet to mothers. A monthly report of the health of every child in the day nursery, or crèche, was provided. Here is one example: "In January, 1895, there were thirty-five babies in the crèche during the month. Two cases of rash were noted and one case was sent to the hospital." The nationality of the babies also was recorded: fifteen were Italian, ten French, and ten German.[52]

This same report also notes that reproductions of paintings on themes likely to be enchanting to children—two by Millet and two by Rembrandt—were hung on the walls. Children and expectant mothers were succored and given a chance to spend time in the countryside. Addams treated all such activities as social occasions so as not to patronize the immigrant parents. She invited Italian women who brought their children to Hull-House for well-baby activities to a Sunday morning breakfast in the Hull-House nursery and offered the children "oatmeal instead of tea-soaked bread."[53] For Addams, this was a social method: to be with people, not to do for them. Some efforts, such as the Hull-House diet kitchen, which attempted to wean immigrants away from poor nutrition and toward a healthier diet, failed for the most part. But attempts to make low wages stretch as far as possible, and to convince mothers that bread soaked in tea—or wine—wasn't optimal for the developing child, seem reasonable. *How* you do these things is all-important. For Jane Addams, the means were as important as the ends. You should not brow-beat your immigrant neighbors into an activity or sit-uation they were unprepared to accept. You should walk the path with them, learn from them, and offer guidance in the awareness that you were being instructed at the same time. In many ways Hull-House was a home movement based on informal gatherings, whether in the parlor or in the kitchen of a tenement.

A Stranger No More: Hilda Polacheck's Story

It was the home atmosphere of Hull-House that beguiled an initially fearful and suspicious Hilda Satt Polacheck, whose family had emi-grated to Chicago in 1892.[54] They arrived on June 16 of that year, hav-ing been overcharged for their tickets, because immigrants "were at the mercy of dishonest agents."[55] Years of bewilderment, penury, and struggle, followed by the early death of Hilda's father, were their lot. At her father's death, young Hilda pondered, What is to become of me?— the desperate fear that links childhoods everywhere, according to Ad-dams. But Hilda, through the mediation of a friend, found an answer. Looking back, she wonders "what kind of life I would have lived if I had not met Jane Addams."[56]

Shortly before Christmas 1896, one of Hilda's Irish Catholic play-mates—tenement dwelling had placed in proximity those who would ordinarily be separated—asked Hilda to accompany her to a Christmas party at Hull-House. A Jewish girl at a Christmas party was out of the question for Hilda: "'I might get killed,'" Hilda proclaims. Her friend is astonished: "'Get killed!' She stared at me. 'I go to Hull-House Christmas parties every year, and no one has ever been killed.'"[57] Per-haps Jewish children in Poland couldn't be on the streets at Christmas. But this was America, the new world. So Hilda summoned up her courage and trundled on over without telling her mother. Everyone seemed to be having a good time. "Then Jane Addams came into the room! It was the first time that I looked into those kind, understanding eyes. There was a gleam of welcome in them that made me feel I was wanted. She told us that she was glad we had come. Her voice was warm and I knew she meant what she said . . . we were all having a good time at a party, as the guests of an American, Jane Addams. We were all poor. Some of us were underfed. Some of us had holes in our shoes. But we were not afraid of each other. What greater service can a human being give to her country than to banish fear from the heart of a child? Jane Addams did that for me at that party."

To banish fear: we are standing with the little Cedarville schoolgirl peering into the open grave, staring death in the face. What will become of me? From that first moment, Hilda became a Hull-House child. She witnesses as Addams supports a mother at the funeral of her child, after she "had placed a small bouquet of real flowers on the coffin." This was a child who had been driven to consumption by poor living conditions and overwork. Hilda starts to take classes at Hull-House whenever she can. Addams herself gives her a tour of the Labor Museum, showing her the spinning and weaving and other beautiful accomplishments of immigrant parents. Polacheck sees a young girl suddenly awed by the discovery that her non-English-speaking mother, of whom she previously was ashamed, could speak German, French, Russian, and Polish, although she had not yet learned to speak English. "To her, the mother was just a greenhorn. For such children the Labor Museum was an eye-opener."

Hull-House opened Hilda's eyes to her own abilities and possibilities. She joined a reading club. Her teacher presented her with a real book at the Christmas party, Elizabeth Barrett Browning's *Sonnets from the Portuguese*. Looking back after fifty years, Hilda realizes just how much her life was molded by Hull-House and Jane Addams. Her story of the day Jane Addams said to her, "How would you like to go to the University of Chicago?" is remarkable. Hilda had displayed promise in her written papers for Hull-House classes. So even though she didn't have a high school diploma and her family had no money, Addams arranged for a scholarship as well as a loan to cover the amount of Hilda's lost earnings so her family wouldn't suffer financially, telling her, "Whenever you are able, you can pay it back." This is a moment that brought tears to Hilda's eyes (and it will do the same to the reader whose heart unlocks to grace and human possibility).

Polacheck offers many vivid images of Addams: defending anarchists, who were generally unpopular but who were making their case peacefully; "following a filthy garbage truck down an alley in her long skirt and immaculate white blouse"; investigating deaths from typhoid fever; cajoling and pleading and finally getting a playground for the neighborhood children. Surely the witness of Hilda Satt Polacheck should count when it comes time to make a reckoning:[58]

Jane Addams was never condescending to anyone. She never made one feel that she was a "lady bountiful." . . . When she did something for you, you felt . . . that she was making a loan that you could pay back. The most forlorn scrubwoman received the same warm welcome as the wealthy supporters of the house. I remember one day the daughter of a wealthy family had come to Hull-House to help in the reception room, and an old shabby woman came in and asked for Miss Addams. Looking down at the poor woman, the young lady started to tell her that Miss Addams was busy and could not be disturbed, just as Miss Addams was coming down the stairs. She quickly told the young lady that perhaps she had better go home. Then she took the old woman by the arm and said she was just going to have a cup of tea and would she join her. Then she led her to the coffeehouse. . . . America has not yet awakened to the realization of what it owes to Jane Addams. No one will ever know how many young people were helped by her wise counsel, how many were kept out of jail, how many were started on careers in the arts, in music, in industry, in science, and above all in instilling in their hearts a true love of country—a love of service.

Revealing Immigrants to Their Children

The realities of immigrant life were complex, as Hilda Satt Polacheck's account indicates. Jane Addams understood the reluctance of the immigrant to leave his or her home of origin. In the powerful chapter XI of *Twenty Years at Hull-House,* she tells the Story of Angelina, Who Was Ashamed of Her Mother.[59] Addams conveys to an Italian girl, Angelina, who is ashamed of her Italian mother ("who wore a kerchief over her head, uncouth boots, and short petticoats"), something of what her mother's life must have been in the Old Country. Addams was probably speaking Italian to the girl, as she could converse in the language. Following this encounter, Angelina could look at her mother from another perspective, having recognized that others were interested in her mother's superb stick-spindling. One of the displays in the Labor Museum—one that featured live action—was that of different styles of spinning and weaving. Addams recalls her story to Angelina:

> I dilated somewhat on the freedom and beauty of that life [the old village life in Italy]—how hard it must be to exchange it all for a two-room tenement, and to give up a beautiful homespun kerchief for an ugly department store hat. I intimated it was most unfair to judge her [the mother] by these things alone, and that while she must depend on her daughter to learn the new ways, she also had a right to expect her daughter to know something of the old ways.
>
> That which I could not convey to the child but upon which my own mind persistently dwelt, was that her mother's whole life had been spent in a secluded spot under the rule of traditional and narrowly localized observances, until her very religion clung to local sanctities,—to the shrine before which she had always prayed, to the pavement and walls of the low vaulted church,—and then suddenly she was torn from it all and literally put out to sea, straight away from the solid habits of her religious and domestic life, and she now walked timidly but with poignant sensibility upon a new and strange shore.

Most immigrant parents finally made the transition, but some with their hearts permanently broken. How could their pain be eased? That was the task Addams assigned to Hull-House, as a new version of the old tradition of hospitality that survived among the immigrants and that the native-born Americans greeting them should surely offer in return. Recall Addams's hope that immigrants come into contact with a "better type" of American, a term that troubles us. She seems to compound the problem by speaking of the "pathetic stupidity of agricultural people crowded into city tenements."[60] These are not politically correct sentiments. Applying sympathetic understanding to what Addams is trying to do helps us appreciate the intentions behind these remarks. By "better type" of American, Addams had in mind no plutocratic elite but something more along the lines of Thomas Jefferson's aristocracy of virtue and talent. She understood that many whom the immigrants first encountered as they made their way were the unscrupulous, or immigration officials who had the power to rip a family apart by turning them back at Ellis Island—and they did turn back many. If you or your child had glaucoma, you weren't admitted. If your child had Down syndrome, you weren't admitted, or the child wasn't. There were dozens of criteria that could keep you from landing on American terra firma.

The "better type" of American tried to understand this, and more. He or she worked to induct immigrants gently if decisively into the ways of the new culture in which they were *obliged* to make their way—it was *not* an option—and did so by offering immigrants the best of what the new world had to offer. As to the phrase "pathetic stupidity," here Addams is making a fairly straightforward claim: people who are all at sea are stupefied: they cannot find their feet. Many have described what happens to people when layer after layer of their identity and dignity is stripped away. South Italian peasants are not stupid people: they are stupefied by what is happening to them.

Addams created space in which the beauty of the Old World could display itself to the new and in which songs and reminiscences were welcomed and woven together to become part of a new culture of the American immigrant city. Do not suppose, she tells us, that the new is always the best. Much of the new she found tawdry, in any case. Small wonder she felt an "overmastering desire to reveal the humbler immigrant parents to their own children." This possibility came to her one day as she watched an "old Italian woman, her distaff against her homesick face, patiently spinning a thread by the simple stick spindle so reminiscent of all southern Europe." This was on Polk Street in Chicago. It was time to heal the yawning chasm between fathers and sons, mothers and daughters, and to prevent it from deepening into an impassable void. For Addams, all of the national styles of spinning, all of the beautiful objects on display in the textile museum, "connected directly with the basket weaving, sewing, millinery, embroidery, and dressmaking constantly being taught at Hull-House," were prized because they put the immigrants "into the position of teachers, and we imagine that it affords them a pleasant change from the tutelage in which all Americans, including their own children, are so apt to hold them."

Every culture establishes forms of "sanctity and meaning," and women's labor often lies at the heart of such efforts. Addams muses on "shifting pictures of woman's labor with which travel makes one familiar; the Indian women grinding grain outside of their huts as they sing praises to the sun and rain; a file of white-clad Moorish women whom I had once seen waiting their turn at a well in Tangiers; south Italian women kneeling in a row along the stream and beating their wet clothes against the smooth white stones; the milking, the gardening, the market-

ing in thousands of hamlets, which are such direct expressions of the solicitude and affection at the basis of all family life."[61] Something terrible
happens when solicitude and affection are denied their normal channels
of expression in and through culturally sanctioned, necessary activity
that fuses form and function. Such activity possesses an undeniable
charm—another favorite Addams word. But being shut up in tenements,
these women were denied their culturally shared expression.

Men who have all sorts of skills in metalworking and woodworking
likewise find themselves stupefied in factories. If they try to brighten
things up a bit, they may find themselves in trouble. Addams wrote, "I
recall an Italian who had decorated the doorposts of his tenement with
a beautiful pattern he had previously used in carving the reredos of a
Neapolitan church." His fate: eviction. A Bohemian man nearly killed
his little girl in a drunken stupor, then committed suicide. His wife was
put up for a week at Hull-House until something else could be
arranged. Addams reports: "One day [she] showed me a gold ring
which her husband had made for their betrothal. It exhibited the most
exquisite workmanship, and she said that although in the old country
he had been a goldsmith, in America he had for twenty years shoveled
coal in a furnace room of a large manufacturing plant; that whenever
she saw one of the 'restless fits' that preceded his drunken periods
'coming on,' if she could provide him with a bit of metal and persuade
him to stay at home and work at it, he was all right." Why hadn't she
been told? cries Addams. Perhaps that artistic ability could have found
an outlet, for "long-established occupation may form the very foundations of the moral life."

If to the dislocations of immigrant life one adds the terrible reality
America has not really faced—"our own race problem"—a picture
emerges of formidable challenges as well as broken hearts and unful-
filled promises. But here the newcomers to our shores might help America face its racial past and present "with courage and intelligence"—especially Mediterranean immigrants. How so? Because "they are less
conscious than the Anglo-Saxon of color distinctions. . . . They listened
with respect and enthusiasm to a scholarly address delivered by Professor DuBois at Hull-House on a Lincoln's birthday, with apparently no
consciousness of that race difference which color seems to accentuate
so absurdly." We proud Americans have a lot to learn, and even more
to live up to.[62] We can learn from many who have come here, yet pre-

serve the best of the old foundations. This was Addams's unshakable credo, and it runs spiritedly against that current that is so much of the American story of striving, overturning the old, shaking up the received, shunning the past and racing into the future because it is bound to be better than whatever was or is. Addams believed in progress, but she knew better. The great woman of Chicago was always the frightened child peering over the edge of the grave in Cedarville—and therein lies much of her greatness.

6

❧

WOMAN'S
REMEMBERING HEART

B Y 1910, THE YEAR HER ACKNOWLEDGED masterpiece and
her most successful book, *Twenty Years at Hull-House,* was published, Jane Addams was an internationally acclaimed figure. *Twenty
Years at Hull-House* has never gone out of print. Kudos for the book
flowed in from all quarters, from common persons, distinguished
scholars, and public figures alike. One Edward Burchard, who describes himself as having been a short-term resident at Hull-House
"nineteen years ago," writes that "you more than ... anyone else"
opened "my mind to the realities and significance and duties of human
relationships." Ellen Frost is especially appreciative of the discussion
of "Social Education" and wishes that it be read by "every college student and graduate." She continues: "Over and over I have been convinced of the truth of your conviction. Thanks for writing the book. It
gives me great strength and courage." Mary H. Swope, who also had
direct experience of Hull-House, writes: "I can't possibly tell you how
I love it. It was a great pleasure to be again at H.h. for which I am always a little homesick." Distinguished economist Richard T. Ely calls
it a "great work—stimulating and encouraging. You grow continually
and continuously as your work expands and enlarges and it seems to
me that you ought to take great satisfaction in your life—as your
friends do." People wrote Jane Addams of being moved to tears, of being touched profoundly, of having their lives changed. In 1910, Addams could not have anticipated the ugly turn American public life

would take with United States entry into World War I, just seven years in the future. It was during World War I that Jane Addams fell from public favor and endured censure and humiliation. Although these events left her deeply shaken, her years in the civic wilderness did not defeat her. She had great resources to draw upon. She was tough-minded and hopeful. She had never assumed that heaven could be brought down to earth. That human life might be somewhat less hellish, yes, that was possible. But the boulder inevitably comes crashing back down the hill. When it does, one takes up the eternal task of Sisyphus and rolls it uphill again.

As the storm clouds began to gather in Europe, Hull-House celebrated the twenty years during which it had made available to its neighbors what should, in Jane Addams's view, be routinely available to any and all citizens of a city, including bewildered newcomers: hospitality, education, art, legal assistance, English classes, courses in citizenship, places to debate social theories and the cutting issues of the day, household arts, cookery, even bathing. Add to that well-baby care and a kindergarten, the Hull-House theater, boys' and girls' clubs, the unions organized out of Hull-House, and the participation of Hull-House more generally in the political and civic life of Chicago, and one is left nearly breathless. When did the good lady stop? The answer is, never, or only very rarely.

We glean glimpses into her habits from the reminiscences of others. There was general concurrence that she worked like a "galley slave." Those closest to her struggled, usually in vain, to take care of her and to urge her to take care of herself. One of Hull-House's major supporters, Mrs. Joseph T. (Louise) Bowen, who had "raised and spent over $100,000 to pay the probation officers and maintain the detention home" of the Juvenile Court Committee, which had its origins at Hull-House, and who served as treasurer of Hull-House for over forty years, describes keeping a "watchful eye" on Jane Addams.

Several of her anecdotes[1] provide amusing insights into Addams's idiosyncrasies:

> Whenever she [Miss Addams] was disturbed or depressed she would move the furniture in all the rooms. . . . If there was no one to help her, she did it herself. Twice she fell off the tall stepladder, once breaking her arm. . . . It was quite customary to hear the resi-

dents at Hull-House say, "Miss Addams is low in her mind today. She is re-hanging all the pictures."

Miss Addams was very provoking at Christmas. While she loved pretty things, her passion for giving them away to others was so great that it was difficult to get her to keep anything. . . . White kid gloves were all the rage then—elbow length—and were very expensive. She always wore them because they made her look dressier, she said, and they made shaking hands with so many people more comfortable. She was always borrowing a pair of mine, so . . . I gave her a dozen pair. Several days later she . . . rather sheepishly asked me if I could lend her a pair of white gloves. She had given away the whole dozen.

Other telling observations on Addams's character come from a letter written by Gertrude Barnum, a Hull-House resident, to Mary Rozet Smith, Jane Addams's closest friend and companion, who was then abroad:[2]

She [Jane Addams] is very tired & has had bowell trouble added to lady-trouble these last few days—of course she did not let either deter her much from tearing about. She preached for the Methodists last Sunday, entertained the colored women of the National Council (Mrs. Booker Washington et al) yesterday and went later to Winnetka . . . she runs over to Mrs. Jones—around to Mrs. Fiellras . . . up to Mrs. Kenyons—off with Mrs. Haldeman down to inquiring strangers & in & out & around about to Italian Fiestas, forced marriages, rows between scabs & unions etc etc etc till my head spins & I sink exhausted while she poses to Mr. Linden & discusses the questions of the day with freshness & calmness that put the finishing touches to my amazement. . . . I wish you could think of some scheme that wd take Lady Jane east for a jaunt & then could meet you & you could come home together. You might know her eastern interests enough to plan something. She says she is not going to lecture at all in September & is going to rest but I don't believe anything but an organized jaunt away will accomplish the recuperation for her which she needs.

Despite Addams's idiosyncrasies, observers described her as a well-mannered, cheerful, reticent lady. Even her dearest acquaintances referred to her as Miss Addams, thirty years after her death. Historian Anne Firor Scott's 1958 unpublished account of her day-long meeting with Hull-House alums and residents—the distinguished Alice Hamilton, together with Margaret Hamilton and Clara Landsberg—is instructive. Scott notes: "The three all speak of 'Miss Addams' with respect—despite—in Alice Hamilton's case—30 years of intimate association. They were unanimous in their view of the greatness of the three principals: Jane Addams, Julia Lathrop, Florence Kelley." All three stress just how much was happening and that it was a "great time to be alive." Hamilton, who went on from Hull-House to a professorship at Harvard, confirms what many others had observed—that Jane Addams never let being tired stop her, and that she had the faculty for quick rest. "She could lie down and in one minute be sound asleep. She didn't take much thought of fatigue," notes Alice Hamilton, to which Margaret Hamilton adds: "She was truly plucky about her physical self." Alice Hamilton then recounts a trip to Europe. She and Addams were traveling together and "there were no sleepers. . . . She would sleep sitting up and disembark next morning ready to meet people, while I took to my bed, though I was a good deal younger." Hamilton also notes: "Women did so much more before they had the vote! It was the women who really were the reformers in Chicago. In those days, Miss Addams and Mrs. Bowen could always count on the Chicago women's clubs. . . . Nowadays those things are purely social."

Summarizing their experiences at Hull-House, the women describe it as "the least institutional place in the world" and not "the least bit feminist in atmosphere." They add that Addams "attracted men who came to work at Hull-House." The three contrasted this atmosphere with "the House on Henry St [the famous New York Settlement] which they felt had a decidedly feminist cast," presumably because it was more exclusively female. Scott concludes that all three were "unanimous in the view that Hull-House in their day was the most interesting place in the world." But they also note that the place called Hull-House of the present date—the late 1950s—is "not the same at all."[3]

Not the same at all. Why not? Presumably because of the bureaucratic cast the welfare state took in the post–New Deal era, an administrative mode that delivered services to clients rather than creating citizens. The early settlement world of friendships—and Jane Addams was always eloquent on the theme of the settlement and friendship—and the search for community it entailed no longer animated what had become social service work. Addams was adamant throughout her life that Hull-House should offer shelter from the storm and a new way of being in the world. It was a place of civic education, a spirited enterprise that served as a vehicle for the creation of community and the sustaining of identities. Indeed, the central role Hull-House played in generating identity is the hallmark of its mission.

A Self Realized Through Fellowship

Social commentator and historian Herbert Leibowitz is one of the few who have grasped Addams's understanding of identity and selfhood, perhaps because what she was up to cuts so powerfully against the contemporary mode of putting oneself first at all times. For Addams, it is in giving the self that one truly discovers oneself. The self requires social and cultural forms and channels through which to flow. Absent these, the self is buffeted, becoming so much flotsam and jetsam on the surging currents of social, political, and economic life. By establishing a framework within which enthusiasms are housed, one creates a cultural form that makes action in freedom possible. Leibowitz appreciates that Addams never embarked on a solo search "for self-fulfillment"; rather, she sought to underwrite a "social covenant that connects one man to another." He adds: "She caresses the word 'fellowship' as if it were an icon of the 'true democracy.'"[4]

There is a parable in *Twenty Years at Hull-House* that illustrates this idea. It is one that many commentators have found curious or have simply ignored, but it is key to understanding Addams's view of the self. This story—an anecdote from her childhood—was Addams's response to doubts and criticisms expressed by a leading member of the Chicago Women's Club about what was going on at Hull-House. The story may be curious, but it is not mysterious to those familiar with the Christian understanding of a kenotic or "emptying" self. Had not the Master taught that those who lose themselves for His sake would truly find themselves? Here, then, is what I call the Story of the Large Toad Who Swallowed the Small Toad.[5]

> When she was a little girl playing in her mother's garden, she one
> day discovered a small toad who seemed to her very forlorn and

lonely, although she did not in the least know how to comfort him, she reluctantly left him to his fate; later in the day, quite at the other end of the garden, she found a large toad, also apparently without family and friends. With heart full of tender sympathy, she took a stick and by exercising infinite patience and some skill, she finally pushed the little toad through the entire length of the garden into the company of the big toad, when, to her surprise, the toad opened his mouth and swallowed the little one. The moral of the tale was clearly applied to people who lived "where they did not naturally belong," although I protested that was exactly what we wanted—*to be swallowed and digested, to disappear into the bulk of the people.*

Twenty years later I am willing to testify that something of the sort does take place after years of identification with an industrial community. [The emphasis is mine.]

Leibowitz, who also finds this story instructive, comments:[6]

What begins as a cautionary lesson about the foolish innocence of do-gooders who attempt to alleviate the isolation of the unfortunate turns into a hymn to caring for those in need. Because in the brutal world the strong do swallow the weak, and predatory social and economic acts are not rare, the club member concludes that she was meddling, that her "tender sympathy" was ineffectual and damaging, but Addams rebuts this view. Identification, as with the early Christians, does not erase identity. The disappearing self is compensated for by the enhanced sense of community and a "constant revelation." The glib commonplace of Social Darwinism is upended: The strong, in a form of communion, feed the weak.

The parable of the small toad is not a tale of self-abnegation or dour self-sacrifice. To the contrary, it reflects a form of care for the self. Addams was insistent that the help she received from her neighbors who visited at Hull-House far outweighed the help she gave them. Fellowship is both the end sought and the means to get there. The mutual process of interpretation that takes place at Hull-House challenges and quickens human sympathies and is a powerful form of social learning. Addams and her remarkable generation of college-educated women were not "career women" as we understand the idea today, but rather, women with a vocation. They lived out a version of strength through solidarity in community. They were maternal, although many—indeed, most in the first generation of Hull-House residents—did not have children of their own.

Addams's rare ability to convey all of this is a tribute to the forthrightness and directness of her style. She knew that the intellect could be stirred through vivid example. There is no cure for the human condition, but there is a cure for a sense of purposelessness, and it lies in the forging of purposeful lives in and through community. One doesn't use community for self-seeking purposes. One participates and in fellowship and friendship finds the self relocated. Appropriately, Addams disappears into the story of Hull-House in her autobiography. The relational identity she highlights is revealed only through the experiences of mutuality in which the self participates. The intimate friendships forged by the residents, and the special friendships within the wider circle, the beckoning and welcoming of others in, the famous Hull-House open door—these are the heart of the matter.

Hospitality may be strained to the breaking point if one is called upon to provide safe haven for those the world deems heretics or pariahs and realizes that one courts opprobrium in doing so; but this, too, is a part of the tradition of hospitality Addams embraced. Do not forget the one in the effort to aid the many. Do not reduce human beings to abstract categories. Do not self-centeredly rush to the excitement of violence and confrontation in the mistaken assumption that this exhibits greater courage than do forbearance and the tedious negotiations of democratic politics, including the often hard-to-swallow pill of compromise. As Leibowitz puts it, noting the striking "absence of bellicosity" in her masterwork: "Addams avoids three errors radicals often commit: She does not talk about people, her neighbors or her adversaries, in reifying abstractions like 'the masses' or 'the bosses' (them and us); she never invokes history as a force inevitably taking her side; and she does not allow her compassion for the injuries of children or for pinched and desperate breadwinners to romanticize the poor."[7]

Addams understood that social change destroys even as it generates; that every new technology leaves people behind; that the fragile threads of intergenerationality are easily and often cruelly and carelessly broken. One of her favorite essayists, Matthew Arnold, influenced her thinking in this matter. In his *Culture and Anarchy,* Arnold asserts that language has the power to wound and to kill spirits. Violent deeds often follow from violent words. He takes to task what he calls "Jacobinism," with "its fierce hatred of the past and of those whom it makes liable for the sins of the past." The work of culture, in contrast, "resists this tendency" through the keen awareness that we are all guilty of our culture's sins, in one way or another, and that "fierce hatred" of what has gone before undermines the living by cutting them off from the dead.[8] To consistently live with such a recognition, without turning morbid, is no small feat.

What Women Do; What Women Represent

A theme Addams evoked repeatedly was that of women's friendships and what she called "woman's remembering heart." Her perspective offers a fundamental challenge to several ways of seeing the world that are indebted to the Western philosophic tradition. For example, two conceptual categories inherited from classical antiquity are necessity, on the one hand, and freedom, on the other. The world of necessity is closely related to nature and is a sphere in which things are determined; hence, the realm of necessity lacks authentic freedom and the ability to act, argued a number of great classical philosophers. Plants and animals belong in this realm; but so, too, do women, given their role in procreation. The world of culture, by contrast, is deemed man's creation, the result of free human action—*free* here meaning action that is not predetermined by an external force such as the inexorable laws of nature. And it is *man*—not in the generic sense of human but in the quite specific biological sense—that the Greek thinkers had in mind. The realm of necessity, of the household, served as a precondition for the realm of freedom: some (male citizen-soldiers) were freed to act, so to speak, by others' provision of daily necessities (food, clothing, shelter, harvest, raising children). Because these necessary matters ranked lower in the overall scheme of things, they were taken care of by the human beings who ranked lower in the overall scheme of things—in other words, by women, servants, slaves, and laborers of many kinds.

Politics was the domain of free speech and action par excellence. In practice, this meant the exclusion of women from the political life of the ancient city and from political discourse as well. This exclusion was essential, not accidental, to accounts of political action as these evolved within Western political theory. Plato denigrated the household and Aristotle downgraded it, although he conceded that the male-female relationship in a household was an ethical relationship of sorts.[9] This schism is implicit throughout much of the subsequent history of Western political thought, even among a number of feminist thinkers.[10] Jane Addams would have found such thinking strange. For her, the realm of necessity is not in opposition to civic life but is an essential feature of it. The sources that supported her in this conviction included Christian social thought that had, from its inception, challenged the classical devaluation of necessity and established new ideals and principles to guide human beings over the course of their lives on earthly pilgrimage. This transformation brought women and another group previously excluded from the ancient city, the poor, within the boundaries of the city newly understood.[11] In assuming the dignity of all as a fundamental belief, it became possible to lift the ostensibly lesser realm of necessity to an importance previously reserved for the sphere of freedom. Addams rejected any presumed split between the worlds of necessity and freedom. In her life and thought she moved to redeem the joys and vexations of everyday life and its values and purposes, its place in helping us become human.[12]

Addams observed that women's lives revolved around responsibility, care, and obligation. These emphases were, in a sense, thrust on them. She made it clear that this fact should not be taken as evidence of women's moral superiority but should be seen instead as a moral necessity that can and often has served as a source of female power and authority. The imperatives of this realm must be extended more generally. That is the rock-bottom ground of her civic philosophy and her social feminism.

Bread-Givers and the City

In Addams's junior oration at Rockford Seminary, she had enjoined women to be bread-givers in an expanded sense. Women do not wish to be men, she argued, but they do desire to rise to new and daunting challenges. What women should bring to the public world is the needs, concerns, and possibilities of concrete, local, specific places. In so doing, she believed they would tap into common, even universal imperatives and concerns. There is genuine vitality and dignity in this world of so-called necessity with which women are associated. The challenge was to embrace these cherished norms and traditions in a broader sense but not to reinforce their devaluation in favor of the world of political action. After all, the world of women was the crucible in which ordinary, sustaining human relations were forged throughout history and remembered in songs, stories, and myths.

So housekeeping was a sphere of action, not an isolated, private haven. Addams aimed to reclaim this world by expanding its boundaries and by bringing it to politics. Politics, in turn, would be compelled to respond. Addams believed that the shared values of centuries of domestic tradition lay behind her approach. The world of women was, for her, a dense concoction of imperatives, yearnings, reflections, actions, joys, tragedies, laughter, tears—a complex way of knowing and being in the world. These she would bring to bear on a public, political world that seemed to place little value on life.[13] In viewing human beings through the prism of a many-layered, complex social world, Addams helped point the way toward an ideal of human solidarity without uniformity, an ideal that underwrites cooperation and yet encompasses, rather than quashing, dissent. A Christian Social Gospel message was central to this task; most of Western political theory was not. There was, however, a nascent literature in the field of anthropology that gave Jane Addams important insights and reinforced her convictions about the importance of women's roles.

Anthropology and Cultural Memory

In 1915, Otis Tufts Mason, then curator of the Department of Ethnology in the United States National Museum, published *Woman's Share in Primitive Culture.* This text provided scholarly confirmation of views that Jane Addams already held about the centrality of women's role in the creation and maintenance of culture. Mason's book appeared in 1915; although Addams had been expounding views consistent with Mason's well before that date, his book bolstered her convictions. The overriding theme limned by Mason is that women did not languish in the backwater as men charged forth to create culture and make history; rather, if one looks at the world of primitive culture (by which he means cultures prior to written languages and with a tribal structure of one sort or another), one finds women serving as food bringers, weavers, skin dressers, potters, beasts of burden, jacks-of-all-trades, artists, linguists, founders of society, and patrons of religion. The "founders of society" category is especially important in light of the fact that the dominant Western political tradition features only male founders of polities. Mason, however, gestures toward female foundings. He believes there is substantial anthropological and paleontological evidence that women were the creators of settled social life. This thesis belied then-ascendant social Darwinism, with its accounts of societal origins in a brutal survival of the fittest.

When Mason sees women pass before him, he sees not "an abject creature . . . the brutalized slave of man," but a creature whose ability to do almost everything helped to create a "higher law of culture . . . the law of co-ordination and co-operation."[14] Women were inventors. Women domesticated animals. Women were the cultural carriers of weaving and of textiles in general—and this is a vital dimension of civilization. Women harvested what nature offered and invented orderly cultivation. They were the "first ceramic artisans and developed all the techniques, the forms, and the uses of pottery."[15] Women were the first to "conceive the idea of shelter for herself and helpless infant." Women invented dyes and the arts of decoration; women linked necessity—protecting the body—to beauty. Lastly, the mother-child pair was the first linguistic unity.[16]

Because motherhood requires stability, women were the primary agents of stable matrimony—an enormous advance for civilization and for women themselves. Women were prophetesses and mourners. They helped create religion. Surely, Mason argues, the progress of civilization and of "intellectuality" should not be "opposed to childbearing." Indeed, if such a sentiment becomes prevalent, a society is doomed. For both pedagogy and the body politic had their origins in female-generated activity.

This is a sharp alternative to accounts of human origins that stress the hunt, including, as I have already noted, the heady cruelties of social Darwinism with its mapping of "nature red in tooth and claw" onto human social life.[17] Although Addams was an evolutionist and familiar with Darwin's account of competition within and between species, she drew her conclusions instead from sources that, like Mason's book, advocated the view that the primordial tasks of women were essential creations of culture. Not only was she an opponent of social Darwinism in her own day; her views also place her in a tradition of thought that fell into disrepute with the demise of the social feminism she advocated and the triumph of an individualist version of feminism in the past quarter century.[18]

What Addams seems to have glimpsed is a form of power that doesn't have as its means violence and doesn't have as its end total control and command. She had been searching, ever since her "Cassandra" speech to the graduating class at Rockford Seminary, for that ever-elusive female authority, the right and the power not only to speak but also to act.[19] She confronted a conundrum: that women have been both powerful and powerless. But it seemed that—at least, for much of history—the forms of power that women wielded and the areas of human life in which they had their say did not grant women the right to speak afforded to men, which flowed to men by virtue of the form of power they exercised and the arenas over which they had effective control. Certainly women have not been uniformly and universally downtrodden, demeaned, infantilized, and coerced. Women have not, however, been afforded the authority of men. The new woman of Addams's age was well advised to seek the source of authority in new versions of women's historic strengths. For, just as Addams had recognized that "there is power in men," so power is to be found in women's history.

Every culture holds an image of a body politic. What Addams insists upon is that the female body—most important, the maternal female body—is the central image of social generativity and fecundity. Clearly, one need not be a mother in the biological sense—although she found this the most vital of all human activities—in order to locate oneself within this image. This body politic is not the classical notion of a kingdom or king's domain. It is, instead, a vision that locates "familied contexts" and "communities of everyday belief and action that regenerate political education without subordinating people."[20] Could Chicago be that sort of body politic, with its stockyards, sweatshops, and tenements? There was a fighting chance, if woman-power and authority as a civic ideal available to all came to prevail.

Municipal Housekeeping, Whose Time Has Come

In 1903, a bill was introduced in the Michigan legislature that provided for the electrocution of infants with mental infirmities—no doubt inspired by the eugenics craze that was then sweeping the United States.[21] Electrocution was quick and didn't involve suffering, or such was the claim. By extension, what better way to rid society of "imbeciles" than to do it quickly and tidily at birth?[22] For reaction to this proposed piece of legislation, prominent persons were polled, Jane Addams among them. She is quoted as saying: "The suggestion is horrible. It is not in line with the march of civilization nor with the principles of humanity. The Spartans destroyed children physically infirm. Are we to go back to the days of Sparta? Feeble-minded children are one of the cares of a community. It is our duty to care for them. Such a bill surely cannot be passed in this country of enlightenment."[23] Addams surely believed that women would be less likely to promote such a policy than men. Why? Were women morally superior? No, not that, but women, with their hands-on primary responsibilities for children, before and after birth, could not treat "imbeciles" as a generic category the world is best rid of or so Addams believed. Addams tells story after story of mothers devoted to their "feeble-minded" offspring. It is clear, at times, that she has some reservations about the toll this takes on the poor women and their families. But the answer is not to destroy those with special needs, it is for the community to pitch in to help. Given her commitment to make the world less violent and cruel, the "feeble-minded" and "mentally deficient" (these words were standard usage in her day, and by no means considered epithets) must come under a capacious civic and ethical umbrella. That is part of municipal housekeeping.

In a commentary on "The Home and the Special Child," Addams indicates her support for, but caution about, experts making judgments about the needs of "special children"—a point that had been argued by the previous speaker on a panel on which she sat. Addams asserts: "It is difficult for a parent to make a clear judgment in regard to his own child, especially in respect to the child's mental or moral capacities. But, if parental affection clouds the power of diagnosis, at the same time, after the diagnosis has been made by the trained mind, parental affection enormously increases the power of devotion which is necessary to carry out the regimen which the trained mind has laid down."[24]

Bowing toward the trained expert without stripping parents (and the mother is central here) of their authority in relation to their child, Addams notes that in going through a socially sanctioned process of child-study and diagnosis, the parent realizes the child is "not an exception" and loses "his peculiar sensitiveness in regard to his child." Furthermore, "the reaction of this change of attitude upon the entire family is something astounding." She then links this process to one of her standard briefs against self-pity, the notion that one is "so isolated," that one (or one's child) is "an exception."25 Parents thus convinced go through a process like this:

> You think you have a child unlike other children; you are anxious that your neighbor shall not find it out; it places you and the normal children in the family in a curious relation to the rest of the community; but if you find out that there are many other such children in your city and in other cities thruout the United States, and that a whole concourse of people are studying to help these children, considering them not at all queer and outrageous, but simply a type of child which occurs from time to time and which can be enormously helped, you come out of that peculiarly sensitive attitude and the whole family is lifted with you into a surprising degree of hopefulness and normality.

She proceeds with a number of anecdotal tales from her own experience that illustrate the extraordinary difference it makes when having a "special child" becomes ordinary, "simply a type of child which occurs from time to time." Only when mothers are freed from a "sense of isolation," when they discover that "there were many other people who had children of that sort who were not thereby disgraced," when "the community recognized such children and provided for them," and needed the mother's cooperation in this—then and only then can that which is broken be somewhat repaired.26 Jane Addams didn't win this battle; the era of massive institutionalization was upon the country. But she helped create what might be called a countertradition, another way of doing and thinking, which one day bore fruit. In lecture after lecture, newspaper article after newspaper article, interview after interview, she stressed the theme of municipal housekeeping as a type of applied morals (her characterization) and as a mode of analysis.

The phrase *municipal* (or *civic*) *housekeeping* is easily misunderstood and dismissed: it seems to imply that politics can be replaced by house-keeping on a grand scale. No doubt some social reformers had precisely that in mind, but Addams was not so naïve. Indeed, she taxed the doctrinaire socialists of her day for the ideological naïveté they exhibited concerning the anticipated glories of the socialist future. She recalled how one ardent socialist during the course of the weekly Hull-House drawing-room discussions held under the auspices of "The Working People's Social Science Club" had declared that "socialism will cure the toothache." A second interlocutor, not to be outdone, upped the ante, insisting "that when every child's teeth were systematically cared for from the beginning, toothache would disappear from the face of the earth."[27]

Even as she deplored fanaticism and the notion that nothing is more important than the right theory, she opposed politics as violence and resolutely refused to glamorize social unrest. Episodes like citywide strikes may be exciting to some, but they turn a town into "two cheering sides" as if one were a spectator at a sporting event. Fair-mindedness goes down the drain. Her quest for balance and for a politics that best fits the quotidian norm a social democracy should embody, takes expression frequently as a determination to *mitigate*. She and Hull-House and similar settlements would mitigate a situation. We rarely use the term nowadays in this way, but she has in mind to make milder and more gentle; to render anger and hatred less fierce and violent; to relax the violence of one's action; to alleviate physical or mental pain; to lighten the burden of an evil of any kind; to reduce severity; to moderate to a bearable degree.

The politics of a socialized democracy was concerned with precisely this kind of mitigation. Addams understood the importance of politics: hence the key role she played in seconding the nomination of Theodore Roosevelt as the candidate of the Progressive Party for president in 1912. She made hundreds of speeches in behalf of her candidate, stumping to the point of physical breakdown. She appreciated that electoral politics was a central feature of American life. But why should something as basic to the well-being of a city as garbage collection be a matter of political influence, deal-making, and contestation?

City Housekeeping As Experimentation

Why not be experimental, for what is a settlement if not "an experimental effort to aid in the solution of the social and industrial problems which are engendered by the modern conditions of life in a great city," she had written in *Twenty Years at Hull-House*.[28] Municipal housekeeping was an experiment. Look at the situation closely. Study it. What do you see? You cannot help but observe that most of the departments in a modern city "can be traced to woman's traditional activity."[29] Two points must be made. The first is that it makes no sense to disallow women to vote on matters that so directly concern them. The second is that in light of their traditional activities, women possess the insights and expert (if informal) knowledge needed by cities in order to deal with the manifold problems that have emerged in the overcrowded immigrant city: unsanitary housing, poisonous sewage, contaminated water, infant mortality at alarming rates, the spread of contagion, adulterated food, impure milk, smoke-laden air, ill-ventilated factories, dangerous occupations, juvenile crime, unwholesome crowding, prostitution, and drunkenness. In times long past, when the city was a citadel, it may have made sense that "those who bore arms" were the only group "fully enfranchised." Addams writes: "There was a certain logic in giving the franchise only to grown men when the existence and stability of the city depended upon their defense, and when the ultimate value of the elector could be reduced to his ability to perform military duty."

But cities no longer settle their claims by force of arms. Instead, the city depends upon "enlarged housekeeping." No "predatory instinct" serves us here, nor does "brute strength"—not when one is dealing with "delicate matters of human growth and welfare." Is it not possible that the city has failed to keep house properly "partly because women, the traditional housekeepers, have not been consulted as to its multiform activities?" Addams stresses that "ability to carry arms has nothing to do with the health department maintained by the city which provides that children are vaccinated, that contagious diseases are isolated and placarded, that the spread of tuberculosis is curbed, that the water is free from typhoid infection."[30] Addams argues for a new civic humanitarianism in which women not only can but must participate:

Because all these things have traditionally been in the hands of women, if they take no part in it now they are not only missing the education which the natural participation in civic life would bring to them, but they are losing what they have always had. From the beginning of tribal life they have been held responsible for the health of the community, a function which is now represented by the health department; from the days of the cave dwellers so far as the home was clean and wholesome it was due to their efforts, which are now represented by the bureau of tenement house inspection; from the period of the primitive village the only public sweeping which was performed was what they undertook in their divers dooryards, that which is now represented by the bureau of street cleaning.

Simple logic and the aspiration to political education all combine to urge upon women and all others municipal housekeeping. Addams speculates on two possible effects if women get the municipal ballot. The first is an "opportunity to fulfill their old duties and obligations with the safeguard and the consideration which the ballot alone can secure for them under the changed conditions and, secondly, the education which participation in actual affairs always brings." She continues: "As we believe that woman has no right to allow the things to drop away from her that really belong to her, so we contend that ability to perform an obligation comes very largely in proportion as that obligation is conscientiously assumed."[31]

Jane Addams's argument, straightforward in its assessment of the problems and a way to meet them head on, is also subtle in its recognition that much of woman's political innocence, which appears as moral goodness, derives from the fact that women haven't had the opportunity or the power to do many of the things—including the horrible and dubious things—that men, who have had both power and opportunity, have done. So if one could "forecast the career of woman, the citizen," it is that she, too, must "bear her share of civic responsibility not because she clamors for her rights, but because she is essential to the normal development of the city of the future."

To an extraordinary degree, Chicago's women had already rolled up their sleeves and tackled the host of problems Jane Addams enumerates. She was intertwined from the beginning of Hull-House—indeed, even before its beginning—with networks of powerful, influential, and civically engaged women. They provided financial backing. They lobbied powerful men—in many cases, their own husbands. They went public with their concerns. They worked indefatigably. This was volunteer activity, not only because many of the women were well-to-do but because they were responding to a deeply ingrained call to service. But they were frustrated by the limits they encountered repeatedly, and were no doubt pained as well as chagrined by the fact that they were not allowed to vote even in municipal elections. Typically, Addams ties the municipal ballot for women to a very practical set of concerns. But she goes on to link woman suffrage as a general proposition to the insistence that women must discharge their civic duty, which they cannot do while separated from the ballot.

In a pamphlet entitled "Why Women Should Vote," penned in 1915, Addams charges contemporary women with failing to "discharge their duties to their households properly simply because they do not perceive that as society grows more complicated it is necessary that woman shall extend her sense of responsibility to many things outside of her own home if she would continue to preserve the home in its entirety."[32] Life in a crowded city quarter affords the meticulous housekeeper no sanctum sanctorum. She may scrub day and night; dust around the clock; close the blinds and shutters (assuming she has windows and can occasionally see sunlight); but the meat she puts on the table may nonetheless be tainted, the drinking water surging with bacteria, and the winter overcoats and cloaks bearing contagions from the sweatshops. Addams educates women who represent many languages and traditions but who share a common concern for the well-being of their children, to understand in what that well-being now consists.[33]

> In a crowded city quarter . . . if the street is not cleaned by the city authorities—no amount of private sweeping will keep the tenement free from grime; if the garbage is not properly collected and destroyed a tenement house mother may see her children sicken and die of diseases from which she alone is powerless to shield them, although her tenderness and devotion are unbounded. She cannot even secure untainted meat for her household, she cannot provide fresh fruit, unless meat has been inspected by city officials, and the decayed fruit, which is so often placed upon sale in the tenement

districts, has been destroyed in the interests of public health. In short, if woman would keep on with her old business of caring for her house and rearing her children she will have to have some conscience in regard to public affairs lying quite outside of her immediate household. The individual conscience and devotion are no longer effective.

Addams illustrates this point with a parable from chapter XIII of *Twenty Years at Hull-House* that I call the Story of the Self-Sacrificing Mother's Spotless House, All in Vain.[34] Addams begins by recalling the typhoid fever epidemic of 1902, in which the 19th ward, "although containing but one thirty-sixth of the population of the city, registered one sixth of the total number of deaths." Hull-House residents had "made an investigation of the methods of plumbing in the houses adjacent to conspicuous groups of fever cases." She continues:

> They discovered among the people who had been exposed to the infection, a widow who had lived in the ward for a number of years, in a comfortable little house of her own. Although the Italian immigrants were closing in all round her, she was not willing to sell her property and to move away until she had finished the education of her children. In the meantime she held herself quite aloof from her Italian neighbors and could never be drawn into any of the public efforts to secure a better code of tenement-house sanitation. Her two daughters were sent to an eastern college. One June when one of them had graduated and the other still had two years before she took her degree, they came to the spotless little house and to their self-sacrificing mother for the summer holiday. They both fell ill with typhoid fever and one daughter died because the mother's utmost efforts could not keep the infection out of her own house. The entire disaster affords, perhaps, a fair illustration of the futility of the individual conscience which would isolate a family from the rest of the community and its interests.

Addams may be a bit rough on the self-sacrificing mother here, but she has a point to make, so she permits herself some heavy-handedness. Participation in municipal housekeeping aimed at helping to keep everyone's children safe is the best shot at protecting your own children. You can bar the door, but germs do not knock before they enter. Don't turn your back on housewifely duties, Addams argues, but extend their purview. You are in part responsible for the condition of the streets, the food, the drinking water, even the schools. You can lobby for playgrounds or watch kids harm themselves or even run afoul of the law through playing in busy city streets or train yards.

Jane Addams knew that much of the work of culture lay in the creation of the boundaries that make free activities possible. But when those boundaries constrict and strangle, when they fairly asphyxiate the patient, it is time to take decisive action. Much of the activity of Hull-House over the years involved pushing boundaries to include people who had been excluded, as well as extending boundaries that were too restrictive in other ways.[35] "Home extension," some have called it.[36] Optimistically, Addams believed that both the family claim and the social claim would be ennobled in this dynamic process; that neither need lose. As she notes in her biography of her friend, Hull-House resident Julia Lathrop[37] (a distinguished figure in her own right):

> Even in the very first years of Hull-House we began to discover that our activities were gradually extending from the settlement to a participation in city and national undertakings. We found that our neighborhood playground, the very first in Chicago, was not secure until it became part of a system covering the whole city; better housing was dependent upon a good tenement house code for which we had worked against many obstacles through the City Homes Association.

The Garbage Wars

The lag in garbage removal in the 19th ward typified the many local problems caused by a lack of political responsiveness to serious public issues. In many cases this lack of responsiveness was due to extensive corruption, or "boodling," which lined the pockets of the few but did not clean the streets for the many. One of the more remarkable early Hull-House stories is that of how Miss Jane Addams, in 1894, became the first woman appointed Sanitary Inspector of the 19th ward. The problem of garbage here was severe. Sidewalks, where they existed, were buried under many feet of compacted refuse. Immigrant families were surrounded by its stench, and vermin were their ever-present companions.

Those in the neighborhood who insisted that garbage was each family's own business assumed that so long as each household disposed of its garbage, the applicable ethical code—that of the household—had been fulfilled. But this assumption had created a problem for the community at large. Activities in the immigrants' world were severely circumscribed according to gender. There were male- and female-defined activities and spheres of movement, with the woman's sphere being *inside* the home (despite the numbers of young girls, unmarried women, widows, and deserted, divorced, and single mothers compelled to work outside the home), and the man's, *outside* the home. Garbage removal seemed far too base a task for men to take seriously—it was an extension of the household. Because no single household could possibly deal with the mountains of accumulating garbage, a civic ethic had to be brought to bear. City leaders had to be made to see that garbage collection was too crucial a municipal function to dole out to "boodlers." It was not so much a matter of salting the city apparatus with social reformers as it was working to ensure that those who took on civic tasks—even chores as humble yet necessary as garbage collection—realized their importance to the whole, and saw their efforts as a vital part of the wider challenge to make the city more livable and more beautiful.

Addams's appointment as a sanitation inspector came only after a protracted battle between Hull-House and Alderman Johnny Powers, a famous and popular "boodler" who delivered turkeys at Thanksgiving time but who was indifferent to the garbage problem despite the mounting evidence of disease and the much-higher-than-average death rates, including infant mortality, in the 19th ward. With some backing from prominent businessmen, Hull-House launched a campaign to unseat Powers and to bring in a reform candidate (who presumably would not reward a Powers loyalist with the garbage inspector appointment). Addams and her colleagues then submitted a bid to the city council in the hope of being awarded the garbage collection contract. In the first round, Hull-House's bid was thrown out. But the effort generated a flurry of citywide publicity: the Hull-House ladies versus the flashy, smooth, and popular Mr. Powers. The upshot was that the mayor, "Major George Swift, a reform-minded Republican," decided to "appoint her [Addams] garbage inspector for the 19th ward—the first woman to hold the $1,000 a year job."[38]

So Addams and another Hull-House resident began the odorous and onerous task of traipsing along after garbage collection teams to make certain that the task was completed to their satisfaction. The Chicago newspapers made much of this, but Addams's own telling of the tale in *Twenty Years at Hull-House* is circumspect (if reminiscent of Charles Dickens in its detail). One sees the "huge wooden garbage boxes" that little children played on and in; the "decayed fruit and vegetables discarded by Italian and Greek fruit peddlers"; the "residuum left over from the piles of filthy rags which were fished out of the city dumps and brought to the homes of the rag pickers for further sorting and washing." Many living in the neighborhood had become accustomed to the foul smells, and those living farther away were unaware of the increasingly dangerous situation. For more than three years prior to Addams's appointment, the Hull-House residents had complained of these conditions. They had encouraged their neighbors to join them in the effort to obtain redress. But only slight modifications had occurred, and the conditions "remained intolerable."

Addams tells us that by her fourth summer at Hull-House she was "absolutely desperate" because her "delicate little nephew for whom I was a guardian, could not be with me at Hull-House at all unless the sickening odors were reduced. I may well be ashamed that other delicate children who were torn from their families, not into boarding school but into eternity, had not long before driven me into effective action. Under the direction of the first man who came as a resident to Hull-House we began a systematic investigation of the city system of garbage collection."[39] The Hull-House Women's Club was drummed into service, with twelve Irish American clubwomen working to investigate conditions in the alleys. At the end of their investigation, the women reported to the health department all of the violations they had observed and recorded : a total of 1,037. One can well imagine the effect this veritable mountain of disastrous information had on the health department chief, accompanied as it was by accusations of city inaction in the face of mounting death rates, especially among children, in the 19th ward.

Addams praises the clubwomen who "had finished a long day's work of washing or ironing followed by the cooking of a hot supper" and for whom "it would have been much easier to sit on her doorstep during a summer evening than to go up and down ill-kept alleys and get into trouble with her neighbors over the condition of the garbage boxes. It required both civic enterprise and moral conviction to be willing to do this three evenings a week during the hottest and most uncomfortable months of the year." But they had persisted. It was "in cheer des peration" at the lack of improvement that she had put in her bid for the garbage removal contract in the 19th ward. Having secured the contract, she and Amanda Johnson dutifully followed the garbage wagons and insisted that the number of wagons be increased to get the job done. They were indefatigable. Landlords were taken to court for not providing proper garbage receptacles. Addams and Johnson arranged for the removal of dead animals whose rotting carcasses had befouled the streets and alleys. And then comes what Jane Addams calls "our greatest achievement"—and it takes a person with a secure sense of identity and a sense of humor to crown herself in this way— "the discovery of a pavement eighteen inches under the surface of a narrow street."

Having uncovered this sign of previous civilization, they "triumphantly discovered a record of its existence in the city archives."[40] She continues:

> The Italians living on the street were much interested but displayed little astonishment, perhaps because they were accustomed to see buried cities exhumed. This pavement became the *casus belli* between myself and the street commissioner when I insisted that its restoration belonged to him, after I had removed the first eight inches of garbage. The matter was finally settled by the mayor himself, who permitted me to drive him to the entrance of the street in what the children called my "garbage phaeton" and who took my side of the controversy.

There was a price to pay for this victory in the garbage wars. Jane Addams had used up some of her political capital. Many "of the foreign-born women of the ward were much shocked by this abrupt departure into the ways of men, and it took a great deal of explanation to convey the idea even remotely that if it were a womanly task to go about in tenement houses in order to nurse the sick, it might be quite as womanly to go through the same district in order to prevent the breeding of so-called 'filth diseases.' While some of the women enthusiastically approved the slowly changing conditions and saw that their housewifely duties logically extended to the adjacent alleys and streets, they yet were quite certain that 'it was not a lady's job.'"[41] This demonstrates clearly that much of the task of municipal housekeeping consisted in convincing women that the clearing away of refuse was an entirely legitimate extension of their range of concerns and responsibilities. The effort not only revealed sidewalks previously buried under compacted refuse but also led to a new report on death rates in the city wards. Following Jane Addams's appointment as sanitation inspector, the 19th ward death rate dropped from third highest among Chicago wards to seventh. Quite literally, garbage removal was a matter of life and death.

Addams fought for further improvements in municipal housekeeping in the 19th ward until the day she died. Although the range of her activities broadened until it could extend no further, she claimed steadfastly that, in one way or another, all of these multiple imperatives and activities were linked. The civic identity she fashioned out of these early years of civic housekeeping was sturdy and up to the task; the interventions of Hull-House were dramatic, and they saved untold numbers of lives in the 19th ward and elsewhere. Typhoid fever epidemics, which arose because sewage water had entered the drinking water supply, were targeted in the best scientific fashion. A bacteriological study undertaken by Hull-House resident and pioneer epidemiologist Alice Hamilton provided the necessary scientific evidence for Hull-House's proposed reforms in health and sanitation by showing that flies breeding in the befouled plumbing could spread infection. But it took a trial before the civic service board to get things moving in the Sanitary Bureau. Hull-House lost subscribers in all the furor over typhoid and garbage, but sanitary conditions improved. Many Hull-House investigations were merged with those of other settlements. By 1920 there were at least 500 settlements, and this added to the clout of each in its own backyard.

A settlement is always led, Addams insisted, from the concrete to the more abstract. You must try to see the relation of the small thing to the whole. She illustrates this point with a story about the tailors' union that met at Hull-House, which once sought the help of the residents there in "tagging the various parts of a man's coat in such wise as to show the money paid to the people who had made it." By the time one added the costs of "salesmen, commercial travelers, rent and management" to those of cutting, buttonholing, finishing, and other aspects of the job, the poor "tagged coat was finally left hanging limply in a closet as if discouraged by the attempt." But this desire to "know the relation" of one's "own labor to the whole is not only legitimate but must form the basis of any intelligent action" for improvement. You must start with the particular, even though you can't end there.

The Excellent Becomes the Permanent

A visitor to Hull-House between 1890 and 1910 might have found Jane Addams following a garbage collector through refuse in the morning; leading a discussion of George Eliot in the afternoon; meeting with backers or with those angered by something she had said or that Hull-House had done; introducing newcomers to Hull-House in moments snatched away from other activities; participating in a rousing discussion of the Working Man's Social Science Club in the evening; working on correspondence and financial matters well into the night; and then rousted out of bed the next day by a crisis involving a child in trouble, a police roundup of suspected anarchists, or some other event. Her work was never done.

The way in which Addams negotiated her own solution to the family claim and the social claim meant that those two claims continued to bear down upon her in full force. She was intimately involved with her own family until her death. She was also the center of a huge extended family of sisters—as the Hull-House residents often described themselves—and in active contact with many of them after they left Hull-House for other opportunities.[42] Given Addams's grueling daily schedule, it is amazing that she kept such a vast and detailed correspondence churning along—not just with Mary Rozet Smith when they were apart but also with many others. I estimate that the letter Addams wrote to Mary Smith on her thirty-fifth birthday (September 4, 1895), even if she were writing quickly, would have taken at least forty-five minutes; and many of the surviving letters she wrote to Smith are of the same length. They are filled with details about what was going on at Hull-

House and are not what we would call personal much of the time. For Hull-House was Addams's life.[43]

The extension of the family claim into the social claim incorporated, at least in Jane Addams's case, the persons with whom she was in intimate contact and with whom she lived out many aspects of her life on a daily basis. What comes through clearly is not that Addams replaced her family of origin with a substitute but that she enlarged the circle of those who could claim her, and whom, in turn, she could claim, in a family way. When Mary Rozet Smith died, in February 1934, letters of condolence poured in from family, friends, and admirers expressing sympathy for Addams's loss of a "dear and wonderful friend" and on the "beautiful friendship" the two had shared.[44] In a letter to Smith dated May 31, 1899, Addams had described their friendship as a bond of "unchanging affection."

How far could such bonds extend? For Addams, the intimate connection of the individual to the many knew no limits. Addams's experiments with life helped focus the energies of an era and brought them to bear in a creative endeavor that opened channels of possibility for countless others. She was the apostle of a healing domesticity in which the strong maternal image sustains and enables instead of smothering or constraining. She was a student of history and was therefore aware of the creative possibilities different epochs had afforded for enlarged female identities and communities. This all cuts much deeper than our dry notion of a role model. Addams sought to develop new ways of being that underwrote forms of autonomy *within* relationships, not in opposition to them.[45]

Her recognition of the importance of human relationships helps account for her decision to publish the eulogies she collected under the title *The Excellent Becomes the Permanent.* It was her conviction that well-lived lives are a deposit of hope and faithfulness to those who live on, but only insofar as they are remembered. If to this conviction one adds her sorrow when links between the living and dead are carelessly or ruthlessly broken, and her determination to remember that certain ways of being in the world can be a gift bestowed on others, this curious text becomes more intelligible. We start out knowing little or nothing about the persons Addams eulogizes in this book; but she draws us in, painting word portraits that are so distinctive that our interest is engaged. Whether our consciences are any longer pricked is another question.

In her introduction to the book, Addams quotes one of her favorite thinkers, Sophocles: "Against our will comes wisdom to us by the awful grace of God."[46] She approaches life-and-death matters, she tells us, with a "spirit of realism." Death is "awe-inspiring" and a dread presence that must be given its due. If one captures this in memorializing the dead, one taps a "quality sufficiently universal to be of interest to those beyond the range of acquaintance."[47] Human affairs may be transitory, but exemplary lives help the excellent to become permanent. So we learn of Jenny Dow Harvey, "ardent volunteer"; of Mrs. Charles Mather Smith, "an early friend to our Music School"; Henry Demarest Lloyd, "a citizen" and a "valiant defender of democracy"; Alice Kellogg Tyler, an artist who gave "lavishly" of her services; Gordon Dewey (son of John Dewey), who symbolizes the "many promising children we had known at Hull-House whose brief lives had been prematurely extinguished"; Judge Tuley, who served the cause of the "poor and helpless"; Joseph Tilton Bowen, husband of Louise de Koven Bowen, Hull-House stalwart, and who himself stood by Hull-House "during various periods of stress and public difficulty"; Mrs. Wilmarth, "a member of our first board of trustees"; Mrs. Coonley Ward, who "gave her house for a discussion of 'Toynbee Hall and Its Offshoots' in the spring of 1889 when both were considered very strange undertakings"; and Samuel A. Barnett, "the founder of Toynbee Hall and the originator of the settlement method."

The leitmotif throughout these eulogies is an exquisite particularity coupled with the articulation of universal themes and identities. The words marking the passing of Henry Demarest Lloyd are fascinating in showing Addams's attitude toward progress. Progress is not a force that exists of itself. It takes human beings to change things. A few "must be willing to take the first steps and assume the risks." Those who charge forward from "blind enthusiasm for human betterment" often do more harm than good. The process of social change is delicate, and to undertake it one "must have a knowledge of life as it is, of the good as well as of the evil"; one "must be a patient collector of facts" and "inspire confidence" in others in order to "arouse" them to action.[48] The only way to bring about alterations for the good is to quicken moral sensibilities and to help others recognize, for example, that a woman need not be "entirely absorbed in her family" but can be a good woman and mother and a citizen as well.

The souls of human beings are "widening / Toward the past" (a quote from George Eliot), meaning that our horizons expand not only in a horizontal direction in our own epoch but also deepen as our historical knowledge grows. And as that knowledge grows, we come to understand the folly of any attempt "to label large bodies of men with obnoxious names and then to treat the men themselves as the public thinks the doctrines indicated by the labels deserve to be treated." She adds, "It is as if our social judgment were insensibly falling back into those ancient categories which once divided men according to race or religion, whereupon they were harshly judged by men of other races or religions who applied their widely differing standards with much self-righteousness, but with no understanding."[49]

Sympathetic understanding, again; and Addams needed all she could muster at Hull-House, given the sheer volume of human misery, chicanery, goodness, folly, and mystery she encountered regularly—never more so than in the event that became the story of the famous devil baby. Addams uses this story to evoke woman's remembering heart and the need to interpret its myths and legends.

The Devil Baby at Hull-House

How it all began, no one ever knew. But a strange phenomenon was centered at Hull-House that seemed to tap primordial myths about a power capable of transmuting present-day experience. Memories of these myths, which coalesced into fable, helped the immigrant poor to keep their moral world anchored even in the wretched situations in which so many of them lived. Addams devotes two chapters in *The Long Road of Woman's Memory*[50] to the Devil Baby phenomenon. It is wonderful grist for her mill, as it affords her a glimpse into the contagion of group emotion and the deeply felt need to make sense of things morally, to be assured that things happen for a reason. Also on display is the saving grace of memory, humanly transmuted, and capable of sustaining the spirit even in the bleakest and most limiting circumstances. The Devil Baby is also a story of old age—specifically, of old women who had been wrenched away from one culture and deposited in another, who were never truly at home in the new world in which they had been compelled to make their way and in which they would one day die.

The Devil Baby story begins thus:

> One day . . . three Italian women, with an excited rush through the door, demanded that he [the Devil Baby] be shown to them. No amount of denial convinced them that he was not there, for they knew exactly what he was like with his cloven hoofs, his pointed ears and diminutive tail; the Devil Baby had, moreover, been able to speak as soon as he was born and was most shockingly profane. The three women were but the forerunners of a veritable multitude; for six weeks from every part of the city and suburbs the streams of visitors to this mythical baby poured in all day long and so far into the night that the regular activities of the settlement were almost swamped.

As Addams and the other residents were swept up into the mania, they realized that different ethnic groups had particular variations on the Devil Baby tale. In the Italian version (which itself had "a hundred variations"), the key protagonists were "a pious Italian girl" and her atheist husband who had "torn a holy picture from the bedroom wall saying he would quite as soon have a devil in the house as such a thing, whereupon the devil incarnated himself in her coming child." When this Devil Baby was born, he reproached his father, and the father caught the thing and brought it to Hull-House. Despite the terrible appearance of the Devil Baby, the residents, in a quest to save its soul, took it to be baptized, but it fled the holy water and was hiding somewhere about the premises.

The Jewish version features a father lamenting over his six daughters, saying he would rather have a devil than another girl, whereupon his perverse wish was granted. Addams notes wryly: "Save for a red automobile which occasionally figured in the story and a stray cigar which, in some versions, the new-born child had snatched from his father's lips, the tale might have been fashioned a thousand years ago." The Devil Baby is a moral fable with ancient lineaments, and its attraction cut across the usual lines of social division. Visitors to Hull-House hoping for a glimpse of the demon infant even included a number of people with medical training who claimed scientific concerns. So the "old wives' tale" continues to stir and to roil the waters for "thousands of men and women in modern society who are living in a corner of their own, their vision fixed, their intelligence held by some iron chain of silent habit."

The word spread, and soon there were lines outside the door of Hull-House. People clamored for admission; got angry when told there was no such baby; offered to pay admission, saying they were told you had to pay, and it was a shame the good residents of Hull-House were trying to make money off such a pitiful thing. At first, Addams tries to ignore the phenomenon; after a time, she finds that she cannot. She begins to pay attention "whenever I heard the high eager voices of old women" because there was "something in the story or in its mysterious sequences" that had "aroused one of those active forces in human nature which does not take orders, but insists only upon giving them."

She then interprets what it all means. The Devil Baby story had stirred old tongues to speak, those who were often silent and inarticulate in their new world because they couldn't understand what was being said even by their own children and grandchildren. But now they were in their element: "The story of the Devil Baby evidently put into their hands the sort of material with which they were accustomed to deal. They had long used such tales in their unremitting efforts at family discipline, ever since they had frightened their first children into awed silence by tales of bugaboo men who prowled in the darkness." For Addams's elderly neighbors, the Devil Baby story was a kind of triumph, as it showed that tales and metaphors were alive and well as a form of moral instruction and social control. The story "seemed to condense . . . mystical wisdom" and to speak to the depths of human nature. Many of the women who came to see the Devil Baby, when invited to take tea despite their disappointment, began to recount their own tales of often tragic and brutal experience—true horrors. One example: "'My face has had this queer twist for now nearly sixty years; I was ten when it got that way, the night I saw my father do my mother to death with his knife.'" Or: "'Yes, I had fourteen children; only two grew to be men and both of them were killed in the same explosion. I was never sure they brought home the right bodies.'" And yet these women seemed to harbor no bitterness toward life; it was as if they had been burnished down to the core and all their resentment had been worn off. Addams puts it this way: "Apparently the petty and transitory had fallen away from their austere old age, the fires were burnt out, resents, hatreds, and even cherished sorrows had become actually unintelligible." These old women had nothing more to expect from life. They had arrived at "quiet endurance" of some sort, but they still required assurance that theirs was a moral universe and that somehow miscreants were punished even if the good were not necessarily rewarded.

The fable of the Devil Baby was so powerful that it even drew one elderly woman out of the poorhouse: somehow she managed to escape, to borrow streetcar fare, and to cajole a streetcar conductor to lift her aboard, as she couldn't climb in on her own effort. One bedridden woman bedeviled those around her so that Addams was fetched to tell her there was no Devil Baby. After she has made her way through a dark corridor and up some stairs to the dying woman's "untidy bed," Addams nearly succumbs to the temptation to describe such a baby in detail. What harm would it do? Addams thinks. But because she cannot bring herself to confabulate about the fabulous, she delivers the woman a terrible disappointment, and then lingers a while to listen to the old woman's stories. She has a prescient sense of the narrative needs of old age: People want to tell their stories. To be cut off from such telling and listening kills the spirit. These stories give evidence of folklorish survival, yes, but they are also a kind of reckoning of the consequences of things, a drawing up of a moral balance sheet. Addams comes to a realization "of the sifting and reconciling power inherent in Memory itself."

Memory helps ease the "inconsistencies and perplexities of life" by melting things "down into reminiscence." A metaphorical account of basic experiences "which are implicit in human nature itself, however crude in form the story may be, has a singular power of influencing daily living." To be more specific: the Devil Baby tale put power, in the form of that elusive authority—*auctoritas*—in the hands of women. The Devil Baby reaffirms Addams's belief that women created fairy tales in an effort to tame their mates and to make them better fathers. To be sure, such tales add up to a "crude creed for domestic conduct," but a creed nonetheless. What weapon did women have in ancient times save "the charm of words," with which they might hope to subdue "the fierceness of the world about them." Clearly, "humble women are still establishing rules of conduct as best they may, to counteract the base temptations of a man's world." The Devil Baby tale provided a direct causal link between "wrongdoing and punishment" that made sense and "restored a shaken confidence as to the righteousness of the universe."

Perhaps it was the dark, demoniac quality of the story that exerted the most potent allure "to those who live under the iron tyranny of that poverty which threatens starvation, and under the dread of a brutality which may any dark night bring them or their children to extinction; to those who have seen both virtue and vice go unrewarded and who have long ceased to complain." That women often pay a price for the misdeeds of others was only too true, and the existence of the Devil Baby seemed to affirm that their words of warning to miscreant men were justified, even if the end result was a *via dolorosa*. At least it was a road of sorrow that made some sense.

At moments, Addams seems to verge on anger in her retelling of the most violent of these tales. She acknowledges the folklorish embellishment that is no doubt intrinsic to their telling. But they conceal a nugget of diamond-edged sharpness, "the great revelation of a tragedy, or sometimes the great illusion of tragedy"; and perhaps, paradoxically (or so it seems), this "has power in its own right to make life palatable and at rare moments even beautiful."

By the time *The Long Road of Woman's Memory* was published in 1916, Addams had passed the pinnacle of her national acclaim. In 1910, with the publication of *Twenty Years at Hull-House,* she was at the height of her powers. She was famous beyond her wildest fancies, lionized, her every word listened to and published, usually several times over. She had fashioned a respectable social identity for ardent young women that put them in the heart of social upheaval and transformation. She had received honorary degrees. Her admirers competed to outdo one another in their praises (lines such as "She walks in the paths which only the great-spirited may tread").[51] The settlement house movement was burgeoning. Hull-House itself had undergone expansion—or, as one historian has put it, "perhaps explosion is a better word."[52]

Amid the flurry of activity at Hull-House, Addams listened, conjured, and interpreted, often well into the night. She heard stories of Devil Babies and many other tales of horror and of redemption. The horrific stories were soon to be swamped by the unspeakable carnage of the Western front. Wars claim many victims, on battlefronts and home fronts alike; and as Addams began to speak out against the war, opprobrium began to rain down on her laurel-laden head.

7

LIFE HAS MARKED US WITH ITS SLOW STAIN

The War at Home

CONTROVERSY DOGGED JANE ADDAMS and Hull-House. The quest for cleaner streets put her on a collision course with Alderman Johnny Powers and his "boodling" operation. Although she won the garbage battle, she lost the war with Powers. It is worth taking a closer look at the campaign against Powers in order to understand why Addams and her colleagues failed in a number of important battles, including their concerted effort to unseat the entrenched alderman at the polls on two separate occasions.

Addams had a distinct advantage in most debates so long as she could cultivate the "extension of household duties" theme as a rationale for social action. But when her desire to mitigate the dire circumstances of the immigrant poor led her to intervene in matters that many thought were not her concern—were not, in general, "woman's business"—she opened herself and the other residents of Hull-House up to sometimes ferocious criticism. Demonstrating that piecework in sweatshops was contributing to higher rates of tuberculosis, or that the mingling of sewage removal and water drinking pipes caused typhoid epidemics, was a legitimate "housekeeping" concern. But to insist that one couldn't deal with such matters effectively unless certain officials were either removed from office or pressured into changing their views—that put Addams into the rough-and-tumble of politics reserved for men.

Jane Addams and the other residents of Hull-House took their interventions seriously. Whenever they appeared at hearings, commissions, and committee meetings, they came with every *t* crossed and every *i* dotted. Addams could outmaneuver even the cleverest opponent in debate.[1] The residents of Hull-House tried to win over the movers and shakers, as well as the proverbial common man or woman, to their view that the moral and ethical implications of every economic and policy question were an intrinsic part of those questions. When one studies what Jane Addams liked to call the "moral balance sheet," one all too often sees a small group's interest leading in one direction, and the public interest and the good of the commonweal, in another. Addams embraced an *ecological* perspective long before the term was in widespread use. Hers was a *social ecology*. She was insistent that environmental impact, as we call it nowadays, included the effects upon the real men, women, and children who will either derive the putative benefits or suffer the drawbacks of some proposed change, even as she decried what she called goody-goody approaches, whether to domestic social policy or questions of war and peace. There was certainly nothing goody-goody about the conflict with the redoubtable Powers. These campaigns threw a bright spotlight on Hull-House in full throttle. In the aftermath of two successive electoral debacles, Addams penned one of her most famous, and most famously rueful, essays, "Why the Ward Boss Rules."[2]

The background to the Powers campaign would be incomplete without consideration also being given to the incendiary *If Christ Came to Chicago*, by muckraking investigative journalist William Stead, an Englishman who went undercover (posing as a job seeker, a bum seeking shelter, and the like) in order to expose conditions in Chicago.[3] Stead spent many hours at Hull-House. The residents shared their research with him. He shared his stories with them. The mutual influence shaped Stead's potent picture of Chicago graft and corruption (the "boodling" business) and of the desperate razor's edge on which lived most of the immigrant poor.

If Christ Came to Chicago: A Militant Social Gospel

William Stead "often visited us at Hull-House, and his brilliant monologues on a Sunday evening or at a prolonged dinner table were very exhilarating although his indictments often seemed unduly severe," Addams observed. This was the winter after the World's Fair of 1893. The Stead visit really got the juices flowing against Alderman Powers, described by historian Anne Firor Scott as "the prototype of the ward boss who was coming to be an increasingly decisive figure on the American political scene." Scott elaborates: "In the first place, he was Irish. In the second place, he was, in the parlance of the time, a 'boodler': his vote and influence in the Chicago Common Council were far from being beyond price. . . . In a single year, 1895, he was able to help to sell six important city franchises. When the mayor vetoed Powers' measure, a silent but significant two-thirds vote appeared to override the veto."[4] William Stead detailed boodling in his hard-hitting expose and labeled it the kind of thing Christ would extirpate—even as He chased the money-changers from the temple—were He to show up on the streets of Chicago unexpectedly on any given night.

The Christ figure whom Stead imagined showing up in Chicago was the Man of Sorrows who said of himself, "The foxes have holes and the birds of the air have nests, but the Son of Man hath not where to lay his Head." This Christ, the embodiment of the common man's highest self, would be saddened and shocked by what he saw, the petty cruelties, the harsh neglect, and the corruption of those who were in positions of responsibility (because all roads in Chicago eventually lead to City Hall). Stead hangs about the Harrison Street Police Station, and finds the "central cesspool whither drain the poisonous drippings of the city which has become the *cloaca maxima* of the world."[5] The worst criminals are stashed there, but so are harmless tramps. The corridors at least are warm, and the tramps make do as best they can, as there is no room for them in any inn.

Stead learned that work was what the men all wanted and could not seem to get. Stead talked with prostitutes, many of whom were penitent, and found it shocking that the doors of churches would be closed to the "Magdalen" when Christ had opened his arms to such. The intimate, mutually beneficial dealings between the custodians of law and order and the "sporting houses" are detailed in the best investigative fashion. An "inside glimpse of the practical working of the Democratic machine in Chicago" could very easily leave you "with a feeling of despair." Stead decides that the dominant, Democratic Party organization, together with the less powerful Republicans, contributes to the situation. But the parties can also stimulate in a positive sense, by inspiring citizens to render service. If you could do even a little something about the large-scale graft that has dangerous consequences for the health and well-being of citizens (like uncollected garbage and dirty drinking water), then the petty graft wouldn't matter so much. You wouldn't achieve a New Jerusalem, but at least you would avoid hell on earth.

Addams was much taken with Stead's perspective and with his long list of things that could and should be done, that Christ Himself would do, were He there in the flesh. She recognized that any serious reform effort had to be well-organized, patient, and determined, and to require of public officials that they be held accountable by the voters. Bestirred by Stead's writings and goaded by her own experiences, Addams decided that Hull-House would take on Powers directly. Stead saw in Addams and Hull-House the hope for social democracy; indeed, if Christ ever came to Chicago, he would stop at Hull-House, for Hull-House was animated by the key question Christ puts to one and all: Who is thy neighbor? For Jane Addams, we are bidden to help the neighbor, capaciously defined. But suppose the neighbor is being harmed by a third party. Are we then required to interdict the evildoer and stop the harmful activities? It seems the answer is yes. Creating a democratic political culture means building up civic life in a robust way. You cannot build a democratic culture if everyone is on the take and cynicism about public life prevails.

Powers proved a tough opponent, not just because he was powerful but also because he helped people get jobs, he bailed out constituents when they were arrested, and he could fix things. Writes Addams in "Why the Ward Boss Rules": "The Alderman of the Nineteenth Ward at one time made the proud boast that he had two thousand six hundred people in his ward upon the public pay-roll."[6] Powers also gave out presents at weddings and christenings. He handed out railroad passes to constituents. He distributed turkeys by the ton at Thanksgiving. Why, then, were Jane Addams and the Hull-House residents so livid about the Powers operation? Turkeys, rail passes, and the other little gifts seemed innocuous enough. But boodling flew in the face of their understanding of the ethical principles that *should* set the horizon within which civic life was conducted. The more than 2,000 souls who came to Hull-House each week to participate in one activity or another indicated by this very act that they yearned for something better, for more than a mutual greasing of wheels. They had aspirations. Powers, in contrast, aimed to freeze politics at a low level of mutual gratification without accountability. The boodling system instills a deep cynicism: America may not be a monarchy, but in Chicago, boodle was king, as William Stead had lamented.

Addams was involved in the Municipal Voters' League, founded in 1896, "in an effort to clean up the Common Council of whose sixty-eight aldermen fifty-eight were estimated to be corrupt." The League aimed to replace as many of the fifty-eight as possible with honest men. In 1896, as part of this campaign, a member of the Hull-House Men's Club ran for the second aldermanic position in the ward and against all expectations was elected. Subsequently, historian Anne Firor Scott notes, "his idealistic backers found that their hero had his price: Johnny Powers promptly bought him out."[7] So Hull-House cranked itself up for 1898, aiming to unseat Powers. Addams went on the offensive, pulling no punches in linking Powers to retrograde forces, labeling him as one who wouldn't permit the community to move forward in its ethical development, who thrived only because he kept people in situations of clientage and hence dependent and defenseless. Their helplessness was his advantage. Addams concludes her analysis of why the ward boss is so successful with an ethical peroration: "If we would hold to our political democracy, some pains must be taken to keep on common ground in our human experiences, and to some solidarity in our ethical conceptions."[8]

Jane Addams set her sights on ethical change because she recognized that politics and ethics are inseparable. The question is, what sort of ethics will prevail? In her analysis, and true to her evolutionary perspective, Addams describes the boodling system as a primitive morality. This morality is much admired by some immigrants, who respect the "good man" who, like a traditional *padrone,* doles out gifts from his largesse. One never inquires as to the source of the largesse, of course, nor faces the fact that what Johnny Powers gives, he can take away. People may be beneficiaries one moment and deprived the next, should they not do exactly as Powers demanded.

By round two of Hull-House v. Powers, Powers was, by all accounts, somewhat shaken by the concerted campaign against him. Journalist Ray Stannard Baker quotes Powers as declaring: "Hull House . . . will be driven from the ward and its leaders will be forced to shut up shop."[9] He had to mend some political fences he had previously taken for granted. He then publicly attacked Addams's associate, Hull-House resident Amanda Johnson, who had taken over from Addams as sanitation inspector. Some newspapers mocked him for savaging a young woman, "shielded by her civil service status" from the boodling dynamic. Powers then moved to "stir up the Catholic Clergy against Miss Addams and the reform candidate," without great success.[10] Signs started popping up in the 19th ward: "No petticoat govt for us." Undeterred, Addams and the others pressed their case, calling on Powers to account for why trolley fares were higher in the 19th ward than in most of the city, why the streets were in such terrible condition, and why the public schools were so crowded. Addams appealed to Italian residents to shake off "bossism."

But it was not to be. Voting in the 19th ward was raucous, with ten saloons open in order to ply Powers's voters and reward them with drink. Powers was victorious once again. But he was shaken by the effort it had taken to defeat Addams. In the aftermath of these campaigns, Hull-House maintained its stance of permanent opposition to a man who "continually disregards the most fundamental rights of his constituents."[11] But it never went head-to-head with him again, and Powers held his post as alderman of the 19th ward until 1913. What Addams gleaned from this experience was an appreciation of the dynamics of boodling, or bossism. Anne Firor Scott points to this episode as a demonstration of how "intensely practical" Addams's approach to politics was. Addams was no abstract dreamer or revolutionary filled with wroth; for her, politics was the realm of the best possible, not the perfect.

Addams learned yet another lesson from her neighbors during these battles. It was a powerful lesson having to do with the cultural importance attached to a dignified burial—even in the case of an abandoned infant. Paying for funerals was a big part of what Alderman Powers had going for him, as it spared his poor constituents the shame of an ignominious burial at county expense for their deceased. Hull-House residents discovered the hold that tending to the final resting place had upon the 19th ward when they unwittingly did something that shocked the "genuine moral sentiment of the community."

As Addams tells the tale, a delicate child had been abandoned at the Hull-House nursery. The residents tried but failed to locate the mother. Despite every effort, the child died. Hull-House decided on a county burial. The county wagon was to fetch the dead infant at eleven o'clock the next morning. News of what was pending circulated among the neighbors, some of whom turned out in protest and took up a collection out of their own largely empty pockets in order to pay for a funeral. Addams describes the ensuing confrontation:

> We were then comparatively new in the neighborhood. . . . In our crudeness, we instanced the care and tenderness which had been expended upon the little creature while it was alive; that it had had every attention from a skilled physician and trained nurse; we even intimated that the excited members of the group had not taken part in this, and that it now lay with us to decide that the child should be buried, as it had been born, at the county's expense. It is doubtful whether Hull House has ever done anything which injured it so deeply in the minds of some of its neighbors. We were only forgiven by the most indulgent on the ground that we were spinsters and could not know a mother's heart. No one born and reared in the community could possibly have made a mistake like that. No one who had studied the ethical standards with any care could have bungled so completely.

It is hard to understand how Addams, given her rich experience, suffused with wisdom drawn from Scripture and from her favorite writers, could have missed this; for the dignity to be accorded the dead is a theme that runs through much of the literature of the West. Perhaps she and the other Hull-House residents thought burial was the key thing, not where the body was buried. In the view of their 19th-ward neighbors, they could not have been more wrong: To be buried in an anonymous pauper's grave was nearly as bad as to have no burial at all. Needless to say, Hull-House didn't make this mistake again. The concern and anger of the neighborhood women left a deep impression on Addams. To understand the significance of a death, including that of a ten-day-old infant, we must be mindful of what life means; and that was one of Addams's great preoccupations.

Criticism of Addams and Hull-House came from different quarters at various times, and it increased or abated depending upon how politically controversial Hull-House, meaning primarily the ever-visible Jane Addams, was at the moment. Addams and Hull-House were denounced from both the left and the right. As Addams recognized early on, she was fated not to please any ideological camp. During World War I, the attacks on her and Hull-House came mostly from what one might loosely call the right, although not all nativist sentiment emanated from under that ideological umbrella. Then, too, there were a good many respectable conservatives who opposed U.S. involvement in this war just as they had earlier opposed American entry into the Spanish-American War.[12]

Throughout its history, Hull-House was also a target of criticism from those on the far left. Hull-House was consistently denounced as the home of do-good bourgeois women who tried to salve their guilty consciences through meager palliative steps that in fact did no good and only deepened the "false consciousness" of the masses, who would otherwise be gearing up for a social revolution. Here's one example, from a New York socialist newspaper (Jane Addams had just given a speech at Carnegie Hall that was received with great acclaim in most of the press, but the *New York Call* was having none of it):[13]

> We have listened to Miss Addams in particular for the last twenty years . . . we have seen innumerable "crusades" suggested, organized, and financed . . . but what has come of it all? Nothing.
>
> Miss Addams is an excellent and well-meaning woman. In fact, "gentle Jane is as good as gold." If the self-sacrifice of an individual could accomplish anything of value, her work should have told effectively. But what has her effort accomplished? We will not say that it has accomplished nothing. Some of her handiwork remains, but what does it amount to? A speck in an ocean of misery, suffering, and poverty.

As it progresses, the article grows more sarcastic and biting in its recollection of "peaceful evenings at Hull-House when some well-known, rampant, rip-snorting Socialist was invited to address the assemblage of timid reformers" and how the "warrior of the red revolution" always was soothed by "the mollifying little artifices of the Gentle Jane as a preliminary to his appearance on the platform."[14] The occasion for this particular attack was another direct foray by Addams into electoral politics, this time on the national stage and in behalf of a figure radicals regarded as a cruel imperialist, Theodore Roosevelt.

An Opportunity for Education:
The Progressive Party

Much to the surprise of her admirers and the chagrin of some others, Jane Addams not only endorsed Theodore Roosevelt for the U.S. presidency but she also seconded his nomination at the Progressive Party convention in August 1912, at the Chicago Coliseum. True to form, she was aiming for what was doable, not what was perfect. The Progressive campaign put her squarely in the electoral arena and made her even more a target than she had been before. She could no longer claim nonpartisanship for her efforts, although she took pains to separate her endorsement of Roosevelt from Hull-House and its activities. The years from 1912 until the end of World War I were tumultuous ones for Jane Addams and the country. At one point, she spun into an orbit of self-doubt such as she had not known since the founding of Hull-House in 1889.

Her involvement in Progressive Party activities is traced in chapter II of *The Second Twenty Years at Hull-House*.[15] Her treatment of the Progressive movement in its incarnation as a third party affords a detailed glimpse into her political pragmatism and her no-nonsense approach. Although she wrote frequently of purifying politics and infusing it with righteous principles (by which she means cleansing it of graft and corruption), she understood that one couldn't get involved directly in the hurly-burly of politics and remain above the fray at the same time. In fact, she sometimes fretted that there might be a form of corruption implicated when individuals do attain a lofty level of individual purity (or claim to) and thereby set themselves wholly apart from the majority. "When the entire moral energy of an individual goes into the cultivation of personal integrity," she writes, "we all know how unlovely the result may become; the character is upright, of course, but too coated over with the result of its own endeavor to be attractive."[16]

Although the campaigns against Johnny Powers had been divisive, Addams's national reputation in 1912 was almost uniformly positive (except among certain radical groups). Addams had amassed a solid record of accomplishments. She and her colleagues at Hull-House had helped push through a pension for mothers, the ten-hour workday (the Illinois Supreme Court sustained the law in 1910), and a juvenile court and a domestic relations court.[17] They had worked to improve the treatment given to charity patients in hospitals, and they had achieved many breakthroughs. Praise of Addams was so fulsome that there was talk from time to time of nominating her for U.S. president.[18] Addams appealed to a broad cross-section of Americans.[19] The reforms that she and her Hull-House colleagues had spearheaded, along with Addams's argument that political corruption and inaction touches all citizens, had touched a responsive chord. As she had written in *Democracy and Social Ethics:* "We are all involved in . . . political corruption, and as members of the community stand indicted. This is the penalty of a democracy,—that we are bound to move forward or retrograde together. None of us can stand aside; our feet are mired in the same soil, and our lungs breathe the same air."[20]

It was this philosophy of moving forward or backward together that propelled her toward Roosevelt and the Progressive Party effort in 1912. Perhaps Addams was thinking of this effort when she wrote, in her introduction to *The Second Twenty Years at Hull-House,* "Even if we, the elderly, have nothing to report but sordid compromises, nothing to offer but a disconcerting acknowledgment that life has marked us with its slow stain, it is still better to define our position."[21] So define it she did. In her characterization of this campaign, she barely mentions Roosevelt; for her, the Progressive campaign was about certain principles and proposals, not about a man.

Her experience in the Powers campaign and Roosevelt's Bull Moose operation convinced Addams that women were too amiable in politics, "too conventional, too afraid to differ with the men, too ill at ease to trust their own judgments, too skeptical of the wisdom of the humble to incorporate the needs of simple women into the ordering of political life."[22] This error she would avoid. The efforts initiated at Hull-House had convinced her that to truly remedy certain wrongs, alliances had to be forged, and the "zeal for reform" that raged throughout the country between 1909 and 1914 must be tapped and coordinated.[23] People had been aroused by various studies and surveys that showed just how dangerous many industrial occupations were, making clear that employers needed to provide safe work environments. The era of muckraking spearheaded by national magazines such as *McClure's*—because local newspapers were often beholden to monied interests—also created a pent-up national political urgency. Taking pains, as she invariably did, to distinguish between the "grief of things as they are" and the injustices that can be changed, Addams insists that the power of compassion can be harnessed politically.

In 1909, President Roosevelt called together a group to consider "the best type of care to be given to dependent children," and this effort helped solidify a consensus in favor of keeping children in their homes (including children with mental retardation) rather than institutionalizing them. The meeting demonstrated the broad concerns of the coalition. The group discussed a range of issues, from industrial safety to safe foods to the length of the workday. A Federal Children's Bureau was created in 1912 and headed by Hull-House resident Julia Lathrop. Addams was elected president of the National Conference of Corrections and Charities. All of this generated some controversy.

Addams believed this controversy was sparked by a misunderstanding of the nature of self-government. Too many Americans, in her view, conflated self-government and local government. They had too narrow a notion of politics and their role in it. Something needed to be done to coordinate the many efforts under way in every state and on the national level and to initiate a nationwide forum for civic education. These reflections provided the backdrop to a session with Theodore Roosevelt at his home in Oyster Bay, New York, in the summer of 1912, exploring the possibility of a third party. Addams had been frustrated by her appearance before the platform committee at the Republican national convention in July, where her efforts to push woman's suffrage onto the agenda were ignored. Roosevelt himself had left the convention. Addams makes certain in her reminiscences to highlight her active role, presumably because she wanted to belie any impression that she had simply been swept along by Theodore Roosevelt's forceful personality. Not only did she attend this launching event, she tells us, but she "wrote some paragraphs which he more or less put into his keynote speech at the Chicago convention."[24]

A national convention for the new, third party was called for August 1912. Addams was a member of the platform committee. As she remembers it, the city of Chicago, site of the gathering, was abuzz with excitement. There were torchlit parades by night; platform committee meetings by day. The platform called for equal suffrage, for direct primaries, for referendum and recall—all of which Addams saw as means for deepening and extending democratic norms and imperatives. Her description of her own position grows sharper: she is an "incorrigible democrat," not just a garden variety one.[25] Incorrigible democrats thrive on political friendship and affection, and this is the heady atmosphere in which she finds herself, despite some reservations.

On the whole, she believed the platform expressed "the social hopes so long ignored by the politicians."[26] It was time for women to speak up. It was time for a party to pledge itself to "the protection of children, to the care of the aged, to the relief of overworked girls, to the safeguarding of burdened men." Such a party was bound to appeal to women and to tap a "great reservoir of their moral energy so long undesired and unutilized in practical politics."[27] She knew that those who had never been caught up on a wave of political enthusiasm, who had never seen themselves as part of an civic effort larger than their own lives, and who had never sampled the fruits of political friendship, would have no idea what she was talking about.

To be sure, Addams notes that the Progressive Party convention was not a halcyon time. Thinking back on it, she decides that perhaps the time was not yet ripe for a platform of this kind. She had had to swallow a couple of bitter pills to gain that platform, so her conclusion that it was probably premature cannot have been a happy one. The compromises she struck earned her anger and ire from many of her erstwhile allies. She had been compelled to compromise on a plank calling for the building of two battleships per year.[28] In the interest of party unity, she accepted another plank calling for the building of huge fortifications in the Panama Canal zone. She had argued against the policy but lost. Maybe she was just rationalizing, she muses, desperate as she was to see a national effort to promote the agenda she most cared about. Addams also fought a losing battle to include southern "colored" delegates. Despite all of this, she seconded Roosevelt's nomination and, by all accounts, was enthusiastically received by the convention delegates.[29]

Addams rolled up her sleeve and went to work for the party and the election of Roosevelt. She reports: "I was sent from town to town in both Dakotas, in Iowa, Nebraska, Oklahoma, Colorado, Kansas and

Missouri. The comradeship which a like minded group always affords, combined with the heartiness of western good will, kept my spirits at high tide in spite of the fatigue of incessant speaking."[30] Not all of Jane Addams's admirers accepted her compromises. Perhaps this is one of the reasons why she gives the platform such lengthy treatment and Roosevelt such short shrift in *The Second Twenty Years at Hull-House.* The famous and the anonymous wrote to her. The writer Hamlin Garland, a supporter of Roosevelt, called her seconding nomination "thrilling both because of its substances and its time and place." Ernest Harvier of the New York Aqueduct Commission, who had heard her, thanked her for her speech. A self-identified New Jersey Socialist and member of the Ethical Culture Society expressed his surprise at finding her name among the delegates and his amazement that Jane Addams could ever support a man like Roosevelt, who had denounced Socialists.

One Jean Gordon, writing from New Orleans, noted her "great esteem" for Addams but refused to sign on with the effort because she could not support Roosevelt, who had had the audacity to suggest that women's suffrage hadn't really accomplished much in the states where it had been instituted. The Colored Women's Civic Club thanked Addams for her "courageous stand," as did W. M. Trotter from Colored Massachusetts, who also implored her not to be "false to [the] colored race and betray [the] cause [of] equal rights by seconding [the] nomination [of] Roosevelt." The medical director of the Frederick Douglass Memorial Hospital in Philadelphia expressed his gratitude for her "firm stand" in behalf of "human rights, without discrimination of race or sex."

Addams also received a number of angry letters charging her with having betrayed the "poor African" by seconding the nomination although her view on the southern delegation question had not been honored. A member of the Ethical Culture Society could not believe that "a man with a record like T.R. could find a supporter in Jane Addams." Charles E. Beals, secretary of the Chicago Peace Society, could not believe that "the Big Sister has swallowed Bull Moosism or been swallowed by it." He was saddened, as was Jenkin Lloyd Jones of the Chicago Abraham Lincoln Center, who addressed her as "Sister Jane Addams" and told her that she was "'too big a man'" to be "identified with any *party* agitation, or as a leader of any *party* enthusiasm," because this "destroys the perspective and does violence to the proportions."[31]

Despite the heroic efforts of Addams and others, the Progressive Party went down to electoral defeat everywhere. But Addams didn't measure success simply by the ballot count. All in all she believed the campaign had been an exercise in political education, although she was surprised at the thoroughgoing electoral repudiation. She moved on, supporting Woodrow Wilson in 1916, in large part because he "kept us out of war." Her support of Wilson soon left a bitter aftertaste in light of what Addams considered his betrayal in the matter of treatment of immigrants and in the coming of World War I, two issues that were inextricably linked. The Progressives' electoral debacle and the volume of disconcerted, puzzled, hurt, and angry mail perhaps helped prepare her for the deluge that was to come.

The Russian Jewish Colony in Intense Excitement

Because Hull-House was home to political debates in which a variety of positions were expounded, it was often accused of harboring or even encouraging outlawry, anarchism, socialism, and other feared and despised doctrines. Accustomed to such attacks (which came from the left as well as the right), Addams maintained calmly that the fact that Hull-House provided a forum for the expression of views did not mean that the views espoused were shared by her or the other residents. Certainly, "the settlements are endeavoring to understand and to allay" what is going on in an "over-wrought community," but the distinction between this and outright incitement is easily forgotten in a time of fear, when "fervid denunciation is held to be the duty of every good citizen, and if the settlement chooses to use its efforts to interpret rather than denounce the sentiments of the foreign colony, its attitude is at once taken to imply a championship of anarchy itself," as she wrote in 1908.[32] Being identified with the interests of immigrants doesn't necessarily mean agreeing with the points of view espoused by many immigrants. It means sharing their interests in decent housing, safe, clean streets, and good schools. It also means helping to calm people who are on the verge of group hysteria and confronting a lurid press doing its best, with help from overeager, out-of-control policemen and other local officials, to stir up civic panic about the anarchist threat. Another interest Addams embraced was challenging attacks *within* radical social movements against their own heterodox members. She found it endlessly distressing that the launching of broadsides and anathemas was more common on the sectarian left than in any other segment of society, immigrant or otherwise. This observation further confirmed her opposition to socialism as a "doctrinaire radical creed." She "disliked their insistence on violent confrontation and on the immutable fact of class warfare and economic determinism—their tendency to view the masses monolithically, as a redemptive force," even though most of the time this amounted to just violent talk, not action.

But many were frightened. Russia was in upheaval at the turn of the century. Waves of immigrants had come to America in the aftermath of the first of what was to be a series of violent disturbances that culminated in the Bolshevik coup of 1917. Many were simply fleeing the violence. But large numbers of American citizens harbored images of their country opening its floodgates to a wave of seditious anarchists and dangerous radicals of all sorts—this despite the fact that since 1903 no known anarchist had been admitted into the United States (anarchism having been added to insanity and vagrancy as grounds for denying entry).[33] Russian immigrants were desperate to find a safe haven. Addams describes seeing the scarred back of a young girl who had barely "escaped with her life from the whips of the Cossack soldiers," and a studious young woman who "suddenly disappeared from the Hull-House classes because she has returned to Kiev to be near her brother while he is in prison." Addams had also been impressed by the distinguished Russian activists who had visited Chicago, foremost among them Prince Peter Kropotkin, who was a guest at Hull-House.

All hell broke loose when President McKinley was assassinated in 1901 by a self-proclaimed anarchist, one Leon Czolgolz. Fears simmering beneath the surface exploded. Hull-House was attacked in the newspapers as a seedbed of anarchy: after all, people like Kropotkin had spoken there. It didn't seem to matter that Kropotkin had also addressed the Chicago Arts and Crafts Society and had spoken at the universities of Illinois and Wisconsin without making these institutions and societies anarchistic, as Addams observed.[34] But Hull-House was unusually vulnerable, given Addams's visible and outspoken commitment to sympathetic understanding and the airing of controversial opinions.[35] Hull-House (as a "place for enthusiasms") had been founded in part to provide a space for political debate and dialogue, including the discussion of unpopular views.[36]

Of the ethnic groups clustered in the 19th ward, the Russian Jewish community came under the most intense scrutiny and suspicion, for a number of reasons. To begin with, Russian Jews arrived in Chicago in an agitated frame of mind, due to the conditions they had fled. They knew that the characterization of physical degeneracy that had been added by U.S. immigration as a reason to refuse entry into the country might well be applied to them, given the commonplace ethnic and racial stereotypes of this era. America had been caught up in the eugenics craze, which lasted until the coming of World War II, and this pseudo-science was reflected in immigration criteria. The physical degeneracy test is astonishing in retrospect, but it was taken in all seriousness at the time. Thus, in 1906, the commissioner-general overseeing immigration at Ellis Island provided an account of the physical test to be administered by medical examiners at immigrant stations. It makes for sober reading, as it shows just how far the theory of innate degeneracy had taken hold and how easy it was for an individual or group to fall under suspicion of degeneracy.

In turn, physical degeneracy was associated with political degeneracy, so to speak, defined as easily falling prey to dangerous and violent doctrines. Even social reformers such as the famous Jacob A. Riis, author of the classic *How the Other Half Lives,* routinely engaged in ugly characterizations of races and peoples. Riis's chapter X, on "Jewtown," speaks of men "with queer skull-caps, venerable beard, and the outlandish long-skirted kaftan of the Russian Jew."[37] He continues: "Money is their God. Life itself is of little value compared with even the leanest bank account."[38] Chinatown is home to those who are the heirs of ages of "senseless idolatry," which have left the Chinese "without the essential qualities for appreciating the gentle teachings of a faith whose motive and unselfish spirit are alike beyond his grasp."[39] With such notions ascendant, it is unsurprising that the storm clouds began to gather and thicken in the neighborhood of Hull-House.[40] Addams's reaction to all this was to deepen her efforts in behalf of immigrants. She was instrumental in helping found a League for the Protection of Immigrants, the first organization in Chicago offering help in legal matters, housing, and employment.

The incident that most tarnished Addams's reputation in Chicago, and that primed the pump for the nationwide, anti-immigrant hysteria of the World War I era, was the so-called Averbuch affair. This was not the only incident through which Addams's name was linked with that of a Russian Jewish "anarchist," of course, but it was surely the most notorious. Lazarus Averbuch was a young Russian Jew who had witnessed but escaped the Kishinev massacre of 1903.[41] He and his older sister had made their way to America, and they had lived in Chicago for two years. Both were described as industrious, quiet, and frugal. Then the nineteen-year-old boy lost his job. He went to the house of the chief of police, alone and unarmed. Having been admitted to the hallway, Averbuch advanced toward the police chief as the latter descended the stairs, said something unintelligible in broken English, and apparently reached out his hand toward the police chief. The chief drew a revolver, and somebody shot Averbuch four times, twice in front and twice in the back as he turned to flee. Three members of the chief's family and his policeman-chauffeur were also on the scene. The chief asserted that Averbuch had come to assassinate him and that he had fired in self-defense. The police chief declared that Averbuch was an anarchist, although Averbuch had no weapon and seemed confused rather than menacing. A dragnet was put out at once for all anarchists. The word *anarchist* had invited panic in Chicago for more than twenty years, since the Haymarket riot.[42] It didn't take much of a provocation to light the fuse. Olga Averbuch was arrested and her rooms were searched. Some printed material of "anarchistic tendencies," and paraphernalia of prayer of the orthodox Jewish faith, were found. "Which of these was the better evidence of the young man's beliefs was never determined," wrote Addams's nephew and biographer, Linn, acerbically.[43]

Addams had long considered the anarchist presence and philosophy a challenge. She viewed the philosophy as one of hyperindividualism—wrong, therefore, from its underlying premises to its political conclusions. But she also found it difficult to respond to anarchist charges against American law and society when people were being thrown into jail on the vaguest suspicions, when apartments were being ransacked and pathetic little libraries seized. Anarchists, of all people, should be given the opportunity to see that justice is impartial. Sporadic acts of violence by desperate men must be averted, if possible, and punished if carried out. But one must also interpret what is going on and ask one-self, how is it "that a boy should have grown up in an American city so uncared for, so untouched by higher issues, his wounds of life so un-healed by religion that the first talk he ever heard dealing with life's wrongs, although anarchistic and violent, should yet appear to point a way of relief?"[44]

The only thing that spares us from the desperate loneliness that leads to a philosophy of murder is "a sense of fellowship": that and that alone can break through the "locked purpose of a half-crazed creature bent upon destruction in the name of justice."[45] Perhaps this was the case with young Averbuch; alas, no one would ever know. The particulars of the case were strange and muddled. Addams's measured re-sponse added to the troubles that already confronted Hull-House, in-cluding the withdrawal of support by early enthusiast and famous Chicago citizen (and wife of the most powerful man in Chicago) Mrs. Potter Palmer. Addams's plea for understanding struck many as beside the point, with the country facing what many believed was an orga-nized, violent threat.[46]

In the aftermath of Averbuch's shooting and the subsequent police roundup, Jane Addams was called upon by many immigrants whose historic memories included experiences of being hounded, subjected to pogroms and the tender mercies of the tsar's secret police, thrown into foul prisons, and deported to Siberia—people who understandably saw a portent of massacre in any untoward incident. Addams took upon herself the delicate task of calming their fears as well as denouncing the police abuses: her famous quest for balance never deserted her. In an es-say about the affair, "The Chicago Settlements and Social Unrest,"[47] Addams is insistent on equality under the law as well as equality of op-portunity—two of the golden rules of her political philosophy.

> Because my first American ancestor bought his land of William Penn in 1684, and because Olga Averbuch has been in America two years, does not make the least difference in our constitutional rights. It does, however, put me under an obligation to interpret to her and her kindred, the spirit and intent of American institutions as they are understood by those who have inherited them, so to speak; it may cause me to reflect that unless their protection shall be extended equally to all, they are slipping from our grasp.

Addams details specific injuries that undermine respect for law and for governmental institutions: assaults on streetcars, a young man forced to leave dental college because of an outburst of anti-Semitism. The out-of-control newspapers simply assumed Averbuch was a dangerous anarchist—why then had he come unarmed?—and when one paper, the *Evening Post,* tried to calm the situation, it couldn't be heard—or read—above the din. By then, the charge lodged by the chief of police, that the settlements were "the first cousins to the anarchists," had taken hold.[48] Some editorials even suggested that Jane Addams, by encouraging anarchists to state their views in the setting of a debate club, had encouraged them to go forth and murder: this would make her an accessory, of course, but the only one murdered was the unarmed Averbuch himself! Given the familiarity of the Russian Jewish colony with the methods of the Russian police, what happened in the aftermath of the shooting of Averbuch seemed like a repetition of the repression they had experienced in the old country. A restaurant that provided food at cost to the unemployed was raided. Libraries were seized. Olga Averbuch was held without bail and lied to—the police claiming that her brother had killed three men in order to startle her into a confession . . . of something. Addams describes the mood in the colony as one of bitter disillusion.[49]

The upshot of the Averbuch affair, according to Addams, was a deterioration of trust in American civil institutions and an increase, not a decrease, in membership in "all the radical societies in the Russian Jewish colony." Addams was clearly worried. She held strongly to the view that the sense of justice—and injustice—could and should express itself through the regular channels of established government. But if those channels are too narrow, or get dammed up, or people are relegated to backwaters and eddies, the stage is set for trouble. Besides, we don't have so much to be proud of, she concludes. From what we know of execution figures in Russia, in any given six-month period their executions do not "equal the number of lynchings in America."

A palpable weariness pervades Addams's reflections on these matters. "At the end of twenty years," she writes, "it seems absurd that the Chicago settlements should be explaining their position to the public upon these grave matters."[50] Surely the Christian path is right: We must include "the least of these," and we are all called to compassionate understanding. Fellowship is our means and fellowship is our end.

This invitation to fellowship extends to African Americans as well. Although the black population of Chicago was small at the turn of the century—overall, Illinois was about 2 percent African American—and blacks maintained their own institutions, especially churches, Addams was visible on this issue as well. She had been the only member of the Progressive Party platform committee who voted to seat a "colored" delegation, and she maintained, over and over again, that race was "the gravest situation" in American national life.

In *The Second Twenty Years at Hull-House,* she wrote that although the abolitionists had already grappled with the evil of discrimination, it sometimes seemed as though the country wasn't even maintaining what had already been accomplished, imperfect as it was. "To continually suspect, suppress or fear any large group in a community must finally result in a loss of enthusiasm for that type of government which gives free play to the self-development of a majority of its citizens," she writes. She cites a study of comparative wages of white and black women that shows that wages for "colored" workers are far below the earnings for white workers doing the same jobs.[51] She foresaw continued strife and difficulty on race matters.

Addams was a charter member of "an organization devoted to securing Negro justice," which later became the National Association for the Advancement of Colored People (NAACP), and her name appeared regularly on various petitions having to do with the race problem. But Hull-House, like other settlements, struggled with the race question. Prior to World War I, few blacks lived in the ward. Addams nonetheless brought prominent African Americans, such as W.E.B. DuBois, to Hull-House as guests and speakers. Hull-House provided active assistance in the formation of a black settlement—the Frederick Douglass settlement—in 1905. As demographics shifted and more African Americans moved into the area, Hull-House commissioned a study of black needs in order to better respond. Photographs of the Bowen Country Club summer camp show that African American children participated. Addams fought the segregation trend.[52]

What she had failed to reckon with was the power of the tabloid press to stir things up; the venality and cowardice of many officials; the recklessness and political stupidity of certain radical groups; and the overall consternation in the country at the sheer numbers of newcomers who were settling in American cities and helping mold and shape them.

It is important to underscore that Addams never claimed that those victimized were always right. Victimization does not confer moral rightness or political acuity: "If the under dog were always right, one might quite easily try to defend him," she wrote in *Twenty Years at Hull-House.* "The trouble is that very often he is but partially right, and often quite wrong; but perhaps he is never so altogether wrong and pig-headed and utterly reprehensible as he is presented to be by those who add the possession of prejudices to the other almost insuperable difficulties of understanding him."[53] For Addams this presents a way to "buoy us up" when we "come to a life outside of ourselves." She begs of her listeners and readers, Do not be afraid of this experience. You will soon discover "the man who seems quite unlike ourselves, and yet whose experiences are so like our own and who is often so forlorn because he does not realize there is any fellowship in this land to which he comes, who thinks that all we want is money and muscle. As our land is growing cosmopolitan in its peoples, let us meet it with a cosmopolitan culture, let us meet it with a cosmopolitan fellowship."[54] Her fellow citizens declined this invitation, with vitriol and with vehemence, in the decades to follow.

The Assault on Hyphenated Americans: Addams in Exile

On March 23, 1904, Jane Addams penned a letter "To the Editor of the *World*,"[55] describing the Hull-House Players' highly praised production of Sophocles' *Ajax*, the first staging of this difficult play in North America:

> Perhaps the chief value of "The Ajax," which was given at Hull House was the fact that it revealed the Greek colony to the rest of the city in a totally new aspect. It not only won for them a new esteem, but established a bond of common tradition and experience. Perhaps nothing is so necessary as this in the so-called problem of "Americanization"—that we should first of all respect and understand the really valuable store of Old World culture which many immigrants bring. To have this expressed in the pure classic form which "The Ajax" afforded was no small contribution to the education of a cosmopolitan city.

Despite the outbursts of public hysteria about anarchy, directed against particular immigrant groups, Addams remained confident that these were temporary dislocations attendant upon widespread and deep social change. Surely things could only get better, as her 1907 book *Newer Ideals of Peace* had confidently predicted. She was to be proven wrong.

Addams clearly had not anticipated the cauldron of hatred and animosity that would be stirred up when the United States entered into World War I. In the prewar years, she shared the optimistic, sunny hopefulness of social evolutionists that the old war virtues—and they were real virtues—were no longer needed in an industrial age and would therefore do what unnecessary organs do: they would atrophy and finally disappear. The entry of women into political and social life would surely help push the war virtues aside and help nurture and sustain a group morality based on a solidarity that did not need external enemies in order to hold itself intact. Although Addams was expressing the standard progressive and evolutionary argument, it is worth probing further into the analogies she used to connect small-scale and international events.

The cosmopolitanism of a congested city quarter like the 19th ward, in which immigrants from many countries, speaking a veritable Babel of tongues and dialects, managed to carry on all sorts of social exchanges without enmity and violence, offered a harbinger of things to come internationally, Addams believed. Surely, one day, the international arena in which states engage one another would find pacific modes of social exchange. The immigrant city had convinced Addams of this possibility. The interesting thing to note is that Addams omits from her analogy the pugnacity often visible in immigrant groups' dealings with one another; the alienation of the younger generation of immigrants from their elders; and the aura of fear and suspicion engendered by overbearing police raids and a hysterical press. These omissions permitted her to avoid the unhappy conclusion that there would *always* be forms of conflict, alienation, turmoil, and suspicion between groups of people in cities as well as between states. Hers is a best-case scenario of the cosmopolitan future.

Necessary to the realization of this vision is the sloughing off of the last vestiges of "militarism in city government," the theme of chapter II in *Newer Ideals of Peace*. This means diminishing the use of "penalties, coercion, compulsion, remnants of military codes, to hold the community together."[56] For Addams, the city, as we've already seen, is a form of housekeeping writ large: one must tend to food, garbage, child-care, misbehavior, the breakdown of social relationships, a budget. Relying on force of arms makes no sense here. Instead, we must invite all into political fellowship. It is political fellowship she has in mind when she talks about social democracy. She doesn't want government to nationalize everything or to dominate and take over. She favors cooperative alliances in government on all levels; but what really animates her is the possibility of fellowship and the repudiation of an attitude of contempt or patronage. Necessary to fellowship is active social intercourse, the creation of channels for social cooperation, and an end to onerous and demeaning tests for voting or for holding office.

As we move to end the demeaning and cruel exploitation of people, we must reject the "Anglo-Saxon temptation of governing all peoples by one standard." We are one people, yes, but Americanization doesn't mean trimming everyone down to the same size. Standardization is a holdover from militarism, Addams asserts. This approach is borne of the spirit of the conqueror toward an inferior people, an ethos that has "many manifestations, but none so harmful as when it becomes absorbed and imitated and is finally evinced by the children of the foreigners toward their own parents." There is every reason to hope that a cosmopolitan bond will be forged that will substitute for the frayed old bonds of militaristic atavisms. Her ideal of the modern city is one in which solidarity does not depend upon sanctions or a "consciousness of homogeneity but upon a respect for variation, not upon inherited memory but upon trained imagination."[57]

Newer Ideals of Peace is a hopeful book; whether it is a persuasive one is another matter. A few years after its publication, Addams must have been shaking her head in puzzlement and sadness at how quickly the dream of cosmopolitanism was becoming a nightmare of assault against so-called hyphenated Americans, the culmination of campaigns exciting fears of a loss of Anglo-Saxon dominance to lesser peoples from Catholic, Mediterranean, and Eastern Orthodox countries; the pseudo-scientific claims of eugenics; the brutalities of social Darwinism; and, of course, the outbreak of war in Europe in August 1914.

What had been anomalous and sporadic before World War I became routine during the war: radical assaults on basic civil liberties; routine abuse of immigrants; and widespread, legally sanctioned vigilantism against any and all who were not "100-percent American." It was as though some malign, contemptuous, and mocking genie had been unleashed upon the land. This makes it all the more remarkable that Addams remained stalwart in her hope for peace at home and abroad.

The wartime mind-set encouraged racists and eugenicists. Many Americans fell under the influence of publicists who foresaw the imminent demise of the white race as the "rising tide of color" swamped Caucasian supremacy. Because the capacity for self-government was linked to a "homogeneous population of Nordic blood," it was political and race suicide to mix Nordic blood with that of non-Nordics, for race was "the basic factor in human affairs," not politics. Such were the sentiments expressed by Lothrop Stoddard, a Harvard Ph.D., in his inflammatory and highly influential text *The Rising Tide of Color Against White World-Supremacy*—a work that helped underwrite and legitimate the 1921 Quota Act excluding whole categories of people from immigrating to America.[58] Fear-inducing fold-out maps with Areas of White Settlement in red, Areas of White Political Control over Colored Populations in Brown, and the like showed the then-current situation and the prognostication of the situation to come in which the red parts shrank as the brown and orange, the colored populations independent of white political control, grew apace. Fear of "reds" fused with hostility toward immigrants, adding to the volatility of the political environment.

The ostensible susceptibility of "lesser" ethnic groups and races to pernicious political doctrines invited an unholy fusion of race and politics that justified everything from immigration quotas to the notorious Palmer Raids of 1918–1921, attacks mounted by Attorney General A. Mitchell Palmer and directed at rooting out agitators wherever they may be. The raids concentrated on resident aliens, who had fewer rights than full-fledged citizens. Now recognized as one of the worst government-sanctioned violations of civil liberties in our history, these raids led to unjust imprisonment and deportation, the shutting down of newspapers, and a whole range of abuses. The coming of the war added pacifists and conscientious objectors to the list of agitators and reds and invited horrors of a particularly poignant sort against pacifist groups that had come to America expressly in order to practice their faith in peace. In *Peace and Bread in Time of War*, one of Jane Addams's most powerful books, she details the often harrowing experiences of the war years. One example is the mistreatment of the Doukhobors, a Russian religious sect, followers of Leo Tolstoy's peace faith, who found themselves under sustained assault after war was declared. Addams tells a particularly horrific tale of one such case. I call it the Story of the Dead Doukhoborets in Military Uniform.[59]

> I found myself appealed to on behalf of a frightened little widow who was at the moment desperately holding at bay the entire military prison system. Her husband had been one of "those obstinate cases who cling to a scriptural text and will not listen to reason." During his long imprisonments [for refusing to be drafted] he had been treated in all sorts of barbarous ways and finally, after a prolonged ducking under a faucet in the prison yard on a freezing day, had contracted pneumonia and died. He had originally and continuously taken his stand against putting on the uniform, and when his wife arrived at Leavenworth to take away the body, to her horror she found that body, at last unable to resist, dressed in a soldier's uniform. Her representative who came to see me, with his broken English, could convey but feebly the sense of outrage, of unfairness, of brutal disregard of the things of the spirit, of the ruthless overriding of personality which this incident had aroused among thousands of Doukhobortsi.

One might recall by way of comparison Addams's story of the outrage of women in the immigrant community at Hull-House's plans to bury the body of an abandoned child in a potter's field maintained by the county—outrage at the indignity and disregard that this implied. How much greater would have been the horror and humiliation of this man's widow, seeing him bedecked in the uniform that to him was a sacrilege and a violation, even an abomination, a departure from his understanding of the way of peace taught by Jesus of Nazareth. Why would one do that to a helpless corpse? These are the sorts of petty cruelties that were encouraged by the general hysteria about *internal enemies*. The notion of a war within had taken hold of the public imagination.

In 1919 and 1920, the United States was swept up in a "deportation delirium." Addams describes colonies of the foreign-born in her neighborhood living in terror at the "sudden descent of uniformed Immigration Inspectors and Chicago Police, who broke into their homes, sometimes without warrants, carried off patrol wagons full of people to the police stations and to the county jail." The number of deportations in 1918 totaled 11,625. Reentry into the United States after deportation was made a felony offense, guaranteeing that "wives or husbands who came on a visit to their families here, who overstayed their permits and were deported, can never be reunited in this country."

One pitiable case after another surfaces in the files of the Immigration Protective League, including cases that are both cruel and ludicrous, such as that of "the Italian child of ten who within three years after having entered the country to join her parents who had been here some years, was sent to a public hospital for a tonsilotomy." Addams continued: "Her parents were unable to pay for private treatment. Thus she became a 'public charge' for having become dependent and cared for at the expense of a public institution within five years of entry, and therefore she was deported to Italy to live with her old grandmother." These records eloquently testify to the cruelty and self-righteousness shown by America in dealings with immigrants.

The record only got worse. Addams did her best to fight the riptide. Meanwhile, the Wilson administration decided that the United States would have no clout in the postwar settlement unless it repudiated its previously neutral status and entered the war, which it did in 1917. The war was then ravaging Europe and destroying its youth in grotesque bloodletting, with British casualties as high as 60,000 for the single day of July 1, 1916, during the Battle of the Somme. The reports from the Western front created a shock wave among citizens around the world. Those like Addams, who had looked forward confidently to what some have called functional integration, were distraught. They had hoped that through increased ties via immigration, commerce, railroads, steamships, telephones, and telegraphs, not to mention international mail service, a truly international culture would grow that would make war between western European states and the United States virtually unthinkable. The war not only destroyed lives; it crushed hopes and inaugurated an era of cynicism about previous optimistic assumptions.

Yet, on the American home front, some progressives saw in the war a solution to the domestic problem of unassimilated immigrants and what, in their view, was a culture that was still too local and parochialized. Per-

haps the war effort could speed up the process of nationalizing both industry and identities. President Woodrow Wilson, who shared these
broadly progressive views, nonetheless issued broadsides that stun a contemporary reader: "There are citizens of the United States, I blush to admit, born under other flags but welcomed under our generous naturaliza-
tion laws to the full freedom and opportunity of America, who have
poured the poison of disloyalty into the very arteries of our national
life. . . . Such creatures of passion, disloyalty, and anarchy must be crushed
out. . . . The hand of our power should close over them at once."[60]

Such rhetorical excesses spurred vigilantism against alleged slackers
and traitors. The lynching of Robert Prager, a young man who had
been born in Germany and had tried to enlist in the U.S. navy but had
been rejected for medical reasons, took place before a cheering crowd
of five hundred near St. Louis. In the subsequent trial, the defense counsel called the mob's leaders' offense "patriotic murder," and a jury returned a verdict of not guilty. Historian David Kennedy quotes a comment by the *Washington Post:* "In spite of excesses such as lynching, it
is a healthful and wholesome awakening in the interior of the country."[61] Similarly, the *New York Times* deplored lynching but con
tributed to the public mood that invited it by attacking radicals as
"treasonable conspirators against the United States."

The culpability of the U.S. government in these activities is genuinely
troubling. For example, a vigilante organization called the American
Protective League received quasi-official status from the U.S. Department of Justice for its efforts to spy on neighbors, "fellow workers, of-
fice-mates, and suspicious characters at any time." Members of the
League opened mail, served as *agents provocateurs,* and led raids
against supposed draft evaders.[62] The Official History of the American
Protective League makes for sober reading.[63] From the viewpoint of the
League, citizens' groups and institutions like Hull-House fell under a
cloud of suspicion. The League is described as a company of detectives
who "served without earlier specialized training, without pay, without
glory," but they did not mind, as they were the voice of "anguished
America." The war, declares Emerson Hough, author of the official history and himself a protective league enthusiast and participant, is
against the German people in toto, whether Germans in Germany or
Germans in the United States. All are "covert, sinister, sneering, confident, exultant."[64]

The Germans had created a web of conspiracy; but two hundred fifty thousand loyal patriots had answered the call and begun to disentangle this web. The city of Chicago was singled out as a hotbed of pro-German suspects, but the Germans and their friends were everywhere, in every hamlet and burg, often centered around the Lutheran Church and its pastorate. With encouragement from the highest offices in the U.S. government, these poisoners of the body politic were rooted out. Hough issues a retrospective warning: "Your house, your neighbor's, was known and watched, guarded as loyal, circled as disloyal. The nature of your business and your neighbor's was known—and tabulated. You do not know to-day how thoroughly America knows you. If you are hyphenated now, if you are disloyal to this flag, so much the worse for you."[65] The Chicago division of the League was particularly active, going after everyone from pacifists to German musicians in symphony orchestras. Their weapons were the threat of deportation and "denaturalization."

The test of loyalty was simple, according to Hough. The loyal person is "he who himself knows in his own soul whether or not he is done with the damnable hyphen which has almost ruined America and yet may do so." How one proves the state of one's soul is not answered. Jane Addams isn't singled out by name, but she certainly fits many of the generous criteria adumbrated for slackers and preachers of sedition, including those giving aid and comfort to the disloyal—especially in Chicago, which is described as the most disgusting place in the country for its "unassimilated rabble," its "polyglot politik-futter."

Addams was less critical than she might have been of Wilson's role in helping generate this climate of opinion, with his occasionally florid rhetoric and the free rein he gave to some of the worst abusers. But instead of attacking the attackers, she devoted her efforts to repairing as much of the damage as possible. In "Immigrants Under the Quota, 1921–1919," in *The Second Twenty Years at Hull-House,* she bemoans the general acceptance of standardization. What happened in this era violated all that was best in the American method, understood by her as one in which citizens reach their own ends "through voluntary action with fair play to all interests involved," which in turn tends toward "wider justice."[66] The Quota Act of 1921—the National Origins Quota System—passed in the aftermath of wartime repression, made clear that Mediterranean and Slavic immigrants were considered undesirable. Many immigrant families that could not afford passage to the United States for all of their members at once, and that did not know of the pending discriminatory legislation, sent some members on ahead, planning to be reunified later, at the first opportunity; the Quota Act prevented the reunification of many such families, including that of husbands and wives.

The Immigrants Protective League compiled one heartbreaking file after another, filled with desperate letters asking how one could, please, get to Chicago, or bring one's husband or wife or child to Chicago. Letters detailed just how hard the person was working to become fluent in the English language. But the Polish quota took no pains over individual cases, leading Addams to bemoan "this callous land of ours," which was apparently determined to discriminate against southern and eastern Europeans because they were swarthy or Catholic, or for some other illegitimate reason.

Addams observed another sadness flowing from America's long-standing problem of racial separation and prejudice: When Mexican immigrants first arrived in America, they "mingled freely with the negroes from the south," and, given their own relatively darker skins, they soon became victims of the same prejudice that confronted the "dark-skinned man. So we witnessed the phenomenon of Italians picking up native-born white attitudes towards Negroes and applying them to Mexicans as well." Friction and hatred followed. In the summer of 1921, a "colored man had been lynched in an Italian neighborhood about half a mile from Hull-House." One friend of Addams's observed ruefully, "Of course this would never have happened in Italy; they are becoming Americanized."

A horrific commentary: a lynching was a sign of Americanization. Should America not be generous and welcoming instead? Surely this was the American way, not one of fear and wrath and contempt. But the prejudice, discrimination, and violence continued unabated for a number of years. Addams's period in the civic wilderness began with her defense of immigrants and her insistence that all in America, whether newcomers who are not yet citizens, or those who can trace their ancestry back to the Mayflower Compact, are owed fair and equal treatment under the law. These efforts alone do not account for her fall from public grace, however. That event can be laid squarely at the doorstep of her pacifist convictions. She had never experienced civic isolation before the war; but with the coming of World War I—and particularly, after her notorious "bayonet charge" speech at Carnegie Hall on Friday, July 9, 1915—many of her early and most faithful supporters abandoned her.

8

⁓∞⁓

SOLIDARITY WHICH WILL NOT WAVER

Jane Addams in War and Peace

NESTLED AMONG THE PAPERS of Jane Addams, amid the many encomiums to her, is a hostile satiric verse—"Lines composed while gazing at a portrait of Jane Addams."[1]

> A nose that's long and shows it doth dote
> On Poking into business not its own.
> A jaw that loves to ape and loudly groan
> O'er other's sins. An eye that doth denote
> Propensity to howl about the vote:
> A nerve that leads her to approach a throne
> And nag great kings in sanctimonious tone
> And prattle how the War has got her Goat.
> O meddler from Chicago! What have we
> E'er done, that you our gizzards thus should vex?
> We longed that when you sailed across the sea
> The waves should sweep you from that Peace-Ships decks
> Eternal ennui you have inspired
> No Hun from Hun-land e'er made us so tired.

This was not the sort of response Addams had become accustomed to, and the change must have seemed abrupt. In 1904 she had been awarded an honorary degree from the University of Wisconsin. In December of that same year, she was invited to deliver a convocation address at the University of Chicago, then as now an honor ordinarily reserved for members of the university faculty. Following on the heels of her revered father in the smaller compass of Cedarville, she was appointed to the Chicago School Board in 1905, at which point her fame was not only national but international. Her 1902 book *Democracy and Social Ethics* had been published to "extravagant praise" and had gone into second and third editions. Her saintly qualities were extolled in article after article. A feature article in *Harper's Bazaar* in October 1904[2] lauded her "divine inquisitiveness." The prose is treacly even by the standards of that day:

> Miss Addams has walked a long road, and she has come at last to a beautiful and windless place, a plateau of high altitude, where a wonderful peace lies brooding. Her melancholy eyes behold much—behold the pageants of earth and the long terrible processions of the poor. The friendship she pours out upon them is the essence of friendship—something spiritualized and made universal. It related itself not to one person nor to a group of persons, but to the whole world. . . . She walks where only the great-spirited may tread.

In light of such effusive praise, her fall from public grace—the result of her pacifist stance during World War I and her defense of immigrants and political radicals, including those who were suspected of disloyalty—is startling. Perhaps, however, the real surprise is that it took a war to turn the occasional negative murmur into a united chorus of disapproval. The criticism of Addams continued unabated throughout the war and much of the 1920s. Addams had long been at odds with her countrymen and -women in the matter of war and peace and the relation between the two; the outbreak of conflict in Europe and America's entry into it brought these philosophical differences to the surface. From 1914 on, Addams's life was dominated by her internationalism and her pacifism rather than by her work at Hull-House (although she still considered these various concerns intimately related).

Addams had grown up in a family that favored the abolition of slavery and supported the War Between the States—meaning that John

Huy Addams's Hicksite Quakerism was of the flexible variety. Revering Abraham Lincoln as she did, Jane Addams always took pains to represent Lincoln primarily as the Great Reconciler rather than as a determined commander in chief who was prepared to bend the Constitution in order to prosecute the war more effectively. Throughout her life, Addams sought out reconcilers. She even made a pilgrimage to the home of one of the acknowledged living saints of pacifism, the great Russian writer Leo Tolstoy. This visit yielded a famously droll story that appears in *Twenty Years at Hull-House* and that culminates in Addams's advocacy of a version of peace at odds with Tolstoy's pure pacifism.[3]

Addams and her closest friend and companion, Mary Rozet Smith, went abroad in May 1896, in part to permit Addams to recuperate from one of her many illnesses—this time, typhoid fever. The highlight of their trip was a pilgrimage to Yasnaya Polyana, home of Leo Tolstoy.[4] Addams tells us that she had "read the books of Tolstoy steadily" and had pored over Tolstoy's *What Then Must We Do?*—an account of the Russian's "futile efforts to relieve the unspeakable distress and want in the Moscow winter of 1881, and his inevitable conviction that only he who literally shares his shelter and food with the needy, can claim to have served them."[5] Tolstoy argues that persistent misery corrodes the human soul and renders people not only unlovely but unlovable. He depicts what happens to men who become wretched because they have been stripped of the habit of earning their bread and the dignity of labor; to women, denuded of family and kin, selling their bodies on dirty cots in order to stave off starvation.[6] Tolstoy's encounters with the poor and miserable jolted him to the depths of his soul. He resolved to do good by stripping himself of his earthly status and riches—for he was a count, a member of the landed Russian nobility—and by sharing the life of the rural poor, the peasants on his own estate.[7]

It is easy to see the attractiveness of Tolstoy's vision to Addams. He was no removed theoretician but a man who practiced what he preached by doing "his daily share of the physical labor of the world." The "prospect of seeing Tolstoy," she tells us, "filled me with the hope of finding a clew to the tangled affairs of city poverty. I was but one of thousands of our contemporaries who were turning toward this Russian not as to a seer—his message is much too confused and contradictory for that—but as to a man who has had the ability to lift his life to the level of his conscience, to translate his theories into action." Tolstoy's saintly halo is somewhat tarnished, however, by Addams's account of their meeting. Tolstoy was provoked by the fact that Addams appeared before him garbed in a traveling gown with sleeves that were "monstrous in size," as befitted the season and the current style. He, in the simple peasant attire he affected following his harrowing life transformation, took hold of "an edge" of one of Addams's sleeves and pulled it out to an "interminable breadth," saying, as he did so, that "'there was enough on one arm to make a frock for a little girl.'" Ignoring the translator's enthusiastic description of the work being done at Hull-House, Tolstoy challenged Addams as to whether the wearing of such garb did not present a "'barrier to the people.'" She managed a reply. Her sleeves, she told him, weren't nearly so "monstrous" as those of "the working girls in Chicago" who strove to keep up with every twist and turn in fashion. Were Addams to adopt a blouse "following the simple lines of the human form," she would separate herself from the people, not draw closer to them. Conspicuously rustic dress would constitute a tacit rebuke to struggling working girls with their hard-won frocks.[8]

Tolstoy's wife tried to rescue Addams at this point by describing her own attempts to "clothe *hypothetical* girls in yards of material cut from a train and other superfluous parts of her best gown until she had been driven to a firm stand which she advised me to take at once." (The emphasis is mine.)[9] Tolstoy did not relent. He peppered Addams with more questions: Who fed her? Who gave her shelter? Addams answered that she owned a farm one hundred miles from Chicago, part of her inheritance, at which point Tolstoy dubbed her an "absentee landlord." Perhaps she should go back to tilling her own soil, he suggested.

Addams admits to being attracted by Tolstoy's "sermon of the deed" as well as his "frantic personal effort" to put himself "into right relations with the humblest people, with the men who tilled his soil, blacked his boots and cleaned his stables." His attempt to live as he taught suggests to Addams that there is too wide a gap between "our democratic theory on the one hand" and the actual facts of American society. What we have done is to wear out hundreds of thousands of human beings by overburdening them with toil. The result is that the "intellectual resources of society," to which all have a right, are unavailable to the overworked laborer and mother. Is this not an indictment of the way things are? But Tolstoy's *imitatio Christi* Addams finds difficult to emulate. She goes on to extol him as a great genius making intellectual contributions beyond price with his writing. Surely he is saintly in his embrace of bread labor. In this way, he and his followers have reduced a great truth to action. (Reduce is a positive word for Addams, remember, connoting a way to translate thoughts into concrete deeds.) But, nonetheless, she finds herself resisting certain aspects of Tolstoy's message,[10] and she leaves Yasnaya Polyana in a state of mortification: she has disagreed with the great man.

Leaving Russia for Germany, where she and Smith spend a month, she delves more deeply into Tolstoy's thought, reading everything of his she can find that has been translated into English, German, or French. She carries on an internal argument with Tolstoy. Perhaps he was "more logical than life warrants." Perhaps it is not the case that "the wrongs of life" can be "reduced to the terms of unrequited labor." Nevertheless, she vows that she will spend "at least two hours every morning in the little bakery which we had recently added to the equipment of our coffee-house" when she returns to Hull-House. However, when she is back on terra firma in Chicago, her lofty, Tolstoyan vow comes crashing down: "The whole scheme seemed to me . . . utterly preposterous." There were people waiting to see her; there were letters to be answered, sponsors to encourage, meetings to attend, politicians to challenge, and essays and editorials to write. Was everything else to wait as she tried to "save my soul by two hours' work at baking bread"?

Addams eventually set aside Tolstoy's doctrine as dogma, even as Addams's admiration for those who followed the doctrine in every jot and tittle remained intact. She became a champion of the pacifist Doukhobors, Russian immigrants imbued with Tolstoy's philosophy and practicing a "literal acceptance of nonresistance" even when they were under assault as endangering the war effort—but she did not attempt to follow their purist path. Although Addams extolled a "newer ideal of peace" (the title of her 1907 book, which went into multiple printings), she struggled with Tolstoy's way the rest of her life.

In a 1931 essay in the *Christian Century*, comparing Tolstoy and Gandhi, she describes Tolstoy's purpose as that of substituting "moral forces for all those forces which are at present aroused in warfare." The bulk of the piece is devoted to an analysis of the doctrine of nonresistance, including the insistence that moral force or power must go up against violence without itself turning into "violent antagonism." The "unceasing effort" to overcome evil by "doing good," which is at the heart of Gandhian as well as Tolstoyan teachings, was initially derived from the message of Jesus of Nazareth.[11] Addams's primary purpose in making this case was to refute charges of irrelevance and impracticability lodged against the theory and practice of nonresistance. She had found a way to separate the message of nonresistance from a war against mutton sleeves and the routine of an alarm bell going off before the crack of dawn to summon her to the bakery.

Addams again engages Tolstoy's thought in her account of the period 1914–1922, in her powerful *Peace and Bread in Time of War*.[12] Although she at first attached hope to the Bolshevik coup—despite her suspicion of what she calls the "military" methods deployed by its inner leadership cadre—for her the real revolution was the phenomenon of Russian peasant soldiers on the Eastern front in World War I "talking to their enemy brothers in the opposing trenches" when news first arrived of the "abdication of the Czar."[13] By the thousands these same men abandoned "the two thousand miles . . . along the Eastern front." Their slogan "Land and bread" touches her.[14] Tolstoy comes back into the picture as she writes of peasants who, having walked away from warfare, made a "pilgrimage to Tolstoy's grave"—he had died in 1910—"and wrote these words upon a piece of paper which they buried in the leaf mold lying loosely above him: 'Love to neighbors, nay the greatest love of all, love to enemies, is now being accomplished.'"

Tolstoy was only one of Addams's many interlocutors on the contentious questions of war, peace, and violence, at times in face-to-face discussions but primarily through the written page. Because Addams habitually questioned her own judgment in all matters, she sought out those who, instead of confirming what she believed, challenged her position. The war years brought enormous political, ethical, and philosophical pressures to bear on her normative, moral pragmatism, especially her insistence that the measure of an idea and its truth is the crucible of experience and the ways in which that truth can be concretely embodied in practice. That this did not happen with pacifism in time of war—at least, not in any effective, compelling, and widespread way—raised questions about pragmatism as well as pacifism.

Unlike most leading progressives, including the great philosopher John Dewey, Addams never made her peace with war. She certainly did not trumpet the social "advances" brought by the war, as industry, educational curricula, and much else was nationalized and centralized in the interest of mounting a unified war effort. Addams would have agreed with Randolph Bourne (another progressive dissenter against the war effort) that a nation-state at war closely resembles a cold-eyed snake.[15] She had disturbed this creature, stirring it to agitation, and it had struck mercilessly against her and her "newer ideals of peace." Nothing she had done at Hull-House, and none of the earlier celebrations of America's greatest woman and foremost public citizen, shielded her from its attack.

From *New Ideals* to *Peace and Bread*

Addams believed that the American state and polity should embody and represent the "better angels of our nature," in Lincoln's words; it should embody the "commonality" of the nation's "compassion." Prior to the outbreak of World War I, Addams, together with most of her contemporaries, rode the waves of a heady optimism, borne along by their vision of a positive state that would actively promote a common good; that would have a nurturant as well as a disciplinary side; and that would take seriously its role as civic educator. Addams believed that the further the state moved in the direction of compassionate tending to citizens, the more it would move away from war.

Her most systematic exposition of what she described as a new, dynamic understanding of peace calls for the strengthening of international law. In *Newer Ideals of Peace,* she asserts that international codes will one day mandate relations between nations analogous to those between citizens and their government in a democratic society. She was convinced that peaceful international relations (with the West leading the way, as it was the most highly developed region) would gradually displace warfare. Even as humankind evolved out of tribal life, so would social morality move steadily forward until it achieved the level of "social affections" of a cosmopolitan nature. In practical terms, this would translate into the assimilation of domestic law into international law. What stands in the way of such a venture? she asks rhetorically. Does not enlightened opinion everywhere recognize a new humanitarianism afoot? Do we not see it operating every day "in the immigrant quarters of a cosmopolitan city," where people speaking a bewildering mix of languages and dialects, and coming from nations and regions that were enemies one to another historically, now find themselves nose to nose and are learning to work and to play together?

The immigrant city would pave the way for a new internationalism: from city to cosmos. Addams had seen this internationalism in operation.[16] She gives the example of a South Italian Catholic being "forced by the very exigencies of the situation to make friends with an Austrian Jew representing another nationality and another religion, both of which cut into all his most cherished prejudices." But he finds it harder to sustain these prejudices in his new situation and he thus "modifies his provincialism for if an old enemy working by his side has turned into a friend, almost anything may happen."[17] In the cosmopolitan city, people "are forced to found their community of interests upon the basic and essential likenesses of their common human nature; for after all, the things that make men alike are stronger and more primitive than the things that separate them." She is daily amazed by the "manifestations of altruism" in the congested quarter of Chicago she inhabits. She sees how people respond to the "demands of social justice." To be sure, for many years to come, the majority would believe "that war is noble and necessary both to engender and cherish patriotism." But even as they trumpet such notions, they daily live in "the kingdom of human kindness." Sooner or later they will weigh these two claims against one another and one—the "nobility of war" claim—will fade: this was Addams's confident, prewar hope. The human race was at long last building a social cathedral, using diverse materials toward a shared end. Industry and commerce were leading the way toward internationalism. New modes of communication meant that no country was, or could remain, isolated. The "progressive goodness of the race" was close at hand. Each nation "quite as a natural process will reach the moment when the virile good-will will be substituted for the spirit of warfare."

This is Jane Addams at her most optimistic and, arguably, her least persuasive. The horror of the slaughter on the Western front makes her prewar optimism seem both naïve and forlorn. The idea of social evolution from militarism to nonmilitant internationalism is no longer convincing. One can sense in Addams's argument for this evolution an abandonment of her quest for balance—the careful tension between competing claims that she sought to maintain (as in her juxtaposition of the family claim with the social claim). Instead, she describes the "military party" or claim in wholly negative terms, as something that the human race can and should abandon altogether. How does this square with her intuition that any perduring tradition bears within it a potent truth that must not be jettisoned? The answer is that it does not. Because she elides national defense and security with militarism and authoritarianism, she glosses over the question of whether there are ways to provide for the common defense that do not incite contempt and cruelty. Instead, she extols the blessings of a new dispensation: civic communion brought about through pacific means. One marker of this new fellowship is generosity in welcoming immigrants to their new civic homes, wherever these may be. Civic communion offers the beguiling prospect of more women taking their place alongside men in civic life. It includes protecting and educating children in a consistent, fair, and compassionate way. It requires the creation of a morality that does not worship at the altar of material success achieved by any means necessary. It eschews warlike methods and rhetoric and rejects "blind adherence" to "my country right or wrong." It brings forbearance and toleration to a new level. We cannot do without patriotism, she insists, but we must cease founding that patriotism on war. Contrasting industrialism to militarism, she defines industrialism as a force that is liberating and reconciling newfound human energies in and through the socialization of industry, whereas the old militarism governs by suppressing those energies.

Addams's evolutionary optimism is tied to her conviction that human beings are more similar than they are different. It follows that what unites us is stronger than what divides us. She rejects what she calls static notions of human nature—notions like those of the eighteenth century, propounded by America's Founding Fathers—along with what she describes as empty talk of "inborn rights." In fact, evolutionary thinking demonstrates that rights are by no means inalienable but, instead, are "hard-won in the tragic process of experience." Social and political equality are not given prima facie but instead emerge through a dynamic process: the engagement of human beings with a social surround that permits them—indeed, requires them—to recognize their commonalities. The human life cycle is the greatest leveler of all: We are all born helpless and dependent; we all need nurture to survive; we grow infirm; we die.

Addams would never again recapture the halcyon days that gave rise to her celebration of newer ideals of peace. With the coming of the war, the naïveté of her prewar vision grew painfully clear. By consistently juxtaposing coercion against nurturance and protection, she had evaded the complexities posed to all pacifists by the pervasiveness of violence as a feature of all human cultures, past and present. She had offered no viable alternative to the state as a monopoly on the means of violence—Max Weber's famous definition—and instead had assumed that human cultures would evolve out of a situation in which collective violence was either necessary or desirable. She knew that in any society, laws must be enforced. Civic order must be maintained if citizens are to live and interact in safety and peace. How is this coercive aspect to human affairs to be handled? Addams had underestimated the difficulties of embracing a strong definition of human similarity while maintaining an equally strong commitment to human distinctness and diversity.

Her ideals of peace rested on an overarching analogy that was fundamentally flawed. Nation-states are not related to one another as are foreign-born immigrants in America's burgeoning cities. Immigrants come into a preestablished context of rules and laws, however badly they may be enforced. The violation of rules and norms carries with it predictable penalties. The use of violence to gain a desired end results in punishment if the offender is caught. There is no such structure in the international arena, as Addams well knew. Presumably she believed that enough was in place—a kind of brittle shell of international law—that it could operate on states the way domestic law does on individual citizens. But it doesn't work that way in practice. A state that has a preponderance of force and that uses it quickly and effectively is not going to be "hauled into court" on charges of having violated the principle of sovereignty. This is one of those frustrating realities that the "civil party" (or peace party), in which Addams placed such great confidence, has never found a way to alter, at least not consistently. By minimizing the ways in which the operation of power at all levels of government helps create and secure the context Addams celebrated—the multinational city in which everyone is a candidate for civic membership—she evaded the distinction between a great city within a nation-state, on the one hand, and the individual sovereign state in its relation to an international arena that lacks an overarching authority. If every state is analogized to Chicago and its internal context, an analogy Addams often made, then what political body plays the role of the U.S. government or its equivalent? Her answer was, some form of international law or international organization that did not yet exist but that must be promoted and eventually secured. This effort dominated the last twenty years of her life.

Women Against War: The Fight for Bread and Peace

If you glance at any effort in American life that can reasonably be called a "peace initiative" during the period 1912–1935, you are almost certain to find Jane Addams's name on its list of officers, board members, sponsors, or some other capacity. The importance of this work to her is signaled by the words she chose for her headstone. She would be remembered, simply, by her association with two efforts: Hull-House and the Women's International League for Peace and Freedom.[18]

As time went on, the peace theme became increasingly dominant in Addams's writings and public activities. Her pre–World War I books, apart from *Newer Ideals of Peace,* do not have peace efforts as their central motif, although Addams makes it clear that she sees a more peaceful world as one of the fruits of spreading democracy. In *The Spirit of Youth and the City Streets,* her favorite among her books, Addams devotes a chapter to the "thirst for righteousness" that she believes animates youth. This thirst encompasses a robust vision of democracy and an enthusiasm for "self government . . . found among the groups of young immigrants who bring over with every ship a new cargo of democratic aspirations. . . ." She continues: "Democracy like any other of the living faiths of men, is so essentially mystical that it continually demands new formulation. To fail to recognize it in a new form, to call it hard names, to refuse to receive it, may mean to reject that which our fathers cherished and handed on as an inheritance not only to be preserved but also to be developed."[19] This faith fits with a gradual and peaceful transition to more peaceful and more socially (not individualistically) structured institutions, from labor to industry to education.

A key aspect of this effort, which Addams calls "conservative"—in the sense of conserving and protecting what is vital—and which she supports enthusiastically, is the movement to secure protective legislation for women and children in industry. To encourage people to support these measures, one must appeal to "the old spiritual sanctions for human conduct, that we must reach motives more substantial and enduring than the mere fleeting experiences of one phase of modern industry which vainly imagines that its growth would be curtailed if the welfare of its employees were guarded by the state."[20] In *The Long Road of Woman's Memory*, published in 1916 before the United States entered the war, Addams devotes a chapter to the ways in which women's inheritance of particular memories and traditions, as well as women's continuing cultural efforts, offer a challenge to war. Chapter V of *The Second Twenty Years at Hull-House* details "Efforts for Peace During Five Years of War, From August, 1914 to August, 1919." The book also covers postwar developments, from alterations in notions of individual freedom, to the clampdown on immigration, and assaults against immigrants. In *Women at the Hague,* Addams describes the international conference that turned her into a citizen-diplomat, touring European capitals in a quest for arbitration and mediation of the conflict then raging. In *My Friend Julia Lathrop,* a loving biography of Hull-House resident Lathrop, Addams notes that she and Lathrop opposed the death penalty. Addams links the death penalty explicitly to the war virtues, which, despite the relapse into war, will slowly but surely pass.

Peace and Bread in Time of War contains Addams's most powerful and poignant reflections on the devastation of war, as well as her account of concrete activities by women in the war years and after to prevent the carnage and to deal with its aftermath. The war was not only a historic cataclysm but a personal catastrophe for Addams. The war dealt a blow to the solidarity and affection she most cherished—namely, civic friendship and fellowship. She felt the sting of ostracism so keenly because she esteemed the succor of fellowship so highly. The starkness of her sense of separation from the democratic fellowship that she had once called mystical comes through in this pained observation: "I concluded that to the very end pacifists will occasionally realize that they have been permanently crippled in their natural and friendly relations to their fellow citizens."[21] How did matters come to such a pass?

So convinced was Addams of the existence of latent antiwar sentiment among women that she opined in the *Ladies' Home Journal* in November 1914—after hostilities had commenced but well before the United States had entered the fray—that the example of neutral nations condemning the war was a sign of partial success for peace efforts. Surely the moment when international arbitration of disputes would become the rule rather than the exception was fast approaching.[22] Her nonstop activity against American entrance into the war, against the continuation of the war, and in opposition to a punitive peace began with a conference at the Henry Street settlement in New York City in September 1914. Addams attended this conference at the urging of Paul Kellogg, editor of the *Survey*, a journal to which she contributed frequently. Kellogg criticized the old, well-established peace organizations, which in following the lead of President Woodrow Wilson in this period of American neutrality remained silent about the horrific bloodshed that was under way. Addams was jolted to the very core by the mass, mechanized slaughter of European youth, who were dying at a rate of ten to twenty thousand a day. In contrast to this horror, reform efforts looked puny and would no doubt be undermined. The Henry Street meeting culminated with a condemnation of the war as a blow to internationalism, which participants at the meeting asserted had been built up through new technologies such as the telephone, the telegraph, and international postal service and through the growth in worldwide travel.[23]

At the same time as American settlement leaders were issuing antiwar statements, many leading figures of the suffrage movement in Europe were protesting the war and calling for mediation of the conflict by the leader of a neutral state—namely, President Woodrow Wilson. European women leaders toured American to plead their case. Addams enhanced their visibility and legitimacy by publicly endorsing their idea.[24] In the six years following the September 1914 Henry Street settlement meeting, a dizzying array of peace organizations were founded, meetings and rallies held, and efforts of all sorts made, in which Addams participated fully until she was halted by illness.

The tempo of peace-oriented activity increased with the establishment of the Woman's Peace Party in January 1915. Civically active American women had become expert in creating associations and networks. The interlocked activities of women's clubs around America had for years been a springboard for new policy initiatives at the local, state, and national levels, on everything from safe drinking water to playgrounds and hot school lunches, from anti-vice and temperance efforts to suffrage. Women peace advocates now were calling for everything from mediation of the dispute to the building of the kingdom of the Lord on earth.[25] For example, an anthem sung to the tune of "The Battle Hymn of the Republic"[26] proclaimed in its refrain:

> The end of fort and battleship! The end of gun and sword!
> The end of shame and misery and vice and crime abhorred!
> The time for us to build on earth the Kingdom of the Lord!
> That day is marching on!

Not all of the women who signed on with the Woman's Peace Party were pacifists. Thousands, no doubt, were acting more from isolationism than internationalism, hoping to keep America out of the conflict. Others were long-standing internationalists. Few were committed pacifists. But this coalition effort buoyed Addams with its enthusiasm and its numbers. At the first convention, in January 1915, Addams delivered the keynote address and was elected chairman. At the height of the Woman's Peace Party effort in the United States, there were 165 groups with a total membership of 40,000 women. The American party became a section in the Women's International Committee for Permanent Peace, which had branches in fifteen countries, and which later evolved into the Women's International League for Peace and Freedom (WILPF).

In April 1915, a forty-two-member American delegation headed by Addams sailed on the ship *Noordam,* bound for the Hague and an extraordinary congress of women, including delegates from countries that were even then engaged in the most destructive war ever to scar the European continent. One purpose of this meeting was simply to demonstrate that it was possible to bring together representatives of warring countries and for these same representatives to demonstrate the possibility of mediation and arbitration even as a war raged.

The crossing was troublesome for the American delegation, and they were detained for five days in the English Channel before being allowed to proceed. Some delegations never made it at all or succeeded in sending only a token number. Remarkably, however, 1,336 women from twelve countries, including both belligerents and neutrals, attended. A consistent theme for the delegates—some of whom had endured considerable grief (including threats and intimidation) in order to attend— was that women needed to build up a political power base if they were ever to be effective in preventing war.

In her opening address, Addams, who was acting as chair, appealed to a basic solidarity between women that was no respecter of national boundaries. She had high hopes for the International Congress of Women and its ongoing efforts. The symbolism of meeting at the Hague, where a World Court of Conciliation and Arbitration had been established in 1899, fortified her. Addams offers a detailed account of her involvement in the Hague Congress and in other antiwar activity in chapter V of *The Second Twenty Years at Hull-House* and in *Peace and Bread in Time of War.*[27]

The resolutions adopted by the International Congress of Women at the Hague are interesting in that they anticipate what was to become the League of Nations and that they argue that arbitration efforts should go on even as a war is being fought—the implication being, of course, that no nation should be required to surrender unconditionally as a precondition for peace negotiations. Other proposals adopted included no transfer of territory without consent; a refusal to ratify the fruits of conquest; the establishment of a permanent international court to mediate disputes; and condemnation of secret treaties—on the dubious proposition that secret diplomacy serves only to contribute to war. Free trade, freedom of the seas, universal disarmament, and extension of the suffrage to women were predictable planks in the platform. A number of proposals that were considered "melodramatic" and "absurd" by Addams and another member of the American delegation, Hull-House resident and Addams's personal physician Alice Hamilton, were rejected.[28]

Whatever one thinks of the specifics of the Hague Congress and its platform, Addams is perceptive in noting, in her post-Congress reflections, that much of the bellicosity of wartime is fueled by the war itself. The fighting of a war generates animosities that may not have been there at the outset. As a war goes on, the reason to keep fighting is in order to punish your foes for the violence you have suffered in fighting. War is self-perpetuating. Addams also points out that much of what the women at the Hague proposed was later included in President Wilson's famous Fourteen Points.

As the Hague Congress concluded, two delegations were empowered to take the cause of continuous mediation to the European capitals. The women sought meetings with leaders, whether the latter were directly implicated in the hostilities or were neutral parties who might play a role in arbitrating the conflict. The Hague Congress formed an

International Committee of Women for Permanent Peace and elected Addams as its president. When the International Committee later founded the Women's International League for Peace and Freedom—as the official history of the League states—"the first elected President of WILPF was, inevitably, Jane Addams."[29] The inevitable Addams was made president for life.

Addams's reminiscences of this period and of her own efforts are tinged with sadness. She recognizes that the majority of women did more than passively support the war effort of their countries—they sometimes shamed young men into fighting and cheered them on as they marched off to slay or be slain. Soldiers themselves wrote bitterly of facing "crowds of women surrounding the railroad trains leaving for the front; urging their lovers, husbands and sons into battle."[30]

Addams's discussion in *Women at the Hague* of the mission of the women delegates to the capitals of Europe is remarkable for its measured tone and matter-of-factness. Together with Rosa Genoni of Italy and Aletta Jacobs of the United States, Addams went to Austro-Hungary (Vienna), Belgium, Britain, France, Germany, Italy, and Switzerland. The second delegation, including Emily Balch, Chrystal Macmillan, Cor Ramondt-Hirschmann, and Rosika Schwimmer, visited the Scandinavian countries and Russia. Remarkably enough, the women's amateur diplomacy was greeted with open doors and great courtesy for the most part, as they met with foreign ministers and even prime ministers at the height of the bloodshed (with ten to twenty thousand men a day being killed on average).[31] Addams's hopes rose for a quick resolution of the dispute and for America's active role as a neutral arbitrator. In late spring 1915, she was confident that President Wilson would keep America out of the war: this was before the sinking of the passenger ship *Lusitania* on May 7, 1915, which inflamed anti-German sentiment and rhetoric among the American public and politicians.

Addams at Carnegie Hall: The "Bayonet Charge" Debacle

In July 1915, Addams returned to the United States, and immediately began to publicize the Hague Congress and its message of continuous mediation. She addressed an enthusiastic and supportive crowd at

Carnegie Hall on July 9, and went to bed that night with thunderous applause still ringing in her ears. She awakened the next morning to outraged accusations in the press that she had calumnied America's brave soldiers and patriots. The public outcry alerted Addams to the depth of sentiment favoring the war, and forced upon her the "consciousness of social opprobrium." She now knew how it felt to be "an easy mark for the cheapest comment."[32] At the age of fifty-five, Addams found herself teetering again on the brink of self-pity—a feeling she had not experienced since her twenties.

Addams's speech at Carnegie Hall had been billed as a report about the peacemaking mission undertaken by her and other participants in the International Congress of Women.[33] A substantial press contingent was on hand, and at least 3,000 people were in attendance.[34] Addams's speech was powerful in its matter-of-factness and its measured reasonableness.[35] Often political advocacy in inflamed situations is hyperbolic and morally overwrought, portraying a world of villains and noble rebels or innocent victims. True to her lifelong habit of refusing to deepen rifts and enmities, Addams observed that young men were fighting bravely and dying horribly on all sides.

If on this occasion Addams had been content to speak only on the theme of women's devotion to peace, she would have fallen into a by-then familiar groove linking women, especially mothers, to pacific thinking. But Addams went further, straying into a male preserve, when she began to speak of soldiers whom she had met near the front lines. Despite the initial exuberant response from her Carnegie Hall audience, it was in part this commentary that sent her reputation into a tailspin in an America aroused by tales of the horrid "Huns" and their unspeakable atrocities.

Addams began by expressing the hope that efforts in behalf of peace might be as "rousing almost as war."[36] She acknowledged the "genuine emotion and high patriotism" of the moment, together with its confusions, the many "wild and weird things" being said. What she will say is neither wild nor weird, because it does not originate in a theory but rather in concrete encounters and direct experience. "One gets afraid of tall talk," she says, "and one does not know where words may lead the people to whom one is speaking." This acknowledgment of uncertainty and ethical concern about the power of words to incite deeds is unusual in a public figure in the heat of the moment.[37] But to Addams, public rhetoric was a form of persuasion, not bullying, and the speaker bore responsibility for the effects of the speech on listeners. The speaker must be careful not to incite animosity, resentment, hatred, or despair. People needed hope. At the same time, the audience should not be gulled into false optimism. Public speaking, thus, required a complex balancing act.

The meat of the speech is Addams's description of her experiences in the countries that were engaged in killing one another's young men in staggering numbers. She found that people, from government officials down to ordinary men and women, spoke freely, once they overcame their initial reserve. What she had learned as a member of "this pilgrimage of ours, if you choose to call it so, going from one government to another, to nine governments in all, as we did in the space of five weeks," was that "everywhere one heard the same phrases, the identical phrases, given as the causes and as the reasons for the war." She continued: "Each of the warring nations, I solemnly assure you, is fighting under the impulse of self-defense. Each of the warring nations, I assure you, is fighting to preserve its own tradition from those who would come in to disturb and destroy those high traditions and those ideals."

The delegation heard over and over again that a "nation at war cannot make negotiations, that a nation at war cannot even express a willingness to receive negotiations, for if it does either, the enemy will at once construe it as a symptom of weakness." It followed that the terms eventually struck would inevitably work to the disadvantage of the state that first suggested negotiations. That state would suffer "as being considered the side that was weaker and was suing for peace"—a pithy, clear-cut articulation of a state-security position. Addams and her compatriots were struck by the tragedy of the whole thing, and by the recognition of that tragedy even on the part of those who proclaimed the war's necessity.

Her interpretation of what she heard was that there was a common desire for the war to end, but two quite different approaches to bringing about that much-hoped-for result. She claimed that one approach—that promoted by the military party—"believes that the matter can be settled only upon a military basis." The second approach belonged to the "civil party, which very much deprecates this exaltation of militarism, which says that the longer the war goes on, the more the military authorities will be established, as censors of the press are established in all sort of places . . . ; the longer the war goes on, the more the military power is breaking down all the safeguards of civil life and of civil government, and that consequently it will be harder for civil life and for the rights of civil life to resuscitate themselves and regain their place over the rights and power of the military."[38] Given her sense of urgency about civilian control and the need to bolster the civil party, Addams asks, Why not start negotiations now, before the military party can further entrench itself? She was heartened by the fact that their delegation met pacifists in every country; and she assumed, probably wrongly, that there were many more covert pacifists who feared to come forward given wartime censure.[39]

The next section of Addams's speech proved her undoing. She reported to her rapt audience that "in each of the warring nations there is this point of similarity; generally speaking, we heard it everywhere—this was not universal, but we heard it everywhere—that this was an old man's war; that the young men who were dying, the young men who were doing the fighting, were not the men who wanted the war, and were not the men who believed in the war. . . ." She continued, "This is a terrible indictment, and I admit that I cannot substantiate it, I can only give it to you as an impression." She then told about the young men she had met who believed there were good *Menschen* in every country, as one young German had told her. The head of a hospital in one German city told her of "five young Germans who had been cured and were ready to be sent back to the trenches," who had instead "committed suicide, not because they were afraid of being killed, but because they were afraid they might be put into a position where they would have to kill someone else."

Similar insights are strikingly evident in the literature of war in general, and stories like these are common in accounts of World War I. The sacrificial theme—I am prepared to die, but I would rather not kill—is potent. One sees, of course, just how abrasive this would be to many American supporters of the war who preferred to see soldiers, at least the soldiers on their side, as stalwart warriors rather than frightened young men who, overwhelmingly, would rather not kill another young man.[40] In the postwar years, an often deeply bitter and ironic literature by veterans emerged, reinforcing the poetry of disillusionment by the so-called war poets (such as England's Wilfred Owen). But that lay in the future. In the thick of things, most people did not want to hear about soldiers' inhibitions but about their gallantry and unflinching determination to persevere.

Those who criticized Addams thought it wrong for her to be speaking about the mentality of soldiers. As a woman, she had not gone through a war experience as a combatant, so what could she possibly know about it?[41] There was particular bite in this criticism, given the importance Addams accorded to direct experience. The experiential claim was one that she took seriously, due to her general sympathy with pragmatism; hence, she made clear that her description of soldiers' reluctance to kill always derived from firsthand reports in conversations with soldiers themselves. She also attempted to debunk the widespread assumptions about a gender divide on this question: "I would like to say just a word about the women in the various countries. The belief that a woman is against war simply and only because she is a woman and not a man, of course, does not hold. In every country there are many, many women who believe that the war is inevitable and righteous, and that the highest possible service is being performed by their sons who go into the army. . . . The majority of women and men doubtless believe that. But the women do have a sort of pang about it."[42] In this matter as in others, Addams was committed to narrowing the gap between men and women.[43]

Addams concluded her speech on a typical note of caution and humility—she was "never so dead sure I am doing the right thing"—and in the matter of the delegations she feared it might seem a folly. But one prime minister, she remembered, said the women's delegation had uttered the first sensible words he had heard in ten months—an opinion that had reassured her that they were on the right track.

Then came the fateful final paragraph, in which Addams described how the young men felt about bayonet charges—the prototypical act of combat in the minds of the public, although such charges counted for a minuscule number of deaths, compared with the number slaughtered by heavy artillery. Addams and the others heard similar statements in all countries regarding what happened before a bayonet charge—namely, that soldiers were provided with stimulants before they "would engage in bayonet charges, that they have a regular formula in Germany, that they give them rum in England, and absinthe in France.

They all have to give them the 'dope' before the bayonet charge is possible. Think of that. No one knows who is responsible. All the nations are responsible, and they indict themselves. But in the end human nature must reassert itself. The old elements of human understanding and human kindliness must come to the fore." The reason for the use of alcohol was clear: to dull the young men's sense of horror at the face-to-face killing—not because of any cowardice on their part but because of their general loathing of killing.[44] At this point Addams stood down to thunderous applause.

The applause was short-lived. Addams tells us why in *Peace and Bread,* in which she expands her "Revolt Against War" discussion (from her *Women at the Hague*) to include the tumultuous outcry against her after the speech at Carnegie Hall. She reflects on the wording she had used, indicating that she should have made it clearer that the young men did not flinch "at the risk of death but because they had to be inflamed to do the brutal work of the bayonet, such as disembowelling, and were obliged to overcome all the inhibitions of civilization." Soldiers, she adds, are in fact the most touching victims of the war, "the heroic youth of the world . . . tragically pitted against each other." Their response to patriotic appeal is heartening and moving in many ways. We admire the soldier not because "he goes forth to slay but to be slain," she claims, citing Ruskin.

Her explanation came too late. In response to Addams's Carnegie Hall remarks, Richard Harding Davis, described as a popular militarist,[45] wrote a letter to the editors of the *New York Times.* The letter was published on July 13, 1915. Addams has besmirched our soldiers, Davis told the *Times.* She has sullied and dishonored them. She has stripped them of their courage. She would have us tell children left partially orphaned by their fathers' deaths that their father did not die for his country "but because he was drunk." He depicts Addams as a "complacent, self-satisfied woman" throwing insults like so many hand grenades on the graves of the hallowed dead. How dare she?

Addams, in turn, describes Davis's letter as claiming that what she had said was "a most choice specimen of a woman's sentimental nonsense." She continues: "Mr. Davis himself had recently returned from Europe and at once became the defender of the heroic soldiers who were being traduced and belittled. He lent the weight of his name and his very able pen to the cause, but it really needed neither, for the misstatement"—that Addams had taxed soldiers with cowardice and drunkenness in order that they might fight—"was repeated, usually with scathing comment, from one end of the country to the other." In retrospect, she offers a clarification:

> I was conscious, of course, that the story had struck athwart the popular and long-cherished perception of the nobility and heroism of the soldier as such, and it seemed to me at the time that there was no possibility of making any explanation, at least until the sensation should have somewhat subsided. I might have repeated my more sober statements with the explanation that whomsoever the pacifist held responsible for the war, it was certainly not the soldiers themselves.

She tried at least once, in a later public address, to clarify her earlier statements, but being again misquoted, "I gave up in despair." In an attempt to understand what exactly the scandal of the bayonet charge speech suggested about the human experience in modern society, she writes:[46]

> I will confess that the mass psychology of the situation interested me even then and continued to do so until I fell ill with a serious attack of pleuro-pneumonia, which was the beginning of three years of semi-invalidism. During weeks of feverish discomfort I experienced a bald sense of social opprobrium and wide-spread misunderstanding which brought me very near to self pity, perhaps the lowest pit into which human nature can sink. . . . Strangely enough he [the pacifist in time of war] finds it possible to travel from the mire of self pity straight to the barren hills of self-righteousness and to hate himself equally in both places.

The period of exile and self-doubt had begun.

Addams's commitment to modern democratic teaching prompted her to question her own judgment. In a democratic society with institutions and structures available to register and to evaluate the popular will, can one stand apart in a time of national crisis? "In the hours of self-doubt and self-distrust the question again and again arises, has the individual or a very small group, the right to stand out against millions of his fellow countrymen? Is there not a great value in mass judgment and in instinctive mass enthusiasm, and even if one were right a thousand times over in conviction, was he not absolutely wrong in abstaining from this communion with his fellows?" She confesses that she desperately missed the comradeship felt by the millions of supporters of the war. For Davis's hadn't been the only public letter attacking her. Many more letters of this sort flooded into the *New York Times.* Wherever she went in the country, the charge that she had called American soldiers drunks and cowards followed her like a determined stalker. She faced humiliation. Some of her speeches were canceled. She was publicly booed for the first time. The press, which for years had been her great ally for the most part, and which had played a key role in lionizing her and turning her into an American hero, now deserted her.

Three incidents that took place in Chicago must have been particularly painful to her. One involved the University of Chicago, to which Addams had powerful connections and which enjoyed an intimate partnership with Hull-House. The second involved the powerful and influential association of civically minded women, the famous Fortnightly Club, whose members had been among her most ardent, earliest supporters, offering both money and influence. The third was the public break with her initiated by an old friend and Chicago-area judge, over the war issue.

In August 1917, Addams was to be honored at a University of Chicago reception by women members of the faculty. Noticing this in the university's "Weekly Calendar," one dissenting faculty woman, Elizabeth Wallace, declaimed in a letter to the president of the university: "However much we honor Miss Addams for her generous work in philanthropy it seems to me ill-advised, to say the least, to give her any special distinction at the present moment when the reason for honoring her might not be entirely clear." Wallace also notes that Addams is not a faculty member. The whole thing is a blunder. Wallace's letter was countered by the formidable Sophonisba Breckinridge, then professor in the School of Social Service and a Hull-House resident alumna. The University of Chicago simply could not dishonor Miss Addams: the whole idea was unthinkable. The university's president sided with Breckinridge: he would never dishonor Miss Addams, although he went on to speak derisively of "so-called peace activities." Wrote President Harry Pratt: "Such activities at this time are merely giving aid and comfort to the enemy, and what that means you know. We cannot permit the University to be used when the nation is at war as a base for anything approaching disloyal operations."[47] That Addams's behavior could be described even vaguely as treasonous is a sign of the temper of the moment.

It was in this overheated atmosphere that Addams was scheduled to speak on "A League of Free Nations" at a meeting of the Fortnightly Club. It was 1919, and she had quit talking about war's folly or even about negotiation and arbitration, finding such discussions politically pointless because no one really heard what she was saying. Instead, she had begun to emphasize the need to feed the malnourished and starving of Europe—a mission consistent with her lifelong theme of women as bread-givers. She had publicly endorsed Herbert Hoover's appeals to Americans to support food aid, an initiative undertaken by the new federal Department of Food Administration. Her work with the food relief effort afforded Addams the opportunity to affirm the work of peace—provision of bread for the hungry—in the midst of chaos and malnourishment. She traveled from state to state, speaking about the need to increase food production and to economize in order to be able to help those who had too little. In other words, Addams promoted what we would nowadays call humanitarian relief or intervention.[48]

Back on familiar terrain, she once more was articulating ancient female concerns as a desperate civic necessity, this time at the international level. But this did not mollify a few stalwarts among the membership of the Fortnightly. They "made their displeasure known to Miss Addams," at which point she notified the Fortnightly board of her decision not to give her paper. This led to a counterinitiative by her defenders, who urged her to present her paper as planned. She did so on January 23, 1919, speaking before what is described as a very large crowd for a January meeting.[49] But the controversy wasn't over. An article lamenting the bitter intolerance expressed in the august Fortnightly Club appeared in the *Chicago Tribune*. Riled Fortnightly members chided the *Tribune* as well as the author of the critique, warning that it was "unwise and unpatriotic before the articles of Peace are actually signed to extend the hospitality of our platform to anyone who is an avowed pacifist." The beleaguered Fortnightly board asserted that it had never meant this matter to become public knowledge.[50]

This contretemps and others like it were just part of the price Addams paid for risking public ostracism, whether partial (in this case) or total (in some quarters of the press and public). For years, every public appearance was like a minefield. Despite Addams's care in selecting both venue and occasion in order that dialogue might ensue rather than hostility and ruptured communication, many old friends deserted her because of her stand on the war issue, and some did so publicly—in order, presumably, to display their own patriotism. On one such occasion—June 10, 1917—Addams was lecturing at the First Congregational Church in Evanston, just to the north of Chicago, on the theme "Patriotism and Pacifists in War Time." In the audience was her old friend, Chief Justice of the Illinois Supreme Court Orrin N. Carter. Most in the audience were members of an adult class that met regularly to discuss ethical issues. When Addams finished speaking, their response was complete silence.

Then Judge Carter rose to his feet and announced that he and Miss Addams were lifelong friends and that he agreed with her most of the time. At this point, Addams interrupted: "That sounds as if you are going to break with me." Judge Carter responded that indeed he was. The judge's argument was the standard one: no one should dare "cast doubt on the justice of our cause" while the war was going on. Perhaps after the war pacifist measures could be considered.[51] But not now. The judge's remarks demonstrate a fundamental misunderstanding of pacifism, which tries to forge alternatives to war—if necessary, in the midst of war. If pacifism must stand down while a war is going on, then pacifism is gutted. The problem for Addams and other pacifists was that they could not find a way to embody pacifism in concrete, sustainable practices during the war. Food relief was as close as one could come— that, and arguing for continuous arbitration and negotiation. It must have riled Addams to no end that her activities and advocacy were being denounced as an example of the very thing she had struggled to avoid—namely, a well-meaning but ineffectual or even dangerous sentimentalism that fails to take account of basic realities.

The Long Road of Woman's Memory Revisited

In her writings both during and after the war, Addams struggled to find in "women's memories" and women's actual experiences—including the horrific realities of the war itself—at least the nascent beginning of a culture of peace. Perhaps pacifists had been overoptimistic in their belief that such a culture was already *there* in some sense and could be enhanced to break the hold of war. In *The Long Road of Woman's Memory,* Addams gives a platform to the many women she spoke with "during the great European war who had sent their sons to the front in unquestioning obedience to the demands of the State, but who, owing to their own experiences, had found themselves in the midst of that ever-recurring struggle, often tragic and bitter between two conceptions of duty, one of which is antagonistic to the other."[52] Creating two fictitious composites from the many women she encountered during her trips to Europe in the war years, Addams first describes a woman whose son was an accomplished professor. She herself had come to regard "the government as an agency for nurturing human life." Her son was shot down, and his body was thrown "into a lonely swamp." In his last letter to her, he had revealed to her that he, a professor of industrial chemistry, had been consulted about asphyxiating gases for use in the war. The woman commented bitterly: "I know how hard it must have been for him to put knowledge acquired in his long efforts to protect normal living, to the brutal use of killing men." Mind you, the mother continued, her son was a "red-blooded, devoted patriot," like other scientists; but they were developing an international mind, as men of science are wont to do, given the fact that scientific developments proceed through a collaboration that recognizes no national boundaries. If such an international community of scientists exists, why not some sort of international government? If scientists can hone such contacts and develop them into what some international relations thinkers now call epistemic communities, why could women not get together? To fail to do so is to disregard an "imperative instinct." A now-famous quote, which Addams attributed to one of her prototypical interlocutors, clearly has Addams's own stamp on it:[53]

> Certainly the women in every country who are under a profound imperative to preserve human life, have a right to regard this maternal impulse as important now as was the compelling instinct evinced by primitive women long ago, when they made the first crude beginnings of society by refusing to share the vagrant life of man because they insisted upon a fixed abode in which they might

cherish their children. Undoubtedly women were then told that the
interests of the tribe, the diminishing food supply, the honor of the
chieftain, demanded that they leave their particular caves and go
out in the wind and weather without regard to the survival of their
children. But at the present moment the very names of the tribes
and of the honors and glories which they sought are forgotten,
while the basic fact that the mothers held the lives of their children
above all else, insisted upon staying where the children had a
chance to live, and cultivated the earth for their food, laid the foundations of an ordered society.

Feminism and militarism are counterposed as two stark opposites
("an unalterable cleavage"). Militarists believe "government finally
rests upon a basis of physical force"; but feminists must, if feminism is
to mean anything at all, "necessarily assert the ultimate supremacy of
moral agencies. Inevitably the two are in eternal opposition." This
might appear to set up the sort of stark duality between the sexes that
Addams generally rejected; but she makes it clear, here as elsewhere,
that the opposition she is describing is not between men and women
but between two contrasting attitudes.

Addams's second respondent contrasts with the sophisticated mother
who could articulate so artfully her opposition to the war (and who
sounds so much like Addams herself). This next woman is simple; her
internationalism is humble and is founded not "upon theories, but
upon the widespread immigration of the last fifty years, interlacing nation to nation with a thousand kindly deeds." It turns out the woman
has a brother in California and she—an Italian peasant—had "visual-
ized America as a land in which all nationalities understood each another with a resulting friendliness which was not possible in Europe."
She has a hard time wrapping her mind around the fact that the shrap-
nel that killed her son came with a Made-in-the-USA label. The old
woman's eyes are troubled and anguished. She remained faithful to an
understanding of moral unity, but not without struggle.

Addams says she "caught a glimpse of an inner struggle, as if two of
the most fundamental instincts, the two responsible for our very development as human beings, were at strife with each other. The first is
tribal loyalty, such unquestioning acceptance of the tribe's morals and
standards that the individual automatically fights when the word

comes; the second is woman's deepest instinct, that the child of her body must be made to live."[54] As Addams had recognized from the beginning of her public life and writing and had stated clearly so many times—most notably, in analyzing the family claim and the social claim—these are both legitimate, not illegitimate, claims. If you assume that you can toss one out because the two may come into conflict, you radically oversimplify the moral life; you violate our deepest moral intuitions. Unsurprisingly, she concludes the chapter by holding up the "eternal Antigone" who "makes no distinction between her suffering brothers who make war on each other." She surely recognized, however, that the key term in the Antigone reference was to brothers. The texture and density and intimacy of that relationship make all the difference. It is difficult to generalize that relationship to include "all young men who might be my brothers" or "all young men who might be my son." But that is what her vision of peace required.

The Quest for Mediation

Addams and her fellow delegates had moved swiftly to secure President Wilson's compliance with the Hague Conference's general commitment to neutrality, if not its specific proposals. Addams met with Wilson and his chief adviser, Colonel House, in July 1915, but no firm commitment was secured. Addams arranged for the publication in major newspapers of manifestos calling for a conference of neutrals with Wilson as its leader. She argued that such a conference would enhance U.S. influence in Europe and American prestige internationally. The White House stalled. The determined women of the Woman's Peace Party flooded it with some twelve thousand telegrams. A message from Wilson, delivered in December 1915, raised hopes not only for continued U.S. noninvolvement in hostilities but for the U.S. to play the role of mediator. Addams believed that Wilson meant to call for a negotiated peace.

The uncertainty surrounding the government's actions encouraged, in the meantime, many private initiatives. The ill-fated "Ford Peace Ship," funded by Henry Ford, was slated to sail for Europe at Thanksgiving 1915, on a mission to bring the war to an end. As head of the Woman's Peace Party, Addams felt obliged to participate, despite urgent warnings from many of her friends that the expedition was ill advised.[55] Ford intended to fund a conference of neutral powers, and to that end he had chartered a ship—the *Oscar II*—and got Wilson to agree he had a right to engage in this venture. He also made a public pronouncement that the boys would be out of the trenches by Christmas. The press had a field day with that, and the entire effort became an object of scorn.

Before the *Oscar II* sailed, Addams fell seriously ill with what was diagnosed as a tubercular infection of the kidneys. The *Oscar II* sailed without her as she lay in a Chicago hospital, no doubt somewhat relieved that she had missed what clearly seemed more of a publicity stunt than a serious undertaking.[56] She kept going, despite her illness, working behind the scenes in favor of neutrality. While she was recuperating, Addams was at first buoyed by Wilson's apparent commitment to play out the U.S. hand from the stance of both power and neutrality. Addams appears not to have realized that the international women's peace movement and President Wilson were functioning at cross-purposes. As she describes Wilson's position: "His first point, 'to unite in guaranteeing to each other absolute political independence and territorial integrity' was not so significant to us as the second, 'to settle all disputes arising between us by investigation and arbitration.'"[57] Addams genuinely believed that the United States would use its "vast neutral power to extend democracy throughout the world" only through democratic ends and that Wilson was committed to a policy of doing this without war. Unsurprisingly, her confidence in the president's determination to keep the United States out of the war led to "absolute bewilderment" when her country joined the fray. For Addams, it was a terrible tragedy. Wilson had had a chance to "dig the channels" through which his purposes could have been achieved without warfare. He not only failed to do this; even worse, "I found my mind challenging his whole theory of leadership. Was it a result of my bitter disappointment that hotly and no doubt unfairly asked myself whether any man has the right to rate his moral leadership so high that he could consider the sacrifice of the lives of thousands of his young countrymen a necessity?"[58]

Her physical illness, although it did not yet forestall her customary flurry of activity, was exacerbated by increasing mental and moral exhaustion, bringing all-too-vivid reminders of her battle with neurasthenia decades earlier. She had always been convinced that those years of illness were the result of her not yet having found a way to translate her high ideals into concrete action. The frustration she felt now was similar: there seemed no way to embody pacifist ideals in the war effort, especially after Wilson had decamped to the other side. She was no more heartened by developments after the war, taking a dim view of the League of Nations—of which Wilson was an architect—because it permitted war "in too many instances, because its very structure and functioning is pervaded by the war spirit, the victorious disciplining the defeated," thus sowing the seeds of future conflict.

"A Line of Moving Skeletons": Suffering Children

The war had created food shortages, in part because so many men were away fighting that crops could not be raised and harvested. More important, the havoc wrought by the war had destroyed food distribution networks. Shipping was disrupted by the U-boat campaign as well as other, typical wartime dislocations. On top of that, the Allies (the Triple Entente powers, which the United States joined in 1917) had established a food blockade aimed at starving their foes (particularly Germany and Austro-Hungary) into submission. After the war ended, an American food relief effort was launched in Europe under the direction of Herbert Hoover, to which Addams offered her support. Addams's understanding of pacifism dictated that she take action to ameliorate the human devastation caused by the war. Her moral stance was not only *against* but *for:* more was required of her than reiterations of her antiwar convictions. The eternal duality—war versus bread—haunted her. She thought of peasant women the world over, who were still doing their part in growing and preparing food. She recalled "them everywhere in the fields of vast Russia as in the tiny pastures of Switzerland; by every roadside in Palestine they were grinding at the hand mills; in Egypt they were forever carrying the water of the Nile that the growing corn might not perish." Under the old diplomacy, there "was no place for woman and her possible contribution," but politics had now become woman's sphere. Perhaps in the orderly feeding of children lay a nascent international morality. Even in time of war this ethic should be honored, not only to help keep alive an alternative but also concretely to prevent starvation and to succor the suffering. The wheat loaf had become a symbol of survival. Addams's service as a spokeswoman in behalf of humanitarian relief helped allay her terrible sense of failure and futility.[59]

In spring 1919, after the hostilities had ceased but before the terms of peace had been negotiated, Addams went to Europe at the invitation of the American Red Cross. Accompanied by Mary Rozet Smith and Alice Hamilton, she began her tour in Paris at Easter. In addition to her service responsibilities, she was fulfilling a family mission during this leg of the trip: Her eldest nephew had "fallen in the Argonne," and she was searching for his gravesite. In July 1919, she proceeded to Germany, where she traveled under the auspices of the American Friends' Service Committee. Later, in *Peace and Bread,* she described the somber landscape through which she passed in the French countryside:[60]

> Day after day as rain, snow and sleet fell steadily from a leaden sky, we drove through lands laid waste and still encumbered by mounds of munitions, exploded shells, broken down tanks and incredibly huge tangles of rusty barbed wire. The ground was furrowed in all directions by trenches and shell holes, we passed through ruined towns and villages in which no house had been left standing, although at times a grey head would emerge from a cellar which had been rudely roofed with bits of corrugated iron. It was always the old people who had come back first for they least of all could brook the life of refugees. There had not yet been time to gather the dead into cemeteries, but at Vimy Ridge colored troops from the United States were digging rows of graves for the bodies being drawn toward them in huge trucks. In the Argonne we still saw clusters of wooden crosses surmounting the heaps of clay, each cross with its metal tag for inscription.

Hoping to ameliorate the worst of the war's depredations, the Congress of Women several times had called for a lifting of the blockade so that food could get to the starving noncombatants in Germany and the Austro-Hungarian empire. Their pleas had been ignored. It is unsurprising that "only the feeding of the hungry seemed to offer the tonic of beneficent activity" to Addams. On the home front, the postwar period was marred by race riots and by assaults on immigrants, evoking in Addams a sense of disheartened alienation from most of her countrymen and -women, and dampening the hopes that Hull-House had represented.[61] Recognizing in herself at the same time the "health-destroying" effects of suppressed energy, she craved more than ever the healing grace of useful activity. She was also convinced that a successful international effort at distributing food might provide a lesson in international organization that could serve as a spur to other, more far-reaching efforts.

The sights, sounds, and overall devastation of postwar Europe convinced Addams of the rightness of many of the resolutions adopted by the International Congress of Women in 1915, including those detailing their conviction that under the conditions of modern warfare, women and noncombatants in general could not be protected from war's ravages. Although the women of the Congress had not envisioned the deliberate blockade on food supplies, that development confirmed its opinion. Addams's trip to Germany was what we today would call a fact-finding mission, aimed at investigating the effects of the Allied blockade after seven months. Her power to convey the scene spread out before her is so keen that one sees the devastation. One of her vignettes, which I call the Story of Winged Shoulder Blades and Feeble Cheers, is unforgettable.[62] It is worth quoting at length, because it helps make clear the intrinsic connection in Addams's mind between the quality of human life and the quality of public policy—which could either work to sustain human fellowship or contribute to the breakage of human relationships.[63] What she saw around her was a shattered social world.

> We were received everywhere in a fine spirit of courtesy. Doctors, nurses and city officials, who were working against tuberculosis, to keep children healthy, to prevent youthful crime and foster education, had long passed the mood of bitterness. What they were facing was the shipwreck of a nation and they had no time for resentments. They realized that if help did not come quickly and abundantly, the coming generation in Germany was doomed to early death or, at best, to a handicapped life.
>
> We had, of course, seen something of widespread European starvation before we went into Germany; our first view in Europe of starved children was in the city of Lille in Northern France, where the school children were being examined for tuberculosis. We had already been told that forty per cent of the children of school age in

Lille had open tuberculosis and that the remaining sixty per cent were practically all suspects. As we entered the door of a large school room, we saw at the other end of the room a row of little boys, from six to ten years of age, passing slowly in front of the examining physician. The children were stripped to the waist and our first impression was of a line of moving skeletons; their little shoulder blades stuck straight out, the vertebrae were all perfectly distinct as were their ribs, and their bony arms hung limply at their sides. To add to the gruesome effect not a sound was to be heard, for the French physician had lost his voice as a result of shell shock during the first bombardment of Lille. He therefore whispered his instructions to the children as he applied his stethoscope and the children, thinking it was some sort of game, whispered back to him. It was incredibly pathetic and unreal and we could but accept the doctor's grave statement that only by a system of careful super-feeding, could any of these boys grow into normal men. We had also seen starved children in Switzerland: six hundred Viennese children arriving in Zurich to be guests in private households. As they stood upon the station platforms without any of the bustle and chatter naturally associated with a large number of children, we had again that painful impression of listlessness as of a mortal illness; we saw the winged shoulder blades standing out through their meagre clothing, the little thin legs which scarcely supported the emaciated bodies. The committee of Swiss women was offering them cakes and chocolates, telling them of the children at home who were waiting for them, but there was little response because there was no vitality with which to make it.

This terrible scene of "death in life" was repeated over and over: the children were starving during the armistice. Addams, Smith, and Hamilton visited playgrounds where children were eating a noonday meal consisting of a pint of war soup—war meal stirred into a pint of hot water. These children "would have nothing more to eat until supper, for which many of the mothers had saved the entire daily ration of bread" because they couldn't bear to hear their children whimper and moan in their sleep from the pangs of hunger and, in some cases, near-starvation. The scene witnessed by Addams and her group in Leipzig is searing, in part because when the children are told that they will have some milk in their soup the day after tomorrow, they break out "into the most ridiculous, feeble little cheer ever heard." For Addams, in these circumstances, the claim of human life to its own preservation exceeded the claim of politics. Feeding these hungry children was a rock-bottom imperative: there was no more exigent claim than this. "Suffer the little children to come unto me," Jesus of Nazareth had said, "and forbid them not, for of such is the Kingdom of God." *Suffer* here means "permit"—permit the children to enter into a way of life based on a radical notion of love and peace. Wherever she went in war-ravaged Europe, Addams saw nothing but dread and suffering, a reduction of the human condition to incessant preoccupation with mere survival. In such conditions, what room was there for any notion of love or peace?

A Pilgrim's Progress Is Complete

The public animosity and isolation experienced by Addams during the war years gradually subsided. Maude Royden, a British pacifist, describes the radical changes in attitudes toward Addams over time:[64]

> In America in 1912 I learned that it was unsafe to mention Jane Addams's name in public speech unless you were prepared for an interruption, because the mere reference to her provoked such a storm of applause. They told me that Jane Addams's mere promise of support to Mr. Theodore Roosevelt was worth a million votes to him. . . . And I was in America again after the war, and I realized with a shock how complete was the eclipse of her fame . . . her popularity had swiftly and completely vanished. . . . How well I remember, when I spoke in America in 1922 and 1923, the silence that greeted the name of Jane Addams! The few faithful who tried to applaud only made the silence more depressing. What she must have suffered! It was the characteristic of Jane Addams that she could not put on armor, not even defensive armor. This is the very soul of peacemaking, when a person's very heart is not defended, and in this sense Jane Addams was the most completely defenseless person in the world. She was defenseless in the profound sense in which Christ was defenseless.

The years of unpopularity were also years of political blacklisting by the Daughters of the American Revolution (of which Addams was a member) and the publication of their famous "Spiderweb Chart" of putative conspiracy against the government of the United States, with Addams as the very heart of the intricate web. But as the war years receded and Addams aged, her public reputation gradually improved. The acclaim and adoration that had been hers before the war were never fully restored; but she had arrived at a venerable age, an age at which people traditionally were spoken of with respect. During the hard years of the Depression and the early years of the New Deal, Addams again became a candidate for public honors, celebrations, and awards.

Her public activities during the 1920s and the 1930s were focused almost entirely on the Women's International League for Peace and Freedom and on internationalist and pacifist efforts generally. She made many more trips abroad.[65] These included trips to the Hague in 1915, to Zurich in 1919, to Vienna in 1921, to Honolulu in 1928, and to Prague in 1929. In January 1923, she began a nine-month journey around the world. Wherever she went, the reception was warm; in some places, even triumphant.

It was in conjunction with this arduous around-the-world tour that Addams responded to requests she had received from various international women's organizations for a Christmas message "to the women of the world." In this message, Addams speaks of fear and apprehension in Europe and argues that we should all "stand shamefaced in the midst of Christmas rejoicing." Did not "He whose birthday we celebrate" give a "basic command to His followers, 'Be just and fear not'?" But what does one see when one looks around? In the United States, there is a government that has "abandoned the solemn covenants made in her name," that has restricted immigration and withdrawn from international responsibility. Addams calls upon China and Japan to reject the sword and the dominance of military authority over civil life. She extols the resolute preparation for citizenship under way in African lands, India, and the Philippines, praising Gandhi as one committed to "the Christian adventure" in a way, clearly, that the West is not.[66]

During this period, Addams maintained Hull-House as her official address, but she was in residence less and less frequently. Maintaining a schedule that would fell an ordinary person, she became more and more prone to illness, with ever lengthening periods of recuperation. In the 1920s she was overtaken by pneumonia and kidney disease. She was operated on in 1923 for a kidney ailment. In 1926 she was diagnosed with angina. She had a tumor removed in 1931 and underwent a mastectomy in Japan. Her closest friend and companion, Mary Rozet Smith, died in February 1934. Letters of condolence poured in, commenting on how extraordinary it was to have, and to lose, such a dear friend. Addams told her close associates that in times of grief and loss, one has only two options: go on or give up. She never gave up. Even in the midst of illness and personal losses, her writing career never faltered. *Peace and Bread in Time of War* was published in 1922; *The Second Twenty Years at Hull-House,* in 1930; *The Excellent Becomes the Permanent,* in 1932; and her final book, *My Friend, Julia Lathrop,* posthumously, in 1935. Perhaps her resolve to continue was strengthened by these recollections of her extraordinary life and of her role in helping "invent an American national community in which each individual was an important and valued part."[67]

The democratic fellowship she sought so ardently for the nation as a whole had been hers in abundance. The cadre of extraordinary women and professionals she helped bring together and inspired to action remained steadfastly loyal throughout her life. As many important social historians have pointed out, the sisterhood of affinity and vocation was a potent relation for nineteenth-century women. To many women who did not pursue marriage and maternity, the "relationship of a sister was perhaps the noblest and purest two adults could have with one another since the ideal embodied disinterested love, devotion, and friendship."[68]

Indeed, the rehabilitation of Addams's public reputation was largely the work of her close friends and of a number of distinguished citizens who were determined to honor her. January 1927 witnessed a dinner celebrating her life and accomplishments. Encomiums were heaped upon her head. Addams rose in response to the tributes and said that she was, in fact, a simple person who was "not at all sure I am right, and most of the time not right, though wanting to be; which I am sure we all know of ourselves. I can only hope that we may go on together, working as we go for the betterment of things, and with thorough enjoyment and participation in those many things which are making for righteousness."[69] More celebrations and anniversaries followed. The facilities at Hull-House had not been expanded since 1913, but the complex continued to flourish and celebrated its 40th anniversary in 1929. Hard upon the heels of that commemoration came Addams's seventieth birthday party, in 1930. In 1931 she was named first among the twelve greatest living women in America by a committee of distinguished men. She popped up on a list of six outstanding present-day Americans. She was even dubbed a "Contemporary Immortal." Through it all, her internationalist and pacifist activities continued. These, too, were eventually honored when, in 1931, she was awarded the Nobel Peace Prize, sharing the award with Nicholas Murray Butler. She was too ill to travel to Oslo to receive the prize in person, having been operated on for a lung tumor at Johns Hopkins and having reacted badly to the anesthetic, and was advised to remain at home and rest.[70]

Julia Lathrop died in 1932, prompting Addams to pen a tribute to Lathrop's life, which became both a paean to collegiality and friendship and a history of the era and the events that the two women and their extraordinary compatriots had shared. Perhaps the greatest tribute of all paid to Addams was a fete on May 3, 1935, in honor of her seventy-fifth year, involving a complicated international radio broadcast that featured speakers from London, Paris, Moscow, and Tokyo. Six months had been required to perfect the arrangement, which were reported to have been the most complicated in the history of broadcasting to that point. Each of the speakers was introduced by a dignitary. In Addams's case, this was Josephine Roche, Assistant Secretary of the U.S. Treasury, who called the tribute to Addams unparalleled and proclaimed that peace was born only of justice, and justice was what Addams's life had been about. Speaking from the NBC studios in Washington, Addams called for the substitution of law for war and political processes for brute force.[71] "We don't expect to change human nature," she insisted, "but we do expect to change human behavior." She was resolutely committed to change and yet was an equally determined anti-utopian: there are things that can be changed, and things that cannot and should not be uprooted.

Back in Chicago, she completed a round of meetings and returned to Hull-House for dinner with the residents. On May 15, 1935, she reported severe pain. Physicians were called in for consultation. She was taken to the hospital on May 17 to be operated on. She understood that her body was beginning to fail her. When the doctors at the Passavant Hospital operated, they discovered an inoperable cancer as well as an intestinal blockage that had been the source of the excruciating pain. She rallied briefly, asking for a drink of water but acquiescing when she was told she could take no liquids at the moment. She joked with one of her doctors: "When I was a child, I had an old doctor friend who told me the hardest thing in the world was to kill an old woman. He seems to have been right."[72] Louise de Koven Bowen, a longtime Hull-House sponsor and Addams's close friend, was among those who kept vigil. She described the events of Addams's last days: Addams maintained her spirits, and continued to read the novel she had brought to the hospital with her, being determined to finish it. At one point, she turned to Bowen and said, "Don't look so solemn, dear."

On Monday, May 20, Addams began to slip into a coma. She died on May 21 in the hospital, surrounded by family, associates, friends, and Hull-House residents, who filled her ninth-floor room and overflowed into the hallway. Her death and funeral evoked an outpouring of public affection and international tribute. A plain light gray casket was selected, and her body lay in state in Bowen Hall at Hull-House. On the day of the funeral, her body was moved from Bowen Hall to the Hull-House terrace. It was a beautiful Chicago day, Louise Bowen writes, and floral and written tributes had flowed in from around the world. Those who passed by as she lay in state included the low and the mighty: no one kept track of how many thousands flowed through Bowen Hall, but at least six thousand per hour moved in single file for a four-hour period in the evening; and around fifteen hundred per hour had gone through during the day. Families were dressed in their Sunday best as a sign of respect. Stores and shops up and down Halsted Street, including the saloons, were closed and draped in purple. People jammed the Hull-House courtyard and adjacent terraces. Loudspeakers carried the service to the Hull-House theater and coffeehouse, and onto Halsted Street, which was also jammed with people. The Hull-House music school provided music for the ceremony. Addams's friend and fellow settlement house pioneer, Graham Taylor, offered the benediction. After the funeral her body was taken by train to Freeport, and thence by hearse to Cedarville, to be buried in the little local cemetery just a short remove from the Addams homestead. A huge crowd greeted the casket's arrival at the Freeport train station. In Cedarville, several thousand visitors had assembled to pay their respects, and they filled the little village to overflowing. The ceremony at the cemetery was brief, with readings of a single Bible verse and two poems.

Tributes continued to pour in for days after the funeral. Many were effusive, describing Addams as "like Mother Earth" or even "like the Mother of God." Addams would have been embarrassed by that sort of thing. More to her liking, surely, would have been the now-famous eulogy written by Walter Lippman:[73]

> She had compassion without condescension. She had pity without retreat into vulgarity. She had infinite sympathy for common things without forgetfulness of those that are uncommon. That, I think, is why those who have known her say that she was not only good, but great. For this blend of sympathy with distinction, of common humanity with a noble style is recognizable by those who have eyes to see it as the occasional but authentic issue of the mystic promise of American democracy.

"The mystic promise of American democracy" may sound alien to our jaded contemporary ears. For Addams, democracy was a form of public action making possible the doing of simple tasks in peace: the daily tasks of tending to bodies, of making a home and a family, of sustaining friendships, of trying to be a decent citizen of a community. It was this affirmation of everyday life that Addams reflected and refracted in her life's work and in her very being. She had many rich sources on which to draw: early life experiences in a small, close-knit town; a fine public education; a strong moral center in her father; and great texts in Western politics, religion, law, and literature to stimulate her mind and to equip her for her pilgrim's progress. If to this one adds her capacity for friendship, one finds at least the "raw materials" that went into the making of such an extraordinary personality.

D URING ONE OF MY VISITS to the Hull-House museum, the director permitted me to examine and to hold Addams's death mask. I was struck by the full face with its fine features and the nose slightly askew. I interpreted her expression as benign, although I'm not sure that's quite the right word. Her face was full, but not fleshy. She had the well-worn look of a woman of seventy-five whose primary concern had not been the preservation of a youthful appearance. Also on display were castings of her hands, which were wonderful, with fine, long fingers. I was struck by the length of the fingernails, especially on the little finger. She had long, almost sculpted nails. Her hands seemed both delicate and sturdy. They were not a scrubwoman's hands, nor those of a society lady, but they bore elements of each. Such a small woman. Such a tremendous force.

AFTERWORD

❧

Return to Cedarville

'Twas in another lifetime, one of toil and blood
When blackness was a virtue and the road was full of mud
I came in from the wilderness, a creature void of form.
"Come in," she said,
"I'll give you shelter from the storm."

I was burned out from exhaustion, buried in the hail,
Poisoned in the bushes an' blown out on the trail,
Hunted like a crocodile, ravaged in the corn.
"Come in," she said,
"I'll give you shelter from the storm."

I've heard newborn babies wailing like a mournin' dove
And old men with broken teeth stranded without love.
Do I understand your question, man is it hopeless and
Forlorn
"Come in," she said,
"I'll give you shelter from the storm."

— "SHELTER FROM THE STORM,"
WORDS AND MUSIC BY BOB DYLAN

JANUARY 6, 2001. I'm in Chicago, where the Society for Christian Ethics is meeting. Having completed my part of the program, I dragoon a friend who has both a free day and a good automobile, and my son Eric, a graduate student at the University of Chicago, to drive me to Cedarville on this sunny but cold day. The snow is piled up in six-foot-high drifts on the side roads. But the trip seems necessary and not entirely unreasonable. I'm nearing the completion of the "Jane book," and I want to make a return visit to her homestead—this time, to see the interior of the old home, at the invitation of the current owners, Tom and Ida Ennenga.

The space that once was the downstairs bedroom where Laura Jane Addams was born on September 6, 1860, is now part of the kitchen. There are five bedrooms, each with a fireplace. A letter written by Jane Addams to her niece Marcet hangs on one wall, framed behind glass. Ennenga tried heroically to transcribe it, but he discovered what every Addams scholar discovers: that her handwriting is atrociously difficult to decipher. Books from John H. Addams's lending library are also stored behind glass. Glancing at the huge barn with the millstone propped up against it, I recall Jane Addams's story about how desperately she yearned for a "miller's thumb" so that she could be, in as many ways as possible, just like her father.

Cedar Creek, which runs along the edge of the vast yard, is home to smallmouth bass and northern pike, writes Ennenga, an ardent fisherman. He continues: "Across the creek is a pie shaped tract lying between the old roadbed of the hiway to Madison and the limestone bluff. It's about 2–3 acres and contains, in the bluff, a cave or crevasse perfect for the amusement of small children. Jane Addams called it her 'fairyland.'" It has been retained as a wilderness area by the Ennengas.

We take our leave of the Ennengas and bear right, heading for the cemetery. The cemetery's circle drive has been cleared, but the gravestones are buried beneath at least thirty inches of accumulated snow. It is easy to spot the Addams family burial site because of the distinctive obelisk that rises above the graves. My friend and my son fairly drag me through the snow to the burial site: My left leg, weakened by childhood polio, is no match for the thirty inches of snow. We manage to get there. As I place a card on the obelisk and lay down three roses, Eric brushes off Addams's gravestone to reveal its inscription: "Jane Addams of Hull House and the Women's International League for Peace and Freedom." We notice recent footprints in the heavy snow, leading directly to her grave and there, frozen solid atop her gravestone, a few red poppies.

We are freezing. My feet, unbooted, are cold and wet.

"We should all thank her before we leave," I say, and we do. As for the flowers: we left a red rose, bearing witness to her passion and her determination; a white rose, to the nobility of her purpose and the flame of an ambition that she submitted to the humbling discipline of public service, and a yellow rose for her love of beauty and her ability to convey the many vivid scenes, some unlovely, out of which nonetheless moments of beauty and grace, dignity and courage, emerged.

Jane Addams's sins were the sins of the large-hearted. She generated a large public purpose that derived from her moral convictions, her keen intelligence, her dream of a generous American democracy, and her own personal pain. She understood that words and convictions, without deeds, or without the space within which to speak and to act, wither on the vine and may well corrode the soul. She never lost sight of the single, unique person in her determination to ease the suffering of the many. How can we forget them: little Goosie, lying still and lifeless on a pile of refuse; the old German woman, clinging to her chest of drawers, emitting animal cries; the four-year-old bundle of human misery crouched against the wall, pulling out basting stitches hour after hour; the silent, shuffling line of malnourished children in war-ravaged Europe, capable of issuing only a feeble cheer when they learn they are to get milk on the morrow.

Perhaps it is well that Addams died before the full horror of World War II was revealed. Would this hideous war have stretched her pacifist convictions to the breaking point? Would she have held firm? My hunch is that she would, but with a broken heart. She certainly would have condemned all of the violations and horrors committed by the participants. She would have been appalled by Hitler and Stalin. She would have criticized her country for its strategic bombing of German cities and for the use of atomic weapons. She would have called for generosity in rebuilding and reconstruction after the war. I believe she would have emerged as a critic of what the postwar welfare state became, with its mode of top-down social provision and its turning of would-be and should-be citizens into clients. There is much about which she would have had something to say. Her voice was so eloquent, it would have been a pleasure to listen, whether one agreed with her or not.

There are days when I think the world has passed her by; that she is so securely lodged in a bygone era that it is impossible to draw her into a conversation about our situation, dominated as it is by impersonal techniques and the rush to turn everything into a commodity. We are buyers and sellers. We see no limits to the use of our powers. Techno-enthusiasm is everywhere. Geneticists are gearing up to clone human beings. The delicate, fragile, indelible, and irreplaceable lineaments of *this* singular, unique self, and none other: what happens if that goes? I think the human race will go mad—not stark, raving mad like someone foaming at the mouth in a "B" movie—but we will lose our bearings. We may be unable to make our way back to what it means to be, simply, human and to respond to that singularity. There is a wonderful phrase used by philosopher Karol Wojtyla in an essay he wrote before he became pontiff, in which he argues that when we deal with human beings and with their unique individuality, we must pause "at the irreducible."

Jane Addams always paused at the irreducible. Her solidarity never wavered, because it was not based on abstract categories that smother persons and strip away their individuality but, instead, on human empathy that was capacious enough to encompass the falling-down drunk and the mentally ill.

This much is clear: All those who were, in one way or another, alien or foreign, she welcomed as neighbors. We are all bidden, she insisted, to welcome them. "Come in," she said. "I'm just having some tea. Would you care to join me?" In this she never wavered. She was braver than we. Whatever her limitations and shortcomings, whatever the limitations and shortcomings of the astonishing institution that she imagined and brought into being, we, as a culture, could do worse, much worse. Indeed, we have.

Come in, she said. There is shelter from the storm.

NOTES

Preface

1. See Jean Bethke Elshtain, *Democracy on Trial* (New York: Basic Books, 1995); Robert Putnam, *Bowling Alone* (New York: Simon and Schuster, 2000); and "A Call to Civil Society: Why Democracy Needs Moral Truths," the 1998 report of the Council on Civil Society, which I chaired.

2. Readers may want to consult the companion to this volume, Jean Bethke Elshtain, ed., *The Jane Addams Reader* (New York: Basic Books, 2001), which includes excerpts from each of Addams's books, as well as many of her essays and newspaper articles.

Introduction

1. The publisher of this history is listed simply as "County of Stephenson." Chapter 6 is devoted to Jane Addams. The information about John Huy Addams appears on p. 70.

2. *History of Stephenson County,* p. 351.

3. Addams's style of dress was so predictably understated that when she departed from it, it became news. Thus the *Chicago Evening Post* of November 17, 1897, noted: "No anachronism can startle now. Francis of Assisi in doublet and hose. Tolstoi in three inch collar and claw hammer coat. Imagination stops at nothing. Jane Addams has appeared in scarlet shoes" (Jane Addams papers, Swarthmore Peace collection).

4. This bit of information was contributed by my son Eric, who has an interest in archaeology and paleontology.

5. Jane Addams, *Twenty Years at Hull-House, with Autobiographical Notes* (New York: Macmillan, 1910), pp. 35–36.

6. See Addams, *Twenty Years at Hull-House,* pp. 92–93. The famous color-coded maps in the Hull-House maps and papers volume show one small area inhabited by African Americans.

7. Addams, *Twenty Years at Hull-House*, pp. 97–98.

8. It is very likely that Addams knew this standard hymn for children, as it was then and remains today very popular. The tune is that of the famous Civil War song "Tramp, tramp, tramp / The boys are marching." After the war, gentler lyrics were set to this tune, to suit what everyone hoped would be a time of peaceful reconciliation.

9. I do not intend to imply that Ruby and Marie can be viewed scientifically as representing a randomly selected population, although their reverence for Jane Addams and their abiding enthusiasm for Hull-House do confirm the contents of other notes and letters I have received and conversations I have had over the years with those who worked with Jane Addams or encountered her in one capacity or another. I have included parts of our conversation here as a piece of illustrative Hull-House lore. This conversation with the two women, who were at first reluctant to talk to me, came about because a Chicago newsman, Marty Kusak, after seeing a list of Guggenheim Fellowship awardees and their respective projects—mine was described as "an intellectual biography of Jane Addams"—contacted me and told me that his mother and his aunt were children of Italian immigrants who had lived in the 19th ward and who had vivid memories of Hull-House. I welcomed the chance to speak to Addams's neighbors, and the interview eventually took place in May 1993. With the permission of Ruby and Marie, I taped the conversation, and I have listened to it several times since then. I did my own transcription, because the two women talked rapidly, often in a cross-cutting and multilayered dialogue, and I could most easily identify which voice belonged to which woman.

10. Ruby and Marie did not identify this program by name. They might have had in mind "The House that Jane Built," which was aired in Chicago the week of November 11–17, 1990. I later watched a tape of this program, which I found boring. The drama and vitality of the Hull-House experience seemed toned down and tamed. Ellen Burstyn, who narrated the program, spoke in the saccharine tone that people sometimes use to convey just how enlightened and wonderful and solemn are the events they describe. There is no hint of the frenetic pace, the hustle-bustle in which the residents lived in those first few years, or of their state of continual near-exhaustion. I know of no adequate documentary or cinematic treatment either of Hull-House or of Jane Addams's life.

11. They were describing the 750-seat Bowman Auditorium.

Chapter 1

1. Jane Addams wrote a biography of the former, titled *My Friend Julia Lathrop* (New York: Macmillan, 1935). Distinguished historian Kathryn Kish

Sklar authored a later biography titled *Florence Kelley and the Nation's Work: The Rise of Women's Political Culture, 1830–1900* (New Haven: Yale University Press, 1995).

2. Christopher Lasch, *The New Radicalism in America* (New York: Vintage Books, 1965), p. 27.

3. Christopher Lasch, ed., *The Social Thought of Jane Addams* (Indianapolis, Ind.: Bobbs-Merrill, 1965), pp. xiii–xiv, xxvi, cv; and Lasch, *The New Radicalism in America*, pp. 3–37. Addams's discussion of applied knowledge, it seems to me, is not at all anti-intellectual and is more complicated than represented by Lasch. Others who have commented on Addams in the context of pragmatism and progressivism include Robert B. Westbrook, *John Dewey and American Democracy* (Ithaca, N.Y.: Cornell University Press, 1991), p. 89. Westbrook echoes Lasch: "It is difficult to say whether Dewey influenced Jane Addams or Jane Addams influenced Dewey. They influenced each other and generously acknowledged their mutual obligation." In their description of the Addams-Dewey link, Westbrook and Lasch are fairer than their counterparts who have more or less ignored Addams despite the recent rediscovery of Dewey and pragmatism. John J. McDermott (see John J. McDermott, ed., *The Philosophy of John Dewey*, 2 vols. [Chicago: University of Chicago Press, 1981]) mentions Addams only in passing, saying that much of Dewey's "range of interests" can be traced to Addams and Hull-House (p. xxxii). The Dewey–Hull-House connection is far more intense than most realize. Dewey's wife was active at Hull-House, and Dewey worked out some of his ideas in his correspondence with Jane Addams. In a letter dated October 12, 1898, Dewey wrote Addams in apology, to "take back what I said the other night": "Not only is actual antagonizing bad, but the assumption that there is or may be antagonism is bad, in fact the first antagonism always comes back to the assumption. I'm glad I found this out before I began to talk on social psychology or otherwise I fear I should have made a mess of it. This is rather a suspiciously sudden conversion but then it's only a beginning. Gratefully yours, John Dewey." Another famous American thinker who praised Addams unstintingly in his correspondence with her is William James. In a letter of February 12, 1907, he enthuses: "Yours is a deeply original mind, and all so quiet and harmless! Yet revolutionary in the extreme, and I should suspect that this very work could act as a ferment thru long years to come. I read precious little sociological literature, and my opinions in that field are worth nothing—but I am willing to *bet* on you."

4. Jacob Riis, *The Trouble with the Slum* (New York: Macmillan, 1902), p. 395.

5. Elizabeth (Mrs. Albert S.) Dilling, *The Red Network* (Kenilworth, Ill.: Published by the author, 1934), p. 51. The book had gone through six print-

ings by September 1936. The discussion of Addams is found on pp. 51–53. Addams also receives the longest entry in Dilling's index of "Who Is Who in Radicalism?"

6. Tom Lutz, *American Nervousness* (Ithaca, N.Y.: Cornell University Press, 1991), p. 28.

7. Rivka Shpak Lissak, *Pluralism and Progressives: Hull House and the New Immigrants, 1890–1919* (Chicago: University of Chicago Press, 1989), p. 20. It is difficult to take seriously Lissak's contention that something called "settlement ideology" had as its overriding raison d'être "disarming the workers of their class consciousness" and assigning them a "passive role in American society" (pp. 22–23). What class consciousness might that be? The consciousness of the immigrant communities was overwhelmingly ethnic, national, religious, and linguistic. Addams notes time after time the reproduction of old world nationalist conflicts in her part of Chicago. Why should this surprise anyone who knows that some three dozen languages or dialects were spoken in and around the 19th ward? The notion that there was a homogeneous, militant "class consciousness" that Addams and the other women of Hull-House worked overtime to extirpate by applying soothing, deradicalizing syrup falls flat when it is brought up against the historic realities of the situation.

8. W.E.B. DuBois (1868–1963) was a professor of economics and history, a cofounder of the National Association for the Advancement of Colored People, and the author of many books about African American experiences (*The Souls of Black Folk* is perhaps the best known among them). In defending Addams against the blanket charge of paternalism, I am not suggesting that she was entirely free from such an attitude. But she was perpetually on guard against such tendencies and she worked hard at self-criticism. Her insistence that she learned as much from her immigrant neighbors as they did from her comes through resoundingly. This is not the stuff of which paternalism is made.

9. Mary Jo Deegan, *Jane Addams and the Men of the Chicago School, 1892–1918* (New Brunswick, N.J.: Transaction Books, 1990), p. 295.

10. James Weber Linn, *Jane Addams* (New York: D. Appleton–Century, 1937). Linn explains in his preface that his aunt turned over to him "all files of her own manuscripts, published and unpublished; all letters, records, and clippings which she had preserved, from her first valentine to her last round-the-world speech in Washington on May 1, 1935." He adds: "My aunt read over and annotated the first draft of the first eight chapters of this book, talked over the next three, and agreed upon the proportion of the remainder" (p. vii). Linn states that his is "not so much an interpretation of Jane Addams as the story of her life," as if the life could be represented absent interpretation.

11. Linn, *Jane Addams*, p. 424.

12. Linn, *Jane Addams,* p. 425.

13. Linn, *Jane Addams,* p. 439.

14. The laudatory comparison Addams would most have cherished is with her hero, Abraham Lincoln. Several plaudits along these lines were evoked by her death. Addams herself frequently alluded to a Lincoln-Addams connection beginning with her father's friendship with the martyred president in *Twenty Years at Hull-House.* Jane was the hero-worshiping, father-adoring daughter of John Addams; it is thus unsurprising that Lincoln loomed so large for her as a child or that as an adult she extolled Lincoln as the man who really "cleared the title" for the American democracy. In *Lincoln in American Memory,* American historian Merrill D. Peterson uses Jennie Addams's recollection of "the shock of Lincoln's death" to illustrate the general reaction to this event experienced by Americans of her generation. Citing Addams's autobiography, he repeats her words at finding her father in tears—"something I had never seen before"—and the combination of lowered flags and the tears of a father coupled with his words "that the greatest man in the world had died" not only summarize the nation's grief but propel young Jennie into "the thrilling and solemn interests of a world lying quite outside the two white gate posts" (Peterson, *Lincoln in American Memory* [New York: Oxford University Press, 1994], p. 5).

15. "Jane Addams," *Life* (Fall 1990), p. 61.

16. "At Chicago's First Settlement House, Clients Are New but Problems Are Old," *New York Times* (June 9, 1989), p. 16.

17. Allen F. Davis, *American Heroine: The Life and Legend of Jane Addams* (New York: Oxford University Press, 1973), chapter V, footnote 45, p. 306. One of Eleanor Roosevelt's grandchildren, Nancy Roosevelt Ireland, wrote a letter to the *New York Times Book Review* expressing her dismay at similar speculations about Eleanor Roosevelt's sex life in the biography by Blanche Weisen Cook. She wrote, "[There is] absolutely no conclusive evidence to support these charges, and I find them irresponsible," and asked, Why must one sexual orientation or another and feminism be linked? Surely there is no such necessary linkage? Besides that, to take "a woman for whom upbringing, etiquette, politeness, and other social mores of the time were the guidelines and restrictions of her behavior—and push 1990s attitudes and so-called liberation upon her is inappropriate, offensive and ill-fitting" ("Letters," *New York Times Book Review,* Sunday, June 14, 1992, p. 34).

18. See Rochelle Gurstein, *The Repeal of Reticence* (New York: Hill and Wang, 1996), for a fascinating discussion of the displacement of the culture of reticence by the culture of tell-all.

19. From the Swarthmore College Collection of Jane Addams's papers, courtesy of Anne Firor Scott.

20. Note that whereas Mary Rozet Smith saved Addams's letters to her, her letters to Addams seem not to have survived.

21. Joan Acocella, *Willa Cather and the Politics of Criticism* (Lincoln: University of Nebraska Press, 2000), p. 47. In connection with this discussion, I recall that best girlfriends did a lot of hand-holding through about age fourteen or fifteen, when I was a teenager in the late 1950s. In the social context of the time, this practice was a typical gesture of close friendship, with no sexual overtones whatsoever.

22. See John C. Farrell, *Beloved Lady: A History of Jane Addams' Ideas on Reform and Peace* (Baltimore, Md.: Johns Hopkins University Press, 1967). This book originated as Farrell's dissertation, and the manuscript was not yet complete when Farrell, who was still young, unexpectedly died. Although *Beloved Lady* offers an evocative interpretation of Addams, the book has remained largely ignored in contemporary scholarship—perhaps because Farrell took Addams seriously as a thinker, going against the standard view of her as primarily a publicist and a social worker.

23. Davis, *American Heroine*, p. xi.

24. Daniel Levine, *Jane Addams and the American Liberal Tradition* (Madison: State Historical Society of Wisconsin, 1971; reprint ed., Westport, Conn.: Greenwood Press, 1980), p. x.

25. Henry Steele Commager, *The American Mind* (New Haven: Yale University Press, 1959).

26. Henry Steele Commager, "Foreword," in Jane Addams, *Twenty Years at Hull-House* (New York: New American Library, Signet Classic, 1960), p. xvi. Another dean of American historians, Ralph Henry Gabriel, in his classic text *The Course of American Democratic Thought* (New Haven: Yale University Press, 1956), mentions Addams in a single scanty reference in his discussion of progressivism. He offers kudos to the progressives for having transcended agrarian parochialism and the humanitarianism of reformers like Jane Addams and Jacob Riis in favor of a more cosmopolitan, less personalistic stance. In *The Age of Reform* (New York: Vintage Books, 1955), Richard Hofstadter characterizes an early essay by Addams, "The Subjective Necessity for Social Settlements" as "fine and penetrating." Addams herself, he declares, embodies "the most decent stream" in the progressive movement, given her awareness of the alienation attendant upon industrialization (pp. 178, 209).

27. Anne Firor Scott, "Jane Addams," in *Notable American Women, 1607–1950*, ed. Edward T. James (Cambridge, Mass.: Harvard University Belknap Press, 1971), vol. 1, pp. 16–21.

28. Jill Ker Conway, "Jane Addams: An American Heroine," *Dædalus* (Spring 1965, pp. 761–780), p. 761.

29. Conway, "Jane Addams: An American Heroine," p. 764.

30. Conway credits Addams with organizational ability and with having pursued an "instinctive search for intellectual excellence"; but because it was instinctive, she downgrades it ("Jane Addams: An American Heroine," p. 767).

31. Farrell, *Beloved Lady,* p. 25.

32. I found a clipping of this article in the Swarthmore College Collection, among the collected notes of Anne Firor Scott. The *Peoria Illinois Journal* (April 17, 1903) similarly noted Addams's habit of getting all her ducks in a row before she began a fight: "When Miss Jane Addams of Hull House, and her cohorts undertake to do anything in the city of Chicago, it is a good time to dodge. Miss Addams does not say much beforehand, she has her data all in and the documents in evidence ready to be submitted before she strikes and then—well, Miss Addams has never yet fouled out, nor been retired in the bench for fanning—she is a safe hitter."

33. Addams would never have described herself as a tough-minded Machiavellian. Given that she repudiated a narrow, power-oriented definition of politics, for her to have embraced a strategic image of herself would have been unthinkable. Davis also detects American chauvinism at work in Addams's writings; but this criticism, too, seems wide of the mark. There is a difference between sharing Lincoln's sense of "the last best hope on earth" and chauvinistically celebrating one's own culture at the expense of other ways of life. Addams resisted the overidentification of public life with narrow nationalism of the sort that precludes criticism of governments, and she openly opposed the advocates of an American mission to "make the world safe for democracy" in World War I.

34. Addams, *Twenty Years at Hull-House,* p. 35.

35. The motivation for her inclusion may be nothing but the desire for inclusiveness; but whatever is at work, at least some high school and college students will get a taste of the American essay in the hands of a morally formed civic character in one of its most compelling incarnations. (My thanks to Christine Hume for alerting me to the inclusion of Addams in the Norton anthology.) Although *Twenty Years at Hull-House* has never gone out of print, Addams's other works have. A few are once again available in reprints. The original Macmillan edition of *Twenty Years* that I have been using, which I purchased from a library, contains a record of "check-outs" from February 19, 1945, to the day I purchased it, in 1990. The book was checked out in 1945, 1946, 1947, 1948, 1949, 1951, 1953, 1955, 1956, 1957, and 1958. But a forty-two-year hiatus follows: no one borrowed the book between 1958 and 1990. And this, remember, is Addams's most popular and most widely read book.

36. Jean Bethke Elshtain, *Women and War* (New York: Basic Books, 1987; 2d ed., University of Chicago Press, 1992).

37. Addams, *Twenty Years at Hull-House* (New York: Macmillan, 1910), pp. 155–156. Herbert Leibowitz, in his very perceptive discussion of Jane Addams in *Fabricating Lives: Explorations in American Autobiography* (New York: Alfred A. Knopf, 1989), uses this same story to illustrate Addams's descriptive powers. I had already made use of the story in an essay on Addams written in the mid-1980s and reprinted in my *Power Trips and Other Journeys* (Madison: University of Wisconsin Press, 1992), before happening on Leibowitz's similar selection. This fact reinforces my conviction that these are passages of unusual power. (Leibowitz cites the story on p. 143 of *Fabricating Lives.*)

38. Jane Addams to Alice Addams Haldeman, February 19, 1889, *Jane Addams Papers on Microfilm*, ed. Mary Lynn McCree Bryan (Ann Arbor, Mich.: University Microfilms International, 1985), reel 2, frames 1017–1019.

39. Flannery O'Connor, "The Nature and Aim of Fiction," in *Mystery and Manners* (New York: Farrar, Straus and Giroux, 1961), pp. 63–86.

Chapter 2

1. All quotes in this chapter are from Jane Addams, *Twenty Years at Hull-House* (New York: Macmillan, 1910), unless otherwise noted. This particular quote is found on page 5, in chapter I, "Earliest Impressions."

2. This formulation is from Herbert Leibowitz, *Fabricating Lives: Explorations in American Autobiography* (New York: Alfred A. Knopf, 1989), p. 132.

3. Addams, *Twenty Years at Hull-House,* p. 1.

4. Addams, *Twenty Years at Hull-House,* pp. 6–7.

5. Letter from Jane Addams to Vallie Beck, March 21, 1877, *Jane Addams Papers on Microfilm* [hereafter, JAPM], ed. Mary Lynn McCree Bryan (Ann Arbor, Mich.: University Microfilms International, 1985), reel 1, frame 0211; letter from Addams to Beck, May 3, 1877, JAPM, r. 1, f. 0221; letter from Addams to Beck, August 3, 1878, JAPM, r. 1, f. 0315; letter from Addams to Eva Campbell, July 25, 1879, JAPM, r. 1, f. 0363.

6. Letter from Jane Addams to Anna Haldeman Addams, October 21, 1879.

7. Letter from Jane Addams to Ellen Gates Starr, January 28, l880. (Addams was then twenty years old and a student at Rockford Seminary.)

8. Joan Acocella's description of the young Willa Cather evokes comparison with Jennie Addams: "She was one of those genius children—a show-off, an explosion, a pest" (Joan Acocella, *Willa Cather and the Politics of Criticism* [Lincoln: University of Nebraska Press, 2000], p. 6). Jennie Addams seems not to have been the tomboy that Willa Cather was, but her incessant challenge to prevailing norms is similar. Any child who starts a regimen of rising at 3 A.M.

in order to plow through Scripture or the classics, no matter how equable that child's temperament, is going to present complexities for a family. Such a child cannot help but be a show-off in everyday conversation because of what she is thinking and what she has learned.

9. Addams, *Twenty Years at Hull-House*, p. 1.

10. Addams, *Twenty Years at Hull-House*, p. 8.

11. Addams, *Twenty Years at Hull-House*, pp. 12, 16.

12. Addams, *Twenty Years at Hull-House*, p. 12.

13. In her strong association with her father and with a wider world of action, Jane Addams was typical of many strong, active nineteenth-century women. Fathers often encouraged their capable daughters to study and to break out of a narrow definition of domesticity. It is unsurprising that a woman seeking a life beyond the terms of domesticity would seek inspiration, guidance, and mentoring from sympathetic men.

14. The holdings of the lending library that John Addams helped found in 1847 were extraordinary. According to John C. Farrell: "While not a large library, nor one that contained the scientific exhibits and apparatus usually connected with libraries in more settled parts of the country, the Union Library Company at Cedar Creek Mills gave its members access to a wide range of information. American history and biography predominated. There were books on scattered scientific, religious and ethical, and economic subjects. The library also contained a surprising number of books of special interest to women. Included were Catherine E. Beecher, *Treatise on Domestic Economy*, Miss Margaret Coxe, *Claims of the Country on American Females*, Hannah More's *Works*, Mrs. Sarah Stickney Ellis, *Daughters of England* and *Wives of England*, and a *Guide to Social Happiness*" (*Beloved Lady: A History of Jane Addams' Ideas on Reform and Peace* [Baltimore, Md.: Johns Hopkins University Press, 1967], pp. 28–29). The young Jane Addams had full access to this library and to her father's large personal collection.

15. Francis Hackett, "Hull-House: A Souvenir," *Survey* (June 1, 1925), pp. 275–279, quoted in Allen F. Davis and Mary Lynn McCree, *Eighty Years at Hull-House* (Chicago: Quadrangle Books, 1969), p. 76.

16. Quoted in Davis and McCree, *Eighty Years*, p. 118. The original volume, described by Davis and McCree as "little-known," was published in 1952.

17. The following excerpt is from Florence Kelley, "I Go to Work," *Survey* [June 1, 1927], pp. 271–274, as quoted in Davis and McCree, *Eighty Years*, p. 36.

18. Published originally in *The Commons* (April 1905, p. 225), the poem is reprinted in Davis and McCree, *Eighty Years*, pp. 99–100.

19. I refer to the first and best known of the two parts, the story of Christian's progress to the Heavenly City. It was this first part that was considered indispensable reading for young Protestant Americans.

20. John Bunyan, *Pilgrim's Progress* (New York: Penguin, 1987), p. 11.

21. As a religious Nonconformist in mid-seventeenth-century England, Bunyan suffered persecution, spending twelve years in the Bedford prison for open preaching. He finished the first part of *Pilgrim's Progress* while serving a second, shorter term in 1672.

22. Bunyan, *Pilgrim's Progress,* pp. 11, 13, 19.

23. Bunyan, *Pilgrim's Progress,* p. 73.

24. Bunyan, *Pilgrim's Progress,* p. 39.

25. Cited in James Weber Linn, *Jane Addams* (New York: D. Appleton–Century, 1937), p. 48.

26. Bunyan, *Pilgrim's Progress,* p. 60.

27. Bunyan, *Pilgrim's Progress,* p. 119.

28. Jane Addams, "Bread Givers," pp. 103–104 in *Jane Addams: A Centennial Reader* (New York: Macmillan, 1960). All quotes in this passage are from this text.

29. Leibowitz, *Fabricating Lives,* p. 134.

30. For a brilliant development of this theme see Michael Andre Bernstein, *Foregone Conclusions* (Berkeley: University of California Press, 1994), p. 84 *et passim.*

31. The quotes are from Bernstein, *Foregone Conclusions,* p. 91.

32. Herbert Macauley was a British essayist (1864–1946).

33. She expresses dissatisfaction with this paper, however, writing her teacher, Miss Potter: "I'm afraid this isn't exactly logical, but when I rewrite it I think I can condense my ideas better." My hunch is that the thesis (that cognition is the very essence of the human being) troubled her, given her rejection of excessive rationalism, but she was not yet able to articulate this to her satisfaction.

34. Her juvenilia include a strange little essay titled "Tramps" that jars, at least initially, because it seems incompatible with the Jane Addams we have come to know. In this essay, young Jane is in a fine dudgeon about tramps. The country is flooded with them and they are "trying to evade the principle set down from the foundation of the earth that a man must give a full equivalent for everything he receives; by disregarding this principle they render themselves abject & mean and merit their universal contempt." Furthermore, "for a man to tramp around it [the country] expecting to be helped & pleased by all is the height of absurdity, it is an utter impossibility, for it is contrary to the laws of

nature." Tramps are different from the minstrels of old who offered song and beauty in return for bread and board. The wandering per se isn't the problem—nomadic peoples do that—rather, it's the presumption that others will provide for you. One might suggest that sympathetic understanding is clearly not on display in this essay. True enough. But Addams's insistence that one should not simply be on the receiving end of charity, but that one owes something in return, is consistent with her thinking later in life.

35. Girolamo Savonarola (1452–1498), a Florentine reformer who sought to establish an ideal Christian state, was unpopular with the ruling classes, the pope, and the clergy due to his scathing attacks on government and church corruption, materialism, and moral license. He briefly held sway over the republic of Florence but was eventually deposed by a party of aristocrats who had him put to death (tortured, hanged, and burned).

36. Addams, *Twenty Years at Hull-House,* pp. 46–47.

37. This is also a tale of the dangers of excess hubris. Bellerophon's pride prompts him to proclaim that he is equal to Zeus. He urges Pegasus even higher, and tries to enter Olympus. But he has flown too far. Pegasus unseats him and he plummets to earth, falling into thorns in an obscure country and compelled to wander the earth as a beggar until he dies. Pegasus goes on to become the carrier of thunderbolts for Zeus.

38. Addams, *Twenty Years at Hull-House,* pp. 17–18.

39. Addams, *Twenty Years at Hull-House,* p. 18.

40. Mary Douglas, *Natural Symbols* (New York: Pantheon, 1970).

41. Addams, *Twenty Years at Hull-House,* p. 19.

42. Addams, *Twenty Years at Hull-House,* p. 20.

43. Addams, *Twenty Years at Hull-House,* pp. 21–22.

44. Nathaniel Hawthorne, *The Complete Novels and Selected Tales of Nathaniel Hawthorne,* ed. Norman Holmes Pearson (New York: Modern Library, 1937), pp. 1184–1196, p. 1185.

45. Hawthorne, *Complete Novels and Selected Tales,* p. 1189.

46. Hawthorne, *Complete Novels and Selected Tales,* p. 1195.

47. Addams, *Twenty Years at Hull-House,* p. 23.

48. Addams, *Twenty Years at Hull-House,* p. 28.

49. Addams, *Twenty Years at Hull-House,* pp. 31–32.

50. She also had in mind to distribute Thomas Carlyle's *Heroes and Hero-Worship,* for she was an avid reader of Carlyle. But, by her Hull-House days, she had ceased to find him entirely compelling. Instead, she writes in *Twenty Years at Hull-House,* "[we] made much of Lincoln" (p. 36).

51. Addams, *Twenty Years at Hull-House,* p. 36.

52. Addams, *Twenty Years at Hull-House*, pp. 26–27.

53. Edith Wharton, *Ethan Frome* (New York: Charles Scribner's Sons, 1939), p. 13. (Published originally in 1911, the year after *Twenty Years at Hull-House*.)

54. Pater was, like Addams, an avid reader of John Ruskin. Each was drawn to Ruskin's aesthetic sensibility and to his determination to engage, as well, in practical tasks such as gathering privileged young men together to do road building.

55. The description is Harold Bloom's (see his introduction to *The Selected Writings of Walter Pater* [New York: Columbia University Press, 1982], p. xxv).

56. *The Selected Writings of Walter Pater*, p. 9.

57. *The Selected Writings of Walter Pater*, p. 110.

58. Thomas Carlyle, *On Heroes and Hero-Worship and the Heroic in History* (London: Oxford University Press, 1968; orig. ed., 1841), p. 62.

59. The term *neurasthenia* was commonly used in medical diagnoses in the late nineteenth and early twentieth centuries to describe a syndrome of chronic mental and physical fatigue that was then believed to be caused by exhaustion of the nervous system. The term is no longer used in medicine.

60. Addams, *Twenty Years at Hull-House*, p. 65. For more on her back problems and their treatment, see Chapter 3 in the present volume.

61. Addams, *Twenty Years at Hull-House*, p. 37.

62. Edward Caird, *The Evolution of Theology in the Greek Philosophers*, 2 vols. (Glasgow: James MacLehose and Sons, 1904), vol. 1, p. 111. Caird, essentially following the method of Plato, taught that one must rise from opinion to truth but that the process of reaching a higher unity must not obliterate ordinary consciousness. He contrasts Carlyle's hero-worship with "the solidary of humanity." For "to be a self . . . is to go beyond the self; and a human being cannot find a centre in himself, except so far as he recognizes himself as part of a wider whole in which he is centred" (vol. 2, p. 99). More food for thought, food that celebrates "the discursive intelligence," that both chastens and exalts the human being, showing humans poised always on the cusp of actuality and possibility, "individuality and universality." Living out a "narrowly limited existence under the conditions of time and space," yet groaning under an "infinite want claiming to be satisfied": this, for Caird, "is the essential problem of human life" (vol. 2, p. 340).

63. Addams, *Twenty Years at Hull-House*, p. 28.

64. Addams, *Twenty Years at Hull-House*, pp. 28–29.

65. Addams, *Twenty Years at Hull-House*, p. 49.

66. Addams, *Twenty Years at Hull-House*, p. 50.

67. Addams, *Twenty Years at Hull-House*, p. 45.

68. Addams, *Twenty Years at Hull-House*, p. 46.

69. Opium in ingestible medicinal forms (gum, laudanum, syrup, pills, and powder) was easily obtained from most pharmacists in the United States with or without a prescription, as well from mail-order houses and mountebanks. One 1885 study cites 3,000 stores in Iowa during this time period that kept medicinal opium products in stock. Trade in and use of opium products in the 1880s was not illegal. The use of opium as a stimulus to the imagination, according to physician Charles E. Terry, was much influenced by the writings of De Quincey. See Charles E. Terry, with Mildred Pellens, *The Opium Problem* (New York: Committee on Drug Addictions/Bureau of Social Hygiene, 1928), pp. 1–25.

70. George Eliot, *Middlemarch* (Oxford: Oxford University Press, 1997; orig. ed. 1872), p. 77.

71. Thomas De Quincey, *Confessions of an English Opium-Eater together with Selections from the Autobiography* (London: Cresset Press, 1950), p. 295. This work was first published in 1821–1822, and later appeared as No. 223 in the *Everyman's Library* (London: J. M. Dent, 1907).

72. Thomas De Quincey, *Selections from De Quincey*, ed. Milton Haight Turk (Boston: Ginn and Company, 1902), p. 8.

73. Addams, *Twenty Years at Hull-House*, p. 51.

74. M. A. Schimmelpenninck, *Select Memoirs of Port Royal* (London: Hamilton, Adams, and Co., 1835), p. 148. Other studies include Ruth Clark, *Strangers and Sojourners at Port Royal* (Cambridge: Cambridge University Press, 1932); M. E. Lowndes, *The Nuns of Port Royal as Seen in Their Own Narratives* (London: Oxford University Press, 1909); and Marc Escholier, *Port-Royal: The Drama of the Jansenists* (New York: Hawthorn Books, 1968).

75. Of special note is the fact that poor families "were relieved by the extensive charities of the two houses of Port Royal" (Schimmelpenninck, *Select Memoirs of Port Royal*, p. 171). For a time, Port Royal had its own surgeons and physicians to attend the poor, doctors who carried with them both medicines and the New Testament in order to minister to bodies and to souls.

76. Addams, *Twenty Years at Hull-House*, pp. 55–56. In fact—or so the records seemingly indicate—Addams and her companions didn't even arrive at the event in time to participate. The story nonetheless illustrates Addams's capacity for self-deprecation.

77. Addams, *Twenty Years at Hull-House*, p. 57.

78. Addams, *Twenty Years at Hull-House*, p. 58.

79. Addams, *Twenty Years at Hull-House*, p. 59. Being a polio survivor, perhaps I will be excused for using the politically incorrect word *crippled*. In any case, I have remained faithful to what was settled parlance in Jane Addams's time.

80. Addams, *Twenty Years at Hull-House*, p. 61.

81. Addams, *Twenty Years at Hull-House*, p. 62.

82. Addams, *Twenty Years at Hull-House*, p. 64.

83. Richard Poirier, ed., *Ralph Waldo Emerson* (Oxford: Oxford University Press), p. 43.

84. Poirier, *Ralph Waldo Emerson*, p. 45.

85. Elizabeth Barrett Browning, quoted in Addams, *Twenty Years at Hull-House*, p. 22.

86. Poirier, *Ralph Waldo Emerson*, p. 50.

87. Poirier, *Ralph Waldo Emerson*, p. 147.

88. *The Portable Matthew Arnold*, ed. Lionel Trilling (New York: Viking Press, 1949), pp. 173–179.

89. Bernstein, *Foregone Conclusions*, pp. 120–121.

Chapter 3

1. Jane Addams, *Twenty Years at Hull-House* (New York: Macmillan, 1910), pp. 66–68.

2. The operation Harry Haldeman performed is described as the Baunscheidt-mus procedure, "after its German inventor," and it "involved injecting irritant into the tissue with needle punctures. The scarred tissue then contracted to pull the spine straight" (John C. Farrell, *Beloved Lady: A History of Jane Addams' Ideas on Reform and Peace* [Baltimore, Md.: Johns Hopkins University Press, 1967], p. 40, footnote 41). Addams wore a back brace when she was up and about. Made of steel, whalebone, and leather, it left her sore but seems to have helped ameliorate the back pain. She abandoned the brace after a time.

3. Gioia Diliberto, *A Useful Woman: The Early Life of Jane Addams* (New York: Scribner, 1999), p. 100.

4. From the Ellen Gates Starr papers as cited in Lionel C. Lane, *Jane Addams as Social Worker: The Early Years at Hull House* (Ann Arbor, Mich.: UMI Dissertation Service, 1963), p. 14.

5. Herbert Leibowitz, in *Fabricating Lives: Explorations in American Autobiography* (New York: Alfred A. Knopf, 1989), uses this evocative language—of sheltered and sheltering selves—and it is certainly apt at many points in Addams's story.

6. Addams did not express this kenotic Christianity in theological terms, but she had certainly absorbed exempla of the category—others who had devoted their lives to service. In a brilliant essay, Dennis Martin details how the *imitatio Christi*—"in the form of a servant"—marked basic forms and fundamental im-

ages of the Christian story "that were central to medieval literature and piety," with Mary's "yes to God" lying at the very heart of the matter. This is difficult for us nowadays to come to grips with, as it looks like self-abnegation or unacceptable self-loss rather than an alternative route to selfhood. Martin's essay, which I possess in manuscript form, is entitled: "'In the Form of a Servant': Trinitarian Victimization and Critical Empathy in Medieval Studies" (27 pp.).

7. Addams, *Twenty Years at Hull-House*, pp. 68–69.

8. Addams, in her typical fashion, doesn't identify the poet here. But it is Matthew Arnold, and the excerpt is from "Self Dependence," in *The Poems of Matthew Arnold* (London: Macmillan, 1885), p. 112.

9. "The English Mail-Coach," *Selections From De Quincey*, ed. Milton Haight Turk (Boston: Ginn and Company, 1902), p. 325.

10. Addams, *Twenty Years at Hull-House*, pp. 70–71.

11. Addams, *Twenty Years at Hull-House*, p. 71.

12. Addams, *Twenty Years at Hull-House*, p. 75.

13. This is one of the many reasons why World War I was so painful to her. Although she did not side with German political ambitions, having been to Germany, she appreciated the strength of the country's music, art, scholarship, and cutting-edge theories in anthropology, child development, and other areas of social science. As a pacifist, she opposed war regardless of the identity of the opponents; but this war was particularly difficult because for her the Germans were not abstract, faceless enemies.

14. The following excerpt is from Addams, *Twenty Years at Hull-House*, pp. 74–75. Addams's complex method of interpretation through sympathy, which implies the gathering of as much empirical and anthropological data as possible, is the subject of Chapter 6 in this volume. This approach to the study of sociology (which was more or less invented as an academic discipline at the University of Chicago in Jane Addams's era) was overtaken by empiricists who considered their methods more scientific. In the process, Jane Addams was erased from the picture as a great pioneer of urban sociology, and the reputations of such thinkers as George Herbert Mead also suffered. For more about these developments, see Mary Jo Deegan, *Jane Addams and the Men of the Chicago School, 1820–1918* (New Brunswick, N.J.: Transaction Books, 1990).

15. What is most interesting is when her method, if it may be called that, fails her—a failure she herself notes, as we will learn. To anticipate: pacifism in the run-up to World War I, during the war, and with the war's aftermath could not be fully realized in extant social and political forms. There are myriad (to use one of her oft-used words) disconnects between perception, moral *desiderata*, words, and deeds. Is a philosophy or conviction that cannot be realized in

practice falsified thereby? Pragmatism is here stretched to the breaking point and goes on faith alone, and this doesn't meet the pragmatic test, as Addams understood it, for truth. The Story of Reddened Hands with White Scars is one of many that show us Addams's moral realism at its freshest and strongest. For her, as for Christian realists in general, one always begins by trying to offer the thickest depiction of the situation at hand that one can so one isn't tilting at windmills.

16. Addams, *Twenty Years at Hull-House*, p. 73.

17. Addams, *Twenty Years at Hull-House*, p. 76.

18. Addams, *Twenty Years at Hull-House*, p. 77.

19. Later she joined Fourth Presbyterian Church in Chicago, which was a powerful, socially engaged congregation—and remains so today. Chicago was the heart of "applied Christianity," a place where liberal public religion was both preached and practiced. In his biography, Linn tells about a "congress of religions" held in Chicago in 1890 at which the audience was so liberal that Professor Herbert Wilett of the University of Chicago was applauded when he declared that "social service should come first and the church afterward; that there was no antagonism of the masses to religion, but only to the non-essentials of religion, and that among denominations only the fatherhood of God and the brotherhood of man should be recognized as essential" (Linn, *Jane Addams*, p. 207). How one is to sustain Christianity without the Incarnate Christ of Christian theology is apparently a lesser concern to Professor Wilett.

20. At the same time, Addams had little use for "the cheap arguments of the village atheist" or for the "telling phrases of Robert Ingersoll"—a professional nonbeliever—"who was then proclaiming 'the mistakes of Moses' throughout the country" (Addams, *My Friend Julia Lathrop* [New York: Macmillan, 1935], p. 24).

21. Letter from Graham Taylor to Jane Addams, June 26, 1897, written from Madison, South Dakota. Thanks to Anne Firor Scott for bringing this letter and the two cited below to my attention.

22. Letter from George D. Herron to Jane Addams, November 20, 1897, written from Iowa College.

23. Letter from Mary MacDowell to Jane Addams, February 7, 1898.

24. Addams, *Twenty Years at Hull-House*, p. 79.

25. Addams, *Twenty Years at Hull-House*, p. 86.

26. This is the trip during which the famous bullfight incident occurred that has been the subject of continuing controversy. The controversy revolves around the fact that Addams's accounts of her reactions to the bullfight in letters to her family and friends express little of the life-rattling effect she ascribes

to the event in her later autobiography. It seems to me that not much of importance is at stake here: clearly, Addams conceived of *Twenty Years at Hull-House* as a tale of spiritual quest and discovery, and therefore shaped her narrative in such a way as to maximize its transforming power.

27. In her book *My Friend Julia Lathrop,* Jane Addams states that she and Ellen Gates Starr, "an old friend from Rockford College," went about Chicago in the winter of 1888–1889 "advocating a New Toynbee Hall" (p. 47).

28. From Richard H. Brodhead's introduction to *The Marble Faun* (New York: Penguin Books, 1990), p. xvii. Brodhead tells us that this novel became "an agent of the civilizing process," which was its very theme. The cult of art appreciation as Brodhead details it is rather unattractive, and one understands why Jane Addams desired so keenly to distance herself from it. A rather stiff and strange novel, *The Marble Faun* was published originally in 1860. Jane Addams read it some time later and commented (in a letter of January 28, 1880) upon just how disgusted she was with the way "Miriam turns out"—Miriam being one of the central protagonists.

29. Addams, *Twenty Years at Hull-House,* p. 84.

30. In the matter of art for the immigrant poor, Allen Davis begins acerbically but softens somewhat: "There is something pathetic about little immigrant girls hanging copies of Fra Angelico angels on the dreary walls of their tenements and all the emphasis on bringing art to the masses in the early days at Hull-House; but the people flocked to see the art, and the Settlement Founders, for all their esoteric nature, had hit upon a basic truth; those who lived in the slums of Chicago did crave to see and touch and make things of beauty" (Allen F. Davis, *American Heroine: The Life and Legend of Jane Addams* [New York: Oxford University Press, 1973], p. 69). Margaret Tims notes that the Butler Gallery "proved more popular and was far better patronized, than the kitchen! This was not due solely to the superior aesthetic sensibilities of the neighborhood; it owed something also to peasant prejudices and unwillingness to adopt new customs, however beneficial these might appear to be" (Margaret Tims, *Jane Addams of Hull-House, 1860–1935* [New York: Fawcett, 1961], p. 50). Why a Sicilian, Calabrian, or Greek peasant would relinquish his or her pungent fare for the bland but "scientifically" nutritious meals prepared in the Hull-House kitchen, Tims doesn't say. Note as well that in Tims's view, if the art gallery was frequented, it was not because one can attribute any "superior . . . sensibilities" to the immigrants of the neighborhood. But if the food was spurned, Tims lays that at the doorstep of the "prejudices" of the peasants, who don't know what's good for them. Addams was far more nuanced and even dryly humorous about why her neighbors in the 19th ward

accepted some Hull-House offerings and were less enthusiastic about others, including the food. Perhaps she saw such moments as providing important object lessons in humility.

31. Lane, *Jane Addams as Social Worker,* p. 8.

32. Farrell, *Beloved Lady,* pp. 30–31.

33. Allen Davis associates Jane Addams's public persona with sentimentalism, finding it the epitome of the nineteenth-century heroine who "never had a selfish thought"—although Addams details selfish thoughts aplenty in *Twenty Years.* He also claims: "She fulfilled the need for a female religious figure—a saint, a madonna, even a Protestant virgin" (*American Heroine,* p. 105). Whence this need arises, Davis doesn't say, and his tone at times is dismissive. He also misinterprets her complex arguments about "The Family Claim"—the subject of the next chapter—as an attempt to overcome that claim, when in fact it was an attempt to negotiate the claim without abandoning it.

34. Farrell points out that the period Addams spent bedridden after an operation performed by her brother-in-law, the physician Harry Haldeman (Alice Addams's husband, as well as stepbrother to both Addams sisters), is covered by a shroud of silence. Addams had enrolled in the women's medical school at Johns Hopkins University in the winter of 1881–1882 and had consulted the famous physician Weir Mitchell during that time (see Chapter 2). She returned to Cedarville for surgery after leaving medical school, having decided that medicine was not her calling. Writes Farrell: "Jane Addams always talked of this period as involving mental recovery, as well as physical recovery from an extremely painful operation" (Farrell, *Beloved Lady,* pp. 39–40). D. G. Shadwell accepts the "6 months strapped to her bed" account and adds the details of a postsurgical plaster cast, followed by a "leather, steel-ribbed jacket or corset" used for support after the cast was removed, until she was strong enough to shed it. (See D. G. Shadwell, *A Rhetorical Analysis of Selected Speeches by Jane Addams* [Ann Arbor, Mich.: UMI Dissertation Service, 1989], p. 16.) Addams herself described this as a period of nervous collapse.

35. Mrs. L. Maria Child, *The Girl's Own Book* (reprint ed., Bedford, Mass.: Applewood Books, n.d.; 1st ed., 1834), pp. 13–14, 36, 110.

36. On the civically incapacitating dimensions of the historic female archetype I call the "Beautiful Soul," see my *Women and War* (New York: Basic Books, 1987; 2d ed., University of Chicago Press, 1994).

37. Edith Wharton, *The Age of Innocence* (New York: Collier Books, 1968; 1st ed., 1920).

38. Wharton, *The Age of Innocence,* p. 290.

39. Henry James, *The Bostonians* (London: J. M. Dent, Everyman Library, 1994; orig. ed., 1886). The excerpt below is found on p. 33.

40. James, *The Bostonians,* p. 163.

41. George Eliot, *The Mill on the Floss* (London: Longmans, 1960), p. 375.

42. Addams, *Twenty Years at Hull-House,* p. 248.

43. Eliot, of course, was immersed in German higher criticism, as a translator of the works of Feuerbach and a freethinker who had rejected traditional belief. Another dimension of Casaubon's impotent folly is his conviction that his systematicity and the grandeur of his ambitions are a uniquely masculine province of knowledge. The heroine, Dorothea, cannot share in this project by definition, for Casaubon, given the debilitating confines of the feminine mind. The novel in question is, of course, Eliot's masterwork *Middlemarch* (New York: Oxford University Press, 1997; orig. ed., 1872).

44. George Eliot, *Daniel Deronda* (New York: Oxford University Press, 1984; orig. ed., 1876), p. 16.

45. Eliot, *Daniel Deronda,* pp. 145, 179.

46. Addams, *Twenty Years at Hull-House,* p. 354.

47. I grew up with a family story about my Grandmother Lind's heroic efforts to save her fifth child, my Uncle Ted, who was born at home and weighed scarcely four pounds. Everyone thought he would die. My grandmother placed him in a little shoebox by the potbellied stove. Every two hours, around the clock, she held him and dribbled a few drops of warm breast milk into his tiny mouth. This went on for days. The baby lived. He had been persuaded to live by milk, warmth, and human life. A face had called him to life.

48. Eliot, *Daniel Deronda,* p. 448.

49. Eliot, *Daniel Deronda,* p. 457.

50. George Eliot, *Romola* (New York: Oxford University Press, 1994; orig. ed., 1862–1863), from the introduction, p. xv.

51. Eliot, *Romola,* p. 269.

52. Eliot, *Romola,* pp. 270–271.

53. Eliot, *Romola,* p. 442.

54. Addams, *Twenty Years at Hull-House,* p. 308.

55. Eliot, *Middlemarch,* p. xxxv in the Introduction, quoting from Eliot's essay on the theme of silly novels.

56. All citations are from Laura Jane Addams, "Cassandra," in *Essays of Graduating Class, Rockford Seminary, 1881* (DeKalb, Ill.: "News" Steam Press, 1881), pp. 36–39.

57. On authority and the power of persuasion see Peter Brown, *Power and Persuasion in Late Antiquity* (Madison: University of Wisconsin Press, 1992); and Jean Bethke Elshtain, *Democratic Authority at Century's End,* 19th Annual G. Theodore Mitau Endowed Lecture (St. Paul, Minn.: Macalester College, 1997), pp. 1–26.

Chapter 4

1. Jane Addams, *Twenty Years at Hull-House* (New York: Macmillan, 1910), p. 258.

2. Addams, *Twenty Years at Hull-House*, pp. 26–27.

3. Addams, *Twenty Years at Hull-House*, p. 148.

4. Addams's nephew James Weber Linn, in his biography of Jane Addams (in a part that had been approved by Addams prior to publication), states that without "Miss Culver's own remarkable understanding of the new 'social settlement,' Jane Addams's experiment could never have grown as it was to grow" (James Weber Linn, *Jane Addams* [New York: D. Appleton–Century, 1937], p. 95).

5. She adds that she hopes for a visit "from you and Marcet [her niece]. . . . I do hope you will plan for it this fall. The idea of its not being sanitary is perfectly absurd." I have preserved the occasional idiosyncrasies in this letter, which are the results of haste. The letter is dated October 8, 1889, less than one month after Hull-House opened its doors. It shows just how rapid was Hull-House's success and the expansion of its tasks.

6. Hawthorne had penned a biting satire of Brook Farm, called *The Blithedale Romance*. Addams doesn't tell us which Hawthorne selection was read, but most likely it was not this satirical effort.

7. Addams, *Twenty Years at Hull-House*, pp. 107–109.

8. Addams, *Twenty Years at Hull-House*, p. 112.

9. Addams, *Twenty Years at Hull-House*, p. 399.

10. Jane Addams, *Forty Years at Hull-House* (New York: Macmillan, 1935), part 2: *The Second Twenty Years at Hull-House*, p. 404. This two-part volume, which includes *Twenty Years at Hull-House* as well as *The Second Twenty Years at Hull-House*, appeared after Addams's death.

11. The excerpt below is from Jane Addams, *My Friend Julia Lathrop* (New York: Macmillan, 1935), pp. 52–53. In a postscript to Addams's introduction to the volume, Alice Hamilton indicates that at Addams's death the manuscript was found "practically ready for publication, although she had not yet made the final revision. It has fallen to me to do this" (p. vi). Julia Lathrop was born in 1858 and died in 1932, three years before Addams.

12. Lionel C. Lane, *Jane Addams as Social Worker* (Ann Arbor, Mich.: University Microfilms International, 1963), contains a chronology of Hull-House buildings: 1889, Hull-House itself; 1890, Butler Building; 1895, Smith Building; 1897, Theater and Restaurant; 1898, Jane Club (a girls' residence); 1899, Gymnasium Building; 1901, Hull-House Apartments; 1904, Bowen Hall; 1905,

Music School, Dining Room and Terrace; 1906, Boys' Club; 1910, Mary Crane Building; 1912, Bowen Country Club (p. 221). The Bowen Country Club was in Waukegan, Illinois. A February 1, 1894, booklet entitled "Hull-House: A Social Settlement," lists seventeen residents, including Addams, of which "twelve were women" (p. 229). The College Settlement in New York opened in the same month and year as Hull-House. At the height of the settlement house movement, there were hundreds of social settlements all over the United States, concentrated primarily in urban areas. There were rural settlements as well and a settlement house effort spearheaded by African American social reformers. For their story see Elisabeth Lasch-Quinn, *Black Neighbors: Race and the Limits of Reform in the American Settlement House Movement, 1890–1945* (Chapel Hill: University of North Carolina Press, 1993). Lasch-Quinn notes that Addams infused the movement with enlightened cultural pluralism, viewing the settlement house as a catalyst for the eradication of prejudice.

13. Clipping from the Jane Addams papers, Swarthmore College Peace Collection. Addams subscribed to a clipping service, and this collection includes notices clipped from newspapers all over the United States—indeed, the world. I thank Anne Firor Scott for permitting me access to her mountains of notes and copies from this collection.

14. Jane Addams, "The Subjective Necessity for Social Settlements," pp. 1–26 in *Philanthropy and Social Progress* (New York: Thomas Y. Crowell and Co., 1893). The book consists of seven papers delivered at the School of Applied Ethics, Plymouth, Massachusetts, 1892, two of which were authored by Addams. All material quoted here, unless otherwise noted, appears within those pages.

15. Clearly, a theory of moral action is brewing here. Specifically, in arguing that an emotion might become a motive and result in action, Addams is embracing a complex anthropology, or a view of the human person, such that he or she can decoct an emotion into something that can be analyzed, formed, and channeled appropriately. We are not mere stimulus-response mechanisms, but beings who respond—or try to—in complex and creative ways to changing situations. Human needs are exigent but they are not simple, and a yearning to be of service can become a real need of the human soul.

16. Here Addams has in mind Alderman Johnny Powers, who became her nemesis and that of Hull House. Addams and her friends tried unsuccessfully on several occasions to unseat him. In *Twenty Years at Hull-House*, Addams explains, in rueful tones, why they kept losing: Powers was a flashy "boodler" (a man deeply implicated in graft and corruption), and "boodling" was the Chicago way at the time.

17. This scriptural metaphor—one of many appearing in Jane Addams's writings without attribution—is borrowed from Psalm 42 (KJV). In the *New Oxford Annotated Bible,* this psalm begins: "As a hart longs for flowing streams, / so longs my soul for thee, O God. / My soul thirsts for God, for the living God. / When shall I come and behold the face of God? / My tears have been my food day and night, / while men say to me continually, 'Where is your God?'" And it concludes: "Why are you cast down, O my soul, and why are you disquieted within me? / Hope in God; for I shall again praise him, my help and my God." The psalmist's frank yearning clearly touched Addams deeply, as she often quoted from these verses.

18. Letter from Jane Addams to Ellen Gates Starr, April 3, 1887.

19. Jane Addams, "The Objective Value of a Social Settlement," pp. 27–56 in *Philanthropy and Social Progress* (New York: Thomas Y. Crowell and Co., 1893). All quotes in this section are drawn from these pages. The long excerpt below appears on pp. 28–30.

20. The phrase *thick description* derives from cultural anthropologist Clifford Geertz's famous interpretive method. *Thick description* means taking note of as many details of a situation as possible, so as to better make sense of a situation. Jane Addams consistently provided just this kind of rich context, elaborately describing sights, sounds, smells, and other observations.

21. Mary Kittredge (Kittredge, *Jane Addams: Social Worker* [New York: Chelsea House, 1988], p. 22) notes Martha's death and says that it made young Jennie more dependent than ever on her father.

22. Lane, *Jane Addams as Social Worker,* p. 14.

23. See Margaret Tims, *Jane Addams of Hull-House, 1800–1935* (New York: Fawcett, 1961), p. 36.

24. The Pullman Strike became the subject of "A Modern Lear"—one of Addams's most memorable essays, although it wasn't published until sixteen years after the event, being considered too controversial by editors. "A Modern Lear" is discussed later in this chapter.

25. Jane Addams found strikes fearful, an importation of military or martial methods into domestic life.

26. Addams, *Twenty Years at Hull-House,* pp. 216–217.

27. Gioia Diliberto describes both Harry's and George's deaths (Gioia Diliberto, *A Useful Woman: The Early Life of Jane Addams* [New York: Scribner, 1999], p. 264).

28. The nonmention of her stepmother in her autobiography was, of course, noticed by many, including family members. Allen F. Davis states that Jane Addams admitted to her niece Marcet Haldeman-Julius that Marcet's grand-

mother had been a "constructive force in her life—in some ways even more than had my grandfather" (an astonishing admission, if true) but then added that it was "all too complicated." Davis interpolates that it is somehow more "natural and believable for a young girl to admire her father and by putting the emphasis on the father-daughter relationship she was describing a situation that was familiar to all who had read American fiction" (see Allen F. Davis, *American Heroine: The Life and Legend of Jane Addams* [New York: Oxford University Press, 1973], p. 160). Addams indirectly complains about her stepmother in *Twenty Years at Hull-House,* in a passage where she contrasts mothers and daughters abroad and bemoans the inability of mothers to understand their daughters' frustrations. Because Jane had been accompanied in her European travels by her stepmother, this passage no doubt offended her stepmother.

29. Mary Addams Haldeman, the sister who died during the Pullman Strike, had lost an infant son as well as her youngest daughter while Jane Addams was touring Europe. One assumes the awful statistics here are not atypical, but the Addams family does seem to have had more than its share of tragedy. The newspaper clipping containing the story of George Haldeman's strange disappearance is from Harry Haldeman's scrapbook, reproduced in *Jane Addams Papers on Microfilm,* ed. Mary Lynn McCree Bryan (Ann Arbor: University of Michigan, 1989). This is but one of many clippings in that microfilm series, containing notices of family tragedies.

30. Excerpt from Jane Addams, "Filial Relations," pp. 71–101 in Jane Addams, *Democracy and Social Ethics* (Cambridge, Mass.: Belknap Press of Harvard University, 1964; orig. ed., 1902), p. 76.

31. The story of Goosie appears in *Twenty Years at Hull-House* on pp. 173–174, and all of the quotes here are drawn from those two pages unless otherwise noted.

32. Addams, *Twenty Years at Hull-House,* p. 174.

33. Addams, *Twenty Years at Hull-House,* p. 168.

34. Addams, *Twenty Years at Hull-House,* pp. 199–200.

35. Addams, "Filial Relations," in *Democracy and Social Ethics,* pp. 71–101. All quotes are drawn from these pages unless otherwise noted. The seven essays here collected had all appeared in print previously, in popular periodicals such as the *Atlantic Monthly* and academic journals such as the *American Journal of Sociology.*

36. Addams, *Democracy and Social Ethics,* p. 1. Here Addams sets forth her understanding of ethics and her insistence that attainment of "individual morality" no longer suffices; one must come to grips with new realities and meet the demands of a "social morality."

37. Clearly Addams is referring here to women of her own milieu. But she also believed that *all* women face some variant of conflict between the family claim and the social claim.

38. An analysis of the discrepancy between Jane Addams's overall social philosophy and the unhappy fact that many at present seem content to live lives focused entirely on themselves and revolving around bodily hedonism, the "cult of frankness" and all the rest, is beyond the purview of this chapter.

39. A complete essay on the Lear theme was not published until 1912, sixteen years after the Pullman Strike. But Addams alludes to observations contained in this longer essay throughout.

40. Addams typically uses an event or series of events as a heuristic device in order to make more explicit the lessons she finds embedded in the event or events. This, in turn, or so she stalwartly and devoutly hoped, would contribute over time to the building of a "higher social morality"—which, for her, meant a democratic culture. Her Pullman essay, "A Modern Lear," was finally published in *Survey* (November 2, 1912, vol. 29, no. 5, pp. 131–137). All quotes are from those pages unless otherwise noted. The essay is remarkable for its moderation, which makes Mary Jo Deegan's characterization of it as "scathing" rather hard to credit. The fate of the piece is fascinating. John Dewey, in a letter of January 19, 1896, calls the paper "one of the greatest things I ever read both as to its form and its ethical philosophy." He continues: "I confess before reading it, I did not see very well how the matter could be touched so soon after its occurrence without doing as much harm as good: but you not only have avoided that, but have said exactly the things that must be realized if the affair is going to be anything more than a brutal and disgusting memory." He then goes on to offer Addams a few minor editorial comments. But others were not so generous. Albert Shaw, editor of the *Review of Reviews,* rejected the piece because one was obliged to "look forward rather than backward"; "anything relating to the Pullman strike" therefore was unpublishable. A. E. Keet, managing editor of the *Forum,* took a similar tack to avoid publishing the essay: the events were two years in the past, and a "paper on the subject now would seem somewhat belated." He continues: "And besides our schedules are so crowded for so long a time ahead that I could not make room for an unexpected paper for several months. For these reasons I am obliged to deny myself the pleasure of using your interesting and startling article." Lloyd Bryce, of the *North American Review,* was more blunt: "I regret to say that I am unable to find space for it in the pages of the Review." Jane Addams appears to have consulted H. D. Lloyd about the piece, as he told her that the "only obstacles in the way of its acceptance are its personal bearing and the fact that ... the strike—has largely passed out of mind." He then suggested that Addams send a new Fabian journal in London a

short essay of nine hundred words about the settlement movement. H. E. Scudder, of the *Atlantic Monthly*, while expressing his great personal admiration for Miss Addams, "questions the wisdom of publication in The Atlantic." Perhaps her "assumption" that Pullman was driven in part by a "philanthropic intent" is incorrect. Too much of the essay turns on Pullman's motive. Besides, "since Mr. Pullman is a living man I should wish to proceed with the greatest caution in The Atlantic. Even capitalists are persons." But Miss Addams assumes throughout that Mr. Pullman was "in the wrong." There are judicial aspects to the case that Miss Addams has ignored, and so on. Clearly the piece, a model of balance, was a hot potato nonetheless. Readers who are interested in pursuing details of the Pullman Strike might find interesting the full text of the United States Strike Commission hearings, "Report on the Chicago Strike of June–July 1894" (Washington, D.C.: United States Government Printing Office, 1895). There are 700 pages of testimony, including that of Eugene V. Debs. (Letters are from the Jane Addams Papers Swathmore Peace Collection)

41. The quotes are from Almont Lindsay, *The Pullman Strike* (Chicago: University of Chicago Press/Phoenix Books, 1942), pp. 62, 64.

42. Giuseppe Mazzini, *The Duties of Man* (London: J. M. Dent, 1894).

43. Mazzini, *The Duties of Man*, p. 16.

44. Addams, *Forty Years at Hull-House*, part 2: *The Second Twenty Years*, p. 196. Addams wasn't opposed to greater latitude in intimate relations but rather to an excessive drive in that direction that precludes a balanced life attuned to civic and larger social questions.

45. Addams, *Forty Years at Hull-House*, part 2: *The Second Twenty Years*, p. 196.

46. Diliberto, *A Useful Woman*, p. 16. Diliberto describes Jane Addams's conflict as one between "her internal drive to power and the stultifying demands of her parents (the dreaded 'family claims,' which she later wrote about movingly)." She did indeed write movingly, but "dreaded" is not an apt characterization of the way Addams thought about those claims. Note the way Addams's references to a "divine urge of intellectual hunger" and a desire to serve become, for Diliberto, an "internal drive to power": this reduction of the powerful "hunger" of which Addams speaks to a kind of Hobbesian urgency that betrays an uncritical endorsement of current cultural preoccupations.

47. Those Addams calls "half-baked," Freud probably would have also, as Freud insisted that a certain amount of repression was necessary in order that human beings learn to "sublimate," to redirect libido that is "inhibited" in its aim (i.e., that does not seek a direct sexual object). That said, there is little doubt that Addams disagreed with the underlying presuppositions that guided psychoanalysis.

48. Addams, *Forty Years at Hull-House*, part 2: *The Second Twenty Years*, p. 194.

49. Addams, *Forty Years at Hull-House*, part 2: *The Second Twenty Years*, pp. 197–198.

50. Jane Addams, *The Spirit of Youth and the City Streets* (New York: Macmillan, 1909).

Chapter 5

1. Quotes in this section are from Jane Addams, "A Personal Experience in Interpretive Memory," pp. 141–168 (chapter VI) in *The Long Road of Woman's Memory* (New York: Macmillan, 1916).

2. It would be easy to write Addams's experience off as a product of evolutionary progressivism—a theory since discredited—which holds that the human race passes collectively through stages, from primitive to more complex, and that the primitive stage corresponds roughly to childhood. There is a bit of that in Addams's account, but she uses the framework of cultural evolution primarily as a heuristic device.

3. Addams, "A Personal Experience in Interpretive Memory," pp. 154–157.

4. She had a harder time penetrating the experiences of men, and she is often tougher in her assessments of what men did or did not do than she is of what women did or did not do. What men did not do that troubled her most was support and stay with their families, even though she understood the indignities heaped upon them in the world of work, half-work, or non-work, and the confusion, perplexity, and diminution they daily experienced. For an essay on the alternative approaches taken by settlement residents and other reformers to family desertion, see Martha May, "The 'Problem of Duty': Family Desertion in the Progressive Era," *Social Science Review* (March 1988), pp. 40–60. Analyses of the deserting father ranged from "charitable" to "punitive," according to May. Family preservation—finding a way to hold families together through the intervention of an outside third party—came to be a preferred mode, and one welcomed, according to Linda Gordon, "by women and children who lacked the ability, the power, or the resources to protect themselves from recreant husbands and fathers" (quoted in May, "The 'Problem of Duty,'" p. 55).

5. The English cognates are readily apparent here, including *idiosyncratic* and *idiocy*. It is interesting that *idiot* was associated with madness until that term was dropped to avoid stigmatizing the mentally ill—although I'm not sure that the hundreds of categories approved instead by the national psychiatric associations really help to do that. They certainly medicalize the terms.

Perhaps one reason *idiot* came into use for such purposes is that one who suffers from a debilitating mental condition is removed from normal intercourse with other human beings and trapped in a terrible aloneness. Marx lived from 1818 and 1883, so his life span overlapped a few decades with Jane Addams's. However, Addams explicitly rejected Marxism and socialism both as ideologies and doctrines and as methods of social change.

6. Ellen Gates Starr to Mrs. John Addams, Florence, January 30, 1888, and Rome, February 5 (letter written in two sittings), in the Swarthmore College Peace Collection.

7. No doubt it is for both better and worse, as I can attest, having grown up in a much smaller place than Cedarville, with its population of 750. My Timnath, Colorado, was home to approximately 185 persons, give or take a few.

8. The quote is from Jean-Paul Sartre, *No Exit,* tr. Stuart Gilbert (New York: Knopf, 1947). I remember seeing a 4-H Club theater production of this play when I was thirteen or fourteen years old. I couldn't figure out what exactly the problem was, although I knew it had to be my problem, because Sartre was a great foreign intellectual; in today's parlance, it seemed to me he should just "get over it."

9. Albert Camus is not included in this indictment, and he never considered himself an "existentialist" in any case, despite the determination of commentators—then and now—to put him in that camp. Sartre, of course, wrote . . . and wrote . . . and wrote. His famous, or infamous, introduction to Frantz Fanon's *The Wretched of the Earth* (New York: Grove Press, 1981) offers up a view of political reality that would probably have caused the redoubtable Jane Addams to blank out temporarily. I only went so far as to fling the book across several rows of washing machines at the public laundromat as I sat reading, tending four children, and washing diapers for the baby.

10. Starr eventually left Hull-House and converted to Roman Catholicism, drawn by the beauty she contrasted with the symbolically beggared forms of Protestantism that prevailed in her day. She remained fast friends with Jane Addams throughout her life.

11. The Chicago Arts and Crafts Society was founded at Hull-House, inspired by the writings of John Ruskin and William Morris. Its constitution, which was adopted October 31, 1897, stated the Society's express purpose as cultivating a "just sense of beauty," fusing beauty of form with efficiency of function—a direct response to the ugliness of modern industrial life and the terrible drudgery that haunted the working person.

12. Ellen Gates Starr, "Art and Labor," pp. 165–179 in *Hull-House Maps and Papers* (New York: Thomas Y. Crowell, 1895). All quoted material is drawn from these pages unless otherwise noted. The preceding quotes are from p. 165.

13. Some of the most powerful and terrible passages in Jane Addams's account of World War I and her visits to war-torn and postwar Europe are those describing the effects of malnutrition and neglect on children: the children are joyless, almost lifeless. The similarities to children exhausted and depleted by horrible work under horrible conditions for too many hours a day are striking.

14. Walter Benjamin, "The Work of Art in the Age of Mechanical Reproduction," pp. 217–251 in *Illuminations,* ed. Hannah Arendt, tr. Harry Zahn (New York: Harcourt Brace, 1968).

15. Ellen Gates Starr, "Art and Labor," in *Hull-House Maps and Papers,* pp. 165–179.

16. I recall a 1979 tour of the Tretyakov Gallery in Moscow, when I was ushered through room after room of socialist realism—appropriately de-Stalinized but with Lenin looming everywhere as heroic bringer of classless society, etc., to the masses—and the extraordinary sensory relief I felt upon happening upon a room featuring Ilya Repin's powerful portrait of a barefoot Leo Tolstoy (1891). The portrait was familiar to me from a reproduction hanging on my wall at home. A few years later, I discovered that this same reproduction hung in Addams's bedroom/study, when I was shown that room (normally closed to visitors) by Mary Ann Johnson, then director of the Hull-House museum in Chicago.

17. The publication of Addams's *The Spirit of Youth and the City Streets* (New York: Macmillan, 1909) evoked an overwhelmingly positive reaction; the famous, near-famous, and obscure wrote her letters of appreciation. Winifred Salisbury, general secretary of Calumet Associated Charities, in Calumet, Michigan, wrote her on January 5, 1910, that, having worked in factories in Milwaukee herself in order to learn more about factory conditions, she could feel the "Spirit of Youth." "I know what it means to toil from seven in the morning until five-thirty at night in a dirty, hot, sticky, nauseating candy factory, with a half hour off at noon to eat one's newspaper-wrapped lunch at the same table where the rest of the day is spent. I know what it is to crawl home at night—two, three, or four miles—partly because riding is costly . . . and partly because the cars at the supper hour won't hold any more. The first few nights I tried to rest by reading or by lying down and trying to relax every muscle in the approved physical culture style. It didn't work. Every muscle, cord, and tendon persisted either in standing out straight and indignant at the way in which it had been abused or else in tying itself into so hard a knot that morning found it still tight. . . . I was fortunate in having a decent place to dance. . . . Knowing what that recreation meant to me I didn't blame the less fortunate girls after that for dancing wherever opportunity offered. Please don't think me impertinent in thanking you from the bottom of my heart for

not only *knowing* the hunger and thirst of the boys and girls but for being able to tell people about it in such a way as to make the most blasé find your book more interesting than a novel." Another letter, dated December 13, 1913, came from Tokyo addressed to "Mr. Jane Addams." Its writer, T. Yokoyama, thanked Addams for her "interesting and instructive" book, told her that in Japan such work had not yet been done, and asked permission to translate the work into Japanese. Thanks to Anne Firor Scott for drawing my attention to these letters.

18. On the beauty and spectacle of war and its deep attraction see my 1987 book, *Women and War*, reissued in 1992 by the University of Chicago Press. See J. Glenn Gray's classic *The Warriors* (New York: Harper and Row, 1970), for his original and troubling analysis of war's aesthetic appeals as a spectacle, affording satisfaction to various sensory lusts. Gray would have the form and spectacle of a heroic peace satisfy as deeply, and at the cost of no human lives: this is a challenge the human race has yet to rise to.

19. Published by Macmillan, in New York, in 1912. Whereas *The Spirit of Youth* had drawn mostly kudos, the reaction to *A New Conscience and an Ancient Evil* was decidedly mixed. William James's enthusiasm for *Spirit* knew no bounds, and this is the moment when he offered up the much-repeated encomium to Addams: "She simply inhabits reality, and everything she says necessarily expresses its nature. *She can't help writing the truth*" [emphasis his]. This appreciation appeared in the *Journal of Sociology* and was also communicated to Jane Addams in a letter of December 13, 1909, mailed from his home at 95 Irving Street in Cambridge. He tells her he is certain that the book will have a "great and vital influence." James was frequently unstinting in his praise of Addams, having called her *Democracy and Social Ethics* of 1902 "one of the great books of our time." Mary MacDowell, a key figure in the University of Chicago settlement project, calls it "charming" and notes that Addams is an "artist who has revealed the beautiful beneath the sordid and the tragic" (letter from MacDowell to Addams, December 29, 1909). Edgar Gardner Murphy of the *South Atlantic Quarterly* especially appreciates Jane Addams's recognition of what happens if the child is ethically and socially isolated. Walter Lippman, however, called *New Conscience* a hysterical book—hysteria being, of course, the putative specialty of women, even one so even-headed and -handed as Jane Addams. Others were clearly troubled by her concentration on vice rather than possibility. This book, with its "white slave traffic" motif, brought in more letters than the other books of a practical kind, especially from lawyers on the front line of these developments.

20. There is a hefty literature on the "playground movement." A few examples include Charles E. Hartsoe, "From Playgrounds to Public Policy," *Parks*

and Recreation (August 1985), pp. 46–48, 68–69; Jerry G. Dickason, "1906: A Pivotal Year for the Playground Profession," *Parks and Recreation* (August 1985), pp. 40–45; and [no author,] "A Brief History of the Playground Movement in America," *Playground* (vol. 9, 1915–1916), pp. 2–45.

21. Addams, *Twenty Years at Hull-House* (New York: Macmillan, 1910), p. 107.

22. Addams, *The Spirit of Youth,* p. 4.

23. Addams, *The Spirit of Youth,* pp. 5–6.

24. Addams, *The Spirit of Youth,* p. 7.

25. Addams, *The Spirit of Youth,* pp. 16–17.

26. This is a very old and a new story, common to the accounts offered by battered women, who so frequently return to their tormentors because "he loves me and I love him," "he needs me," "he doesn't really mean it," and so on. This particular story appears in Addams, *The Spirit of Youth,* on pp. 40–42.

27. Addams, *The Spirit of Youth,* p. 44.

28. Addams, *The Spirit of Youth,* p. 53.

29. Addams, *The Spirit of Youth,* pp. 55–56.

30. Here are more tales from the juvenile court ledgers: "(1) Stealing thirteen pigeons from a barn; (2) stealing a bathing suit; (3) stealing a tent; (4) stealing ten dollars from mother with which to buy a revolver; (5) stealing a horse blanket to use at night when it was cold sleeping on the wharf; (6) breaking a seal on a freight car to steal 'grain for chickens'; (7) stealing apples from a freight car; (8) stealing a candy peddler's wagon 'to be full up just for once'; (9) stealing a hand car; (10) stealing a bicycle to take a ride; (11) stealing a horse and buggy and driving twenty-five miles into the country; (12) stealing a stray horse on the prairie and trying to sell it for twenty dollars" (Addams, *The Spirit of Youth,* pp. 56–57).

31. Addams was widely read in evolutionary theory. The evidence on child exposure (abandonment) is fairly massive; on child sacrifice in certain cultures, less so. Although some pagan moralists had begun to question child exposure, "the opposition of official Christianity was absolute, though this was not expressed until postapostolic writings. . . . From the beginning of their new religion, Christians established extensive social networks that may have saved children from possible or actual exposure by assigning them to families in need of, or able to provide for, extra members. With Constantine's conversion to Christianity, the process of restricting and outlawing the practice began. To this end, subsidies were provided to indigent parents. Valentinian criminalized exposure; and Justinian in 529 completed the process begun by Constantine, ruling that all exposed children were to be free, whatever their previous status.

Although Christians couldn't entirely end the practice, it had ceased to be morally neutral, and involved both a legal and moral onus." See G. W. Bowerstock, Peter Brown, and Oleg Grabar, *Late Antiquity: A Guide to the Post-Classical World* (Cambridge, Mass.: Harvard Belknap Press, 1999), pp. 373–374. W. V. Harris ("Child-Exposure in the Roman Empire," *Journal of Roman Studies,* vol. 8 [1994], pp. 1–22) states: "The exposure of infants, very often but by no means resulting in death, was widespread in many parts of the Roman Empire. This treatment was inflicted on large numbers of children whose physical viability and legitimacy were not in doubt. It was much the commonest, though not the only, way in which infants were killed, and in many, perhaps most, regions it was a familiar phenomenon. While there was some disapproval of child-exposure it was widely accepted as unavoidable." The author goes on to add that Christians habitually denounced the practice and it was brought to a halt over time, though this process took many years and was uneven.

32. Addams, *The Spirit of Youth,* p. 69.

33. Stuart Joel Hecht, "Hull-House Theatre: An Analytic and Evaluative History," unpublished dissertation prospectus, Northwestern University, Department of Theater, June 1983, p. iii. Hecht notes that there were three particular Hull-House groups that embodied the "most successful and innovative theatre: the Hull-House Players, active from 1897 to 1941; director Edith de Nancrede's Hull-House children's theatre, active from 1902 until 1946; and the theatre directed by Robert Sickinger, active from 1963 until 1969. All three groups share elements. . . . Each evolved directly from the basic ideologies and objectives of the Hull-House settlement; each produced dramatics continuously over a significant period of time; and each had profound impact on participants, actors and audience, and often on Hull-House itself" (p. 2). The reader will recall the profound impact of the theater on Marie and Rose, my lively interlocutors in Chapter 2 of this volume, who "grew up" at Hull-House. The connection Jane Addams forged between art and ethics is reminiscent of Plato's discussion of music and the ordering of ethical life.

34. Addams, *The Spirit of Youth,* pp. 78–79.

35. Addams, *The Spirit of Youth,* pp. 76–77.

36. Jane Addams, "What the Theatre at Hull-House Has Done," *Charities* (March 29, 1902, pp. 284–286), p. 284.

37. Untitled article from the *Kansas City Star,* January 14, 1904, as reprinted from the *Boston Evening Transcript* (n.d.), from the clipping service to which Addams subscribed. A permanent exhibition at the National Museum of American History in Washington, D.C., gives a snapshot of the extraordi-

nary variety of Hull-House activities. Hull-House program bulletins from October 1890, March 1892, and spring 1901 make readily apparent the emphasis on classical learning, evident from course offerings in Greek, elementary Latin, Caesar, and Virgil, and from lectures focusing on ancient Greece and Rome as well as on modern politics. The people's university at Hull-House offered everything from a diet kitchen to an introduction to economics.

38. Letter of October 26, 1899, written from the Palmer House, Chicago, now in the Jane Addams Collection at the Swarthmore College Library.

39. Addams, *The Spirit of Youth*, p. 100.

40. Addams, *The Spirit of Youth*, p. 101.

41. Addams, *The Spirit of Youth*, p. 155.

42. Addams, *The Spirit of Youth*, pp. 156–157.

43. Imogene S. Young, *Jane Addams and Child Welfare Reforms, 1889–1899* (Ann Arbor, Mich.: University Microfilms International, 1967), p. 20. This is a dissertation in social work, completed at the Catholic University of America.

44. Young, *Jane Addams and Child Welfare Reforms*, p. 63.

45. Addams, *Twenty Years at Hull-House*, p. 220. Of course, we all know the ways in which compassion can become paternalistic or maternalistic.

46. The estimate is Anne Firor Scott's, taken from a note written in the course of her attempt to document Jane Addams's daily activities over several decades.

47. The general diffusion today of a negative view of the Progressive era naturally extends to the juvenile court system. As an example, see John Dutton, "The Juvenile Court and Social Welfare: Dynamics of Progressive Reform," *Law and Society Review*, vol. 19, no. 1 (1985), pp. 107–145, which considers the juvenile court movement part of a broader package of "child-control through the legitimizing vocabulary of Progressivism." In other words, the primary aim was to control kids; the language of Progressivism was mere window-dressing beneath or behind which lay the iron bars of coercion. The juvenile court movement was part of a "trend toward bureaucratization" and was "primarily a shell of legal ritual within which states renewed and enacted their commitment to discretionary social control over children. . . . The data give no support at all to hypotheses that juvenile court reform was accelerated by the entrepreneurial ambitions of charity reformers, by the obduracy of legal institutions, or by the felt need to control and socialize immigrants" (p. 142). As with most sweeping conclusions, there is no doubt a grain of truth in Dutton's analysis. The problem is its general ahistoricity. We are offered no concrete picture of the actual situations confronted by children in trouble in the turn-of-the-century immigrant city. What were the alternatives? To let kids run amuck;

to throw them in with criminals; to ignore the problem entirely, and so on. This particular approach is predicated on the assumption that if human beings, including kids, are left to their own devices and go about "unregulated," all will be well—or at least better. No compelling account of child development guides such critiques; nor do they take account of the fact of coercion in every social arrangement. The question is how that coercion functions—whether it is supple and subject to change, open to persuasion, accountable, and so on. Addams is not referenced in Dutton's article. Presumably she is absorbed into that abstract entity that the author refers to as "Progressivism." I myself have written critically about features of the Progressive movement, including the state as therapeutic entity, tending to the "mental health" of citizens in an intrusive way. I do not see this sort of thing operating in Jane Addams's life and work. That some Progressive reforms went sour is true. But it is important always to ask what the real alternatives were in the real situations in which people found themselves. There is an unstated premise in much radical critique of liberalism and Progressivism that if busybodies like Jane Addams hadn't been running around, America would have had a real socialist revolution of some sort. This is a silly pipe dream, but it doesn't stop folks from dreaming it. I'm not claiming Dutton does this; but in a way, dismantling all Progressive-era reforms as just a fancied-up way of "controlling" the immigrant poor fits in nicely with such a hypothesis, one on display explicitly in Rivka Shpak Lissak's *Pluralism and Progressives*. A more positive assessment is proffered by Graham Parker in "The Juvenile Court Movement: The Illinois Experience," *University of Toronto Law Journal* 253 (1976), 26, pp. 254–306. Parker describes the "rare climate of reform" and the presence of an extraordinary group of women among whom Addams was *primus inter pares*. He argues that Addams truly understood "urban problems" and that she "had a warm passion for those citizens, particularly migrants, who lived in the big city 'without fellowship, without local tradition or public spirit, without social organisation of any kind'" (p. 257). Behind and surrounding Jane Addams, walking along with her, were the formidable Chicago Women's Club, the Fortnightly, and other great organizations spearheaded by women. Parker finds many attacks on these reforms "underhanded" and ill informed. He does rue the metamorphosis of Addams-type social engagement into "social administration."

48. Young, *Jane Addams and Child Welfare Reforms*, p. 246. Young details the use made by Hull-House residents of empirical and experiential data in determining their approach to juvenile offenders. Jane Addams's good friend and Hull-House resident Julia Lathrop, the subject of Addams's last, posthumously published book, played the central role in activities touching on juveniles and the courts. Arrest records used by Hull-House in preparing a report showed in-

teresting patterns of arrests in 1898: "Of 77,441 arrests, 508 were children under 10 years of age, and 15,161 were of persons between the ages of ten and
twenty years" (Young, *Jane Addams and Child Welfare Reforms*, p. 247).

49. The answer to this question is directly linked to the child's development,
and Addams believed reading was key to that development. In addition to its
own lending library, Hull-House housed a reading room of the Chicago Public
Library. On the interesting goings-on with the Chicago Public Library see the
Official Proceedings of the Board of Directors of the Chicago Public Library
from July 12, 1900, to June 26, 1902, vol. XIII, and from July 9, 1906, to June
22, 1908. Addams lobbied unsuccessfully for an actual branch—not just a
large reading room—of the public library to be accommodated at Hull-House.
It was one of her very few defeats in Chicago city politics. (On the national
scale, she suffered political defeats aplenty with the coming of World War I, as
detailed in Chapter 7 of this volume.)

50. This matter is taken up in Chapter 7 of this volume. Addams's views on
strikes were well known, but she was trusted by strikers and often called upon
to listen to workers' grievances and to serve as an arbitrator or mediator.

51. A more detailed explanation of this follows in the next chapter.

52. Young, *Jane Addams and Child Welfare Reforms*, p. 39.

53. Young, *Jane Addams and Child Welfare Reforms*, p. 41.

54. Hilda Satt Polacheck, *I Came a Stranger: The Story of a Hull-House Girl*
(Urbana: University of Illinois Press, 1989), p. xi (from the introduction by Lynn
W. Weiner). Polacheck was told at first that no one was interested in the autobiography of an "obscure woman." Her story was published only after the new
social history of women began to generate an interest in such materials. The story
of her family's immigration to America is similar to many other tales: Her father
wanted to come. Her mother, who had buried six children in the Jewish cemetery
in their town in Poland, did not; all that she knew would be left behind. But they
departed, facing confusion and fraud, as did so many immigrants.

55. Polacheck, *I Came a Stranger*, p. 27.

56. Polacheck, *I Came a Stranger*, p. 42.

57. The account that follows is from Polacheck, *I Came a Stranger*, pp. 52ff.

58. Polacheck, *I Came a Stranger*, pp. 74–75.

59. Addams, *Twenty Years at Hull-House*, pp. 244–245. The Hull-House
museum wasn't the only museum effort in which Jane Addams was engaged. It
was also on her initiative and that of Mrs. Emmons Blaine and the Chicago
City Homes Association that the Municipal Museum of Chicago was founded,
"devoted to the collection and interpretation of material illustrating the physical and social condition and the administration of the cities" (Lenora Austin

Hamlin, "Municipal Museum of Chicago," *Charities and Commons* [1906], among the materials collected by Anne Firor Scott).

60. Polacheck, *I Came a Stranger,* p. 232. All quotes, unless otherwise noted, are from chapter XI ("Immigrants and Their Children"), pp. 252–258.

61. Addams, *Twenty Years at Hull-House,* p. 243.

62. Addams is not without her own cultural shortsightedness, of course, especially in the matter of an anticlericalism that at least some Catholic prelates construed as tantamount to anti-Catholicism. Hull-House was openly celebratory of Italians like Garibaldi, and Addams thought that anticlericalism, being a tradition, was rightly recognized. Addams got on well, by all accounts, with her Italian neighbors. She had allies among some in the Catholic hierarchy in Chicago; others found her suspect, worrying that Hull-House initiatives aimed to supplant Catholicism's network of schools and charitable organizations. Still, they existed side by side through the years. A full account of Addams's views of Catholicism and her relationship with the Chicago church would make a book in itself.

Chapter 6

1. Quoted in Muriel Beadle and the Centennial History Committee, *The Fortnightly of Chicago: The City and Its Women: 1873–1973,* edited and with a foreword by Fanny Butcher (Chicago: Henry Regnery Co., 1973), p. 142.

2. From Anne Firor Scott's collection of notes. Letter dated August 16, 1899. Mary Rozet Smith, daughter of a distinguished, wealthy Chicago family, had come to Hull-House to be of service early in the 1890s. She supported financially but also helped out in dozens of other ways. She was just twenty years old when she first came to Hull-House and she remained there forty-three years, until her death. James Weber Linn (in *Jane Addams* [New York: D. Appleton–Century, 1937]) notes Smith's self-effacing personality and the fact that she dedicated herself early on to helping make Jane Addams's peripatetic life as easy as possible. That, much more than her activity in the boys' clubs and with music and drama, was to be her life's work. During Addams's periods of invalidism, in her later years, the Smith home was a refuge; and she and Mary Smith summered together in Bar Harbor, Maine.

3. From Scott's notes of her conversation, dated July 10, 1958, unpaginated.

4. Herbert Leibowitz, *Fabricating Lives: Explorations in American Autobiography* (New York: Alfred A. Knopf, 1989), p. 130.

5. The excerpt that follows is from Jane Addams, *Twenty Years at Hull-House* (New York: Macmillan, 1910), pp. 308–309.

6. Leibowitz, *Fabricating Lives,* pp. 131–132.

7. Leibowitz, *Fabricating Lives,* pp. 144–145.

8. Matthew Arnold, *Culture and Anarchy: An Essay in Political and Social Criticism and Friendship's Garland* (New York: Macmillan, 1911), pp. 25, 36.

9. For a lengthy discussion of Plato and Aristotle on the public and the private, see Jean Bethke Elshtain, *Public Man, Private Woman: Women in Social and Political Thought* (Princeton: Princeton University Press, 1981; 2d ed., 1993), chapter 1.

10. See, for example, Simone de Beauvoir's disdain of the world of necessity by contrast to a transcendent realm where great men get to do great deeds. Even women's bodies are at best a nuisance, with all sorts of superfluous parts (such as the breasts, which may be "excised" at any time without doing any real harm to the women, according to Beauvoir). Only when women take the world as theirs to manipulate and command will they indeed enter the realm of world historic male history-making. I criticize Beauvoir in detail in the concluding chapter of *Public Man, Private Woman.* The book referenced is, of course, Beauvoir's famous *The Second Sex,* tr. H. M. Parshley (New York: Bantam Books, 1968.)

11. By the sixteenth century, Christian philosophy was relegated to "religion," as the Machiavellian assault against Christian social and political thought moved to the forefront of Western consciousness.

12. This is the world I have limned in the concluding chapter of *Public Man, Private Woman,* which is entitled "Toward an Ethical Polity." Some of the precise words and most of the general ideas of this discussion of necessity and freedom are drawn from that chapter.

13. It is important to note that for Jane Addams, to write and speak of the world of everyday life, the ordinary, the women toiling at their daily tasks, was neither a literary conceit nor a grand, sweeping gesture that put on display her capacity for "poeticizing" everything. That, I suspect, is much of what separates her from Emerson, whom she much admired but most often found unhelpful. In his famous "American Scholar" address, Emerson declaims (and one can practically hear the trumpets signaling a major pronouncement): "The literature of the poor, the feelings of the child, the philosophy of the street, the meaning of household life, are the topics of the time. It is a great stride. It is a sign,—is it not? Of new vigor, when the extremities are made active, when currents of warm life run into the hands and feet. I ask not for the great, the remote, the romantic; what is doing in Italy or Arabia; what is Greek art or Provençal minstrelsy; I embrace the common, I explore and sit at the feet of the familiar, the low." It is rather difficult to conjure up an Emerson who would trek up four flights of stairs in a rodent-infested, ill-lit, poorly

ventilated tenement to sit with a bereft mother, to help lay out a dead child, or to make concrete provisions for daily needs. The common, for Addams, is no literary category: it is a concrete, living reality, the presence of her neighbors before her.

14. Otis Tufts Mason, *Woman's Share in Primitive Culture* (New York: D. Appleton and Co., 1915), pp. 6, 139.

15. Mason, *Woman's Share in Primitive Culture*, p. 91.

16. Mason, *Woman's Share in Primitive Culture*, pp. 171 ff.

17. Unlike social Darwinists, Darwin did not draw from his account of origins the conclusion that society must necessarily be riven by rank inequalities, racial divides, and the like. In *The Origin of the Species,* Darwin asserts that membership in a single, human species provides a basis for human sympathy and harmony (Charles Darwin, *The Origin of the Species* [Cambridge, Mass.: Harvard University Press, 1975], p. 244).

18. It's worth noting here that Addams subscribed to no matriarchal theory. Her account puts women in a co-equal position with men—perhaps even slightly above them—in the creation of human culture, but it is not an argument of female superiority.

19. She would be gratified by recent research that shows that women wielded "considerable power within the context of the peasant household and community" and that male dominance did not fully solidify until modernity. See Peggy Reeves Sanday, *Female Power and Male Dominance* (Cambridge: Cambridge University Press, 1987); and "The Power and Powerlessness of Women," pp. 134–148 in Jean Bethke Elshtain, *Power Trips and Other Journeys* (Madison: University of Wisconsin Press, 1992).

20. John O'Neill, "The Body Politic," pp. 67–90 in John O'Neill, *Five Bodies* (Ithaca, N.Y.: Cornell University Press, 1987).

21. Imogene S. Young, *Jane Addams and Child Welfare Reforms, 1889–1899* (Ann Arbor, Mich.: University Microfilms International, 1989), p. 68, footnote 1.

22. It is difficult to imagine what the legislators who proposed this measure could have been thinking. A mini-electric bed on which to place and to execute defective newborns in every delivery room? The image is so grotesque as to be stomach-churning. Thomas Edison himself had demonstrated the glories of electrocution by electrocuting an elephant. A grainy old film exists that shows the great elephant being led to a special stand. The elephant is wired up. A switch is pulled. The great creature totters as smoke curls upward; its knees buckle; it is felled. This is a gratuitous display.

23. The quote is found in "Killing Imbeciles Not in Favor as a Law," *Examiner* (May 22, 1903, n.p.), in the Jane Addams newspaper clipping file, Swarth-

more College Peace Collection. In this "country of enlightenment," of course, persons labeled mentally retarded, mentally ill, or epileptic on the basis of sloppy diagnoses (or no diagnosis at all, in many cases) were shunned and institutionalized. The United States Supreme Court in *Buck v. Bell* sanctioned the practice of involuntary sterilization of "imbeciles." Nowadays, diagnostic procedures are deployed prior to birth in order to promote selective destruction of "defective" fetuses. The medical establishment as a whole is geared in this direction, under the rubric of "choice." The pressure on women pushes them in the direction of not burdening themselves or society with a "defective."

24. Jane Addams, "The Home and the Special Child," *National Education Association Journal of Proceedings and Addresses* (1908, no volume, Proceedings of the 46th Meeting, pp. 1127–1131), p. 1127. Addams's vision of cooperation between parents and experts gave way during the 1920s and 1930s, when "mother love lost favor among childcare experts. Maternal affection was assumed to be especially dangerous for deaf children." For decades the overriding policy of experts was to take children with special needs out of the home, the sooner the better, no matter how the child pined and failed to thrive due to homesickness. See Emily K. Abel, *Hearts of Wisdom: American Women Caring for Kin, 1850–1940* (Cambridge, Mass.: Harvard University Press, 2000), p. 241.

25. Addams, "The Home and the Special Child," pp. 1127–1128.

26. Addams, "The Home and the Special Child," pp. 1127–1128.

27. Addams, *Twenty Years at Hull-House*, pp. 179–180.

28. Addams, *Twenty Years at Hull-House*, p. 125.

29. This was a central motif of Addams's argument for the municipal ballot for women. This quote and the ones that follow, unless otherwise noted, appear in a newspaper column, "Jane Addams Declares Ballot for Woman Made Necessary by Changed Conditions," *Chicago Record Herald* (April 1, 1906), p. 3.

30. The preceding quotes are from Jane Addams, *Newer Ideals of Peace* (New York: Macmillan, 1907), pp. 183–184. The excerpt that follows is from pp. 184–185.

31. Addams, *Newer Ideals of Peace*, p. 207.

32. Jane Addams, "Why Women Should Vote" (1915). The eight-page text is available on line at www.douglass.speech.nwu.edu. The National Woman Suffrage Association pamphlet original is in the Swarthmore College Peace Collection. A version of the piece also appeared in *Ladies' Home Journal*, vol. 27, 21–1, (Jan. 1910).

33. This excerpt is from the online version of Addams's "Why Women Should Vote," p. 2. An important book tracing the political origins of social

policy in the United States is Theda Skocpol, *Protecting Soldiers and Mothers* (Cambridge, Mass.: Harvard University Press, 1992). Skocpol shows the particular ways in which social provision emerged in the United States given the structural features of the American political system, especially its decentralized federal system. She also notes that assistance and protective measures went to two large categories of persons who were deemed worthy of public assistance, namely, soldiers and mothers. Central to the process of creating this system was the role of the many hundreds of women's and mother's clubs and associations that required government assistance in order to meet their stated goals. What was unique about all of this, at least at the outset, was the manner in which female leaders were "strongly tied to vital local voluntary groups across the nation" (the two examples she gives are Julia Lathrop and Jane Addams) (p. 535). When this vital connection got lost, welfare policy took on a decidedly paternalistic or maternalistic cast, grew less responsive to changes in local needs, and often became a burden on the very groups the policies were initially set up to help.

34. Addams, *Twenty Years at Hull-House*, p. 297.

35. There is a considerable literature on this theme. See Laura Gellott, "Staking Claim to the Family," *Commonweal* (September 20, 1985), pp. 488–492. Gellott observes, correctly, that the "family claim" is renegotiated by Addams in such a way that the public sphere is called upon to protect and serve the values of the family at its best. Virginia Kemp Fish ("Hull-House: Pioneer in Urban Research During Its Creative Years," *History of Sociology*, vol. 6, no. 1 [Fall 1985], pp. 33–54, using my early work on the public/private distinction, shows the dramatic ways in which Hull-House residents and pioneers altered the working *definitions* of public and private. Lionel C. Lane (*Jane Addams as Social Worker* [Ann Arbor, Mich.: University Microfilms International, 1963]) insists that the mothering theme in Addams's vision of social life cannot be overemphasized. Her argument against "systematic charity" is dictated in part by the way such charity perpetuates popular disdain toward those who are being "helped."

36. See, for example, Rebecca Louise Sherrick, "Private Visions, Public Lives: The Hull-House Women in the Progressive Era," a dissertation in history at Northwestern University. In the introduction, Sherrick argues that Hull-House aimed to "integrate public and private space" (p. 4) rather than seeking "access to the mechanisms and privileges of the male world." They— the Hull-House women—"sought a new social order founded on the humanitarian principles of woman's sphere" (p. 5).

37. Jane Addams, *My Friend Julia Lathrop* (New York: Macmillan, 1935), p. 74.

38. Gioia Diliberto, *A Useful Woman: The Early Life of Jane Addams* (New York: Scribner, 1999), p. 6.

39. Addams, *Twenty Years at Hull-House,* p. 284. All quotes are from chapter XIII, pp. 281–309, unless otherwise noted.

40. This excerpt below is from Addams, *Twenty Years at Hull-House,* pp. 286–287. It helps, of course, to be able to bring the mayor himself to your side. But this doesn't take away anything from what was done. It shows that organized women could, with admittedly formidable leadership, corral the forces of governmental power and bring them over to their side, at least from time to time.

41. Addams, *Twenty Years at Hull-House,* pp. 287–288.

42. A letter dated July 29, 1899, from Jane Addams to Mary Rozet Smith, notes, "Sister Kelley's return is a great joy and I felt the stimulus the moment she hove in sight."

43. The letters to her sister Alice are rather painful to read at times. It seems that Alice was easily wounded and often felt neglected—unwarrantedly so, in Addams's view. Addams's nephew and biographer, James Weber Linn, tells us that by the time Jane reached the age of sixty years, in 1920, "She had many grandnephews and grandnieces, one in each family named for her . . . , and she began looking backward." About a year before she died, one of her nephews, himself verging on sixty, remarked: "At what age does one begin to feel that he is over that famous crest, and on that famous downhill slope of life, one reads so much of?" "I don't know," she said. "Apparently not at seventh-three. At that age one still has the odd sensation of being in the front line trenches, if you don't mind my using a nonpacifist figure of speech" (Linn, *Jane Addams,* p. 360).

44. Allen F. Davis, *American Heroine: The Life and Legend of Jane Addams* (New York: Oxford University Press, 1973), p. 289, calls Smith's death a "great blow."

45. Medieval communities of women organized for spiritual contemplation and charity are an example of this type of autonomy; for as the new social history has shown, such communities afforded a remarkable degree of autonomy to the women who submitted to their discipline. Addams would have been much interested in the new social history and the way it centers around the growth of cities and the organization of charity.

46. This quote also became a favorite of Robert Kennedy's after his brother's assassination.

47. Jane Addams, *The Excellent Becomes the Permanent* (New York: Macmillan, 1932), p. 10.

48. Addams, *The Excellent Becomes the Permanent,* pp. 39–40.

49. Addams, *The Excellent Becomes the Permanent,* p. 133. Here she is eulogizing Canon Samuel A. Barnett and no doubt thinking of the assaults on "an-

archists," although she would have meant this clear statement against generic labeling to apply equally to such ideological categories as "class" and "race."

50. Jane Addams, *The Long Road of Woman's Memory* (New York: Macmillan, 1916). The long excerpt below is found on pp. 2–3. The two chapters devoted to the story are chapter I, "Women's Memories: Transmuting the Past, As Illustrated by the Story of the Devil Baby," pp. 1–24; and chapter II, "Women's Memories: Reacting on Life, As Illustrated by the Story of the Devil Baby," pp. 25–52. Addams also uses the Devil Baby story to frame chapter III, "Women's Memories: Disturbing Conventions." My discussion is drawn from chapters I and II. The Devil Baby story also appears in Jane Addams, *The Second Twenty Years at Hull-House*, part 2 of *Forty Years at Hull-House* (New York: Macmillan, 1935).

51. *Harper's Bazaar* (October 1904), quoted in Davis, *American Heroine*, p. 159.

52. Daniel Levine writes: "These activities grew helter-skelter, responding not to an overall plan but to the imperatives of the neighborhood, the ingenuity of the residents, and the stresses of a rapidly changing society. At one moment a new club might be formed for Greek women; at the next Hull House influence might touch the Illinois court system, the Chicago city council, the United States immigration service, the Greek restaurant association, the employees of the garment industry, newsboys, the University of Chicago. The Hull House year book for 1920 mentions as regular activities and organizations connected with the House: Jane Club, Women's Club, Men's Club, regular recreation in the gym, a basketball team, a music school, Hull House theatre, a concert series, a day nursery, regular dances, a lecture series on Russia, the Municipal Museum, recreation in the playground and meetings of the Illinois Equal Suffrage Association, the Christian Socialists, the Chicago Peace Society, the National Consumer's League, the Legal Aid Society, the Juvenile Protective Association, and many labor unions. There were classes in the Bible, poetry, German, French, elocution, mathematics, civics, beginning English, United States history, Esperanto, Shakespeare and Browning, arts and crafts" (Daniel Levine, *Jane Addams and the Liberal Tradition* [Madison: University of Wisconsin Press, 1971], pp. 66–67).

Chapter 7

1. As an example of the detailed research that went into Hull-House positions, see Jane Addams, "The Housing Problem in Chicago," an address delivered at the Sixth Annual Meeting of the American Academy of Political and Social Science and published in *Social Legislation and Social Activity* (1902,

pp. 99–107). This is a report based on solid empirical research, replete with details about length of average tenancy, room size of flats, density of residence, rates of rents, and displaying Addams's hardheaded realism. She writes: "A conference should not consider the workingman of its imagination, nor yet the workingman as he ought to be, but the workingman of to-day as he finds himself, with his family, with his savings, with his difficulty of keeping a place very long, due to sudden changes in the methods of his trade" (pp. 102–103). This is a dig, of course, at revolutionaries and radicals, who were always positing an ideal world to be attained and, in Addams's view, paying insufficient attention to the way things actually were at any given moment and what the realistic possibilities for altering the situation might be. Addams's thoroughgoing advance preparation made her a formidable opponent. The *Chicago Daily News* (September 25, 1902) and the *Woman's Journal* (October 4, 1902), quoting the *Chicago Record-Herald,* describe a contretemps between "Miss Jane Addams of Hull House" and "President A. B. Stickney of the Chicago, Great Western railway." Evidently Mr. Stickney "presented the employers' side of the question in a way that stirred Miss Addams to take up the cudgels for the workingmen, and she did so with good effect." Addams's displeasure was evident as Stickney spoke, and when he finished his remarks, she calmly "and cleverly . . . reviewed each of Mr. Stickney's arguments in detail. She riddled them as absolute fallacies before an admiring audience." These and other accounts make it clear that Addams was an effective stump speaker, although she is said never to have raised her voice or to have betrayed much emotion in her public speaking. Her mastery of details was part of her success. That she could marshall all of these facts without losing sight of the broader and more important purpose is much to her credit.

2. As she often did with her work, Addams "recycled" this essay, restyling it as chapter VII ("Political Reform") of her first authored book, *Democracy and Social Ethics.*

3. William Stead, *If Christ Came to Chicago* (Chicago: Laird and Lee, 1894; reprint ed., Chicago Historical Bookworks, 1990). Stead, one of the most famous journalists of his day, went to a watery grave with great dignity in the sinking of the *Titanic.* He was not a sensationalizer in a vulgar sense, but his investigative work often had a sensational effect due to what he had uncovered and the potent language of description in which his characterizations were cast.

4. Anne Firor Scott, "Saint Jane and the Ward Boss," *American Heritage* (December 1960, pp. 12–17, 94–97), p. 12. There is a strong case to be made in behalf of city political machines, to be sure, if not in behalf of each and

every minor boss like Powers. A blanket condemnation of "bossism" is unwarranted, as is blanket enthusiasm. But it is easy to see how it would have grated on Hull-House residents to observe dire poverty, misery, and sickness, on the one hand, and then to note Johnny Powers gliding through the 19th ward in gilded splendor.

5. Scott, "Saint Jane and the Ward Boss," p. 19.

6. Jane Addams, "Why the Ward Boss Rules," *Outlook*, vol. 58 (April 2, 1898, pp. 879–882), p. 879.

7. Scott, "Saint Jane and the Ward Boss," *American Heritage*, p. 94.

8. Addams, "Why the Ward Boss Rules," p. 882.

9. Ray Stannard Baker, "Hull House and the Ward Boss," quoted in Mary Lynn McCree Bryan and Allen F. Davis, *100 Years at Hull-House* (Bloomington: Indiana University Press, 1990, pp. 53–57), p. 54. In this essay Baker details the public school situation. There were 3,000 fewer seats than pupils in this single ward. "It was the duty of Alderman Powers, as the people's representative, to secure more schools, but he not only neglected to do this, but when Hull House circulated a petition, and had it approved by the School Board, the Council Committee of which Powers' partner, O'Brien, was Chairman, quietly pigeon-holed it, at the same time providing new schools in other wards where they were much less needed. In all of these matters of public interest, which an Alderman is especially elected to advance, Powers has been a distinct impediment." Baker goes on: "The Streets and alleys of the ward were notoriously filthy, and the contractors habitually neglected them, not failing, however, to draw their regular payments from the city treasury. At last it fell to the women of Hull House to take the initiative."

10. In a letter dated March 20, 1898, Jane Addams writes to Mary Rozet Smith that Mary Kenney, Hull-House resident and herself Catholic, has been assigned the task of "going into the Catholic opposition question. . . . As nearly as I can make out the opposition comes from the Jesuits . . . and the parish priests themselves are not in it and do not like it." On March 5, 1908, one John Handley, C.P., wrote to Addams, noting that he had received a "sheaf of Chicago newspapers today from which I learned that some Catholics—and Catholic clergymen—have been displaying in public towards you not only a lack of Christian courtesy but also most deplorably a lack of understanding which is positively portentous. As a fellow Catholic and priest, I am deeply mortified." This was written in the midst of a fracas about whether or not Hull-House encouraged anticlericalism with its Giordano Bruno club and the like. Certainly, Addams's vision of an Italian republic (a vision shaped by Mazzini's writings) was of a regular nation-state in which

the church had no official political status. But there's clearly more here than meets the eye. I've seen little evidence that Addams was openly anti-Catholic, although she no doubt shared the almost universal (among American Protestants) view that Catholicism was ignorant, backwards, undemocratic, etc. In a 1911 essay on "Religious Education and Contemporary Social Conditions," Addams frankly calls for religious education to track precisely with the humanitarianism of progressive social reform. The authentic religious educator must be marked with both "scientific and humanitarian aspects"; and she accepts the received wisdom—that we now know to be wrongheaded—that the Renaissance was all light and glory, in contrast to the "grotesque Ecclesiasticalism" that previously pertained. So there is little doubt that she was anticlerical. But an anti-Catholic would have favored restriction on immigration from predominantly Catholic countries and would have supported many other measures that Addams not only did not support but found repugnant and openly said so. See Jane Addams, "The Social Situation: Religious Education and Contemporary Social Conditions," *Religious Education: The Journal of the Religious Education Association,* vol. VI, no. 2 (June 1911), pp. 145–152. By the way, the essay that follows Addams's in this journal is by G. Stanley Hall, then president of Clark University, in praise of eugenics as the progressive wave of the future. This is particularly creepy when one thinks about what lay down the road just a couple of decades in Nazi Germany and when one considers what was already going on in the United States, including coerced sterilization of the "feeble-minded," blessed by the Supreme Court in *Buck v. Bell* in 1927.

11. Scott, "Saint Jane and the Ward Boss," p. 98.

12. The distinguished philosopher William Graham Sumner comes to mind here. He demurred at the time of the Spanish-American War on the grounds that a false sense of patriotism ruled the roost. He wrote: "Patriotism is being prostituted into a nervous intoxication which is fatal to an apprehension of truth. . . . The field for dogmatism in our day is not theology, it is political philosophy. 'Sovereignty' is the most abstract and metaphysical term in political philosophy. Nobody can define it. For this reason it exactly suits the purposes of the curbstone statesman." However, Sumner's voice was drowned out by others. (See William Graham Sumner, "The Conquest of the U.S. by Spain," in *War and Other Essays,* ed. Albert Galloway Keller [Freeport, N.Y.: Essay Index Reprint Series, 1970], pp. 297–334.)

13. "Radicals Attack Hull-House," *New York Call,* quoted in Bryan and Davis, *100 Years at Hull-House* [pp. 122–124], p. 122.

14. Bryan and Davis, *100 Years at Hull-House,* p. 124.

15. Jane Addams, *Forty Years at Hull-House* (New York: Macmillan, 1935), part 2: *The Second Twenty Years at Hull-House,* chapter II, pp. 10–48. All quotes are from these pages unless otherwise indicated.

16. Jane Addams, *Democracy and Social Ethics* (Cambridge, Mass.: Belknap Press of Harvard University, 1964; orig. ed. New York: Macmillan, 1902), p. 275.

17. Enthusiastic as she was about juvenile and domestic courts, Addams no doubt went too far in postulating that these courts should be places of friendship, where human troubles could be sorted out. The problem with such a formulation is that it glosses over the element of coercion that is present in *any* litigation, however strong its commitment to mediation. On the issue of mothers' pensions and other forms of social provision in the U.S. context, see Theda Skocpol's important work *Protecting Soldiers and Mothers.* According to Skocpol, the idea of a pension for mothers took off in part because of the activities of the National Congress of Mothers, which "formally endorsed mothers' pensions and nationally dramatized strong maternalist and social-justice arguments on their behalf" (p. 448). The social feminist ideal of extending "the domestic morality" into "the nation's public life" was "a remarkable source of moral energy and political leverage for the female instigators of the first U.S. programs on public social provisions destined to endure . . . through the New Deal and down to the present day" (p. 3).

18. An editorial in the *New York Evening Post* (August 10, 1909) reads, in part: "The advocacy by women suffragists of Miss Jane Addams as President of the United States has only one possible objection: its impracticality. From the standpoint of civilization, no one could be a better candidate. As a representative of all the people, she would be ideal. . . . She sympathizes with the rich and poor, with the morally fortunate and the morally unfortunate, with all stripes and varieties of genuine social feeling and theory, with all foreign and domestic qualities. . . . She is a great reconciler, a great harmonizer, and this not in a merely negative sense, but instead with a vivid imagination for the future. And this is not the result of mere idealistic fancy, for Miss Addams' knowledge of actual conditions is wide, accurate, and varied. Pointing to the future, she partly belongs there, and this is one reason why she will not be elected president."

19. Addams was described in a *Chicago Tribune* editorial (April 22, 1910) as an "enlightened conservative," because she supported reforms such as the ten-hour day without demanding abolition of "the liberty of contract doctrine." In other words, she wasn't pushing state socialism. Although her thinking was not contract-oriented, she knew that much of what went on in the

country was, and she recognized the impossibility of attacking the prevalence of contract and market imagery in any broad sense. She wouldn't have wanted to attack the idea in any case, as human agency was implicated in decisions to contract. Her concern was, and would still be were she alive today, to avoid attempts to explain and define *all* human relationships under the rubric of contract.

20. Addams, *Democracy and Social Ethics,* p. 256. Part of Addams's work in spreading the gospel of social democracy involved breaking down the conceptual apparatus by which personal worth is defined solely in terms of wealth rather than strength of character or hard work. This was a direct dig at Powers: "To the chagrin of the reformers . . . it was gradually discovered that, in the popular mind, a man who laid bricks and wore overalls was not nearly so desirable for an alderman as the man who drank champagne and wore a diamond in his shirt front" (p. 257). So reformers had to battle not only entrenched plutocratic interests but a popular mind-set caught up in what could be called the "social imaginary" of the Gilded Age.

21. Addams, *Forty Years at Hull-House,* part 2: *The Second Twenty Years,* p. 6.

22. Addams, *Forty Years at Hull-House,* part 2: *The Second Twenty Years,* pp. 109–110.

23. Unfortunately, at the beginning of the chapter devoted to "Social Service and the Progressive Party," in *The Second Twenty Years at Hull-House,* Addams uncritically uses a quote in which the phrase *human engineering* describes reform efforts. Indeed, she seems to have accepted the "scientific social engineering" idea in some capacity. That this approach runs counter to her incessant stress on "sympathetic understanding" she either doesn't recognize or would prefer not to discuss. So such language pops up from time to time and grates. In contexts in which she talks about scientific knowledge of human affairs and the like, she also deploys the phrase *social workers,* which she otherwise tends to avoid, although for her, clearly, the word designates a commitment of a civic kind centered on the well-being of the less well off, primarily women and children.

24. Addams, *Forty Years at Hull-House,* part 2: *The Second Twenty Years,* p. 27.

25. Addams, *Forty Years at Hull-House,* part 2: *The Second Twenty Years,* p. 29.

26. Addams, *Forty Years at Hull-House,* part 2: *The Second Twenty Years,* p. 31.

27. Addams, *Forty Years at Hull-House,* part 2: *The Second Twenty Years,* p. 33.

28. Her rationalization of the battleship plank was that the number of industrial accidents had risen to equal the number of deaths in wars in which the United States had been involved; some fifteen thousand workers died each year, and half a million were crippled. She had to strike a bargain—such was the nature of politics.

29. William Allen White, well-known Progressive journalist and editor of the *Emporia Gazette,* wrote in his classic autobiography of the "volcano of emotion and applause" that greeted Addams when she rose to second Roosevelt's nomination, and "eyes . . . filled with grateful tears." Just four years later, Roosevelt was "fulminating against the pacifists, he cried out: 'Poor bleeding Jane Addams!'" See *The Autobiography of William Allen White* (New York: Macmillan, 1946), p. 531.

30. Addams, *Forty Years at Hull-House,* part 2: *The Second Twenty Years,* pp. 38–39. Anne Firor Scott estimates that Addams had at least twenty-seven speaking dates for the Progressives in October and November 1912, but the number was surely higher.

31. All of these letters are in the Swarthmore College Peace Collection. All except those of Charles E. Beals (October 1, 1912) and Jenkin Lloyd Jones (October 10, 1912) were dated between August 6 and August 12, 1912. Addams read all of her mail, or tried to, and she would have been saddened and troubled by the negative reaction. But she decided in the end that it was not all in vain. The social justice planks, although perhaps ahead of their time, afforded a grand opportunity for political education.

32. Jane Addams, "The Chicago Settlements and Social Unrest," *Charities and the Commons* (May 2, 1908, pp. 155–166), p. 155. In an address to the University Settlement Society of New York, Addams struck similar themes, arguing that the majority takes "very little pains to find out what they [the immigrants] think of us, and the picture they draw is by no means flattering. . . . There is room in a Settlement for all sorts of social creeds."

33. John R. Commons, *Race and Immigrants in America* (New York: Augustus M. Kelley Publishers, Reprints of Economic Classics, 1967; orig. ed., 1920), p. 232. Commons supports these "higher standards" for immigration because the "inferior, defective, and undesirable classes of immigrants" must be kept out. He continues: "The Commissioner of Immigration at New York estimates that 200,000 of the million immigrants in 1903 were an injury instead of a benefit to the industries of the country" (p. 230). Commons defends the restrictive legislation as an "improvement of immigration." The list of undesirables kept expanding through legislation: In 1882, lunatics, idiots, paupers, and Chinese were excluded. In 1885, laborers under contract

were for the first time to be excluded, but exceptions were made for actors, artists, lecturers, singers, domestics, and skilled workmen for new industries. In 1891, the list of ineligibles was again extended, so as to shut out persons convicted of a crime, "assisted" immigrants, polygamists, and persons with "loathsome or dangerous contagious diseases." In 1903, anarchists were added to the list. Commons complains that the average quality of immigrant is going down nonetheless because so many of "poor physique" are getting in. This was an era very concerned with "physical degeneracy" (see pp. 231–233).

34. Jane Addams, *Twenty Years at Hull-House* (New York: Macmillan, 1910), pp. 401–403. All quotes are from these pages, unless otherwise noted.

35. Addams also came to the defense of Abraham Isaak, editor of an anarchist newspaper and a Russian Jew, who was the first person arrested in a police dragnet following McKinley's assassination. Isaak was held without being permitted access to a lawyer. The mayor agreed to let Jane Addams see him. Her primary aim in intervening was to help becalm the public. Eventually Isaak was released. But Addams was more and more associated in the public mind with controversial defense of radical immigrants.

36. Addams so clearly, consistently, and forthrightly came to the defense of immigrants that contemporary accusations that she was somehow coercing and "homogenizing" them are perplexing. As Mary Jo Deegan notes: "The consistent misinterpretation of Addams' stance on immigrants is truly difficult to understand. Although condescending passages can be found . . . , her overwhelmingly more frequent and articulate stance against such attitudes far outweighs these other portions of her writings. One reason to assert this, beyond the change in her thought and the sheer volume of her statements, is her clear and unwavering stance against the nativism expressed in the war fever prior to, during, and immediately following World War I. . . . Addams had a profound understanding of the immigrant experience" (Mary Jo Deegan, *Jane Addams and the Men of the Chicago School, 1820–1918* [New Brunswick, N.J.: Transaction Books, 1990], p. 295).

37. Jacob A. Riis, *How the Other Half Lives* (New York: Charles Scribners Sons, 1897), p. 104. Thanks to Irene Rosenfeld for lending me her pristine copy of the original edition.

38. Riis, *How the Other Half Lives*, p. 107. To be sure, Riis isn't pushing the pseudoscience of eugenics; but this sort of typecasting surely overlaps with that of the eugenicists—absent their scientific pretension.

39. Riis, *How the Other Half Lives*, p. 92.

40. Even as newspaper attacks in Chicago grew more frequent and vitriolic, Addams's national reputation sailed along unscathed. In March 1908, the

Ladies' Home Journal (which was then taken seriously as a political publication) named Addams "the foremost living woman in America" for having "accomplished the most for womankind and, for that matter, for humankind" (from the Swarthmore College Peace Collection).

41. "As bad as all the pogroms were (and a pogrom is a government-sanctioned action against a group of people, usually the Jews), the massacre which took place at Kishinev seemed to symbolize them all. The Czar was Nicholas II who did nothing to tone down the vicious verbal attacks against the Jews; he did nothing to counter physical attacks either. . . . There were conspiracies and revolutionaries, religious and secular leaders vying for power, palace intrigue and the like. Ultimately it was the Jews who were blamed for it all as we had been for years. In Kishinev, located in Bessarabia, fifty Jews were killed, six hundred wounded and 1500 shops and homes were plundered or destroyed." From a weekly article written by Rabbi Peter Grumbacher and published in the OR-BIT [archives], "The 20th Century," Kishinev 1903, available at http://www.bethemeth.com/html/focus-viii.html (cited 10/6/99), pp. 1–3, p. 1. In *Forty Years at Hull-House* (part 2: *The Second Twenty Years*), Addams notes: "Hull-House was opened three years before a great massacre occurred at Kishinev, Russia. A large number of Russians of Jewish origin came to this country, and hundreds of them settled in our neighborhood. Partly because of our personal contacts with some of their relatives and partly because of our knowledge of the ability of those who had been persecuted and driven away from their own country, we felt an enormous interest in the whole situation. We were also concerned with the effect upon our national existence of the sudden coming of a large number of persons who might easily be filled with hatred and a spirit of revenge. I read with a group of those Russians a book of Tolstoy's in English translation in which he works out cogently his theory of nonresistance. When I think of that group I have an impression of something very vivid. They had an intense desire to master the English language because they had something very vital to say, and could not say it unless they could find the English words. It is surprising what a stimulus such a situation provides!" (p. 409).

42. The Haymarket riot was a mass public meeting held on May 4, 1886, that went terribly wrong. There was some sort of explosion—presumably, a homemade bomb was thrown. Seven policemen were killed and many were injured. Eight alleged anarchists were tried and found guilty of murder. Four were executed on November 11, 1887. One committed suicide in prison, and the remaining three were pardoned in 1893. It was never clear whether the eight who were rounded up and tried were involved in the bombing.

43. James Weber Linn, *Jane Addams* (New York: D. Appleton–Century, 1937), pp. 219–220.

44. Linn, *Jane Addams,* pp. 408–409.

45. Linn, *Jane Addams,* pp. 408–409.

46. In her autobiography, Hull-House resident and distinguished physician Alice Hamilton says that many sociologists missed the evils that most pained Jane Addams—that is, they "got" the indices of social and economic inequality but ignored the social ostracism of the "Dago," "Polack," "Hunky," "Greaser," and this, to Jane Addams, was "harder to bear than political corruption and rotten city government." In Alice Hamilton, M.D., *Exploring the Dangerous Trades: The Autobiography of Alice Hamilton, M.D.* (Boston: Little, Brown, and Co., 1943), p. 59.

47. Jane Addams, "Chicago Settlements and Social Unrest," *Charities and Commons* (May 2, 1908), pp. 155–166. The extract below is from pp. 155–156.

48. Clipping from the *Evening Post,* March 1908, in Swarthmore College Peace Collection, Anne Firor Scott file.

49. Addams, "Chicago Settlements and Social Unrest," p. 158. Matters grew ever more bizarre, involving a burial, an exhumation, and a reburial of Averbuch's body. One expert pronounced that "traces of anarchy had been found in the brain" [of Averbuch]—leading Addams to comment acerbically, "as if the words were written across the front lobes." There were incidents all over the country involving attacks on anarchists and on immigrants suspected of something.

50. Addams, "Chicago Settlements and Social Unrest," p. 163.

51. Addams, *Forty Years at Hull-House,* part 2: *The Second Twenty Years,* pp. 400–401.

52. On the black settlement house movement see Elisabeth Lasch-Quinn, *Black Neighbors* (Chapel Hill: University of North Carolina Press, 1993). Also see Mary White Ovington, *The Walls Came Tumbling Down* (New York: Arno Press, 1969); and David W. Southern, *The Malignant Heritage: Yankee Progressives and the Negro Question 1901–1914* (Chicago: Loyola University Press, 1968), for a detailed discussion of the activities of Mary White Ovington and Oswald Garrison Villard in the battle for Negro rights, including their enlistment of a "small but distinguished group of Americans, including Jane Addams," in the effort. Southern describes Addams as a "tireless worker for Negro rights" and a crusader "for a variety of human rights, whether for Indian, immigrant, or unwed mother." He adds, "The liberal press . . . true to form . . . [was] primarily hostile to the sentiments of . . . Jane Addams." Southern also offers an account of the "lily-white" Progressive party platform committee, in which Jane Addams was the only member to support a Negro-rights plank (see pp. 59–65). The report commissioned by Hull-House is excerpted in

100 Years at Hull-House. The author was Dewey R. Jones. Jones asserted that Hull-House hadn't enjoyed much success with the Negro community, not because of any policy but because its assumption that "if an institution was in the heart of the community and had facilities, everyone who needed them would take advantage of them." He continued, "That didn't happen in the case of the Negro because the experience of Negroes has been that when they assume too quickly that whatever facilities are available, are available to them, they have found they are not intended to participate at all" (p. 231). Black women also participated with white women in "the tremendously popular Women's Christian Temperance Union," seeing "for the first time, a chance to create a community of Christian women who looked past skin color to acknowledge a common humanity, a model of interracial cooperation that might expand and encourage more shared labors in the future" (Christine Stansell, "A Brief Shining Moment," review of Glenda Elizabeth Gilmore, *Gender and Jim Crow: Women and the Politics of White Supremacy in North Carolina, 1896–1920* [Chapel Hill: University of North Carolina Press, 1997], *New Republic* [May 12, 1997, pp. 43–49], p. 45).

53. Addams, *Twenty Years at Hull-House*, p. 423.

54. Jane Addams, "Work and Play," *Chautauqua Assembly Herald*, vol. 30 (August 18, 1905), pp. 1–2.

55. Letter from Jane Addams to the Editor of the *World*, March 23, 1904, p. 6, *Jane Addams Papers on Microfilm*, edited by Mary Lynn McCree Bryan (Ann Arbor, Mich.: University Microfilms International, 1985), reel 46, frame 1251.

56. Jane Addams, *Newer Ideals of Peace* (New York: Macmillan, 1907), p. 34. All quotes in this section are from chapter II (pp. 31–61) unless otherwise noted.

57. Addams, *Forty Years at Hull-House*, part 2: *The Second Twenty Years*, p. 367.

58. Lothrop Stoddard, *The Rising Tide of Color Against White World-Supremacy* (New York: Charles Scribner's Sons, 1921), introduction by Madison Grant. Stoddard's position at Harvard and the respectability and prestige of his publisher indicate that the views he advocated were not those of a marginal group of crackpots but were widely shared and approved even in elite circles.

59. Jane Addams, *Peace and Bread in Time of War* (New York: King's Crown Press, 1945 [Anniversary Edition]; orig. ed., 1915), p. 126.

60. Excerpt from President Wilson's third annual message to Congress, cited in David M. Kennedy, *Over Here: The First World War and American Society* (New York: Oxford University Press, 1980), p. 24. Kennedy's is one of the best treatments of the frightening mind-set that took over in this era.

61. Kennedy, *Over Here,* p. 68.

62. Other semiofficial organizations included the American Defense Society, the National Security League, the Home Defense League, the Liberty League, the All-Allied Anti-German League, the Anti-Yellow Spies of America, the Seditious Slammers, and the Terrible Threaterers.

63. Emerson Hough, *The Web* (New York: Arno Press and the New York Times, 1969; orig. ed., Chicago: Reilly and Lee Co., 1919), p. 10. The title page includes the phrase *The Authorized History of the American Protective League* and this explanatory note: "The Web is published by authority of the National Directors of the American Protective League, a vast, silent, volunteer army organized with the approval and operated under the direction of the United States Department of Justice, Bureau of Investigation."

64. Hough, *The Web*, p. 25.

65. Hough, *The Web*, p. 32.

66. Addams, *Forty Years at Hull-House*, part 2: *The Second Twenty Years,* pp. 289, 295, 305. All quotes are from chapter IX (pp. 263–303) unless otherwise noted.

Chapter 8

1. Swarthmore College Peace Collection, *Jane Addams Papers on Microfilm,* ed. Mary Lynn McCree Bryan (Ann Arbor, Mich.: University Microfilms International, 1985), reel 45. The poem is "Respectfully dedicated to Ruth Comfort Mitchell" and is signed, but the signature is indecipherable.

2. Cited in Allen F. Davis, *American Heroine: The Life and Legend of Jane Addams* (New York: Oxford University Press, 1973), p. 159. Davis also notes the importance of Addams's having been published in the *Ladies' Home Journal,* which had "one of the largest circulations" of any American magazine, enabling her to reach a large popular audience.

3. Addams devoted chapter XII (pp. 259–280) of her *Twenty Years at Hull-House* (New York: Macmillan, 1910), to "Tolstoyism." A good chunk of the chapter recounts Addams's journey of discovery as she went from a reaction against her own activities in Chicago—feeling that they were insufficient or that she had made too many compromises—to a similar reaction against the strenuous scrupulosity of Tolstoyism, which she considered impractical and hence ineffective as an active doctrine of peace. The story of Addams's visit with Tolstoy appears on pp. 267–273.

4. Addams and Smith were accompanied by Alymer Maude, described by Addams's nephew as "the authorized translator of Tolstoy's works" (James Weber Linn, *Jane Addams* [New York: D. Appleton–Century, 1937], p. 291).

5. Addams, *Twenty Years at Hull-House,* pp. 260–261. (All quotes in this section are drawn from pp. 259–280 unless otherwise noted.)

6. Leo Tolstoy, *What Then Must We Do?,* tr. Alymer Maude (London: Oxford University Press, 1950; orig. ed., 1925). Addams would have read the text in an earlier English translation published by Thomas Crowell. The Russian edition was first published in 1886 and was supposedly inspired by the recent Moscow census. Tolstoy had been personally involved in the gathering of the census data, seeing it as a "good opportunity for starting my charity in which I wished to exhibit my goodness. . . . So I planned the following: to arouse sympathy for town poverty among the rich; to collect money, enrol people willing to help in the affair, and with the Census-takers to visit all the dens of destitution" (p. 17). The book contains many searing descriptions of human suffering and degradation.

7. Tolstoy, *What Then Must We Do?,* p. 96.

8. Many working-class people did take umbrage when middle- and upper-middle-class student radicals in the 1960s affected the appearance of factory workers and farmers by donning overalls. I recall my grandfather—who was semi-invalided by years of backbreaking farm labor as well as by the residual effects of a childhood accident in which he had been hit by a troika driven by a reckless drunk in the streets of Saratov, Russia (after which he had received no medical attention)—grunting with disgust when he saw scenes of student counterculturalists gyrating to psychedelic music, wearing laborers' clothes. To him, the clothing was not a symbol or an affectation but an everyday reality born of necessity.

9. The "firm stance" suggests that Sofia Andreevna Tolstaya had put her foot down and refused to continue with this experiment, which she had presumably begun only at her husband's urging.

10. For example, Addams concluded that Tolstoy drew too severe a distinction between physical and moral coercion. One of Addams's correspondents, the distinguished scholar of "Applied Christianity," George D. Herron, had written her in 1897 that making one's life a true witness was indeed "the question" but that Tolstoy had not "rightly answered it." At bottom, his was an *egoistic peace.* As Herron explained: "My wishes go with him—it is the simple solution; but my *voices* tell me that after all, it is not the noblest or selfless one. It is peace for one's self, but not for the world. 'My peace I give unto you,' is something different" (Letter from Herron to Addams, dated November 20, 1897, Iowa College; in the Jane Addams papers, Swarthmore College Peace Collection).

11. Jane Addams, "Tolstoy and Gandhi," *Christian Century* (November 25, 1931, pp. 1485–1488), p. 1486.

12. Jane Addams, *Peace and Bread in Time of War* (New York: Macmillan, 1922). The quotes below are from pages 91 and 93.

13. One would not turn to Addams's account as a reliable history of that event. The power of her narrative does not lie in her initial astonishment at and support for the Russian Revolution—which she erroneously construed as the work of the peasantry—but in her vivid description of the efforts of herself and other women during that period to press for a negotiated settlement to the war and in her pathos-laden depiction of postwar conditions in Europe.

14. Of course, what actually happened in the aftermath of the Bolshevik coup was state monopolization of agriculture and the murder of millions of peasant smallholders, the *kulaks,* with millions more deported, immiserated, and uprooted. The portrait she paints of a few landholders against an undifferentiated peasantry is based on Bolshevik propaganda.

15. Another famous phrase, which recurs like a refrain in Bourne's unfinished manuscript on "The State," is "War is the health of the state"—for Bourne, a bitter irony (see Olaf Hanson, ed., *The Radical Will: Randolph Bourne: Selected Writings, 1911–1918* [New York: Urizen Books, 1977]). "The State" is an attempt on Bourne's part to undercut an American version of Hegelianism that extols the state as a source of right and law, which he believed could well culminate in a *Kriegsstaat,* a martial state. This essay and others written by Bourne in this period are blistering attacks on his fellow Progressives, especially Dewey, which eventually got him banned from the pages of the *New Republic* (at Dewey's behest). Bourne fretted that a "semi-military state socialism" might be the result of the war, a kind of Bismarckian warfare/welfare state on American soil. The prospect horrified him. His denunciation of Dewey, hence of the fundaments of Dewey's pragmatism, is found in a number of essays; but for sheer scathing denunciation nothing matches Bourne's "Twilight of the Idols." Here is a sample: "A philosopher who senses so little the sinister forces of war, who is so much more concerned over the excesses of the pacifists than over the excesses of military policy, who can feel only amusement at the idea that any one should try to conscript thought, who assumes that the war-technique can be used without trailing along with it mob-fanaticisms, the injustices and hatreds, that are organically bound up with it, is speaking to another element of the younger intelligentsia than that to which I belong. Evidently the attitudes which war calls out are fiercer and more incalculable than Professor Dewey is accustomed to take into his hopeful and intelligent imagination, and the pragmatist mind, in trying to adjust itself to them, gives the air of grappling, like the pioneer who challenges the arid plains, with a power too big for it. It is not an arena of creative intelligence our country's

mind is now, but that of mob-psychology" (pp. 336–337). Addams read these essays, but she cannot have agreed with them fully, given her friendship with Dewey. The sources on Dewey are voluminous, including admiring biographies by Robert Westbrook and Alan Ryan. See also John Patrick Diggins, "John Dewey in Peace and War," *American Scholar*, vol. 50 (Spring 1981), pp. 213 230. The anti–World War I literature is vast. One hard-hitting critique is a short piece by Henry Fairlie, published in the seventy-fifth anniversary issue of the *New Republic* (November 6, 1989, pp. 58–62). Fairlie makes a strong case against American involvement and is highly critical of "Wilsonianism." He challenges the "conventional wisdom" that America had a prima facie case for entering the war. He is no isolationist, however; he argues that there were a number of ways to "intervene" other than through arms. He asserts that Wilson "tragically warped America's own sense of itself," referencing the "whipped up hysteria" and the "incessant war propaganda" of those years. There are a number of books on Bourne. Two worth checking out are Casey Nelson Blake, *Beloved Community: The Cultural Criticism of Randolph Bourne, Van Wyck Brooks, Waldo Frank, and Lewis Mumford* (Chapel Hill: University of North Carolina Press, 1990); and Leslie J. Vaughan, *Randolph Bourne and the Politics of Cultural Radicalism* (Lawrence: University of Kansas Press, 1997). Vaughan points out that vigilantism was rampant, but schools and universities embraced a curriculum geared to the war effort. On this see also my book *Women and War* (especially pp. 106–120), which shows that Bourne's worries were, for World War I, not far-fetched in many telling respects.

16. Addams called for a "sturdy and virile" internationalism to take form in institutions that perdure (Addams, *Twenty Years at Hull-House*, p. 307). Addams's use of this language is no accident. She understood the importance of making peace a challenge that had about it some of the traditional élan of war.

17. Addams, *Twenty Years at Hull-House*, p. 308.

18. Addams believed that the "passing of the war virtues" was linked to the "utilization of women in city government," because the activities in which women engage require a level of peace in order to flourish. Although in the past it perhaps made sense to reserve the franchise for men on whom the city relied for its defense (when "the ultimate value of the elector could be reduced to his ability to perform military duty"), that situation no longer pertained. Cities do not suddenly go to war against one another; rather, the "modern city is a stronghold of industrialism." That being the case, the new city must concern itself with "unsanitary housing, poisonous sewage, contaminated water, infant mortality, the spread of contagion, adulterated food, impure milk,

smoke-laden air, ill-ventilated factories, dangerous occupations, juvenile crime, unwholesome crowding, prostitution and drunkenness" (Jane Addams, *Newer Ideals of Peace* [New York: Macmillan, 1907], pp. 181–182). Women must be concerned with these issues. To separate women from civic life was to narrow the compass of women's lives unacceptably, because they could no longer perform their traditional tasks unless these problems were dealt with. It also deprived civic life of women's knowledge and expertise. The link to peace was clear, in Addams's mind. The more one diminished military virtues, the more one cultivated industrial virtues—the virtues of socialized civic peace.

19. Jane Addams, *The Spirit of Youth and the City Streets* (New York: Macmillan, 1909), p. 146.

20. Addams, *The Spirit of Youth*, pp. 148–149. Here, again, it seems not to have occurred to Addams that a state powerful enough to engage in the protective and redistributive efforts she endorses will also be powerful enough to engage in war or warlike activities. These efforts demand a degree of social organization and even a level of centralization that put enormous power into the hands of the state. It is unsurprising that so many Progressives supported the war with precisely this goal in mind, having convinced themselves, through tortured logic, that World War I would be the last major war. This war was, remember, the war to "make the world safe for democracy."

21. Addams, *Peace and Bread in Time of War*, p. 197.

22. This latter quote is from John C. Farrell (*Beloved Lady: A History of Jane Addams' Ideas on Reform and Peace* [Baltimore, Md.: Johns Hopkins University Press, 1967]), who discusses the neutrality effort with precision and sympathy. The Addams essay appears in *Ladies' Home Journal*, vol. 21 (November 1914), p. 5.

23. Farrell, *Beloved Lady*, p. 148.

24. These European luminaries included Emmeline Pethick-Lawrence, of England, and the redoubtable Rosika Schwimmer, of Hungary. There was considerable overlap between women's activities and socialism in central Europe, and the internationalist motifs of socialism also fueled this antiwar activity. The antiwar sentiment that was supposed to surface in the working class, cutting across lines of nationality and country, should a war be declared, did not surface. Moreover, men of the working class enthusiastically supported the war, at least initially. Addams helped organize a short-lived group in Chicago in December 1914, the Chicago Emergency Federation of Peace Forces—a precursor to the Woman's Peace Party—and delegates were called to a national peace meeting. See Farrell, *Beloved Lady*, pp. 150–151. See also Sandi E. Cooper, "Women's Participation in European Peace Movements: The Struggle to Prevent World War I," pp. 51–74 in Ruth Roach Pierson, *Women and Peace: The-*

oretical, Historical and Practical Perspectives (London: Croom Helm, 1987).

25. A variety of proposals were put forward, including a suggestion proffered by a University of Wisconsin professor of English, Julia Grace Wales, to create an international commission of scholars to mediate the war. The "ivory tower" naïveté of such a suggestion is breathtaking, and this is what generally discredited peace efforts. Addams was keenly concerned to avoid looking "ridiculous." All sorts of strange proposals for dealing with international conflict were made before, during, and after the war years, including the suggestion by Addams's friend and a Hull-House supporter, the distinguished American philosopher from the University of Chicago, George Herbert Mead. Mead's *Mind, Self, and Society* (Chicago: University of Chicago Press, 1974; orig. ed., 1934) is an acknowledged classic. Addams was familiar with his early writings and his insistence on the communal dimensions of selfhood. Mead had reviewed, and praised, Addams's *Newer Ideals of Peace* for its thesis that immediate human relations—not militarism or military ideals—should provide the basis for government. Mead was a fascinating thinker, but when it came to war his thinking was out of touch, to put it mildly. For example, he proposed war insurance—protection against the damages of war—that would be underwritten by nations and overseen by an "International Board of Trustees with no political powers or obligations," thus guaranteeing its neutrality. Because of the board's political powerlessness, no "single trustee" could control funds. The insurance would guarantee against natural disasters but would also use the interpretation of contracts in cases of dispute, and "there would be no appeal" against its decisions. Presumably, this would "insure against war and would serve to prevent war by an additional rule," namely, that if a nation "had a war with another, the insurance trustees would never directly inquire as to the moral justification of this war but would ask: Who committed the first act of war? No nation would receive insurance compensation for any expenses due to a war in which it committed the first act of war." See Rev. Francis Eugene George, O.M.I., *Society and Experience: A Critical Examination of the Social Philosophies of Royce, Mead and Sellars* (Ph.D. dissertation, Department of Philosophy, Tulane University; Ann Arbor, Mich.: University Microfilms International, 1970), pp. 69–70. What is fascinating is the way this cuts against the grain of Mead's elaborate accounts of symbolic interaction that by no means reduce human motivations to monetary incentives. Other interesting accounts of Mead and his thought include: Dmitri N. Shalin, "G. H. Mead, Socialism, and the Progressive Agenda," *American Journal of Sociology*, vol. 93 (January 1988), pp. 913–950; John S. Berger and Mary Jo Deegan, "George Herbert Mead on Internationalism, Democracy, and War," *Wisconsin Sociologist*, vol. 18, no. 2–3 (1981), pp. 72–83.

26. The words to this hymn were written by the famous feminist Charlotte Perkins Gilman. An account appears in May Wright Sewall, *Women, World War and Permanent Peace* (San Francisco: John J. Newbegin, 1915), p. 28. Addams, to be consistent, would have to take at least partial exception to this sort of thing, given her arguments against socialism as an ideology—that it promised everything, including a world with no more toothaches. Addams was clearly far more attuned to the way human beings work at cross-purposes than were many others active in the peace movements.

27. She associates the efforts of the women meeting at the Hague with the work of Grotius and Kant, but also, more important, with the tens of thousands of men and women over the years who had contributed to internationalism through their emigration.

28. Farrell describes this in *Beloved Lady* (p. 155). Indeed, the documents that were debated and adopted are an interesting combination of the eminently sensible and politically feasible with the elaboration of hopes for a liberal peace that are no more preposterous than Immanuel Kant's famous essay on perpetual peace. Kant's document is taken seriously even by those who, like me, find it both naïve and troubling in many respects; but the proposals adopted by the International Congress of Women were both derided and lauded.

29. Gertrude Bussey and Margaret Tims, *Women's International League for Peace and Freedom, 1915–1965: A Record of Fifty Years' Work* (London: George Allen and Unwin, 1965), p. 9.

30. I discuss this phenomenon at length in my *Women and War,* as a form of women's participation in armed civic virtue.

31. The delegates were received by Prime Minister Asquith and Foreign Minister Grey in London; Reichskanzler von Bethmann-Hollweg and Foreign Minister von Jagow in Berlin; Prime Minister Stuergkh and Foreign Minister Burian in Vienna; Prime Minister Tisza in Budapest; Prime Minister Salandra and Foreign Minister Sonino in Rome; Prime Minister Viviani and Foreign Minister Delcasse in Paris; and Foreign Minister d'Avignon in Havre. Delegates also visited the heads of countries not directly involved in the war.

32. Addams, *Peace and Bread in Time of War,* p. 48.

33. Jane Addams, Emily G. Balch, and Alice Hamilton, *Women at the Hague* (New York: Macmillan, 1915), describes the Congress of April 1915 and the activities that led up to, and followed upon the heels of, this extraordinary meeting.

34. The meeting had been put together by a coalition of organizations that included suffrage advocacy groups, labor groups (e.g., the National Woman's Trade Union Leagues), and other civic entities as well as peace organizations.

35. Other members included, in Hamilton's words, "Dr. Jacobs of Amsterdam" and "Frau Wollften Palthe of the Hague," as well as herself. Astonishingly, they got in everywhere and consulted at the highest levels of government. Addams details this in her contribution to *Women at the Hague,* and later recycles and reframes this material in *Peace and Bread in Time of War.* In the former, she used strong language: "The Revolt Against War" on the part of both some soldiers as well as some civilians; in the latter, she ratcheted down the rhetoric to "Personal Reactions During the War" (this version followed the public onslaught on her Carnegie Hall speech).

36. "Address of Miss Jane Addams, Delivered at Carnegie Hall, Friday July 9, 1915," a stenographic transcription of her remarks, was first published as a supplement to the *Christian Worker* (July 31, 1915, pp. 145–148). The speech would have lasted about an hour if she spoke at a moderate pace, including a number of brief interruptions due to applause.

37. Delvania Gale Shadwell, *A Rhetorical Analysis of Selected Speeches by Jane Addams* (Ann Arbor, Mich.: University Microfilms International, 1989), p. 14. Shadwell's book is the only one I know that takes up in a systematic way Addams's record as a rhetorician. She does not track Addams's entire career but only the arguments supporting pacifism in speeches she delivered between 1900 and 1935. Addams was well educated in rhetorical theory. She had mastered the standard rhetorical curriculum "based largely on classical writings," according to Shadwell. She also had paid for elocution lessons while at Rockford Seminary.

38. This, of course, did not happen as uniformly as Addams foresaw. Some countries returned to an essentially civilian life, as did the United States, although many kept wartime restrictions in place. Others, with different political traditions, reacted in other ways. Those that suffered the most and bore the guilt for the war in its aftermath (as part of the peace settlements) boiled with resentment underwritten by the postwar economic devastation, which helped pave the way for extreme nationalist movements such as National Socialism in Germany.

39. At this juncture she may not have been distinguishing between committed pacifists and old-fashioned isolationists (the latter subscribed to a form of the narrow nationalism she decried). She further believed that the peace movement everywhere was hampered by wartime censorship, hence the impossibility of uninhibited communication both within and between warring nations.

40. In my *Women and War,* the theme of sacrifice is explored at length; it predominates in chapter 6. To be sure, this is a theme that has died down with the trend, in the United States, toward a professional army and the notion of the soldiers as experts trained in tasks others of us are not trained for. In Ad-

dams's era, when the soldier was essentially a civilian raised on a diet that stressed not so much self-aggrandizement and entitlement as sacrifice for the good of others, the sacrifice motif makes more sense.

41. On the theme of epistemological privilege derived from direct experience, see the first chapter ("Not a Soldier's Story") in my *Women and War.*

42. Women who derive civic identity, honor, and status from the service and sacrifice of their warrior sons, and who can be counted on, most of the time, to support the wars of their countries, are examples of a classic historic archetype, the Spartan Mother. Addams mentions one woman who said she had five sons and a son-in-law in the trenches and she wished she had more to give. This is classic Spartan Mother talk. The United States has had its own version in the tradition of Gold Star Mothers. During World War II, the champion American Gold Star Mother was Aletta Sullivan of Waterloo, Iowa, who lost five sons when one battleship was destroyed. All five were serving together aboard the same ship, as they had requested, when the ship was sunk off Guadalcanal. The tragedy led the Navy to promulgate the so-called Sullivan rule, which prohibits siblings from serving together. This tragedy was the subject of a film called *The Fighting Sullivans* (1944) that worried some who feared the sadness of all five sons going down might actually detract from, rather than bolster, the war effort. See *Women and War,* p. 191, for a discussion of Aletta Sullivan in particular and the Spartan Mother in general. In the film *Saving Private Ryan,* the Spartan Mother theme is played out in a tragic, not militant, way. Three brothers die in combat in different places, and George C. Marshall, to justify sending a party into harm's way to rescue the only remaining brother, reads Abraham Lincoln's famous "Letter to Mrs. Bixby," written by Lincoln to a woman who had lost five sons, in which Lincoln refers to the "solemn pride that must be yours to have laid so costly a sacrifice upon the altar of freedom." Addams surely knew of this letter.

43. In a 1915 interview published in the *Ladies' Home Journal,* Addams proclaimed: "I am strong in my belief that men and women should work together on all questions of public interest. It has a better effect on both, and it is moreover the ideal condition that men and women shall do things together. One result of equal suffrage is that women and men work shoulder to shoulder and not apart" ("As I See Women," an interview with Jane Addams, *Ladies' Home Journal* 32 [August 1915], pp. 11, 54).

44. The use of stimulants in battle is well known. In his classic work *The Face of Battle* (New York: Penguin Books, 1983), the great British historian of war John Keegan, in offering a detailed account of the Battles of Agincourt, Waterloo, and the Somme, describes alcohol as a central ingredient of battle. In

such classic war films as Stanley Kubrick's great *Paths of Glory*, the distribution of alcohol also is depicted.

45. By Shadwell (*Rhetorical Analysis*, p. 94).

46. Addams, *Peace and Bread in Time of War*, p. 139.

47. Beadle, *The Fortnightly Club*, p 149 The Fortnightly had voted Addams an honorary member in 1904, when Mary Wilmarth, a supporter of Addams and Hull-House, was president of the club. But the years from 1917 to 1919 were another story: The members of the Fortnightly, along with every other civic institution, mobilized themselves for the war effort, putting together their own "Preparedness Committee" in the conviction that in so doing they were supporting a great and noble need. They also placed an American flag on the platform during their meetings—evidently a war-inspired innovation.

48. Farrell, *Beloved Lady*, p. 179. Addams was back to the theme of woman as nurturer. The federal department in question was set up August 10, 1917.

49. Oddly enough, the minutes of the meeting make no comment about what Addams said, and this is described in the official history of the Fortnightly as "highly unusual" (Beadle, *The Fortnightly Club*, pp. 150–151).

50. *The Fortnightly Club*, pp. 152–153. The Fortnightly approved, on February 17 of that same year, a resolution supporting the creation of the "League to Enforce Peace" (p. 153).

51. "Chief Justice Rebukes Miss Jane Addams," *New York Times* (June 11, 1917), p. 2. Other papers picked up the story and ran it under what in many cases were sensationalist headlines—e.g., "Jane Addams' Address on Peace Rouses Ire of Judge O. N. Carter."

52. P. 115. All quotes in this section, unless otherwise noted, are drawn from Jane Addams, "Women's Memories—Challenging War," chapter V in *The Long Road of Woman's Memory* (New York: Macmillan, 1916). The first page of this chapter contains a fascinating footnote in which Addams speaks of her "two women" as a "composite made from several talks held with each of two women representing both sides of the conflict. Their opinions and observations are merged into one because in so many particulars they were either identical or overlapping. Both women called themselves patriots, but each had become convinced of the folly of war."

53. The quote below is from Addams, *The Long Road*, pp. 126–127.

54. Addams, *The Long Road*, pp. 136–137. This commitment to nurturance is part of what Addams considered "Woman's Special Training for Peacemaking," *Proceedings*, II (1909) of the American Peace Congress, pp. 253–254.

55. Many of Addams's closest advisers, including Louise de Koven Bowen, urged her not to participate.

56. The whole thing began to break down almost as soon as it began, in part because the hyperinflated rhetoric of Ford doomed the venture to failure. Addams engaged in damage control but refused to call the peace ship pure folly. She was, however, at pains to distinguish it from the Woman's Peace Party.

57. Addams, *Peace and Bread in Time of War*, p. 53. That Wilson was equally committed to both points shows the general incoherence of his position. You cannot guarantee absolute political independence—or political sovereignty—to every nation, including those small nations brought into being after the war, and at the same time demand that all disputes be settled by investigation and arbitration. If arbitration is to be effective, it must be enforceable. But it is not enforceable if you are committed to state sovereignty. Subsequent quotes in this section are from *Peace and Bread* unless otherwise noted.

58. The quote is from Addams, *Peace and Bread in Time of War*, pp. 64–65. Needless to say, this is a question that has never been answered satisfactorily, especially not in the case of an optional war, which World War I clearly was for the United States.

59. Hoover, who was then working with the U.S. Food Administration, was impressed by the food distribution system in Belgium, which received some $15 million a month on loan from the United States. Three million bushels monthly of North American wheat went to Belgium and northern France, by Hoover's estimate. Addams's involvement in this effort and her service as a spokeswoman in behalf of humanitarian relief helped allay her distress over the use of bread as a weapon of war by the Triple Entente powers.

60. Addams, *Peace and Bread in Time of War*, pp. 154–155.

61. These were the famous, or infamous, Palmer raids, named for the U.S. Attorney General who spearheaded them, A. Mitchell Palmer. Palmer planned and conducted a series of dragnet raids to ferret out unpatriotic and disloyal elements. Farrell reports that Palmer was disconcerted to find that Illinois state agents had beat him to the punch and conducted a raid in Chicago before he could. "Consequently, in Chicago there were two 'Palmer raids': the first conducted by state agents on New Year's Day, and the second by federal agents the following day" (Addams, *Peace and Bread in Time of War*, p. 174). This was in 1920. These organized activities further isolated peace advocates like Addams. Addams's pacifist stance also discredited her among the association of National Social Workers, as her onetime associates found to their consternation when, at national meetings in the postwar period, the name of Jane Addams often evoked criticism and disparagement. It is hard to underestimate the continuing effect of this on the remainder of Addams's life and career. Addams's two biographers—James Weber Linn and Daniel Levine—take quite different stances toward Addams's peace activities. Linn, unsurprisingly, extols her activities and stresses their possible immediate

and possible future results. Levine is quite critical, suggesting that the events of the war years never led "Jane Addams . . . for a moment" to consider "altering her basic attitudes about the nature of human beings. What she saw did not move her one iota toward the view that men were inherently passionate, irrational creatures with an inborn drive to kill, maim, and blow up their fellows. The assumption of potential human goodness was so deeply a part of her that it could never come up for re-evaluation" (Levine, *Jane Addams and the American Liberal Tradition* [Madison: University of Wisconsin Press, 1971], p. 211). What isn't clear from this criticism is whether Levine believes that human beings are inherently driven to kill—presumably he does. Certainly a belief in *potential* human goodness need not be labeled naïve, so long as one also acknowledges the likelihood, given the historic record, that human beings also have a very large potential for doing very bad things. Levine also criticizes Addams for being "vague" and for not being "very good at thinking analytically in larger theoretical terms." Her intellect proved "inadequate" when it came to thinking through the connections between "nationalism, public opinion, the relationship between leaders and the led, the power of irrationality, or competing economic and political systems" (p. 211). Her thinking was inadequate, as I also argue, but it is not so easy to find intellectuals who were up to the mark.

62. The extract is from Addams, *Peace and Bread in Time of War*, pp. 169–170.

63. Edith Abbott and Sophonisba P. Breckinridge (*The Administration of the Aid-to-Mothers Law in Illinois*, first published under the auspices of the Children's Bureau [No. 82, 1921], and republished under the title *The Family and Social Service in the 1920s* [New York: Arno Press and the New York Times, 1972]) note a cardinal law of settlement and social feminist doctrine: "It is against sound public economy to allow poverty alone to cause the separation of a child from the care of a good mother, or to allow the mother so to exhaust her powers in earning a living for her children that she cannot give them proper home care and protection" (p. 5). This concern with community on what social scientists call the micro-level was connected by Jane Addams to the so-called macro-level, bearing in mind that for her this macro-level was best captured by looking at what was happening on the ground.

64. Linn, *Jane Addams*, pp. 347–348.

65. Linn, *Jane Addams*, p. 355.

66. Linn, *Jane Addams*, p. 358.

67. Lana Ruegamer, *The "Paradise of Exceptional Women": Chicago Women Reformers, 1863–1893* (Ann Arbor, Mich.: University Microfilms International, 1982), p. 17.

68. Ruegamer, *The "Paradise of Exceptional Women,"* p. 45.

69. Linn, *Jane Addams,* p. 373.

70. I have relied on Linn *(Jane Addams)* for these bits and pieces about Addams's final years. He gives details about the awards and the amounts of prize money attached to many of them.

71. Linn, *Jane Addams,* p. 416.

72. Linn, *Jane Addams,* p. 421.

73. Lippman's eulogy, which was syndicated and published in newspapers across the country, is quoted in Davis, *American Heroine,* p. 291.

Index

ABOUT THE AUTHOR

Jean Bethke Elshtain is the Laura Spelman Rockefeller Professor of Social and Political Ethics at the University of Chicago. She was elected a Fellow of the American Academy of Arts and Sciences in 1996 and is a member of the Board of Trustees of the National Humanities Center in Research Triangle Park, North Carolina. She is the author of more than four hundred essays published in scholarly journals and journals of civic opinion and a contributing editor of the *New Republic*. Among her books are *Women and War* (1987) and *Democracy on Trial* (1995), both published by Basic Books. *Democracy on Trial* was a New York Times "Notable Book" in 1995.